CONTENTS

Acknowledgements 4
Introduction 7

Part 1: A Brief History of the Trolley Coach in Canada 11

    The Builders 12
    Canadian Car & Foundry Co. Ltd. 12
    New Flyer Industries Ltd. 14
    Brown Boveri/General Motors Company 15
    Associated Equipment Co. 15
    Leyland Manufacturing Corp. Ltd. 18
    Canadian Brill Company 18

    St. Louis Car 18
    Mack Trucks Inc. 18
    Pullman-Standard Car Mfg. Corp. 19
    Marmon-Herrington Co. Inc. 19
    ACF-Brill 19
    Motor Coach Industries (MCI) – a footnote 20

Part 2: Canadian Cities That Operated Trolley Coaches

Halifax, NS (1949-1969)
    Nova Scotia Light and Power Co. Ltd. 24
Saint John, NB (1947 ordered and cancelled)
    New Brunswick Power Company 35
St. John's, Nfld. (1947 planned)
    Newfoundland Light & Power Company Ltd. 36
Montreal, QC (1937-1966)
    Montreal Tramways Co. /
    Montreal Transportation Commission 38
Ottawa, ON (1951-1959)
    Ottawa Transportation Commission 48
Cornwall, ON (1949-1970)
    Cornwall Street Railway Light & Power Co. Ltd. 56
Toronto, ON (1922-1925 and 1947-1993)
    Toronto Transportation Commission /
    Toronto Transit Commission 64
Kitchener, ON (1947-1973)
    Kitchener Public Utilities Commission 82
Hamilton, ON (1950-1992)
    Hamilton Street Railway 88
Windsor, ON (1922-1926)
    Sandwich, Windsor & Amherstburg Railway –
    Hydro Electric Railway, Essex Division 98
Port Arthur-Fort William/Thunder Bay, ON
(1947-1972)
    Port Arthur PUC and Fort William Transit /
    Thunder Bay Transit 102

Winnipeg, MB (1938-1970)
    Winnipeg Electric Co. /
    Greater Winnipeg Transit Commission /
    Metro Winnipeg Transit 114
Regina, SK (1947-1966)
    Regina Municipal Railway /
    Regina Transit System 126
Saskatoon, SK (1948-1974)
    Saskatoon Municipal Railway /
    Saskatoon Transit System 134
Edmonton, AB (1939 to 2009)
    Edmonton Radial Railway /
    Edmonton Transit System (ETS) /
    Edmonton Transit (ET) 140
Calgary, AB (1947-1975)
    Calgary Transit System 174
Vancouver, BC (1948 to present)
    British Columbia Electric Railway Company /
    British Columbia Hydro and Power Authority /
    Urban Transit Authority of British Columbia –
    Metro Transit Operating Company /
    BC Transit /
    TransLink–Coast Mountain Bus Company 188
Victoria, BC (1945 demo)
    British Columbia Electric Railway Company 213
Nelson, BC (1945-1949 planned)
    Nelson Street Railway 217

Colour Section 219

Colour Postcards 235

Appendices

    Appendix A: Complete Equipment Roster for Each City 241
    Appendix B: Preserved Equipment 252
    Appendix C: Trolley Coach Drawings 256
    Selected Bibliography 269
    Index 270

ACKNOWLEDGEMENTS

This history of the trolley coach in Canada came about as the result of an early childhood affliction. I was relocated to Cornwall, Ontario in the middle of Grade 6 at a very impressionable age. The eldest son of a railway fan, I had already been exposed to a goodly share of steam locomotion, circus trains, museum trains, and streetcars (while living in Toronto) and had learned to tolerate diesel locomotives.

So it was not surprising that I took great interest in the Cornwall trolley coach (and electric freight) operations for more than their convenience in getting me from point A to B. Cornwall was also a place where a young transit fan could see mainline early-generation Canadian National Railways diesels, get an unofficial cab ride for five minutes in an aging Canadian Pacific Railway steamer, and watch the New York Central switch freight cars with exotic names on their sides. All this was accessible by trolley coach or bicycle and filled many summer days.

Many years later, somewhat older, but no less a transit fan, my wife and I moved to Edmonton and my interest in trolley coaches was re-kindled. As a member of the Canadian Railway Historical Association/Alberta Pioneer Railway Association I investigated the history of Edmonton's trolley coaches and wrote articles about them. The idea of an all-Canadian book on trolley coaches sprang from those articles and several summer trips to other Canadian cities incorporated research. The intervention of the invitation to expand my Edmonton trolley coach knowledge into a portion of Railfare's *Edmonton's Electric Transit* delayed the project. Life, children and a subsequent move to Ottawa further pushed the project into the file cabinet. But, it never quite went out of mind, and when Railfare's Dave Henderson approached me in the fall of 2007 as I was reviving my Calgary trolley coach material for the forthcoming *Calgary's Electric Transit*, asking me to bring back this project, I embraced it eagerly.

A few inquiries to trolley coach acquaintances brought a flood of interested parties and I am greatly in debt to all those who encouraged, contributed, critiqued or in any way helped. If I have missed a name, please forgive me.

In alphabetical order thanks to: Jason Ashton from OC Transpo who helped secure copyright for Ottawa photos; Barry Blumstein in far-off Australia for photos; Ian Bowering, archivist at the Cornwall Museum for access to Cornwall Street Railway (CSR) files; John Bulloch for Cornwall details; the late Peter Cox for clarification on Can Car and many cities' details, and his daughter Val's generous permission to use Peter's photos now in the Canadian Transit Heritage Foundation collection; Derek Cheung for Vancouver fleet information; John M. Day, former editor of *Canadian Coach* magazine for photos, information, and vetting the Vancouver, Victoria and Nelson chapters, and contributing many valuable additions; Ken Dahl, City of Saskatoon Archives; Terry Dejong for photos of Edmonton and Vancouver; Bernie Drouillard who shared his Windsor history and reviewed that chapter; Tom Grumley who dug up and connected me to Ottawa information; Colin Hatcher in Edmonton – my erstwhile co-author of two previous transit histories – who miraculously dug up information on several systems, reviewed the Saskatoon chapter and the Edmonton additions, supplied many photos from the Edmonton Radial Railway Society's archives, and was a great support through the thirty some years of this project; Ted Hamill who clarified many of the Lakehead systems details; Scott Henderson for slide scanning; Patricia Hughes and Erin Blay of Halifax Metro Transit who gave me access to Paul Leger's photo collection that they had just scanned; April Johnson, Thunder Bay Archives & Record Centre who scanned and sent much valued material; Brian Kelly for Vancouver information and anecdotes; Rich Krisak who kindly sent several photos from his father's collection; Dave Knowles of the Craig Library and Archives in Ottawa for Cornwall information; the late J.D. Knowles of Toronto who supplied many beautiful colour photos of Toronto and other information, cleared up a Cornwall mystery and sent the Canadian Transit Association Symposium paper which supplied much colour information; Mike Larisey, Jim Jones and Glen Knapp of Maritime Hobbies & Crafts in Halifax for identification information; Carl Lantz, Illinois Railway Museum, Strahorn Library for all the Ohio Brass photographs as well as the Scalzo collection; the late Denis Latour, author and Daniel Laurendeau, CRHA Montreal Secretary for much of the Montreal material; Paul Leger of Halifax for that history, photographs and St. John's information; Bill Linley for many wonderful photographs; Tom Luton and Kevin Nicol (Hamilton Street Railway) for much of the Hamilton detail – Kevin also vetted that chapter; Jeff Marinoff for Winnipeg material, all the trolley coach postcards and Mack photos; Peter McLaughlin of the *busdrawings.com* website for his photos; Angus McIntyre for photos, vetting the Vancouver chapter and wire-mapping of Vancouver; Jim Mcpherson for an elusive Vancouver photo; Tom Morrow of *trolleybuses.net* (Tom's North American Trolley Bus Pictures) website for many images; Peter Newgard, former Ottawa Transportation Commission Equipment Manager who verified rosters and helped clear access to the Ottawa photos; Art Peterson for many of the Glenn Andersen, Mac Sebree and John Williams photographs from the Krambles-Peterson Archives; Doug Shields for corrections to the Winnipeg chapter; Harry Porter, former editor of *Trolley Coach News* and former master of NATTA – the North American Trackless Trolley Association for much information; Jesse Roberts, Head of Reference Services and the staff at the Thunder Bay Library who searched and scanned many articles on the Port Arthur/Fort William/Thunder Bay system; the late Steve Scalzo for colour photographs and for supply-

Tom Schwarzkopf

TIRES AND WIRES

The story of electric trolley coaches serving sixteen Canadian cities

To Jane for all your support.

Railfare ❉ DC Books

ABOUT THE AUTHOR

Tom Schwarzkopf's introduction to urban transit was at age five with a move to Toronto where, when riding on the Peter Witt streetcars, he competed with the conductor in calling out car-stop names. Whether getting up at 6 AM to see the Barnum & Bailey Circus train unload or riding the new PCC streetcars, railways and transit have always been an integral part of Tom's life. In his Cornwall, Ontario years, Tom enjoyed riding the new (for him) electric trolley buses, thus starting a life-long interest in this urban "trackless trolley" transportation mode. The photo demonstrates this as an eleven-year-old Tom collects his brother's fare on his backyard version of a Cornwall trolley coach. A lack of rope or ambition limited the trolley bus/wagon to a single pole and overhead wire – streetcars were long gone from Cornwall by then.

Many moves and years of train-chasing and riding followed, but relocation to Edmonton in 1973 renewed his contact with trolley coaches. A mutual interest in electric transit led to a friendship with Colin Hatcher, culminating in their co-authorship of *Edmonton's Electric Transit*. The collaboration continued with *Calgary's Electric Transit*, despite Tom having returned to Ottawa, where he continued also working on this book – a project started in his Edmonton days.

In addition to Tom's historical writings, he is the author of the popular children's series "The Angela and Emmie

Adventures" and dabbles in short story and youth fiction writing. In between travel, gardening and introducing his grandchildren to trains and all things transit, Tom is also working on several other transit writing projects.

Book designed and typeset in Adobe Garamond Pro, ITC Garamond, and Myriad MM.
Overall book design by Ian Cranstone, Osgoode, Ontario.
Printed and bound in Canada.

© Copyright 2018 Railfare Enterprises Limited.

Legal Deposit, *Bibliothèque et Archives nationales du Québec* and the National Library of Canada, 1st Trimester, 2019.

Library and Archives Canada Cataloguing in Publication

Title: Tires and wires : the story of electric trolley coaches serving sixteen Canadian cities / Tom Schwarzkopf.

Names: Schwarzkopf, Tom, 1943- author. | Canadian Transit Heritage Foundation, issuing body.

Description: Includes bibliographical references and index.

Identifiers: Canadiana 20189067241 | ISBN 9781927599488 (softcover)

Subjects: LCSH: Street-railroads–Canada. | LCSH: Trolley buses–Canada.

Classification: LCC TF726 .S39 2019 | DDC 388.4/132230971–dc23

For our publishing activities, Railfare*DC Books gratefully acknowledges the financial support of:

Société de développement des entreprises culturelles Québec

No part of this publication may be reproduced or stored in a retrieval system or transmitted in any form or by any means, electronic, mechanical, recording or otherwise, without written permission of the publisher, Railfare*DC Books.

In the case of photocopying or other reprographic copying, a licence must be obtained from Access Copyright, Canadian Copyright Licensing Agency, Suite 1100, 69 Yonge Street, Toronto, ON M5E 1K3. email: info@accesscopyright.ca

---

Railfare DC Books

Ontario office:
1880 Valley Farm Road, Unit #TP-27, Pickering, ON L1V 6B3

Business office and mailing address:
5 Fenwick Avenue, Montreal West, QC H4X 1P3
email: railfaredcbooks@gmail.com   web: www.railfare.net

Co-publisher: Canadian Transit Heritage Foundation

ACKNOWLEDGEMENTS

Although this Cornwall postcard dates from the early 1950s, the scene was much the same when the eleven-year-old author of this account moved there. The tracks were truncated from the streetcar days to leave a Y for the electric locomotives, and the approaching trolley coach is completing its loop on the BELT LINE. (POSTCARDS OF CORNWALL WEBSITE, COLLECTION OF LILY WORRALL)

ing many copies of *Trolley Coach News* as well as many of the base wire maps; Brian Tucker for the last twenty years of Edmonton trolley coach history, Mark W. Walton, former editor of *Transit News Canada* for Winnipeg material among other trolley tidbits, and for reviewing the Winnipeg chapter; Ted Wickson for providing resource material from many cities, a treasure trove of *Canadian Transportation* articles, and amazing photographs, and for reviewing Toronto, Kitchener and Hamilton texts as well as the segment on manufacturers, and being 'drafted' into becoming the book's photo and copy editor. Ted provided a wealth of trolley coach images coast to coast and arranged to have them scanned by Bell Arte Photo in Hamilton; Lily Worrall, a Cornwall historian who supplied many photo locations and Cornwall tidbits; Hal Wright at Sandon, BC for information on their collection of trolley coaches; David Wyatt of the comprehensive website *All-Time List of Canadian Transit Systems* for answering queries of all sorts and supplying photos; and a special thanks to long-time transit historian, collector and photographer Wally Young, another former editor of *Canadian Coach* magazine, who kindly sent my requests for help all over Canada and the US, putting me in touch with many of the above-mentioned. Wally was my go-to man for much of the details that needed to be filled in and rarely failed to find the data or someone who did know. Wally also supplied most of the Victoria material, as well as his personal treasure trove of clippings on Cornwall, Regina, Vancouver, Halifax, Port Arthur/Fort William and other systems. He also reviewed the Saskatoon, Victoria, Nelson and Vancouver chapters.

Grateful thanks to all the archivists and librarians who replied to my enquiries and sent what information or monographs they had, especially the Ottawa Public Library which provided many interlibrary loans of key resources, much of which came from the National Library of Canada. Without such expertise and services, we historians would be so much poorer.

Thanks to Dave Henderson of Railfare*DC books for believing in this project for over thirty years and shepherding it through the trials of publishing a special interest book in Canada. Dave also helped with identification of Montreal photos from the time he lived there as a young, trolley-coach-riding lad. Finally and most importantly, Dave's expertise along with Ted Wickson's connections to the Canadian Transit Heritage Foundation (CTHF) made this book happen. I am much indebted to the CTHF and its president, Chris Prentice for taking this history of Canada's trolley coaches from a dream to a reality.

There are two Canadian organizations most deserving of a special mention: New Flyer Canada and Kiepe Electric, who provided generous and much-appreciated support for this project. Without their help, the publication of this book would not have been possible. Here is some information about how these two companies fit into Canada's, and the world's, trolley coach picture:

New Flyer Canada ULC and New Flyer of America Inc., subsidiaries of NFI Group Inc.

Founded in 1930 in Winnipeg, the company got its start in the trolley bus field when the Toronto Transit Commission (TTC) partnered with them in rebuilding their fleet.

5

This might have been what the author saw on a warm summer day with a westbound coach turning at the New York Central Station loop just past the Howard Smith Paper Mills. Our author worked summers at the mill where his father engineered several digester replacements in the building in the background above the eastbound coach. These immensely-tall pressure vessels required dismantling the entire brick wall in order to be removed. That coach is passing a favourite watering hole for mill workers on May 17th 1970. Today nothing remains of the mill except the chimney.
(TED WICKSON)

In 1972 Flyer began producing a new chassis, body, and running gear while TTC rebuilt and reinstalled the rest.

By the early 1970s complete electric trolleys were designed and tested, not only for the TTC but for the San Francisco Municipal Transportation Agency (SFMTA), and soon after for Hamilton Street Railway. Through a 1971 agreement with AM General Corporation in 1971 to assemble bus shells in AMG's Mishawaka, IL plant, Flyer was able to supply trolley coaches into American markets such as Dayton, San Francisco and Boston, while also providing coaches to Edmonton and Vancouver.

New Flyer later developed the first sixty-foot articulated trolley bus with centre- and rear-drive motors, whose propulsion enables coaches to travel up San Francisco's steep inclines. New Flyer also became the first company to introduce low-floor buses to North America, creating a new industry standard. Orders from Southeastern Pennsylvania Transportation Authority (Philadelphia) followed for trolley buses equipped with an emergency back-up generator on board for operation in the event of a power outage. More recently, New Flyer has delivered the Xcelsior® trolley coach models in forty- and sixty-foot lengths to both SFMTA and King County Metro (Seattle), all of which are equipped with Kiepe electrical components.

Kiepe Electric

In 1906, Theodor Kiepe set up a "repair workshop for electrical arc lamps" in Düsseldorf, Germany. The company's focus soon shifted to the manufacture of electrical components for machine tools, cranes and electric vehicles. Kiepe delivered its first electro-pneumatic equipment for a trolley bus for Aachen in 1950. A further order in 1952 for 700 trolley bus equipment sets for Buenos Aires led to international recognition.

ACEC, a Belgian group active in the field of electrical engineering, purchased Kiepe in 1973, which had been family-owned until then. In 1980, the prototype of three-phase propulsion equipment was delivered to the Essener Verkehrs-AG (Essen) and in 1986, the prototype three-phase electric motor with direct pulse inverter technology was put into operation in a trolley bus for Salzburg.

The parent company of Kiepe, ACEC, was taken over in 1988 by the French group ALSTOM S.A. Five years later AEG purchased Kiepe, but sold it in 1996 to Schaltbau Holding AG. Kiepe was subsequently purchased by Vossloh AG of Werdohl in 2002 and renamed Vossloh Kiepe a year later.

In 2003 Kiepe was awarded a major electrical equipment order for 262 trolley buses for Vancouver in partnership with New Flyer Industries Inc. This order became the springboard for Kiepe and New Flyer Industries' success with trolley coaches across North America. Today, Kiepe Electric is a member of the Knorr-Bremse group of companies and Kiepe equipment powers electric buses and rail vehicles around the world.

INTRODUCTION

From sea to sea, literally, Canadians in the mid-20th century rode on the most advanced form of urban transit – the electric bus. The trolley coach or trolley bus, as it was variously called, was the post-war clean, quiet, modern way of getting from point A to B in most major, and in some not so major, Canadian cities. For example, in 1952 the trolley coach served in fifteen cities using 1,036 coaches and orders were on the books for more.[1]

Today only a fragment remains – lonely Vancouver – of what was touted as the most progressive way of moving people around growing municipalities. All too soon, politics, aesthetics, economics and ownership changes spelled the end of most forms of electric transit – streetcar as well as the trolley coach – across the country. Still, the workhorse of urban transit from the late 1930s through to this century is fondly remembered by many, and here I have attempted to tell its story in as much detail and colour as we could find in dusty basement hoards, archives, newspaper clippings and photographs.

It is interesting that as one walks through these pages of trolley coach history, a number of names keep cropping up, for example consultant Norman D. Wilson favoured the use of trolley buses in a number of cities (Edmonton, Calgary, Halifax, Ottawa) and the firm Urwick, Curry Limited was retained to advise – usually in favour of discontinuing all forms of electric transit – in Ottawa, Toronto, Halifax, and Saskatoon. Again the salad years of electric transit, and especially the trolley coach, were often the result of electric utilities owning the city's transit system (Halifax, Cornwall, Windsor, Hamilton, Winnipeg, Vancouver), and either their reluctance to stay in this business or the municipality's desire to operate its own transit usually resulted in the trolley coach's demise. There were other factors that influenced decisions made by transit commissions on their bus fleet purchases including lack of builders of next generation trolleys, and the popularity, lower price and perceived flexibility of the modern motor bus (gasoline or diesel).

There were marked exceptions: Toronto owned its system from the get go with trolley coaches, and was responsible for the revival of the trolley bus in the 1970s with new coaches from Flyer Industries Ltd. and new lines (Bay Street, Mt. Pleasant Road) and route extensions, but then abandoned this transit form despite other system operators – Vancouver, Edmonton and Hamilton – investing in new coaches. In all fairness Hamilton bowed out slightly before Toronto, but one wonders if they had held on a little longer whether the green revolution might have found their trolley coach systems viewed in a more favourable light.

Still, the future of the trolley coach in Canada looks bleak, even in this age of energy crises. Edmonton has discontinued its seventy years of electric buses in favour

A snapshot of trolley bus service in Canada[2]

City	Date Opened	Current Status
Calgary, AB	June 1, 1947	Ended – March 8, 1975
Cornwall, ON	June 8, 1949	Ended – May 31, 1970
Edmonton, AB	Sept. 24, 1939	Ended – May 2, 2009
Halifax, NS	March 27, 1949	Ended – Dec. 31, 1969
Hamilton, ON	Dec. 10, 1950	Ended – Dec. 29, 1992
Kitchener, ON	Jan. 1, 1947	Ended – March 26, 1973
Montreal, QC	March 29, 1937	Ended – June 18, 1966
Ottawa, ON	Dec. 23, 1951	Ended – June 26, 1959
Regina, SK	Sept. 6, 1947	Ended – March 5, 1966
Saskatoon, SK	Nov. 22, 1948	Ended – May 10, 1974
Fort William, ON Port Arthur, ON Thunder Bay, ON	Dec. 15, 1947 Dec. 10, 1947 Jan. 1, 1970	Ended – July 16, 1972
Toronto, ON	June 19, 1922 June 19, 1947	Ended – Aug. 31, 1925 Ended – July 17, 1993
Vancouver, BC	Aug. 16, 1948	Still operating
Windsor, ON	May 4, 1922	Ended – May 1926
Winnipeg, MB	Nov. 21, 1938	Ended – Oct. 30, 1970

Trolley bus demonstration lines ran briefly in Vancouver and Victoria, BC late in 1945. Saint John, NB ordered trolley buses, but cancelled the order and never ran them. St. John's, Nfld. contemplated trolley buses but never followed through. Nelson, BC voted on them, but did not proceed.

of new, hybrid technology in the belief that lower initial cost will best higher fuel prices. Time will tell if they voted right on this one. This leaves only lonely Vancouver – a city that has never followed the transit crowd, as evidenced by its Advanced Rapid Transit or ART SkyTrain lines that use linear electromagnetic propulsion. Though it entered the trolley coach fraternity later than most Canadian cities, it has steadfastly looked for innovative ways to revitalize and extend the fleet, using modern electric buses and introducing low-floor and articulated units.

Elsewhere in North America the picture is varied – from Mexico City that seemingly runs anything that has wheels and two poles (including a lot of castoff Canadian equipment) to Boston, Philadelphia, Dayton, Seattle, and San Francisco that are retaining or vigorously expanding fleets. Overseas, many European cities, with many more years of dealing with high fuel prices and large populations on the move, are keeping electric buses alive and well.

But our task here is to visit once more the glory days of the trolley bus in Canada, where fifteen (sixteen if you split Thunder Bay into Port Arthur and Fort William) cities sported that most modern, efficient, quiet and ecologically-friendly form of transit. Herein I have tried to give a snapshot in relative detail of each city's flirtation with the trolley coach, but have not gone into such fine detail as fares, detailed routes, rollsign designations and timetables; for that please read the appropriate chapters in the references I used for that city such as Railfare's books on Cornwall, Winnipeg, Saskatoon, Edmonton and Calgary systems and their *Ontario's Grand River Valley Electric Railways*. Where there is no such reference the story here

Canada likes the TROLLEY COACH

The modern, electric ride on rubber is on the increase in Canada. Many of the Dominion's transit managements are including the trolley coach in their plans to modernize equipment and improve service. During the first quarter of 1947 alone, 10 Canadian properties had either started initial trolley coach operation, or had announced plans to do so. Orders for over 300 trolley coaches, to be operated on these 10 properties, have been placed and many of them have already been delivered. Moreover, as of February 15, 1947 three Canadian properties, which had been operating trolley coaches for several years, had ordered 112 additional vehicles for the expansion of this popular service.

Several years' successful experience with these vehicles has proved to Canadian operators that:

Trolley coaches operate efficiently in temperatures as low as 45 degrees below zero... Trolley coaches climb easily the steepest hills while fully loaded... Trolley coaches operate with an absolute minimum amount of maintenance... Trolley coaches consistently return high net profits... Trolley coaches are popular with the public and build riding and good will wherever they are installed.

No wonder this modern electric service is becoming so widespread throughout the Dominion of Canada.

MANSFIELD, OHIO

CANADIAN OHIO BRASS CO., LTD.
NIAGARA FALLS, ONTARIO

is what I pieced together from as many sources (noted) as I could find, and that may be the first and only telling of that city's trolley coach history.

Finally a note on nomenclature: post-WWII, when many Canadian systems were converting streetcar systems to the electric bus, the most common word used for it was "trolley coach". Trade journals used this term extensively as did manufacturers. In the latter years, the remaining systems' marketing people started using "trolley bus" or alternated it with "trolley coach". But, for internal use (garage staff, rolling stock engineers), these vehicles were usually referred to as "trolley coaches". Post-war ads placed by Canadian Car & Foundry, maker of the Canadian Car-Brill referred to the vehicles as "trackless trolley coaches". In some US cities, such as Boston and Philadelphia, the term more commonly used was "trackless trolley" or simply, "trackless". However, all the US manufacturers used the term "trolley coach". In Vancouver, the public and transit staff most often used the simple short form, "trolley" which was common in other places like Hamilton and Toronto, but this can be confused with "trolley car", a.k.a. "streetcar" (or "tram" overseas). I have tried to stick to "coach" where possible but have occasionally alternated with "bus" for stylistic reasons. However, when I reference or directly quote an official site or source, their nomenclature is what I used. Hence, "trolleybus" sometimes shows up as one word. Thanks to Ted Wickson for this bit of trolley 'coach' history.

To be consistent, the author has adopted the convention of using imperial measurements throughout the text, given the timespan of the book's content and the tendency of earlier records to be rounded off. In addition, Canadian spelling has been used in this publication about trolley coaches in Canada.

Footnotes:

1. *Canadian Transportation*, April 1952 p. 205.
2. Edmonton Trolleybus Operations: Future Directions. Edmonton > Transit > What's New > Trolleybus Operations – Q and A, with this author's date amendments, corrections and the additions of Saskatoon and Windsor, and title change. *http://www.edmonton.ca/portal/server.pt/gateway/PTARGS_0_2_2869118_0_0_18/* visited February 2007 but no longer active.

Opposite: This c1947 Ohio Brass ad boasted of thirteen Canadian locations that were or were about to use the trolley coach. Unfortunately St. John (sic) never materialized and Hamilton, Ottawa and Cornwall had not yet joined the parade.
(OHIO BRASS COLLECTION, THE STRAHORN LIBRARY, ILLINOIS RAILWAY MUSEUM.)

Index (starts on page 270)

Corporate names for transit systems (trolley coach operators) that are the principal subject in this book are not indexed as a broad term. For these, many narrower terms are given, as well as broad terms for predecessor systems (e.g. street railways) that existed prior to trolley coach introduction in their respective municipalities. Rolling stock fleet numbers normally are not indexed, except for vehicles with unique specifications, histories or featured in special events or accidents.

Common acronyms and short forms used in this work:

ACF	– American Car & Foundry Co.
ACF-Brill	– short for trolley coaches built in the US by ACF-Brill Motors Co.
A.E.C.	– Associated Equipment Co.
BAH	– Booz Allen Hamilton (consultants)
BBC	– Brown Boveri & Cie.
B.C.E.R., BCE	– British Columbia Electric Railway Co., British Columbia Electric
Brill	– This term is used often as a short form for Canadian Car-Brill trolley coaches manufactured at Canadian Car & Foundry's Bus Division in Fort William, Ontario.
CCF, CC&F	– Canadian Car & Foundry Co. Ltd.
CCL	– Canada Coach Lines
CMBC	– Coast Mountain Bus Company (Vancouver)
CNG	– compressed natural gas
CNR	– Canadian National Railways
CPR	– Canadian Pacific Railway, CP Rail
CSR	– Cornwall Street Railway Light & Power Co., Limited
CTS, CT	– Calgary Transit System, Calgary Transit
E.E.C.	– English Electric Co.
ERR	– Edmonton Radial Railway
ETS, ET	– Edmonton Transit System, Edmonton Transit
FDC	– Federal District Commission
GE, CGE	– General Electric, Canadian General Electric
GM, GMC	– General Motors Company, General Motors Diesel of Canada
GVRD	– Greater Vancouver Regional District
GVTS	– Greater Vancouver Transit System
GWTC	– Greater Winnipeg Transit Commission
HSR	– Hamilton Street Railway Company
K&M	– Kummler+Matter
LRT	– light rail transit
MCI	– Motor Coach Industries
Motor bus	– non-electric bus fuelled by gasoline, diesel, or propane
MTC	– Montreal Tramways Company / Transportation Commission
MTOC	– Metro Transit Operating Company (Vancouver)
MUCTC	– Montreal Urban Community Transit Commission
NB Power	– New Brunswick Power Company
NSL&P	– Nova Scotia Light and Power Co. Ltd.
NYC	– New York Central Railroad
OER	– Ottawa Electric Railway
OTC	– Ottawa Transportation Commission
PCC	– Presidents' Conference Committee (streetcar)
PUB	– Public Utilities Board (Halifax)
PUC	– Public Utilities Commission (e.g. Kitchener, Port Arthur)
SMT	– SMT (Eastern) Ltd.
STS	– Saskatoon Transit System
SW&A	– Sandwich, Windsor & Amherstburg Railway
TRAMS	– Transit Museum Society (Vancouver)
TTC	– Toronto Transportation / Transit Commission
UBC	– University of British Columbia
UTA	– Urban Transit Authority (Vancouver)
VICL	– Vancouver Island Coach Lines
WEC	– Winnipeg Electric Co.

PART 1:

A Brief History of the Trolley Coach in Canada

The trolley coach or bus or trackless trolley was not a North American invention as such; it seems to have originated in an 1882 Siemens & Haske trackless trolley in Germany which was an open wagon with an electric motor, its power supplied by a flexible cable. That same year, a Dr. Finney of Pittsburg devised a two-wire overhead system for omnibuses. Other ideas were tried in America throughout the late 1880s and early 1900s including a two-coach line in 1910 operated by the Laurel Canyon Utilities Company near Los Angeles,[3] but the first established transit use was in 1913 in Merrill, WI. The manager of the Merrill Railway & Lighting Company, E. S. King, arranged to have a version of a battery bus made that would run under twin overhead wires. It was a short-lived arrangement, and trackless electric transportation languished until a system appeared in 1921 on Staten Island, NY.

Canada can lay claim to entering this new, unproved field early, as on May 5th 1922, Windsor, ON started a trolley bus line on Lincoln Road using a St. Louis Car Company vehicle that had been built for the 1921 exhibition in Detroit across the river. A 29-seat vehicle with a body-on-frame construction, it was 26 feet long, and weighed just 10,500 pounds. Its success was manifested in the purchase of three additional coaches, and a second line opened on August 1st 1922.

Toronto next stepped into this new form of passenger transportation. When the Toronto Transportation Commission took over a private transit concern in 1921, it found a citizenry demanding streetcar service along Mount Pleasant Road. Wishing to avoid the considerable expense of laying track, the Commission offered trolley coaches. Four were ordered from Canadian Brill in November and placed in service the next June 19th. Streetcar service was eventually extended along Mount Pleasant, and by August of 1925, trolley coach service had ended in Toronto. Windsor's system closed shortly afterward in May 1926 and for another decade streetcars retained their supremacy over the trolley coach in Canada.[4]

It wasn't until the late 1930s that the trolley coach returned to Canadian urban transportation with systems inaugurated in Montreal (1937), Winnipeg (1938) and Edmonton (1939).[5] Over the next fifty or so years, the trackless trolley took over almost entirely from the streetcar as post-war conditions of worn-out track and trams and unavailability of new ones offered a perfect breeding ground for the electric bus. Also, much of the existing traction power supply and associated wayside infrastructure could be reused and adapted for trolley coach operation. While they were scheduled mostly on heavily travelled routes in concert with motor buses on feeder routes, Halifax operated trolley coaches exclusively for many years, Winnipeg used them alongside diesel buses and Toronto utilized them on medium feeder routes for the subway system. From a small cadre of 49 coaches in 1945, by 1950 there were 880 trolley coaches in Canadian service, swelling to 1256 in the mid-50s.

But the trolley coach was too early for the green revolution; its popularity with patrons and transit companies waned. Politics, aesthetics, the move from private to public ownership, and the desire to have a homogenous transit form, led to its dying out in nearly all of the cities that had previously embraced the trolley coach as the savior of the transit system.

It did not help, perhaps, that the technology hadn't changed much in five decades, but then "Why meddle with success?" Aside from bus bodies wearing and rusting out, electric motors and controllers went on and on. That one key fact led to a minor resurgence in the trolley coach in Canada led by Toronto in 1970 (following testing of a Western Flyer prototype 1968-69), putting new Flyer bodies around salvaged and refurbished Brill/GE electrics. Hamilton, Edmonton and Vancouver cautiously embraced the new trolleys and a few other manufacturers stepped forward. Despite bumps in the process, with new safety regulations and new electronics – some of which performed with spectacular fireworks – these properties persisted. Unfortunately, Toronto and Hamilton dropped out; their reasons will be covered in their respective chapters. Edmonton discontinued that passenger-popular transit offering in 2009. Vancouver has re-committed significantly to the trolley coach with low floor, standard and articulated versions. However, by the end of the 20th century, the only other cities in North America still operating trolley buses were: Boston, Philadelphia, Dayton, Seattle, San Francisco, Mexico City and Guadalajara. Whether this new century's energy crises and green movement will push this most passenger- environmentally- and fiscally-friendly form of public transit back into our transit futures, only time will tell.

Opposite: By June 1951 every Canadian city that would have trolley coaches, with the exception of Ottawa, was operating Can Car-Brills wholly or in part. Ottawa would follow that December with another ten T-48As. (SCHWARZKOPF COLLECTION)

Old trolleys never die, they just get recycled into New Flyers. Various trolley coach bodies are stored at a scrap yard in the winter of 1970-71 after re-usable electrical parts were stripped from them for Toronto's ambitious rebuilding program. From the left: ex-Cornwall, Toronto, Halifax and Cornwall (again) Brills. (TED WICKSON)

The Builders:[6]
Canadian Car & Foundry Co. Ltd.

In 1909 the Canada Car Company, Rhodes Curry Company, and Dominion Car & Foundry joined forces to become Canadian Car & Foundry Co. Ltd., headquartered in Montreal. It became a well-respected railroad car builder, and in 1944 was licensed by the American bus manufacturer ACF-Brill to "manufacturer and sell, for use throughout Canada… buses and trolley coaches of our design – these to be manufactured under the trade name 'Canadian Car-Brill' ".[7] World War II intervened and the Fort William plant turned out military aircraft instead, but once the outcome of the war became clear, the plant was in danger of closing. The Hon. C. D. Howe, who would become Minister of Reconstruction after the war, strongly supported the retooling of CC&F's Aircraft Division for bus production. Preparations began immediately following the March 1945 announcement of the new Bus Division at Fort William.[8]

Many lines of equipment were explored, but CC&F finally settled on manufacturing buses for the Canadian market. A happy marriage of the acquisition of ACF-Brill of Philadelphia's motor bus designs and the skill derived from producing aluminum aircraft gave Can Car a distinct advantage over other suppliers. By 1946 the need for an electric bus was determined and a 44-passenger coach was designed, again to Brill specifications, with Canadian General Electric propulsion and controls. It had a heat-treated aluminum frame, mostly aluminum structural members, and aluminum body sheeting. In fact, aluminum was even used for the step wells. A demonstrator was produced in late 1946 that travelled to many Canadian cities, first to Winnipeg and Calgary, and then Toronto, also Saskatoon and Montreal, and was eventually sold (used) to Cornwall in 1951. The first production T-44s (shop serial numbers 1-10*) were delivered to Kitchener in 1947. They were well-built buses with about two-thirds Canadian components. In the post-war years nearly all Canadian transportation systems that converted to trolley coach used Can Car-Brills. A companion line of gasoline and diesel models, notably the very popular C36 model, was also offered to customers. As a side note, ACF-Brill, seeing the success of the 1946 Canadian aluminum coach, changed its production design to a very similar one to CCF's and also called it a T-44.

When production of the larger 48-seat T-48 started in 1949, most properties saw the economy of the larger bus and went for it, the exceptions being Montreal and Halifax. The double front doors of the T-48 allowed a flow of passengers entering and exiting the bus simultaneously. In cold weather only one door could be opened if passengers were only alighting or entering. Production of both the T-44 and T-48 topped out at 1094 units – far more than ACF produced in the US. Initially all Can Car buses and trolley coaches were nearly 100 per cent aluminum (a few high stress posts were steel), until about 1949 when the introduction of heavier gasoline, and later, diesel engines required a steel frame to support them. Soon after, most of the existing models – diesel or electric – used the steel frame and had the A added to their model designation. Use of steel was also mandated due to restrictions on the use of strategic metals (aluminum) imposed during the three-year Korean War. A spotting feature to differentiate a T-44A from a T-44 was the use of lifting, as opposed to a sliding sash in the passenger windows. Otherwise the basic bus stayed the same for eight years. CCF-Brill also sold twenty T-44s to Tranvia Municipal de Bogota, Colombia.[9] In total, Canadian Car built 648 T-44s, 35 T-44As, 204 T-48s and 227 T-48As – a remarkable production of well-built buses. *Canadian Coach* magazine in April 1969 noted that their output of trolley coaches, "numbering about 1100, and having an average age of 20 years, are almost all still in service, and with a minimum of maintenance they will be running as long as their owners want them to." Would it only have been so! Still, the longevity of

*Shop serial numbers are not to be confused with the assigned serial numbers that were stamped into the builder's plate affixed to the finished vehicle. These were in three series – the original T-44 and T-48s in the 5000 series; the T-44As in the 6000 series and the T-48As in the 8000 series.

Opposite: A 1954 advertisement shows off a T-44 coach and highlights repeat orders from all across the country. Unfortunately, this was the last year of trolley coach production at Fort William; their legendary longevity would prove to be the undoing of any replacement orders. (PAUL A. LEGER COLLECTION)

A BRIEF HISTORY OF THE TROLLEY COACH IN CANADA

New orders prove competitive strength...
Repeat orders prove customer satisfaction

CANADIAN CAR-BRILL
TRACKLESS TROLLEY COACHES

In operation right across Canada with fast, smooth power and acceleration, low cost operation, silent performance, modern design for efficiency and curb loading.

Automotive Division

In the U.S.A. it's A. C. F. Brill

CANADIAN CAR & FOUNDRY COMPANY LIMITED

Head Office, Montreal, Que.
Plant, Fort William, Ont.

TTC operators confer after a training run in the Can Car demonstrator coach at the Lansdowne Carhouse, January 1947. The coach finished out its life as Cornwall Street Railway Light & Power Co. No. 115. (J.D. KNOWLES)

these Made in Canada coaches was such that repeat orders dwindled. The last T-44A order went to Halifax in December 1954, and the last T-48As were sent to Edmonton (shop serial numbers 340-345) that year-end.[10]

CCF-Brill's output throughout the years is indicated in the chart. Details of individual orders, fleet numbers, serial numbers and model are listed in each city's roster in Appendix A.

The Fort William/Thunder Bay plant was taken over by A.V. Roe Canada, a member of the Hawker Siddeley Group of England in 1955, and was revitalized in the early 1980s as Can-Car Rail, a joint operation between Hawker Siddeley and UTDC (Urban Transportation Development Corporation, an Ontario Crown corporation created in the 1970s to build advanced light and heavy rail cars for mass transit systems). Sold to SNC-Lavalin in 1986, re-sold soon after to the Government of Ontario, CC&F assets were finally acquired by Bombardier Transportation. The Fort William plant now makes light rail vehicles, subway cars and commuter rail cars.

New Flyer Industries Ltd.

In 1930, Western Auto & Truck Body Works was founded by John Coval, a Ukrainian immigrant who had settled in Winnipeg, Manitoba. As the company turned more and more to bus manufacturing, it changed its name in 1948 to Western Flyer Coach Ltd.

In 1966, the Toronto Transit Commission reconsidered its position about trolley coach service. Most of its trolley

Table 1: CCF-Brill production[11]

Year	Model	Units	Total for Year
1946	T-44	16	16
1947	T-44	311	311
1948	T-44	206	206
1949	T-44	49	
	T-48	96	145
1950	T-44	46	
	T-44A	4	
	T-48	106	
	T-48A	46	202
1951	T-48	2	
	T-48A	111	113
1952	T-44A	27	
	T-48	4	31
1953	T-48A	44	44
1954	T-44A	4	
	T-48A	22	26

A detailed list of CCF's production with the associated transit properties by year can be found at Allan Gryffe's website:
http://www.angelfire.com/ca/TORONTO/builders/ccftc.html
Data amalgamated from Sebree/Ward, *Transit's Stepchild, The Trolley Coach* pp. 148-9 with corrections by the author.

buses' mechanicals and bus bodies were wearing out; however electric components were still useable. But there were no North American trolley coach producers, and sourcing new buses from Europe was cost-prohibitive. TTC then turned to finding a supplier that would work with them in rebuilding the fleet. On May 2nd 1967, fleet No. 9020, a Can Car-Brill T-44, was shipped to (then) Western Flyer Coach, rebuilt and returned to Hillcrest shops July 22nd 1968. This prototype was tested in Toronto for a year and then returned to Western Flyer for further modifications and further testing. Based on this, TTC mapped out a rebuilding program with Western Flyer to produce a new chassis, body, and running gear, and the TTC to install all

At the Winnipeg Flyer plant, a row of E800 trolley coaches is being assembled for Edmonton.
(FLYER PHOTO; JEFF MARINOFF COLLECTION)

electrics, interior appointments and final painting. About sixty per cent of the cost of completing the assembly of each coach was borne by TTC forces.

By the late 1960s, Flyer had shifted their focus toward the production of city buses and became known as Flyer Industries Limited in 1971. In that same year it signed an agreement with AM General Corporation, a wholly-owned subsidiary of American Motors, for Flyer bus shells to be assembled in AMG's Mishawaka, IL plant to export new design trolley coaches into the US. The success of these trolley coaches prompted the Manitoba government to put money into a home-grown production facility, and a new plant was built to produce both diesel and electric buses. In 1986, a Dutch interest purchased the company, changing its name to New Flyer Industries Limited.[12] In 1972, Hamilton purchased forty of the new E700A buses. Edmonton, Hamilton and Vancouver followed with orders for the E800/E800A models and later Vancouver ordered the improved E900 model.

Under its new ownership, New Flyer became the first company to introduce low-floor buses to North America, creating a new industry standard. In 2004, they received an order for 188 newly-styled E40LFR low-floor trolleybuses from the Greater Vancouver Transportation Authority, followed by an order for forty E60LFR low-floor articulated trolley buses. The first E40LFR was delivered in July 2005 for verification and testing, and the rest of the units were delivered in late 2006.[13] The E60LFR trolley buses entered Vancouver's transit service in 2007.

Brown Boveri/General Motors Company

In 1982, Brown Boveri & Cie (BBC), the Swiss electrical equipment maker, supplied Edmonton Transit with 100 new trolley coaches. For this order, BBC contracted with General Motors Diesel Division in St. Eustache, Quebec, for the supply of bodies using their 40-foot new look 5307N design. Designated model HR150G by BBC, these coaches featured solid state chopper controls. The first one, ETS 100, was completed and tested at GMDD's plant in St. Eustache while the 99 other shells had electrics installed in Edmonton by Bennett & Emmot, a local contractor. There were, however, no other purchasers. Even though BBC bid on a 1981 Vancouver order, they were unsuccessful, primarily because the GM body was judged non-conforming to the bid specifications.

Associated Equipment Co.

It may seem odd perhaps that Canada's largest French-speaking city would order English (UK)-built trolley buses, but in 1937, Montreal experimented with coaches

Text continues on page 18

Above: A Flyer body destined to become TTC 9201 arrives in Hillcrest Shops August 13th 1970.

Left: Installing rebuilt electrical control circuits.

Opposite Top: All seats and upholstery were fabricated at Hillcrest Shops (this coach 9282 was the next to last one built July 20th 1972).

Opposite Left: Masking prior to painting.

Opposite Right: Final touches put on coach 9020.

(ALL PHOTOS BY TED WICKSON)

Edmonton Transit BBC/GM model HR150G, the only trolley coach model built by GM, passes its diesel brother as they duck under the CN line on 101 Street in Edmonton, May 26th, 1985. These coaches later served on lease in Toronto, then were returned to Edmonton and ended trolley service in that city in 2009. (TED WICKSON)

that had chassis by Associated Equipment Co., bodies by Metro-Cammell-Weymann and English Electric propulsion and control equipment. These buses were unique in that they had three axles with two sets of rear tires – both driven. Similar forty-seat coaches were also ordered by Edmonton who later made one set of axles freewheeling as this reduced the wear and complexity of the differentials. In all, only ten units were shipped to Canada; seven to Montreal and three to Edmonton in 1939.

Leyland Manufacturing Corp. Ltd.

Another English (London) firm, Leyland was well known the world over as a superb coach builder, but only Edmonton ordered these imports. The bodies on these 39-seat trolley coaches were by Park Royal and there were only six in total to cross the Atlantic. The shipment of first three was in progress when war broke out in September 1939, but all reached Canada safely.

There were three other Edmonton coaches from the UK – they were ACC-Park Royal buses, whose design was a blend of the earlier A.E.C. and later Leyland coaches.

Canadian Brill Company

The Toronto experiment with trolley buses used a Canadian-Brill design employing American technology. These were Brill bodies, constructed at Preston, Ontario (the former Preston Car plant), mounted on Packard's standard 3½ ton chassis and using a Westinghouse 508-A electric motor. They bore a striking resemblance to motor buses, right down to the hard rubber tires and protruding hood and radiator cowling. Initially they used a single pole with a harp at the top that housed swivel collectors. The change to two poles came soon after they determined that this arrangement was much more efficient. Ultimately the trolley coach was replaced by the streetcar and the four Toronto "Brill-Packards" were stored; three were scrapped in November of 1928, but one was discovered in a farmer's field near Bewdley, Ontario in May 1974 and moved to a museum in Cobourg. It was acquired by the Halton County Radial Railway museum in October 1978.[14]

St. Louis Car

Founded in 1887, St. Louis Car was a major builder of streetcars, locomotives and trolley coaches. It commenced trolley coach building in 1921 and continued until 1954, but the only Canadian order ever was for Windsor. Slightly earlier than Toronto, Windsor experimented with trackless trolleys as a precursor to full streetcar operation on new routes. The St. Louis coaches differed from other builders in that the body was built directly on the chassis instead of being built separately and then mated to a truck chassis. The initial coach, built for the demonstration line in Detroit, was added to a 1922 order for three more and shipped to Canada. St. Louis didn't build any more trolley coaches until 1930 and no Canadian property was interested in the trackless trolley then. By the time Canadian cities resumed investing heavily in trolley coaches, the home-grown Canadian Car-Brill coach was in production.

Mack Trucks Inc.

Based in Allentown, PA, Mack had a long history of truck and bus manufacturing, and after WWI decided to enter

Sherwin-Williams paints ran this ad in January 1938, proudly showing off Montreal's new A.E.C. trolley coach resplendent in their paint.
(SCHWARZKOPF COLLECTION)

the emerging trolley bus field. These vehicles were built like the proverbial Mack truck – strong and, unfortunately, heavy. Mack did offer a forty-passenger model to Edmonton in 1938 but didn't get the order. Winnipeg started with Macks and had sixteen before slackening sales ended Mack's production in 1943, with only five to Winnipeg and three units to Edmonton delivered under wartime supply restrictions.

Pullman-Standard Car Mfg. Corp.

Pullman (Chicago) had a long and well-deserved reputation as a premier streetcar builder, but its Bradley plant in Worcester, MA turned out hundreds of trolley coaches starting in 1932, mostly for New England properties. A few – 31 in fact – made it to Canada. These were during WWII when transit companies took whatever they were allowed to purchase by the wartime Dominion Transit Controller and US Office of Defense Transportation. Edmonton (the collector of many manufacturer's nameplates) took eight in 1944 and another eight the next year; Winnipeg got fifteen in 1945. The Edmonton models were 44Ts and Winnipeg's 44AS, all 44-seat models. One of the Edmonton coaches, No. 116 has been preserved by Edmonton Transit and renumbered 113 to represent the first of the order.

In addition to new coaches, a number of second-hand coaches were brought to Canada in the 1950s as US transit agencies began phasing out their trolley coach operations. Halifax bought six and Winnipeg eighteen model 44CXs from Providence, Rhode Island, while Vancouver purchased 25 from Birmingham, Alabama.

Marmon-Herrington Co. Inc.

No products of this Indianapolis, IN manufacturer were ever bought new by any Canadian transit company, but some came north as used units, notably Toronto's acquisition of ex-Cincinnati and Cleveland Marmons. The company started as a luxury car producer, then turned to co-design the Jeep in its wartime origins, and found its final success with the trolley coach. Its 1946 introduction to a transit world emerging from war deprivation was an instant success with a light-weight, monocoque body and a strong frame. It became the best-selling (US) trolley coach of the post-war era. Marmon-Herrington also produced 46-, then 48-, and finally 50-seat models, but trolley coach saturation saw the company's fall from grace, and it ceased manufacturing trolley buses in 1959.

ACF-Brill

J.G. Brill & Company manufactured streetcars and buses in Philadelphia, PA. It was taken over by the American Car & Foundry Company in 1926. Brill developed

Left Upper: Looking forlorn and not in the best of shape, this is how the only surviving Canadian Brill coach appeared when found in a farmer's field in 1974.
(TED WICKSON)

Left Lower: After being rescued, TTC 23 is undergoing restoration at the Halton County Radial Railway museum near Guelph.
(ROBERT LUBINSKI)

Opposite Top: In December 1939, a Winnipeg Mack coach is being given a leak test at the Mack Truck facility in Allentown, PA.
(MACK PHOTO, JEFF MARINOFF COLLECTION)

Opposite Bottom: The Winnipeg Macks had roomy interiors with bright lighting, wide windows and comfortable seats.
(MACK PHOTO, JEFF MARINOFF COLLECTION)

a trackless trolley (which it called a rail-less car) in 1921 and sold a few, notably to Baltimore. However, the trackless trolley didn't catch on until about 1930 when Brill became a major producer of these vehicles in the United States. As with most bus and streetcar manufacturers, production was co-opted for war needs, and it wasn't until after the war that ACF-Motors Company resumed production of buses and trolley buses at the Philadelphia plant. In 1944, the two holding companies – Brill Corporation and American Car & Foundry Motors Company – were merged as ACF-Brill.[15] Production of electric buses ceased in 1952. As a Canadian footnote, the J.G. Brill Company had acquired Ontario's troubled Preston Car Company in 1921, allowing it to bid on a major streetcar order for Toronto (the fifty "Brill" Peter Witt cars) as well as supplying the TTC with four trolley coaches (see Canadian Brill Company above). The plant was closed suddenly in late 1923, with balance of Canadian orders completed at Philadelphia.

Only one Canadian transit property, Edmonton, bought post-war ACF-Brills new (two), and only Winnipeg and Calgary acquired used versions – Calgary the older model TC-44, and Winnipeg the newer post-war model T-46 which was similar to the Can Car-Brill coaches.

Motor Coach Industries (MCI) – a footnote

MCI started in 1933 in a Winnipeg repair shop, where owner Harry Zoltok sketched his design for an eleven-passenger body on a Packard chassis on the factory floor. The company, then known as Fort Garry Motor Body and Paint Works Limited, became Motor Coach Industries in 1941. In 1948, Greyhound Lines of Canada, MCI's major

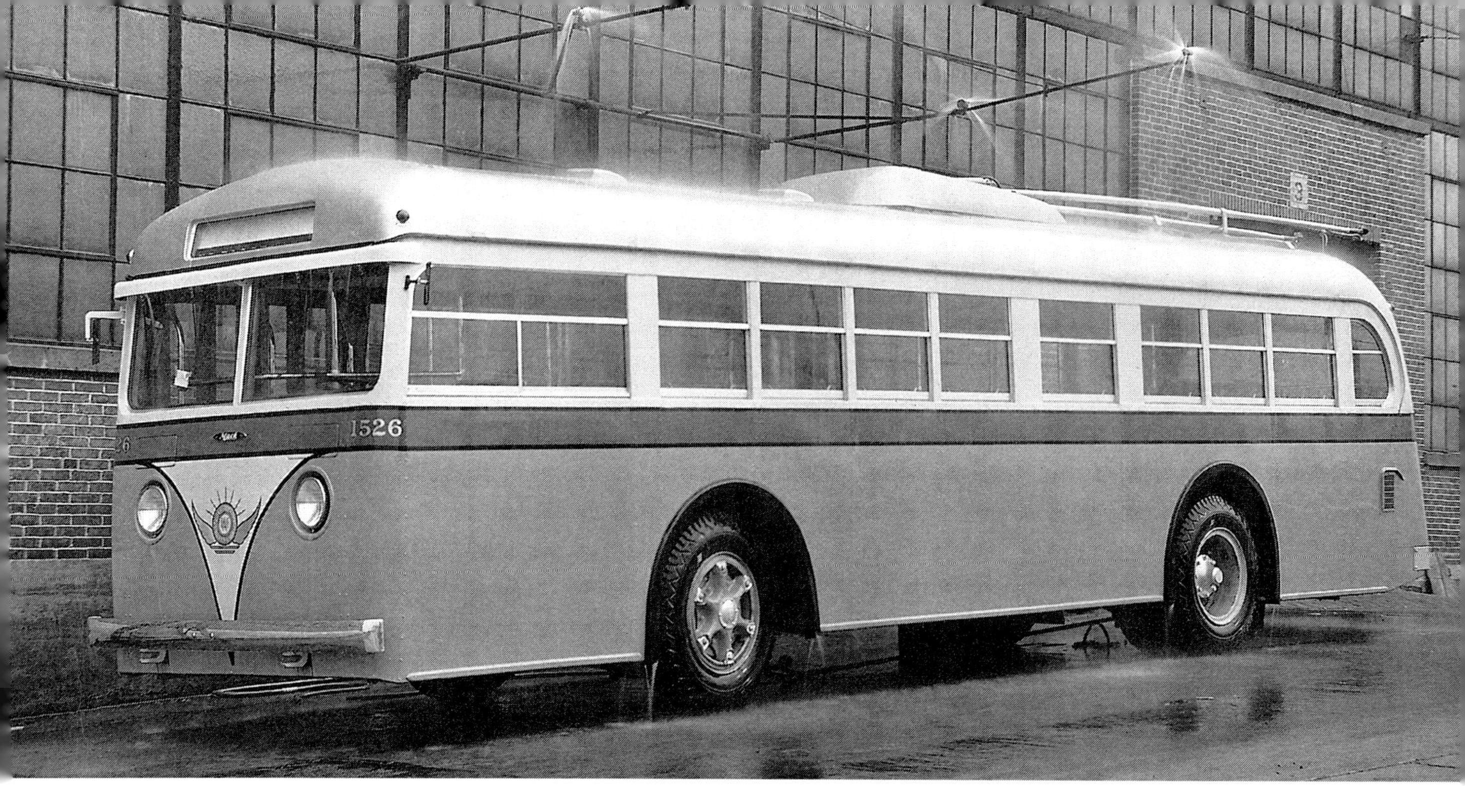
1526

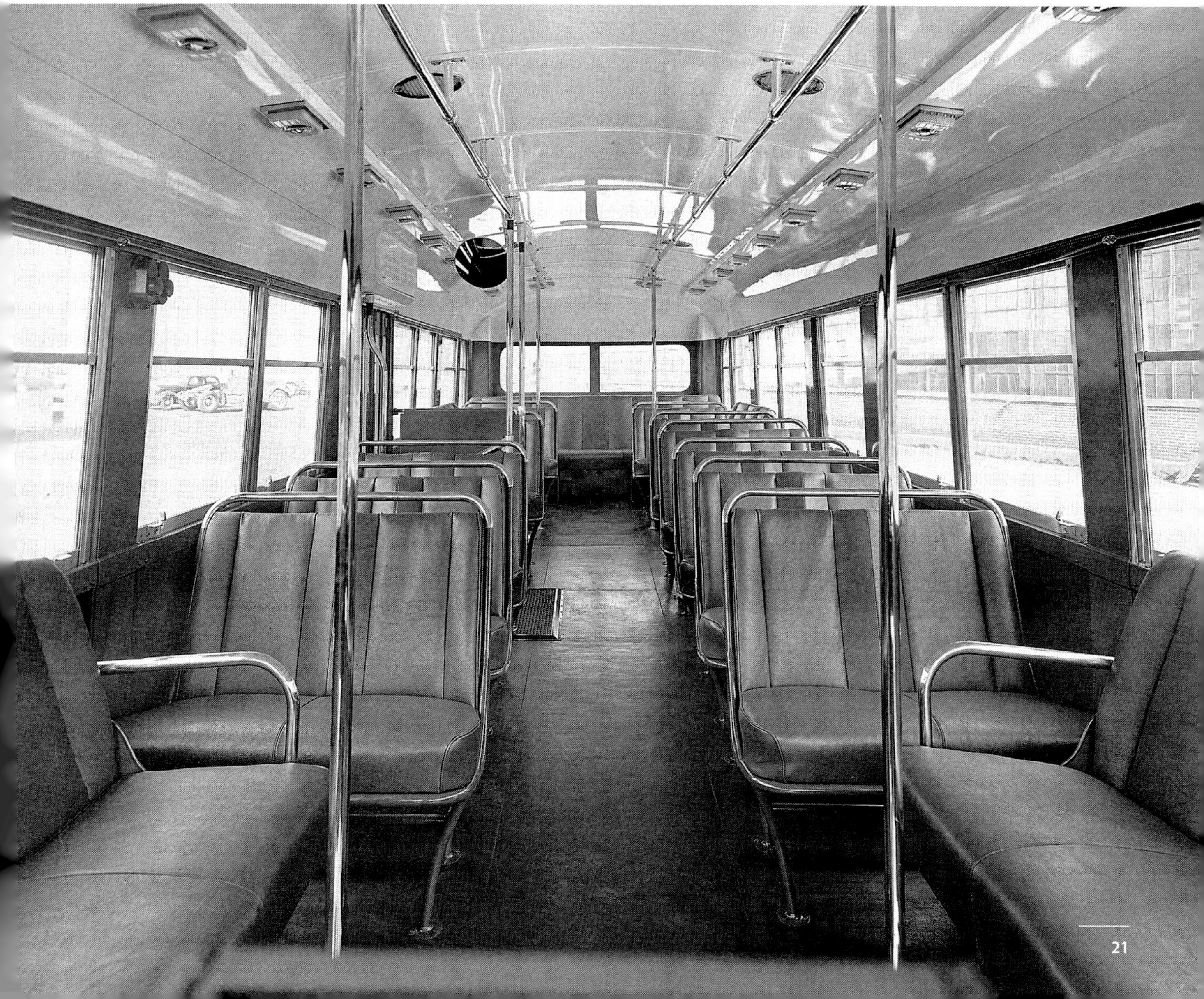

Newly arrived at TTC's Hillcrest shops, Cincinnati Marmon-Herrington 1350 is about to be cleaned up, re-painted and will join Toronto's fleet as 9130. June 26th 1953.
(TTC PHOTO; JEFF MARINOFF COLLECTION)

customer, purchased 65 per cent of the company and in 1958 purchased it outright.

Primarily a highway coach manufacturer, MCI also built urban transit coaches including the 1939 Model 150, a new transit-type coach with the windshield over the radiator, the first use of exterior stainless steel panels and a pancake engine mounted amidships under the floor.

In late 1941, MCI designed and built the first electric trolley bus manufactured in Canada since the Canadian Brills of 1922, designated Model 40TRY with Westinghouse controls and motors. It was delivered to the Winnipeg Electric Company (WEC) on February 20th 1942 and ran as unit 1532 for 25 years. A forty-passenger coach on an all-steel frame, it had Cor-Ten steel exterior panels. Cor-Ten was a proprietary steel designed to ward off corrosion. The bus was an attractive one for its day, and a contract for thirty coaches was signed by WEC, but by then the MCI plant was churning out war production and no more coaches were built. Thus, with this sole unit, Canada's role in trolley coach building took a hiatus until Canadian Car entered the field in 1946.[16] The coach was stored in a Winnipeg scrap yard for a number of years, but was eventually scrapped.

In December 2015, Motor Coach Industries was acquired by New Flyer Industries Inc., now NFI Group Inc., from KPS Capital Partners, L.P.

Footnotes:

3. *Transit Journal*, Vol. 78 No. 10, September 15, 1934 p. 355.
4. Sebree, Mac and Paul Ward, *Transit's Stepchild, The Trolley Coach* (Interurbans Special 58), Interurbans, Los Angeles CA, 1973. pp. 11, 17-18.
5. Sebree, Mac and Paul Ward, *The Trolley Coach in North America* (Interurbans Special 59), Interurbans, Ceritos CA, 1974 pp. 292-346.
6. Sebree/Ward, *Transit's Stepchild, The Trolley Coach* pp. 149-251 with additional information on CCF-Brill, MCI, Flyer and GM/BB as noted below.
7. Brill, Debra, *History of the J.G. Brill Company* as extracted in Google books. http://books.google.ca/books?id=eqKKrMi3FIIC&pg=PA212&lpg=PA212&dq=canadian+car+brill&source=bl&ots=D6vUhW8FwQ&sig=ZVGLlW3z31zDVo3PdSw_6etIN1o&hl=en&sa=X&ei=NyEhUIuRJ9Hp6QGuuoFg&ved=0CFQQ6AEwBjge#v=onepage&q=canadian%20car%20brill&f=false visited August 7, 2012.
8. Wickson, Edward, May 2018 edits.
9. John M. Day and Peter Cox, e-mail correspondence with Wally Young regarding this author's questions.
10. Letter from J.F.A. Painter, Dir. Public Relations Hawker Siddeley Corporation to author, May 11, 1978. Also quoted on Wikipedia Canadian Car and Foundry page with reference *Trolleybus Magazine* No. 283, January–February 2009, p. 11. National Trolleybus Association (UK). ISSN 0266-7452.
11. Data amalgamated from Sebree/Ward, *Transit's Stepchild, The Trolley Coach* p. 149 with corrections by the author.
12. Extracted from busexplorer.com "Flyer, New Flyer and AMG transit buses" by John Veerkamp. http://busexplorer.com/NABus/FlyerNewFlyer-Text.html visited December 2012.
13. New Flyer website http://www.newflyer.com/ visited February 2008.
14. Transit Toronto web site: The First Generation … http://transit.toronto.on.ca/trolleybus/9501.shtml visited October 22, 2012.
15. Sebree/Ward *Transit's Stepchild, The Trolley Coach*, p. 127, and Brill, Debra, *History of the J.G. Brill Company*, Indiana University Press, ISBN 0-253-33949-9 as excerpted in Google Books (no longer posted).
16. *Canadian Transportation*: April 1942, p. 226 and a later issue, unknown month on author's copy, 1942.

Opposite Top: MCI's only trolley coach, Winnipeg #1532, is posed at the main carhouse not far from the Fort Garry Hotel – probably Spring 1942.
(WESTINGHOUSE PHOTO, WILLIAM VOLKMER COLLECTION)

Opposite Bottom: The interior of the MCI coach. The back had a sign over the rear window reading "This trolley coach built in Winnipeg".
(WESTINGHOUSE PHOTO, WILLIAM VOLKMER COLLECTION)

7 NOTRE DAME
77 N. DAME
ENTER FRONT
1532

NO SMOKING PLEASE
1532

Above: The ribbon is cut and trolley coach service inaugurated as a young enthusiast snaps away with his Brownie. Courtesy of Metro Transit, these snapshots by Harold Snider captured the moment, Sunday, March 27th, 1949.
(PAUL LEGER COLLECTION)

Below: Coach 274 loads in the turnaround in front of the Simpsons-Sears building at the end of Chebucto Road. The #5 ARMDALE sign will change to #5 QUINPOOL, and the coach will leave Simpsons, turn right onto Chebucto Road, go around the Armdale Rotary and head up Quinpool Road. Judging from the flags and shields this is June 1953, around the time of the Coronation of Queen Elizabeth II.
(OHIO BRASS COLLECTION, THE STRAHORN LIBRARY, ILLINOIS RAILWAY MUSEUM. LOCATION INFORMATION – MIKE LARISEY)

PART 2: CANADIAN CITIES THAT OPERATED TROLLEY COACHES

Halifax (1949-1969)
Nova Scotia Light and Power Co. Ltd.

One of only two cities in North America, and the only one in Canada, that went from streetcars to all trolley coaches, this system also served two municipalities, crossed a major waterway and coped with narrow streets and hilly terrain – all home territory for the trolley coach. But, when the system passed from private electric utility to public hands, the trolley coach passed away.

It might be said of transit planning in Halifax, "It's the geography!" is the ruling mantra. Canada's eastern continental port city lies on a peninsula with four-fifths of that coastline. Squeeze into that area downtown, docks, public buildings, a seat of government and living quarters, toss in a few military compounds and several historical and tourist areas, and you have a densely packed population navigating narrow streets. Oh, and did we mention hilly areas rising sharply from the waterfront over long grades?

It was no wonder then that the city's street railway consisted of 58 single truck Birney trams (as the locals called them) weaving through the narrow streets and climbing the hills carrying large volumes of riders who were conditioned by the constricting geography of their city to get about using public transit. But, nine million passengers in 1938 climbed to 19 million in two years as Canada's war contribution doubled the city's population. Even an additional 23 ex-Toronto Birneys could not handle the strain on a system which reached 33 million passengers by 1943, and equipment deteriorated to the point that when peace came, both rolling stock and rails were worn out. New trams suitable for Halifax's geography were no longer being built, and good second-hand ones were increasingly hard to come by. Rehabilitation of the infrastructure seemed an overwhelming task – one third would have to be rebuilt, one third reconstructed and the remainder suffered from deferred maintenance.[17]

City Council called in Norman D. Wilson, a transportation consultant of renown, and commissioned a report on whether they should continue with trams, or switch to buses, which would cause Nova Scotia Light and Power Co. Ltd. to get out of the transportation business. As was the case in many Canadian cities, the power company had entered the transportation side of things as a shrewd way of using surplus power and making a profit. Generally the symbiotic relationship with the city worked well to each organization's advantage: the city had an effective transit system without the investment and NSL&P had a revenue-generating stream.

Wilson spent ten days conducting an exhaustive analysis of Halifax's transit needs and situation. It became readily apparent that a complete rebuilding of the track was in order if trams were to continue. The narrow streets limited what equipment could be run – short wheelbase single truck Birney cars – that could in theory be rebuilt, but to last how long? Although the PCC streetcar was now available, it could not cope with Halifax's topography.

Wilson's report stated "it can be seen that it is good economics and sound business, to conform to the trend of the times and change over now to trolley coach or bus operation."[18] He then gave eleven reasons why the trolley coach was preferable; among these that it had great hill-climbing ability, greater passenger capacity, flexibility and curb loading, better handling under winter (snow and ice) conditions and with fixed routes less subject to the "whims of politicians who desire petty variations or extensions." No routes in Halifax, he said, were so weak as to require motor buses – they can all use the trolley coach though a few are borderline.[19] Apparently City Council did not take offence to the "whims" comment, and coupled with NSL&P's desire to continue to operate transit in Halifax, they voted in favour of the trolley coach. With that decision, Halifax joined the other major Canadian cities that had or were about to convert to the clean, quiet and fast electric bus.

The planning had to take into account the drop-off in Halifax's war-time worker population – fifteen million seemed like a good estimate by the time the system could be implemented. Wilson felt sixty coaches would handle peak loads; actually 57 and three spares.[20] By March 1947 the order was placed for sixty, 44-seat coaches from Canadian Car, which would cover conversion of all streetcar lines. NSL&P also considered briefly using motor buses on two extension routes with lighter passenger traffic. Though initial costs were higher for the trolley coach, motor buses required different maintenance training, oil and gasoline, modifying the garage and six buses vs. five trolley coaches. L. Currie Young, NSL&P's transit superintendent travelled to Boston to study its conversions, and perhaps that investigation, plus a more detailed study on the total costs, favoured more trolley coaches. In February 1948, an additional five coaches were added to the order from Can Car.

However, the anticipated summer 1948 changeover was thwarted by public opinion of the negative kind. Some residents along the routes objected to overhead wires and coaches in their areas that were previously un-serviced. Others welcomed public transit – wires and all. Films of trolley coach operations in the US, highlighting its advan-

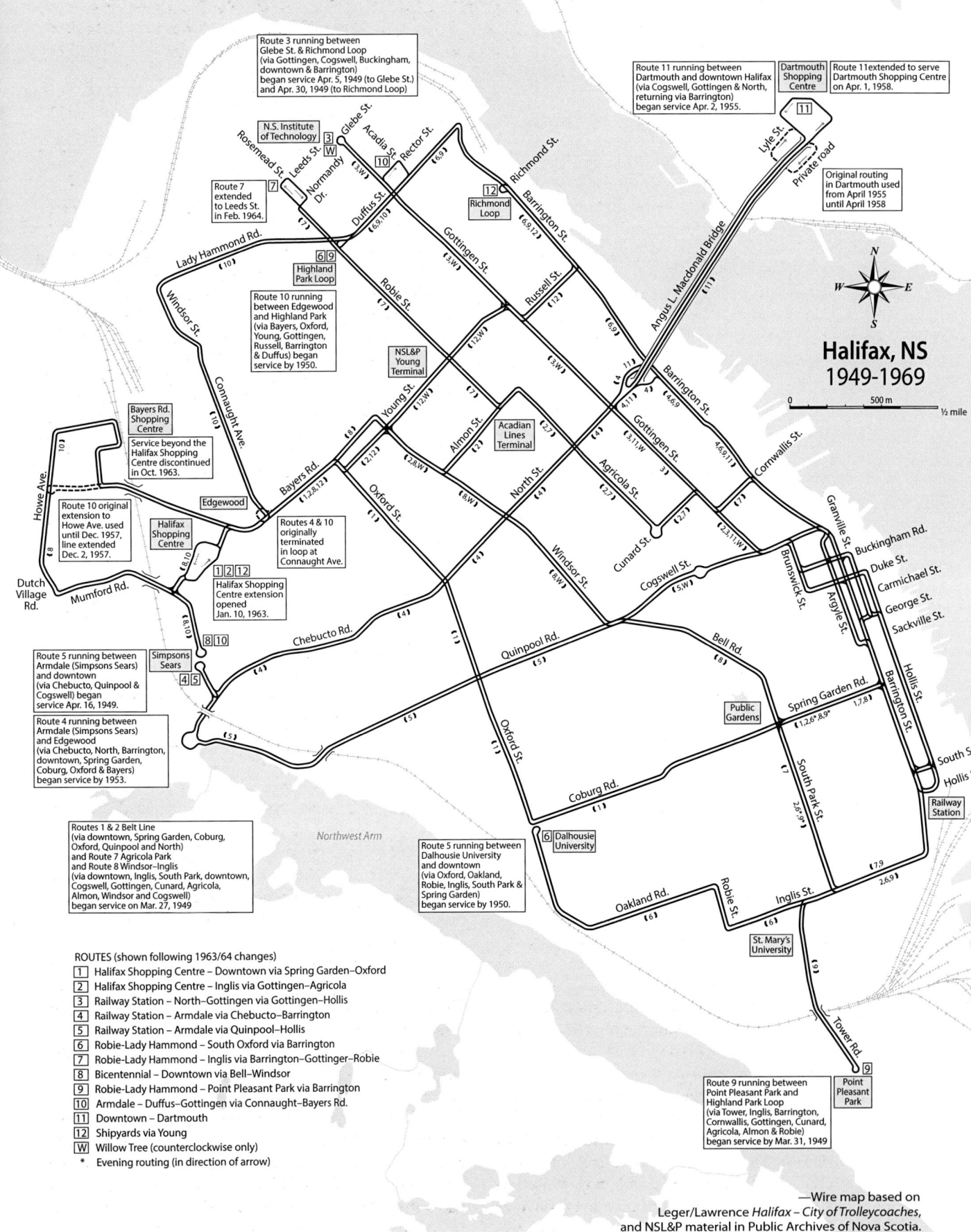

Above: The conversion of Halifax's aging trams to the new trolley coach service was cause for Reddy Kilowatt to light a cigar in celebration of his new arrivals.
(PUBLIC ARCHIVES OF NOVA SCOTIA)

tages of cleanliness, silence and speed eventually convinced the naysayers, but the controversy pushed the conversion into 1949.

The coaches started arriving in the fall of 1948. A war surplus hanger was bought, dismantled and moved from Debert to Young Street to be converted into a new garage. Three TTC School of Instruction Inspectors were brought in to train operators on the new trolley coach[21] and some tram operators were sent to Fort William where the coaches were built, as well as to Toronto and other cities using trolley coaches.[22] Conversion proceeded swiftly even though half of the new routes were following the tram ones so new wiring was erected alongside and over existing tram wire and special work. Finally on Sunday March 27th 1949 the first three lines – #1 and #2 BELT LINE, #7 AGRICOLA–SOUTH PARK and #8 WINDSOR–INGLIS changed over, eliminating trams from the city centre. That Sunday, traffic was 45,000 – more than double the normal Sunday load, and all 33 trolley coaches in operation were full to capacity. Halifax had a hit on its hands. The *Mail-Star* of March 28th recounted the story of a little boy, dressed in his Sunday best, who made his nickel go a long way that day. He had received his five cents after the Sunday ser-

vice and boarded a BELT LINE coach. His fascination with the new, silent trolleys eclipsed his dinner and then supper times, and it wasn't until the police constable checked the buses at 8:30 PM looking for a long-lost boy that he was returned home, "not too tired and happy."[23]

In advance of this, NSL&P placed ads in the papers cautioning patrons to Pay as You Enter on trams and trolley coaches. Earlier ads had not only detailed the new routes but also whimsically shown the trolleys arriving via stork, *a la* a new baby. More seriously, articles cautioned passengers not to cut in front of the bus when alighting as they "pick up speed much more rapidly than trams." Also, they warned that there would be less parking spots available due to bus stops as the new trolleys would load at the curb. Another safety caution was that patrons not step on to the street as a signal that they wished the coach to stop. The trolley would pull over to the curb and stepping in front of it was not to be recommended.[24]

The next day saw an official inauguration with a ribbon cutting, speeches, a pipe band and a lunch at the Lord Nelson hotel.[25] Col. J.C. MacKeen, President of the Nova Scotia Light and Power Company told civic and provincial leaders at the luncheon that when the changeover was completed, "Haligonians will not only boast of having the finest harbour in the world, but also the finest transit system – the only transit system on the North American continent using nothing but trolley coaches."[26]

Aside from riders' enthusiasm, Haligonians living on the routes also applauded the new buses. They noticed how much quieter their streets were compared to the house-shaking rumble of the trams. "The escape from the noise of the trams is simply lovely," said one resident in a *Mail-Star* article. Others echoed his enthusiasm. But there were little quirks to work out – passengers had to get used to stepping down on the treadle step to open the rear door. Also the new routes isolated some tram routes: ARMDALE and four other routes ran shuttle services from as little as days to months as conversion progressed. By March 31st Route 9 TOWER ROAD line was changed over; GOTTINGEN STREET followed on April 5th; the complete ARMDALE line route 5 on April 16th; and RICHMOND – the oldest line in the city – on April 30th. With the opening of that last of the ten routes, Halifax's quirky little Birney streetcars no longer graced its pavements. Trolley coaches now serviced 22.1 miles of street as compared to fifteen by the trams.[27]

The trolley buses performed well on the hilly terrain and damp weather, unlike their predecessors, and ridership increased eighteen per cent annually. In fact, a Canadian Ohio Brass advertisement touted a 14.5 per cent gain just in the last eight months of 1949.[28] With this large increase in passengers carried, NSL&P placed another order for six more coaches that went into service in December of 1949.

Though NSL&P did not own any gasoline buses, there were two feeder routes needed to serve the new military residential areas: EDGEWOOD PARK and MULGRAVE PARK. Wartime restrictions had negated extending tram lines into these areas, so NSL&P contracted gasoline buses to service them. The conversion to trolley coaches had opened up the opportunity to extend existing lines into these areas and replace the contract buses. With rising ridership, NSL&P placed an order in 1950 for an additional fifteen coaches and two more in 1952.

By 1954, the 77 coaches carried 27,397,592 passengers compared with a projected 15 million in 1949. Headway was thirty seconds in rush hours – an enviable schedule even by today's standards. "It is the opinion of management that the trolleycoach is the ideal vehicle for the Halifax area and has so proven under adverse weather conditions" said NSL&P in 1952.[29] Hali-gonians averaged 168 rides per year compared to 113 in Quebec City and 103 in Ottawa in 1961. The geography of the peninsula encouraged public transit usage and of the original ten routes, nine served downtown and eight travelled along Barrington Street – the main shopping area. Unlike most other Canadian cities, Barrington was a narrow two lanes – no parking allowed, with heavy pedestrian shopper traffic. Despite this, trolley coaches maintained a peak headway of thirty seconds even there!

Again, the concentration of trolley coach routes was partly due to geography. The City of Halifax, and therefore the territory NSL&P could operate in, was essentially the peninsula. Beyond that, where most of the newer housing was being built, Acadian Lines' motor buses provided service. Across the narrows, the City of Dartmouth was growing exponentially, but it too was serviced by a separate transit system. A ferry spanned the gap, or one could drive around the Bedford basin – a fifteen-mile trip. Clearly there was a need to connect the cities and integrate public transit.

That occurred on April 2nd 1955 with the opening of the Angus L. Macdonald suspension bridge. Connecting

Right: The public liked them and so did NSL&P. By 1951 Haligonians had enthusiastically embraced their all-trolley coach transit system.
(SCHWARZKOPF COLLECTION)

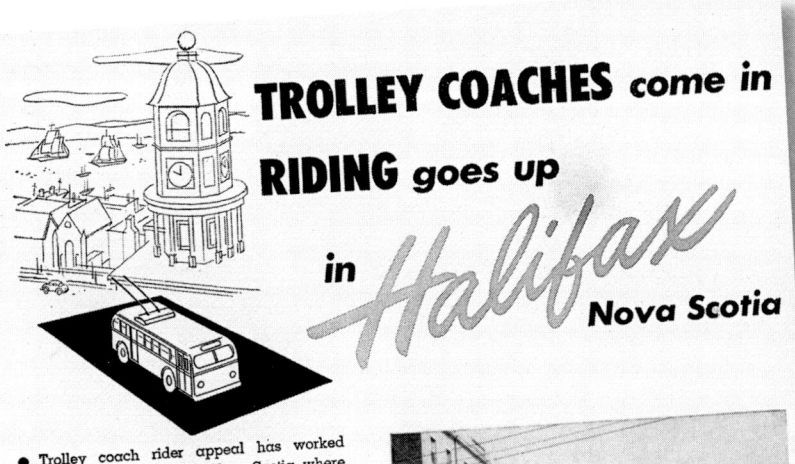

Good examples of Halifax's all-trolley coach system, Brills 213, 255 and 225 at Barrington and Sackville streets in 1953.
(OHIO BRASS COLLECTION, THE STRAHORN LIBRARY, ILLINOIS RAILWAY MUSEUM)

Halifax and Dartmouth, it was built with trolley coach capability and, in anticipation of its opening, NSL&P ordered four more coaches – the last T-44 Can Car coaches to be built in Canada. However, the connection between the two cities was not without difficulties. NSL&P wanted to operate trolley coaches across the bridge to downtown Dartmouth's Portland Street. Bell Busses Ltd., the Dartmouth operator, wanted to cross the bridge into Halifax downtown. The bus advocates played on fears of electrocution if trolley wires came down on the steel bridge. The Public Utilities Board shared that concern until NSL&P brought in experts and showed how their extra circuit breakers would open before a wire even fell. Eventually the Board agreed, but did side with Bell and disallowed trolley coaches from downtown Dartmouth. In fact the extension was to terminate in a loop below the Dartmouth end of the bridge with a minimal passenger shelter.

However, NSL&P made good use of the occasion, posing three of their new trolley coaches side-by-side on the bridge for the media even before the wires were in place. And, despite the restrictions on entering Dartmouth, the route quickly became the most heavily travelled – 74,700 passengers in its first month. By August, ridership was estimated to be the equivalent of one million a year. Much of this came not from former ferry foot traffic, but from the new suburbs booming in Dartmouth.[30] When the four new Can Car coaches couldn't handle the surge of passengers, six used Pullman buses were bought from Providence, Rhode Island since Can Car had stopped production of trolley coaches. In lieu of paying tolls individually each time a trolley coach crossed the span, NSL&P paid an annual fee of $5,000 to the Bridge Commission. Halifax could now proudly claim to be the largest all-trolley coach operation on the continent and the only all-trolley system in Canada. Total one-way routings were 39.9 miles and in 1954 NSL&P reported 2,704,316 coach miles and 24,941,191 revenue passengers.[31]

Across from the bus/trolley coach transfer terminal, the new Dartmouth Shopping Centre rose in 1956, and soon the out-of-the-way stop became an irritant, not only to cold, damp transit riders, but also to shopping centre merchants, seeing potential customers driven away. On April 1st 1958, a new terminus was opened in the Dartmouth Shopping Centre, built by the shopping centre and sanctioned by the PUB. But this wasn't the only shopping centre extension NSL&P had to consider. While trolley coach

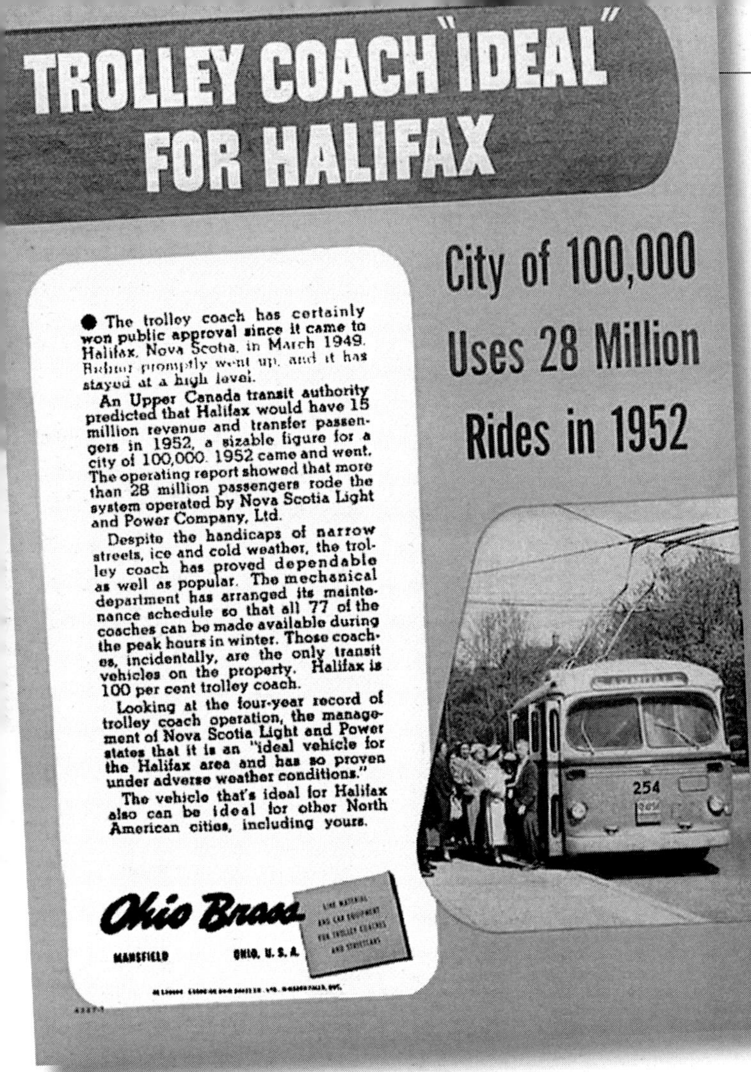

Two years later (October 1953) Ohio Brass again featured the all-trolley coach Canadian city in its advertising. (OHIO BRASS COLLECTION, THE STRAHORN LIBRARY, ILLINOIS RAILWAY MUSEUM)

route 4 looped at Simpsons (later Simpsons-Sears) near the Armdale Rotary, a new shopping mall on Bayers Road was the impetus for NSL&P to extend route 10 to serve both the centre and the under-served neighbourhood. The one-mile extension opened on December 2nd 1957 with frequent service. Just to the south, another mall was under construction, the Halifax Shopping Centre, to become the largest such shopping mall east of Montreal. Still, trolley coach service was more than 900 feet away from the mall, and Christmas shoppers were not impressed. A temporary shuttle service, provided by the mall, alleviated the situation, but a permanent solution was wanting. Not that NSL&P did not want to come into the centre, but negotiations were complex, with land, trolley pole location, insurance concerns and financial help from the mall all debated. The city also got involved, expressing concern over traffic flow as buses turned across busy Bayers Road. A lead editorial in the *Mail-Star* perhaps goaded the city into creative thinking mode, and coordinated traffic signals finally resolved that problem, but the extension of route 4 did not get completed until January 10th 1963, albeit with much fanfare.

While the Halifax system was highlighted with these two major route expansions, smaller changes continued throughout the trolley coach era. Until the 1960s, the trolley coach routes, with the above exceptions, followed those of its predecessor – the streetcar. So it was appropriate that in 1963 NSL&P planned a revamping of the system's routes, coincidentally with the introduction of two diesel bus routes, thereby losing the city's status as an all-trolley coach operation. The new plan organized the routes as point-to-point and added two new routes (the motor bus ones) to the northwest area where the city had grown extensively after the war.[32] With the exception of ROUTE 5, all routes were re-organized effective August 11th but not all successfully. By October, with traffic surveys and numerous customer complaints in hand, the system tweaked, and in some cases changed routes completely. Now the first reorganization had resulted in Halifax's first – and only – route cut. Service on the outer end of the BAYERS ROAD line was cut back to the Halifax Shopping Centre. The second shuffle resulted in a new route, #12, running cross town from the aforementioned shopping centre to the shipyards. In addition to the twelve lines, there was also a special school run, called WILLOW TREE after a famed tree in Quinpool Road, using two trolley coaches and a diesel bus. With reorganization also came route name changes with only #5 retaining its original. More routes served the shopping malls and with the second reorganization fewer passengers were waiting for a connection that had just left. Still, Haligonians are picky or passionate about their public transit – your choice. By February 1964, NSL&P had to adjust routes a third time in response to complaints about scheduling. The third time was a charm as the saying goes, as it was the last of any consequence while the trolley coach held sway. This adjustment also resulted in another extension – sadly the last of the system – #7, to serve the new Nova Scotia Trades and Technical Institute. Another small change was to Sunday service. Previously NSL&P combined the original six routes into three on Sundays, since many routes operated over the same streets in part, while several routes were ignominiously served by diesels on the Sabbath. In fact, of the seven Sunday routes in this service iteration, only three were trolley coach served.

Another peculiarity of Halifax service was the absence of printed route timetables. While service in the heavily travelled areas was frequent enough that one could just show up and count on a bus coming by relatively soon, other areas had half-hour frequency. This hold-over from the streetcar era of no public timetables finally ended in the summer of 1965 when the system issued twice-yearly three-fold timetables, each route in one of five different paper colours. In fairness to NSL&P, there had always been system maps, operator timetables and an inspector downtown to ensure these were followed and to answer public questions. No doubt, the latter subsided once the

Coach 219 takes a time point on the ARMDALE run in a bucolic Halifax setting on west Quinpool Road in 1953. The house is still there.
(OHIO BRASS COLLECTION, THE STRAHORN LIBRARY, ILLINOIS RAILWAY MUSEUM. LOCATION INFORMATION – GLEN KNAPP)

riding public had its own copy of the schedule. According to the newspaper advertisement placed by NSL&P in June 1965, this was a Canadian first – a stretch of imagination on the transit company's part.

While transit fares remained reasonable, by the mid-1950s patronage was decreasing. Traffic congestion was increasing and affecting service levels such that NSL&P urged the city to develop a master traffic plan. Indirectly NSL&P blamed decreasing ridership on this and on other factors, from nice weather (people walked more) to revised tolls on the Angus L. Macdonald Bridge (formerly each passenger paid; now it was per automobile). All this conspired to force the company to apply in 1957 for the first fare increase since 1928. The city also improved traffic flow, but neither served to stem passenger declines. More fare increases were instigated, talk swirled around on whether the city should subsidize or even buy the transit operation. Finally by 1962 the City commissioned a report on the whole transit situation. Meanwhile, requests for fare increases were met with opposition by the City, but approved by the Public Utilities Board and relations became somewhat strained. An additional fare headache was the crossing of the Macdonald Bridge, where a complicated system of tickets and transfers and a bridge fare on top of the regular fare were meant to integrate the Halifax and Dartmouth systems… but the three operators (NSL&P, the Bridge Commission and Dartmouth's Bell/D.T.S. bus lines) differed on the split, so NSL&P finally went to the PUB to discontinue it and substitute a straight toll per passenger for the bridge. The PUB ruled in favour of an integrated fare and subsequent attempts by NSL&P to limit their losses by reducing frequency were also rebuffed.

Concerned with the trend of declining ridership that was being reflected all over North America, NSL&P retained Urwick, Currie Limited in 1962 to survey Halifax's transit system and recommend the best way to serve public transit needs. They were familiar with this situation, as many properties across North America had moved from private to public ownership as private operators increasingly lost money and were mandated by utility boards to retain or increase service. To say that the October 1962 report was controversial would be an understatement. Public hearings, numerous newspaper editorials and general debate greeted it, and though it was comprehensive and had solid recommendations, in the end, nothing was done in terms of ownership of the system, fares or service changes. The report gave high marks to system upkeep and the appearance of the equipment, but pointed out deficiencies and poor practices, poor routing that did not keep up with demographic changes, overlapping routes and too tight running times. As to the coaches, they found them to be an "attractive, clean and silent means of transportation," and popular with the riding public. However, the coaches were getting up in years and maintenance costs were rising. Also, the sole Canadian supplier, Can Car, now under Hawker Siddeley ownership, hadn't produced a trolley bus since 1954 and had no orders on the books.

The report recommended that the city purchase the system immediately since, they said, it was apparent that NSL&P had lost the love for its transit division that was underperforming and eating up revenue. The route patterns also needed revising and the report suggested four different scenarios.

Finally, Urwick, Currie Limited recommended that motor buses were the best transit vehicle for Halifax's needs and outlined a five to seven year phase-in of buses and phase-out of trolley coaches.[33]

Harold Snider snapped these photos of the opening of the Angus L. Macdonald bridge with union flags and the crest of Nova Scotia decorating trolleys 278 and 279. Taken from Paul Leger's scrapbook, they record the excitement of the opening of trolley coach service into Dartmouth.
(PAUL LEGER COLLECTION, COURTESY METRO TRANSIT)

NSL&P agreed with the overall report recommendations, but differed on some of the details. President A. R. Harrington said that many of the recommendations and observations were the same as NSL&P had been making to the city for some time. It seemed odd though, that Mr. Currie, in meeting with aldermen, praised the trolley coaches and their excellent condition, and the work of the private operator in using them as a public relations tool, but his report still recommended scrapping them. Nevertheless, provincial legislation prevented Halifax from operating a transit system, so only the report's recommendations as to diesel bus introduction and routing changes were implemented by NSL&P. The new diesel buses were also deployed for charter business, an area not previously possible with trolley coaches, and in the mid-60s exterior advertising appeared on some of the trolley coaches. Both these initiatives obviously contributed to the utility's bottom line as did a unique form of ad – a pennant attached to the trolley pole retriever rope that fluttered showing the advertiser's name as the coach sped past.[34]

However, NSL&P's deficits mounted, ridership dropped and vehicle traffic intensified. Traffic congestion made it difficult to maintain efficient operation and attract new riders; falling passenger revenue contributed to deficits, and this made it extremely difficult for the company to justify spending $2-million to replace the trolley coach fleet. In a presentation to City Council, the utility offered to go together to seek provincial and/or federal money, and Council, while sympathetic, mused that now might be the time to have a municipal transit system, incorporating Halifax, Dartmouth and Halifax County. Reports, debates, presentations and negotiations dragged on, compounded by the approaching (1970) annexation of six communities – all served by Acadian Lines. Legally, NSL&P was obligated to provide service, while still hemorrhaging financially. Although it could at any time abandon the transit portion of their mandate, NSL&P stuck it out in a sense of corporate civic responsibility. Federal transfer payments promised to ease the deficit, NSL&P offered to incorporate a transit company with a lease back to the city, and the city debated how to maintain the status quo. In 1968, street reconfigurations necessitated route changes and additional wire would have to be strung. The Cogswell Street interchange would not allow overhead wire, so NSL&P needed to order sixteen diesel buses, but the city delayed approving it. Then Hollis Street was to be converted to one-way, forcing more relocation of trolley service and ten more diesels would be needed.

NSL&P had enough. Civic pride can only run so long, and in September 1968 they applied to abandon their Transit Division. Poor progress with the city on remediation of the transit system, falling revenues, construction,

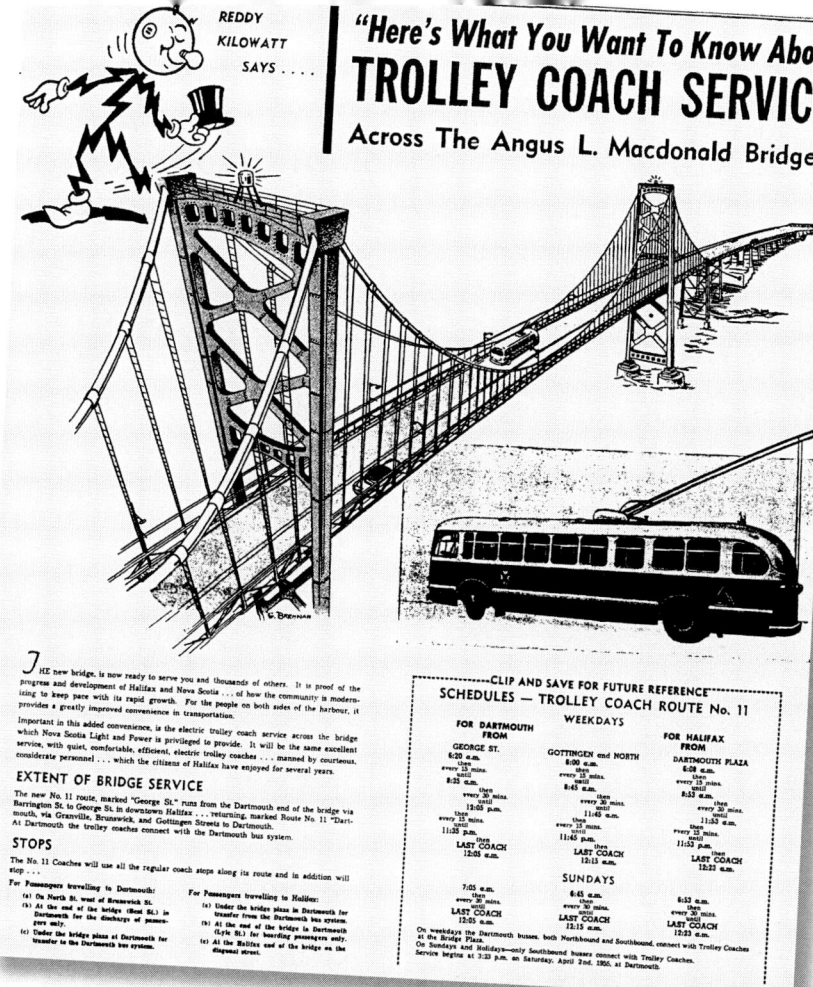

In this excerpt from a special edition of the *Halifax Mail-Star* commemorating the opening of the Angus L. Macdonald Bridge, Reddy Kilowatt tells Haligonians all they need to know about the new trolley coach service.
(PAUL A. LEGER COLLECTION)

coach 273 was stored and then shipped by ferry to the Kennebunkport Seashore Trolley Museum in 1971.

Ten trolley coach systems remained in Canada after Halifax's demise and many faced similar problems. Shortly after Halifax's conversion, Cornwall and Winnipeg went all-diesel; Thunder Bay converted in 1972, Kitchener in 1973, and Saskatoon and Calgary each a consecutive year later. By the early 1990s, Toronto and Hamilton exited while Edmonton hung on until 2009, leaving Vancouver today as the sole Canadian operator of electric coaches. However, Halifax will be remembered as the city that could and did run "all-electric" despite geography, politics and interchange issues with its twin city and surroundings… and the little coaches that could did so bravely right up to the end.

ridership and worn out equipment were cited. Twenty-year-old coaches were at the breakdown point and NSL&P had stockholders to be responsible to as well. City Council debated either taking over the system or subsidizing the existing arrangement – debate and votes swayed back and forth from June, through September and into 1969. Council passed, then rescinded or reversed previous decisions. NSL&P reversed its plan to have a subsidiary transit company. Finally the Council agreed to let NSL&P order diesel buses to arrive by fall. At last a decision was made that stuck – Halifax would get into the transit business. A transit commission was struck and a name and colour scheme chosen. An earlier decision to gradually phase out the trolley coaches was cancelled as the condition of the current fleet and an all-new route system obviated that. The changeover to all diesel buses was to be immediate.

That change over was not without controversy. Anti-pollution advocates and Halifax Transit sparred in the press, each with statistics to support their position. However the arguments presented to Council and the need to serve the annexed communities meant that motor buses were the only reasonable solution. On December 31st 1969, the last electric buses in Canada's only (one-time) all-trolley coach city ran their last runs, ending just after midnight with coach No. 243.[35]

Many of the coaches were sold to individuals for storage or construction buildings, ten went to Toronto to be cannibalized for parts, and the rest were scrapped. However,

Footnotes:

17. Tenant, R.D., *The Electric Street Railway: Halifax's Symbol of Municipal Worth*, p. 35ff. Public Archives of Nova Scotia Vertical File Halifax: Trolley Coaches.
18. Leger, Paul A. and Loring M. Lawrence, *Halifax – City of Trolleycoaches*, Bus History Association, Windsor, ON, December 1994 (Vol. 15, No. 62 issue of *Bus Industry*). p. 6.
19. Wilson report p. 14, Public Archives of Nova Scotia Vertical File Halifax: Trolley Coaches.
20. Wilson report p. 33, Public Archives of Nova Scotia HE5635 H17 W75 copied September 1979.
21. Halifax *Mail-Star*, Thursday April 14, 1949, Public Archives of Nova Scotia Vertical File Halifax: Transit.
22. *Canadian Transportation*, June 1949 p. 333.
23. Halifax *Mail-Star*, March 28, 1949, Public Archives of Nova Scotia Vertical File Halifax: Trolley Coaches.
24. Halifax *Mail-Star*, March 29, 1949, Public Archives of Nova Scotia Vertical File Halifax: Trolley Coaches.
25. Leger/Lawrence p. 27.
26. Halifax *Chronicle-Herald*? n.d. but day after official opening viz. March 29, 1949.
27. *Canadian Transportation*, June 1949 p. 333.
28. *Canadian Transportation*, June 1951 p. 10 author's collection.
29. Leger/Lawrence p. 31.
30. Leger/Lawrence pp. 36-40.
31. *Canadian Transportation*, June 1955 p. 338.
32. Correspondence, September 1963, Public Archives of Nova Scotia Vertical File Halifax: Trolley Coaches.
33. Summary Report, C.W. Kingston, Urwick, Currie Limited, Public Archives of Nova Scotia HE 5635 N17 U83 No. 2.
34. Leger/Lawrence p. 79.
35. Leger/Lawrence p. 99.

Above: Coach 279 brakes going down Duke Street crossing Barrington heading toward the waterfront. This terrain was typical of the hilly routing that Halifax's trolley coaches excelled at.
(JOHN R. WILLIAMS, KRAMBLES-PETERSON ARCHIVE.
LOCATION INFORMATION – MIKE LARISEY)

Below: Getting the green light, NSL&P 280 crosses Sackville on Hollis Street on an October day in 1968.
(JOHN R. WILLIAMS, KRAMBLES-PETERSON ARCHIVE)

TWO BRIEF FLIRTATIONS WITH THE
TROLLEY COACH IN ATLANTIC CANADA

Saint John, NB
(1947 ordered and cancelled) New Brunswick Power Company

*The trolley coach was contemplated
and equipment even ordered, but buses
were never delivered nor placed in service.*

Saint John ordered nine CCF-Brills and Canadian Car assigned serial numbers to the order, putting it into their production scheduling, but then the order was cancelled before delivery.[36] The conditions that led up to the order were familiar ones to transit systems at the end of WWII. The reasons for the cancellation were more complex.

At the end of the war, the street railway system, operated by New Brunswick Power Company (NB Power), was left in the worst condition of any time in its history. Streetcars broke down regularly and equipment was badly in need of repair. To compensate, NB Power bought some motor buses and added extra bus routes, planning to replace the streetcars with either buses or trolley buses when they received an exclusive bus franchise.

Earlier the company had such a franchise, but lost it in 1934. There was a brief skirmish with an upstart bus company, a legal battle, and finally a court decision to prohibit bus competition. Soon after this, NB Power introduced two new bus routes. A 1937 report recommended the city buy the assets of the New Brunswick Power Company and use them to form a bus company. NB Power was itself considering going to all buses, but at the end of the Depression, with better economic times, it decided to retain the streetcar system. The outbreak of WWII forced the company to use buses where it could and run the streetcar system to capacity and beyond. Saint John was a busy port with all the attendant commuting passenger loads. But another company was also interested in bus services in Saint John – SMT (Eastern), and they claimed that NB Power had no right to run buses at all.

In March 1942, SMT filed a proposal with Saint John City Council to operate a transit system in the city. On October 15th 1943, New Brunswick Power officials, including President Fred C. Manning, Vice-President and General Manager Fred M. Sutherland and their legal counsel approached Council to offer to run an all-bus transportation system even though it meant the loss of a power customer – the electric railway. They committed to continuing to run the current system, even if it did not receive a franchise, but Mr. Manning emphasized that the situation was unsatisfactory and with winter approaching, handling a large number of passengers caused them concern.

October 22nd saw SMT returning to Council to remind them of their previous proposal and asking for a transit franchise. It also brought in its President, W. W. Rogers, Vice-president T. Moffett Bell, and directors K. C. Irving and F. J. Brennan. Council agreed to ask both companies to submit proposals in November, with a proviso that the City could take over the transportation system on a year's notice with a fair valuation.[37]

A six-year agreement between NB Power and the City was finally reached in 1945 for the purchase of new modern buses, the construction of a trolleybus system, and the gradual phasing out of the streetcars. The agreement was opposed by SMT who appealed it, saying it was illegal for the Power Company to run buses without a specific licence. The objection was dismissed and streetcars were replaced over the next few years as NB Power purchased motor buses.

Then, the provincially-owned New Brunswick Hydro Corporation took over the New Brunswick Power (NB Power) Company's electric assets, leaving only the transportation and gas systems. The people of Saint John also voiced their opinions that the modernization of the transit system was not proceeding fast enough. The Power Company claimed it was about to order new trolley buses but it had suffered setbacks. Then their car barn caught fire, burning some buses and a streetcar. The City was now leaning toward a bus system managed by SMT. Nonetheless, NB Power went ahead and placed the order with Canadian Car for nine T-44 trolley buses.[38] That order went so far as to be listed in *Canadian Transportation* magazine's annual report on trolley coach operation in June 1946, showing (then) twelve coaches on order for delivery in that year.[39] This was again mentioned in a major article in December 1946 on the commencement of Can Car trolley coach production[40] and again in June 1947.

However, by February of 1948, the City Council had enough and went to the Provincial Legislature to cancel all of the transportation rights given to NB Power. That April, a bill was introduced and, after a heated debate, was passed. The City gave the New Brunswick Power 75 days of notice before their transportation rights were cancelled, claiming that the Power Company had not lived up to its 1945 agreement and that the "1914 vintage street cars" were "a menace to public safety" and they were "a laughing stock to Canada".

The City then granted SMT a transit franchise, whereupon SMT immediately formed City Transit Limited and started bus service. NB Power continued to run a competing bus service, then dropped buses and operated a single tram line with a single car until August 7th 1948, the conclusion of their franchise and of electric transit operations in Saint John.[41]

In the fall of 1975, rumours surfaced that trolley coaches were again under consideration. It was also stated (unsubstantiated) that the original abandonment of the trolley coaches order was due to the system being bought out by bus and oil interests and that the ordered coaches were sent to Halifax instead.[42] Subsequently it was said that there was a major shakeup in the consulting firm conducting the Saint John transit bus study, and that had dimmed the trolley coach's consideration.[43]

Footnotes:

36. Sebree/Ward *Transit's Stepchild, The Trolley Coach* p. 40.
37. *Canadian Transportation*, December 1943 or January 1944 – not clear from author's copy.
38. Sebree/Ward *Transit's Stepchild, The Trolley Coach op. cit.*
39. *Canadian Transportation*, June 1946 p. 321.
40. *Canadian Transportation*, December 1946 p. 683.
41. From the Heritage Multiplex web site, Heritage Resources and New Brunswick Community College – Saint John. *http://www.saintjohn.nbcc.nb.ca/~heritage/streetcars/EndOfEra.htm* – Their source was *Loyalist City Streetcars* by Fred Angus, Railfare Enterprises Limited, and the New Brunswick Museum.
42. *Trolley Coach News* #34 Fall & Winter 1975 p. 90.
43. *Trolley Coach News* #35 Spring 1976.

Right and Opposite: This 1947 ad shows both "St. Johns Nfld." and "St. John N.B." (both misspelled) as having trolley coaches on order. However, neither city consummated the deal.
(COURTESY PAUL LEGER AND LORING LAWRENCE)

St. John's, Nfld. (1947 planned)
Newfoundland Light & Power Company Limited Company

Slightly before its entrance into Confederation, in a situation similar to Saint John, NB, the street railway company flirted with trolley buses, and then abandoned electric transit totally.

A Canadian General Electric Company Ltd. advertisement from 1947 extols the virtues of trolley coaches with GE motors and controllers, and lists ST. JOHNS, NFLD. (sic) as having ordered trolley coaches along with ST. JOHN, N.B. (sic). The equipment shown in the advert was a Can Car-Brill coach.[44] However, Newfoundland Light & Power terminated its transit (streetcar) operations in September 1948, so what happened?

Throughout the war years, St. John's had two public transportation systems: streetcar service and bus – both in private hands. Streetcar operations were started in 1900 by Newfoundland Light & Power Company of Montreal. The bus system arrived in 1939 via a Nova Scotia company – Golden Arrow Coaches Limited. As was often the case, the streetcar system operated at a deficit for many years, while the bus operation was profitable.

St. John's in the mid-1940s was a city of about 44,600, mainly concentrated in the area between Water Street to the south, and Le Marchant and Harvey Roads to the north. However, the city was experiencing rapid growth in a northern area which would eventually be called Churchill Park. An extension of the streetcar system to this suburb meant a substantial capital investment. Streets would have to be widened, track laid, and new streetcars purchased, as much of the existing stock had deteriorated during the war years because of the difficulty in acquir-

swing to trolley coaches has extended to Newfoundland and United Service Corp., Ltd., St. John's has placed an order for eighteen vehicles."[46] The magazine also said in a June 1948 sub-headline for an article on Trolley Coach Operation in Canada, "At the end of 1947, according to an authoritative calculation, there were 371 trolley coaches in operation, or about to be placed in operation, on Canadian transit properties, with an additional 195 on order for Canadian properties and fifteen on order for operation in St. John's, Nfld." The article went on to detail that "… Golden Arrow Coaches of St. John's Nfld., had 15 trolley coaches on order at the end of 1947."[47] United Service Corporation of Halifax was the parent company of Golden Arrow coaches.[48] Now whether Newfoundland Light & Power ordered the coaches initially, and Golden Arrow assumed the order before officially getting the franchise is not clear, however, Golden Arrow, after promising new buses once Water Street was paved, instead imported used Toronto motor buses and continuously failed to provide new buses as per its agreement with the City. In May 1949, Golden Arrow found itself in a labour strike that stretched on and on. Finally, fed up with poor, and now no transit service, the City revoked Golden Arrow's franchise in October 1949.[49] When the trolley coach order was cancelled is not clear, but given Golden Arrow's reluctance to purchase new buses, one can assume it was soon after they got the franchise. It is also possible that the purchase was delayed until the referendum on joining Confederation was resolved, as up to that point in Newfoundland, vehicles were driven on the left side of the street. That was changed in 1947 prior to joining the rest of Canada, and so the order would have had to specify which side the doors would be on. What is clear is that by the time Newfoundland entered Confederation, the trolley coach on The Rock had become only a footnote to Canadian transit history.

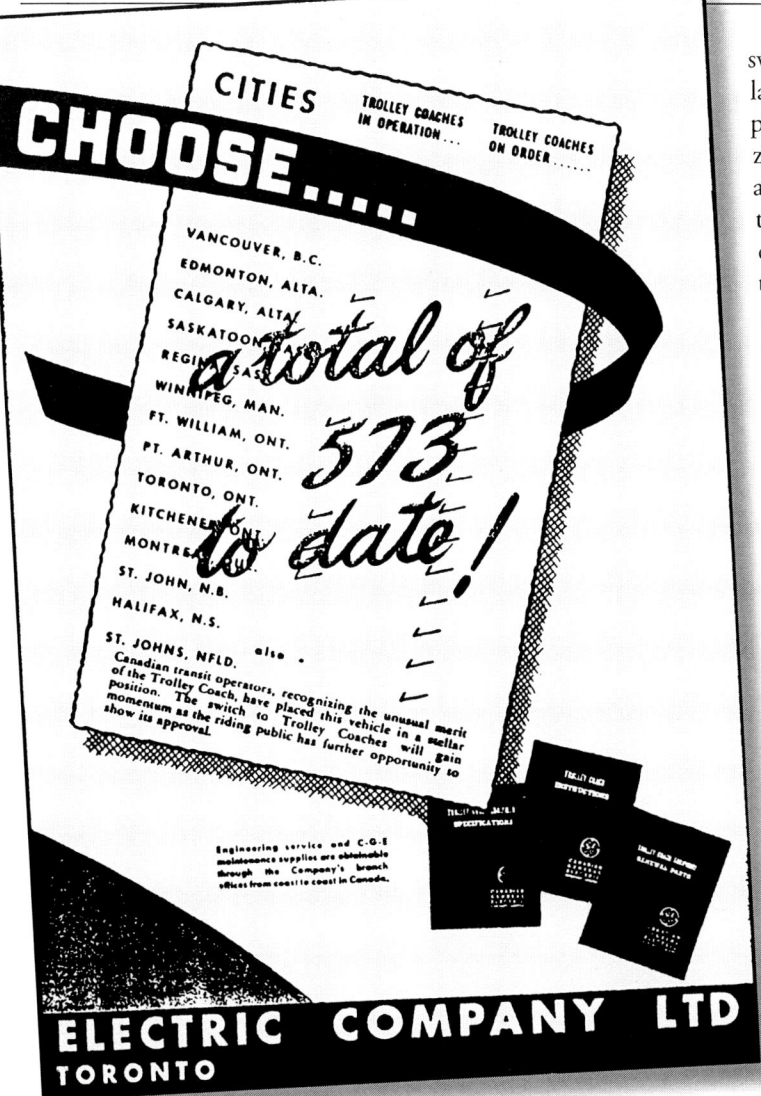

ing parts. Accordingly, buses were considered the best vehicle to meet St. John's future transportation needs. This was further strengthened in January 1947 with the release of a City Council-commissioned report by a Toronto consulting engineer who had been hired to examine the city's traffic problems. His recommendation was for the City to go with a single transportation system under one management. Although the franchise of the Newfoundland Light & Power street railway had ended in 1946, the company had kept the system running until the future of transportation services in St. John's was decided, but the company had terminated any thoughts of continuing to run a money-losing transit system when the consultant's 1947 report was released.

In July 1948, City Council gave an exclusive franchise to Golden Arrow and on September 15th 1948, streetcars ran for the last time in St. John's.[45] As best as can be determined, Newfoundland Light & Power Company had investigated the possibility of trolley coaches as early as 1946, hence the CGE advertisement's reference. In fact *Canadian Transportation* magazine in June 1947 reported "The

Footnotes:

44. Leger/Lawrence p.15, and Richard C. DeArmond
    The Electric Trolleybus web page: Proposed Trolleybus Systems
    http://www.sfu.ca/person/dearmond/morph/Cities.Almost.htm#M
    visited January 2013.
45. Baker, Melvin, ORAL HISTORY AND MUNICIPAL GOVERNMENT: A HISTORY OF THE BUS SERVICE IN ST. JOHN'S, NEWFOUNDLAND, 1948-1957. A paper presented to the Fourth Atlantic Oral History Association Conference, held in September 1982 at Memorial University of Newfoundland, and printed in Report of the Fourth Annual Meeting of the Atlantic Oral History Association: 1982, compiled by Shannon Ryan, 1982.
    http://www.ucs.mun.ca/~melbaker/busing.htm
    visited January 2013.
46. *Canadian Transportation*, June 1947 p.322.
47. *Canadian Transportation*, June 1948 p.326 and 331.
48. Leger, Paul, phone conversation with author, June 4, 2013.
49. Oral History *op. cit.*

Above: A.E.C.-E.E.C. trolley coach 4004 is posed outside the Montreal Tramways Youville Shops early in its career. Note the front crest that incorporated both companies' logos. (MONTREAL URBAN COMMUNITY TRANSIT COMMISSION; COURTESY J.G. CHAMBERLAND)

Right: The inside of the English coaches was luxurious for a bus, with leather seats, and could those be ash trays on the arm rests? (MONTREAL URBAN COMMUNITY TRANSIT COMMISSION; COURTESY J.G. CHAMBERLAND)

Montreal (1937-1966)
Montreal Tramways Co. / Montreal Transportation Commission

The first modern trolley coach system in Canada and the only one in Quebec, Montreal's modest system survived from the end of streetcars to the Metro era – nearly three decades.

"Not since the early 'twenties have trackless trolley coaches been operated in Canada....." began an article in a trade publication in April 1936.[50] It went on to refer to the early coaches in Toronto and Windsor, and opined that then, the trackless trolley was in its experimental stage. However, it went on to report that the Montreal Tramways Company (MTC) has announced that now it "is sponsoring the resumption of trackless trolley coach operation in Canada and operation of these vehicles in Montreal has been approved by the Montreal Tramways Commission." (The Commission was the body overseeing the Tramways Company). MTC Vice President and Managing Director R.N. Watt was quoted as saying "The company proposes to purchase the finest type of bus now on the market. It will seat 40 passengers and will include all the modern improvements in lighting, seating arrangements etc."

The company proposed purchasing seven vehicles and the accompanying illustration showed a three-axle coach very similar to that being produced in England. Subsequently MTC ordered seven units from Associated Equipment Co.-English Electric Co. A.E.C. was pleased enough with this entry into the Canadian market that they placed a full-page ad in *Canadian Railway and Marine World* announcing the "receipt of an order for seven A.E.C.-English Electric Trackless Trolley Buses from the Montreal Tramways Company introducing Regenerative Control for trolley buses to North American Operators."[51] The coaches were an interesting mix of manufacturers, not unlike many electric buses then and today: the body was designed and built by Metro-Cammel-Weymann; electrical equipment by English Electric Co.; with the chassis and assembly by Associated Equipment Co., all in England.[52]

By early March 1937, the new buses had arrived in Montreal, along with an English expert to instruct the Montreal drivers. The *Montreal Gazette* reported on April 30th that a group of well-known citizens had gathered at the St. Denis shops of Montreal Tramways Co. to inspect the new trolley bus service as luncheon guests of Mr. Watt. The trolley coaches were to go into service on the 2½-mile #26–BEAUBIEN route, replacing gasoline buses that had plied it since late 1931. This route was a heavy crosstown route that intersected seven main streetcar lines and one main bus route. It had the dubious distinction of crossing 92 intersections along a heavily travelled street. It was mainly a short-haul route between the major trunk routes.[53]

At one end, the trolley coaches looped around several blocks with streetcars on three sides of this turn back; at the other end the coaches turned using a wye.[54] While this Y configuration was often used for streetcars, it was more unusual for trackless trolleys; however, several early trolley coach properties used it. In essence the coach would run forward up the left side of the Y, then reverse (carefully so as not to dewire the poles) around the yoke of the Y, and then be positioned on the right leg facing forward for the return routing. The route ran from Sixth Avenue along Beaubien Street to St. Lawrence Boulevard, south to St. Viateur Street and up Park Avenue to Bernard Avenue, and then back up St. Lawrence to Beaubien.[55] The *Montreal Star* felt it of value to tell its readers that the electric buses were more economical than gasoline buses, and that they had "two trolleys, and two wires from which the electric power will be conducted to the buses (which) have

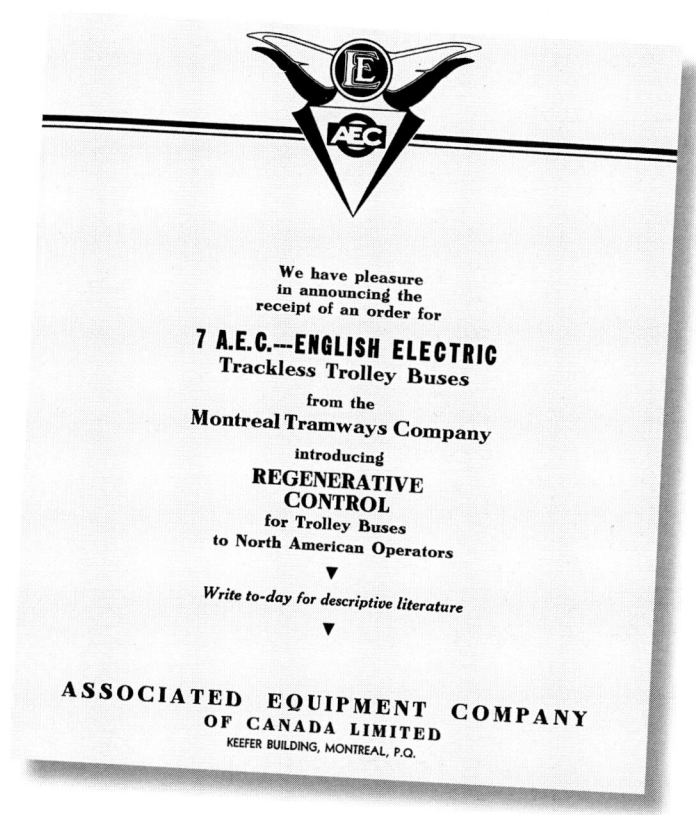

Associated Equipment was obviously proud of its initial entry into the Canadian market. However aside from Montreal and Edmonton, English-built trolley coaches made no further inroads. (SCHWARZKOPF COLLECTION)

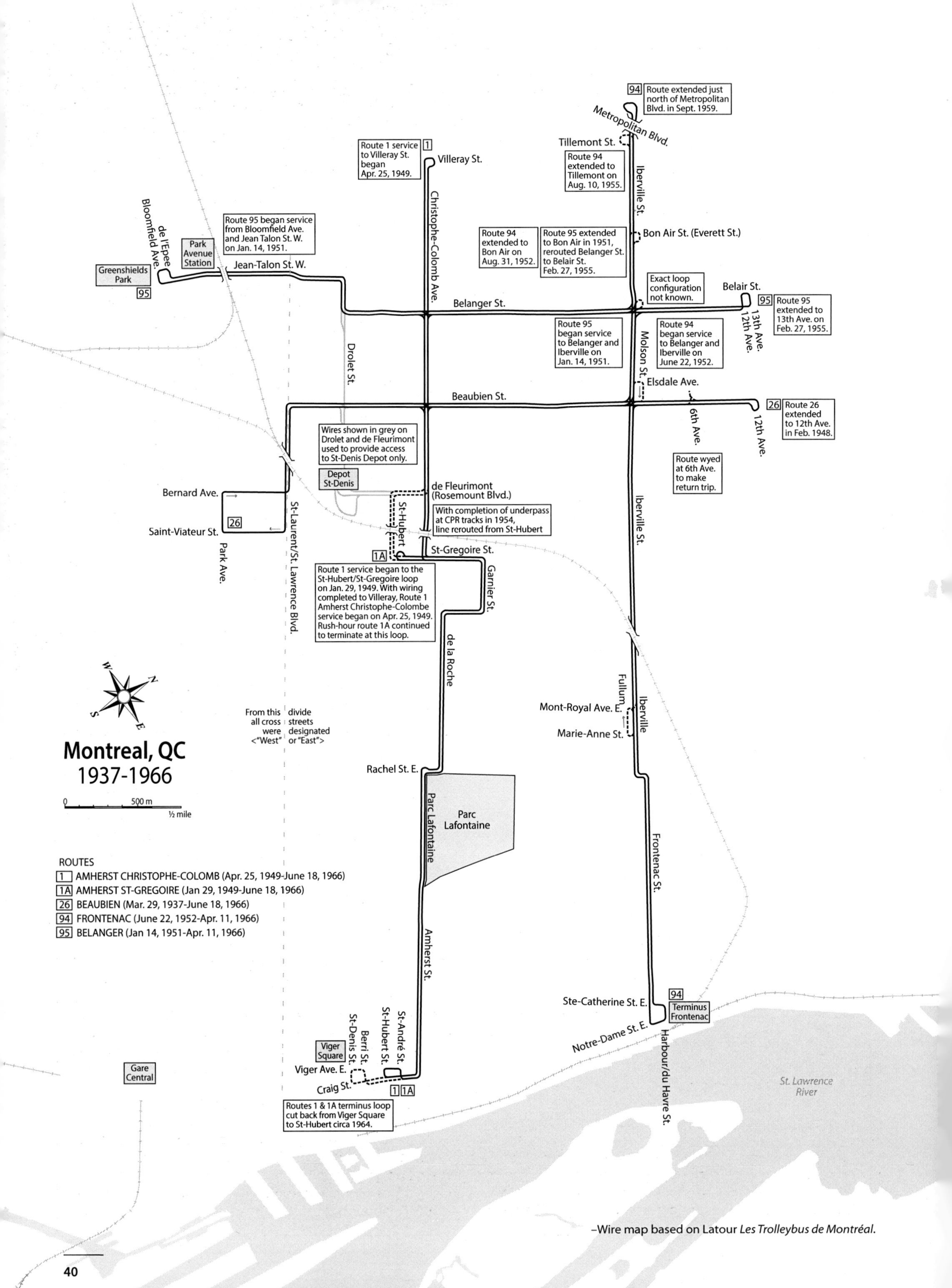

–Wire map based on Latour *Les Trolleybus de Montréal.*

This advertisement by Montreal Tramways introduced the public to the first modern trolley coaches to operate in Canada.
(SCHWARZKOPF COLLECTION)

already been installed along the route beside the regular streetcar wires ... ." It went on to illustrate that the buses ran on rubber tires instead of tracks, mentioned the buses' large passenger capacity, curb loading, smooth stopping and starting, absence of noise and fumes.[56] Much of this mirrors word-for-word articles in the transportation press and was likely taken from A.E.C. press releases issued from their Montreal office. The cost of placing them in operation was $150,000.[57] We assume that included the cost of the coaches as an ordinary Montreal citizen could purchase a new Pontiac 224 Sport Coupe with Opera Seats for $925, or a less fancy Chevrolet Business Coupe for $725, each delivered at the factory in Oshawa (taxes, freight and licence extra).[58]

The buses were given an official trial run with the mayor, aldermen, MTC commissioners, federal and provincial representatives, transportation experts, leading business men and press delegates from across Canada, in total 205 guests, on March 22nd.[59] The seating capacity seems to have shrunk slightly to 38 and the report stated that several improvements were incorporated that were designed by Montreal Tramways Co. engineers. One feature was the coaches' ability to operate on reserve power for a mile.[60] Mr. R.M. Binns, Supervisor of Traffic Studies for Montreal Tramways Co., said at a Canadian Transit Association symposium that the 80 ampere-hour battery could actually propel the vehicle a distance of two miles at a speed of one mile-per-hour.[61] After this auspicious official welcome, the coaches then went into full, public operation on the 29th.

Despite their novelty and the fact that the new trolley coaches led the way in Canadian urban transportation, the company was careful to state that they were not a replacement for streetcars. Vice-president Watt stated that " ... on account of their carrying capacity, economy of space and rapidity of regular movement, the subway and the street car must remain the principal public carriers, with the two types of buses [motor and electric] as auxiliary, or 'feeder' services used to cope with special traffic conditions, and linking up new and unserved territories with the major lines of travel."[62] In referring to subways he was citing London and New York that were phasing out their trams in favour of gasoline and trolley buses, and he emphasized that as subway cities they were not in the same league as Montreal. In fact MTC still maintained 963 streetcars and 169 gasoline buses and boasted 301 miles of track

Montreal Directions – Compass Confusion?

For anyone visiting Montreal or researching its history, it is always difficult to determine "the right way to go" until coming to the realization that Montrealers were never guided by the old song that began "East is East, and West is West..." At least as far as street directions were concerned, the city officials were definitely not governed by the compass.

Therefore, the accompanying map of Montreal's trolley coach routes and their wire diagrams needs an explanation.

Most city streets are laid out in grid fashion, and the Montreal nomenclature is based on the assumption that travellers from Toronto are eastbound, and those from Quebec City or the Maritimes are heading west. Skiers to the Laurentien mountains are going "up north", while the train across Victoria Bridge takes one "to the South Shore."

Historically, the city's "Anglos" referred to Boulevard St-Laurent as "St. Lawrence Main" because, then as now, it is the dividing line beyond which all intersecting streets carried a "W" for those heading "westbound" towards Toronto, and an "E" for the same thoroughfares continuing in the opposite direction on the other side of the city's "Main" street.

All text and photo captions utilize "Montreal directions" unless otherwise noted, even though an observation of the compass in the map demonstrates how far from "True North" those street directions really are. To assist readers, the map is positioned up-and-down on the page respecting the city's unique directional nomenclature, hence "north" is at top of the map.

English Electric Company, the maker of the motors and controllers for Montreal's trolley coaches placed this ad in 1937 hoping to secure more A.E.C.-E.E.C. bus orders.
(SCHWARZKOPF COLLECTION)

"... approximately the distance between Montreal and Toronto."[63] This sentiment was repeated by Watt a year later when he said, "The place of the trolley bus lies between the streetcar and the autobus. While the modern trolley bus is a relative new vehicle, it appears to be ideally suited to medium and medium-heavy travelled routes where fairly high capacity is required throughout the day."[64] Still, the new form of transportation was recognized as far away as Winnipeg, where again Mr. Watt was quoted as saying that their noiselessness, smooth running, ease of operation and absence of exhaust more than made up for the dependence on overhead and its route limitations.[65]

The travelling public in north Montreal embraced the trolley coach sufficiently that the company noted this in its annual report in *Canadian Transportation* magazine. However any plans for expansion were cut short by the onset of WWII with its attendant shortages of tires (and gasoline for the then 224 motor buses). As a result, all available streetcars were pressed into service to cope with pas-

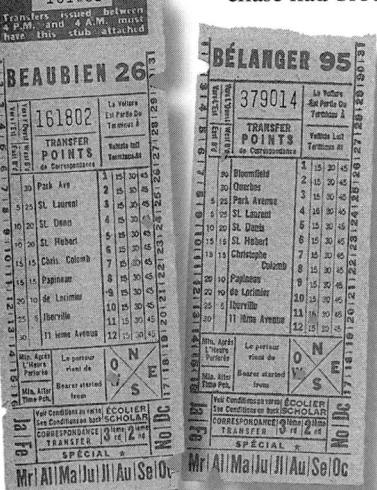

These transfers from the early 1950s are from two of the Montreal trolley coach routes: BEAUBIEN and BELANGER.
(TOM GRUMLEY COLLECTION)

senger traffic that neared four hundred million a year. As happened with many transit systems, the war's end saw an infrastructure heavily in need of rehabilitation with an attendant large expense. In addition, the Montreal Tramways Co.'s contract was due to expire at the end of the decade. Nonetheless, after a demonstration of the new Can Car T-44 coach in 1947, they placed an order for forty units, 28 of which were to supplement the seven on BEAUBIEN. With these coaches the route was extended from 6th to 12th Avenue in February of 1948, making it just under three miles in length.[66] The remaining Can Car coaches were to be used to convert the AMHERST streetcar line service in 1949. This route changed over in stages: January 29th 1949, trolley coaches operated from Viger Square, Downtown to the off-street loop at St. Hubert and St. Gregoire Street only. Meanwhile the service wire under the Canadian Pacific Railway tracks on St. Hubert, which turned west into the St. Denis Depot at de Fleurimont (now Rosemont Blvd.) was extended east on the latter to Christophe-Colomb, then north to Villeray. This permitted regular service on the Christophe-Colomb segment to begin as route 1–AMHERST CHRISTOPHE-COLOMB April 25th, while the St. Gregoire segment was labelled route 1A as a rush hour service. Interestingly, in 1948 there were ten additional vehicles originally ordered for Montreal that were diverted to Toronto instead.[67]

In 1950, another forty Can Car-Brills were ordered and put into service on January 14th 1951 on the 95–BELANGER route, initially operating from Bloomfield and Jean Talon to Belanger and Iberville, but extended soon thereafter to Iberville and Bon Air (later Everett). The 1950 purchase had brought the total to 86 coaches on 21 miles of routes.[68] The public liked them, with perhaps the exception of the visually impaired; the Montreal Association of the Blind complained to the company that many blind persons were afraid to cross a street because they could not hear a trolley coach coming. MTC management liked them as high revenue producers, operating at low costs and reducing the fixed assessment with a higher net return. With no tracks to maintain and using the existing power facilities, the trolley coach also appealed for its flexibility and reliability. The company also liked that with excellent traction the trolley coach had no difficulty in deep snow, and regenerative braking gave excellent control on icy roads. Charles I. Lynch from the

Above: Winter 1937 and A.E.C. coach 4004 passes 4002 on Beaubien at St. Hubert looking north-west. Note that despite the wooden utility pole nearby, MTC used sturdy metal poles for their overhead. On the right is a carbon arc streetlight that was serviced by unwrapping the rope seen dangling below the splay arm and lowering it to street level. Dave Henderson remembers, "In 1942, we lived a few blocks further along Beaubien (you can almost see it.) Using the nickel my mom gave me to buy gum at corner store, I decided, at four years of age, to take my first solo trolley coach ride. It was aboard No. 4004. Since I boarded behind a nice lady, I kept my nickel (kids!) Fortunately, the operator remembered where I'd boarded after I did not disembark at the end of the line, and sent me home, late but well-travelled. The coach steps were way up there! The operator wore leather leg-sheaths. The seats inside had a big additional step-up over the huge wheels."

(OHIO BRASS COLLECTION, THE STRAHORN LIBRARY, ILLINOIS RAILWAY MUSEUM. LOCATION INFORMATION – TOM GRUMLEY)

Below: A.E.C. coach No. 4005 meets unit 4004 on Beaubien looking "north-east" in Montreal parlance (more like true north) at the corner of Iberville in the winter of 1937. The park on the north side of Beaubien Street was called Molson Park, split evenly across Iberville. Molson was the next street, the far "eastern" boundary of the park. One side had a carousel stand for a band to play on. Could that be a horse cart just beyond the intersection?
(OHIO BRASS COLLECTION, THE STRAHORN LIBRARY, ILLINOIS RAILWAY MUSEUM. LOCATION INFORMATION – RALPH MARCOGLIESE/TOM GRUMLEY/DAVE HENDERSON)

Above: Taking on passengers across from St. Edouard (French spelling) church, A.E.C. coach No. 4006 is heading east on Beaubien at St. Denis on a brisk fall day. Note the unique coach stop sign on the post that bears a resemblance to an astrolabe – the symbol of Montreal Tramways, the name of which was in raised letters on it.
(OHIO BRASS COLLECTION, THE STRAHORN LIBRARY, ILLINOIS RAILWAY MUSEUM. LOCATION INFORMATION – TOM GRUMLEY)

Below: Resplendent in their new paint, the first order of Brill trolley coaches basks in the sunshine at St. Denis Shops c1948 awaiting the call to serve.
(MONTREAL URBAN COMMUNITY TRANSIT COMMISSION; COURTESY J.G. CHAMBERLAND)

Ottawa Evening Journal, visiting Montreal in anticipation of Ottawa introducing trolley buses, noted the trolley coach "is able to dodge in-and-out of traffic like a football player carrying a ball in a broken field." [69]

With the expiry of the Montreal Tramways Co. contract, the Province created the Montreal Transportation Commission (MTC) which took over urban transit in metropolitan Montreal on June 16th 1951. The new Commission's mandate was to replace the outdated tramway system with buses and trolley coaches. However they leaned more to the former than the latter, and the last order of Brill coaches, 25 in all, was delivered in 1952 and put into service on the 94–FRONTENAC route June 22nd operating northward from Notre Dame and Harbour (du Havre). Its northern terminus was Belanger and Iberville using a modest 'off-street' loop on the east side on vacant lot. At that time the last operating English units were retired. While trolley coach routes were then only seven per cent of the total system mileage, their routes were extended: the 94–FRONTENAC to Bon-Air (now Everett) on August 31st 1952, duplicating the Iberville segment of the 95–BELANGER line until February 27th 1955, when the 95–BELANGER route was extended eastward on Belanger to 13th Avenue.[70] Meanwhile, the completion of the underpass on Christophe-Colomb under the CPR tracks in 1954 allowed route #1 to go directly south on the newly-extended street, now leaving the St. Hubert and de Fleurimont wires without passenger service.

By 1955 there were 15.09 one-way miles.[71] However, the streetcar system ceased operation in 1959 and with that, the other form of electric transit felt the hot breath of demise on its back. Still, the trolley coaches operated trouble-free for the most part, and there were several more extensions to mesh with the bus routes that replaced the streetcar lines. The northern terminal of the FRONTENAC line moved from Bon Air to Tillemont Street August 10th 1955, and later to a loop at Metropolitan Boulevard in September 1959. All routes had rush hour service plus short-turn service, and as the fleet aged, motor buses supplemented their service. In summer trolley coaches only ran on weekdays; winter in Montreal showed the electric coaches' mettle, and with this superior performance they survived opposition until 1966. Two years earlier, plans had been made for a system of one-way streets to improve traffic flow, and so downtown trolley wires for routes 1 and 1A were relocated from St. Denis to St. Hubert a few blocks further east, but still at Craig Street. These expenses, plus the age of the equipment and the necessity of keeping electric substations, feeder cable and other specialized equipment influenced the inevitable decision: trolley coaches were to be phased out by June 24th. The imminent surplus of diesel buses due to the introduction of a subway (Metro) system was another contributing factor, even though 103 of 105 trolleys were serviceable. Easter weekend (April 11th), trolley coaches disappeared from the FRONTENAC and BELANGER routes, and the end of the remaining routes (AMHERST CHRISTOPHE-COLOMB and BEAUBIEN) came June 18th 1966 as the last revenue trolley coach, number 4095 pulled into the depot from route 1 at 2:00 AM shortly after coach 4050 ended 29 years of service on BEAUBIEN. A farewell tour was operated June 19th and then the power permanently turned off. The four substations were dismantled and the properties sold. The coaches were stored at their depot – the St-Denis Division carhouse. One hundred units were originally to go to the Belgian Congo, but when this deal failed, they were eventually sold to Mexico City where they continued to serve for many years in company with Brills from several other Canadian properties. One coach was privately purchased, and unit 4042 donated to the Canadian Railway Museum

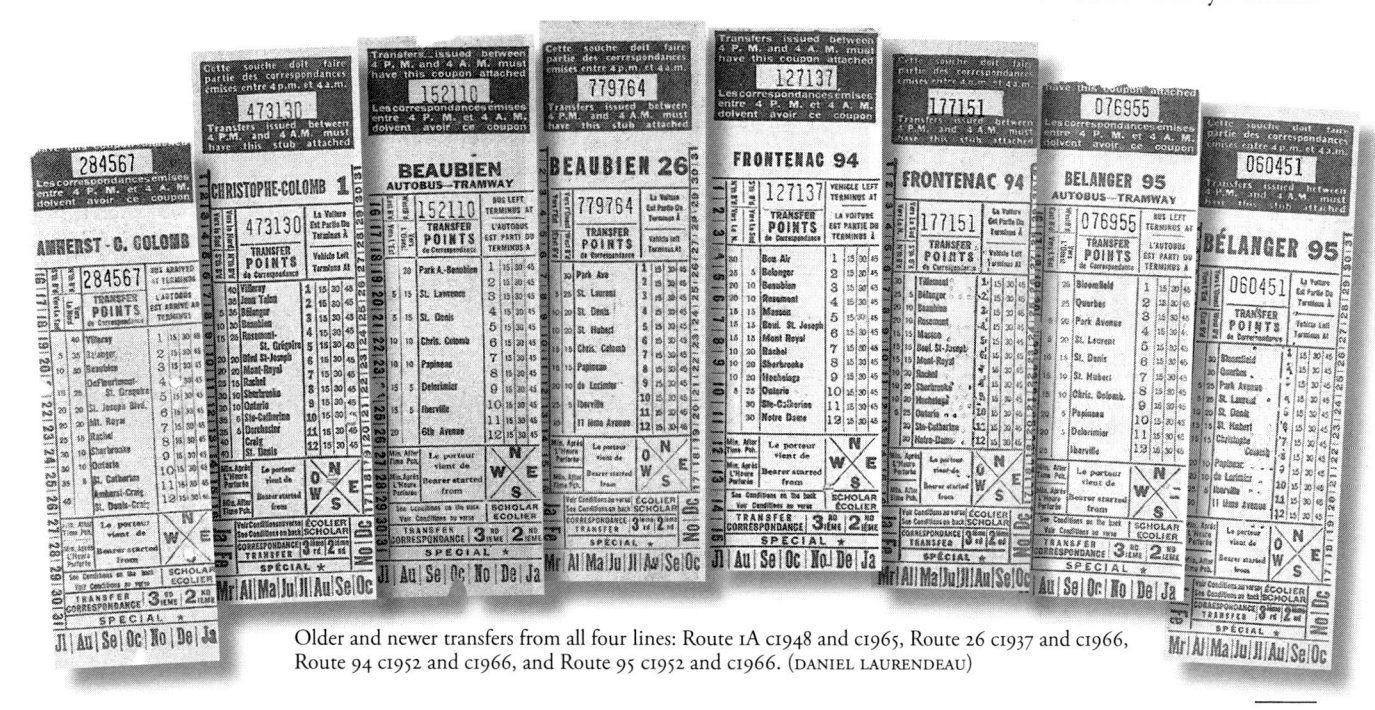

Older and newer transfers from all four lines: Route 1A c1948 and c1965, Route 26 c1937 and c1966, Route 94 c1952 and c1966, and Route 95 c1952 and c1966. (DANIEL LAURENDEAU)

After closure, unit 4067 was taken out of storage for this photo by MUCTC's Jean-Guy Chamberland in April 1977. Although No. 4067 was held for preservation, it was eventually scrapped. (SCHWARZKOPF COLLECTION)

(now Exporail). Subsequently it was traded to the Canadian Museum of Science and Technology in Ottawa.[72] Another unit, No. 4067 was kept by the Montreal Urban Community Transit Commission (successor to the MTC), but deteriorated to the point where it was scrapped.

Montreal remains the first city in Canada to have operated modern trolley coaches and the only one in the province of Quebec.[73] While they no longer slip silently down Montreal streets, there has been renewed interest in bringing the silent, efficient and non-polluting trolley coach back to the island city. As late as 2009 the Société de transport de Laval, Hydro-Québec and the Quebec provincial government engaged in a joint study into the idea of creating a network of trolley buses. However, the report issued in 2010 only recommended that further study be done on various forms of electric transit. So far nothing more has emerged. Time will tell if the trolley coach will be reincarnated in la belle province.

Footnotes:

50. *Canadian Railway and Marine World*, April 1936 p. 136 (most likely as name cut off).
51. *Canadian Railway and Marine World*, June 1936? Provincial Archives of Alberta, APRA Collection 75-11 box 5.
52. "The Place of the Trolley Coach in Urban Transportation" Canadian Transit Association symposium, June 12, 1946 p. 8.
53. C.T.A. Proceedings 1946 pp. 6-7.
54. *Ibid.* p. 6.
55. *The Montreal Daily Star*, March 8, 1937 Provincial Archives of Alberta, APRA Collection 75-11 box 13.
56. *Ibid.*
57. *The Montreal Daily Star*, March 22, 1937 Provincial Archives of Alberta, APRA Collection 75-11.
58. *The Standard, Montreal*, March 27, 1937 Provincial Archives of Alberta, APRA Collection 75-11 box 13.
59. *Ibid.*
60. *The Montreal Daily Star, op. cit.*
61. Canadian Transit Association symposium *op. cit.* p. 8.
62. *The Standard, Montreal*, Saturday, March 27, 1937, Provincial Archives of Alberta, APRA Collection 75-11 box 13.
63. *Ibid.*
64. The Municipal Review of Canada, July/Aug. 1948 in a reply to the City Improvement League Inc.
65. The *Winnipeg Evening Tribune*, May 7, 1937, Provincial Archives of Alberta, APRA Collection 75-11 box 13.
66. *Canadian Transportation*, June 1948 p. 328.
67. Latour, Denis, *Canadian Rail*, March 1977 No. 302 "Montreal's Last Trolleys" pp. 67-82.
68. *Ohio Brass Traction News*, Volume 23 Number 5 May 1951 p. 2.
69. *Ohio Brass Traction News*, Volume 23 Number 5 May 1951 pp. 3-4.
70. Laurendeau, Daniel, Exporail Vice President, email January 22, 2018.
71. *Canadian Transportation*, June 1955 p. 337.
72. *Canadian Rail*, March 1977 *Op. Cit.* pp. 70-71 and 76.
73. *Canadian Transportation*, June 1955 *Op. Cit.*

They're all gone: White Rose, A&P and the Mercury Monterey, not to mention Brill No. 4110 on Belanger at 8th Avenue on October 5th 1959. (SCALZO COLLECTION, ILLINOIS RAILWAY MUSEUM)

Above: Line crews hang special work on a curve as they convert the AMHERST streetcar line in January 1949. This route changed over in stages: starting January 29th 1949 trolley coaches operated from Viger Square in the south, to St. Gregoire Street, then on April 25th 1950 the Christophe-Colomb (northern) segment opened.
(OHIO BRASS COLLECTION, THE STRAHORN LIBRARY, ILLINOIS RAILWAY MUSEUM)

Below: A cold, snowy winter's day and southbound coach 4010 signed AMHERST S GREGOIRE takes on passengers at de la Roche and the intersection of Rachel, which was also named Parc-La-Fontaine for a one block stretch. This was shortly after conversion of the AMHERST line from streetcar to trolley coach in January 1949. At that time, the trolleybus route went only to St. Gregoire and St. Hubert and a bus service went all the way to Villeray. In April 1949, the trolleybus route was extended to Villeray where a loop was installed on the east side of Christophe-Colomb. Note the horse being led across Rachel Street.
(OHIO BRASS COLLECTION, THE STRAHORN LIBRARY, ILLINOIS RAILWAY MUSEUM. LOCATION INFORMATION – DAVE HENDERSON/DANIEL LAURENDEAU)

Above: The OTC White tow truck gingerly pulls a new trolley coach from a CPR boxcar, June 24th 1951.
(CAPITAL PRESS SERVICE, CITY OF OTTAWA ARCHIVES CA-1682 WITH PERMISSION OF THE ESTATE OF DUNCAN CAMERON)

Below: The new Can Car trolley coach is "inspected" by a variety of OTC personnel: operators, mechanics and shop personnel on August 15th 1951 at the Albert Street garage.
(CAPITAL PRESS SERVICE, CITY OF OTTAWA ARCHIVES CA-1683 WITH PERMISSION OF THE ESTATE OF DUNCAN CAMERON)

Ottawa (1951-1959)
Ottawa Transportation Commission

The distinction of having the shortest trolley bus line both in length and time, the smallest fleet and perhaps the most politics, goes to nation's capital.

Ottawa, Ontario – the nation's capital – had been a city well served by electric transportation since 1891. With its fleet of nearly 100 streetcars prior to WWII, Ottawa fulfilled all the requirements of a first class urban transit system. The system went where people lived, was efficient and environmentally friendly using locally-produced power. However, as with most Canadian cities, the onset of the Second World War put a damper on procuring new vehicles and maintaining aging track. By the war's end, the system was tired, worn out and decidedly un-modern in the new era of increased private automobiles and post-war affluence. In 1946, Mr. G. K. Bunnell, a consultant with the Ontario Department of Planning and Development, and an ally of Jacques Gréber, the master planner of the nation's capital, opined that the streetcar had "had its day" and was one of the major impediments to smooth traffic flow.[74] *The Evening Citizen* newspaper followed Bunnell's report with an editorial suggesting the trolley bus as an excellent alternative. Rapid acceleration, manoeuverability, low costs, quiet, fumeless operation and an abundance of electric power were all listed in the trolley coaches' favour.[75]

In 1947, the foremost transportation consultant in Canada, Norman D. Wilson, was brought in to examine the system. Wilson, since the 1920s, had examined most systems in Canada, and although he was thought to be a streetcar man, he definitely favoured the new trolley coach. Coincidentally Bunnell was Wilson's long time partner,[76] and since Wilson had recently helped Halifax plan conversion of its entire tram system to trolley coaches, his conclusion – to maintain the existing system as best possible in order to manage debt, and then gradually convert it to rubber-tired electrics – was no surprise. David N. Gill, general manager of the Ottawa Transportation System suggested in the fall of 1948 that extensions of the transit service to new residential areas and housing developments would be by trolley or motor bus, but that this did not spell the end of the streetcar.[77]

By 1949, Gill was quoted as saying that "every city is considering the use of trolley coaches." Gréber's master plan, however, reared its head when he was said to be " … opposed to overhead wires for the Ottawa of the future and has expressed opposition to trolley buses for that reason."[78] W. R. Creighton, Ottawa Transportation Commission (OTC) chairman, mused that "The new development (of trolley coaches) has definite advantages. But it is a matter for future development … we have just purchased, at a considerable investment, the present equipment (streetcars) of the Ottawa system and it cannot just be junked."[79] He was referring to the City's purchase of the privately-held Ottawa Electric Railway. Again, the concept of trolley coaches for feeder and outlying lines was suggested, and the City Controller suggested that trolley coaches on Springfield Road in Lindenlea would be preferable to laying tracks. Eventually, he said, trolley coaches will replace the greater part of the streetcar system, and that all over North America, trolley coaches were replacing streetcars.[80] Not every one was as enthusiastic. With the impending takeover of part of Nepean by the city of Ottawa, Creighton shot down suggestions that trolley coaches would be instituted on Richmond Road as a sort of testing ground, insisting that there were no plans to purchase any trolley buses.[81]

Throughout 1950 the OTC looked further at the merits of trolley coaches versus free-wheeling buses. Supported with the knowledge that many American cities were replacing streetcars with trolley coaches, and that many Canadian cities had done partial replacements, with Halifax completely converted to trolley coaches, they gave serious thought to a trial using the new electric coach.

More to the point, the last streetcars delivered in 1948 cost $50,000 each while a new trolley coach in 1950 was $24,819. The trolley coach had better manoeuverability than a tram, faster pickup and quiet operation. These factors, coupled with a longer life expectancy, the cost of operation being half of that of a motor bus's fuel and oil, and an absence of fumes, gave the trolley coach a distinct edge in the Commission's eyes. Additionally, streetcars were contributing to street congestion by blocking traffic every time they took on or discharged passengers. Ottawa's trackage design also had little flexibility in routing, with only a few special junctions that permitted detouring in the event of a car failure or a portion of the electric system blacking out. The die was cast for the introduction of the trolley bus in the Nation's Capital.

The 26-BRONSON–WELLINGTON route was selected for the trial replacing the "E" car line. With its 44 stops the Commission calculated headway could be cut from 22 minutes with streetcars to fifteen minutes with trolley buses. Accordingly, ten T-48A coaches were ordered in February from Canadian Car for June 1951 delivery.[82] Canadian Car boasted that with this order, 1,012 trackless trolley coaches were in operation or on order in Canada. OTC Commissioners were less definitive: one was quoted

Above: Coach 2001 sits outside the Albert Street garage with poles up, waiting for public approval, June 1951.
(CAPITAL PRESS SERVICE, CITY OF OTTAWA ARCHIVES CA-1687, WITH PERMISSION OF THE ESTATE OF DUNCAN CAMERON)

Below: OTC Commission officials, FDC officials, Ottawa Police and City Council officials ride in coach 2004 to inaugurate the new electric bus service, December 23rd 1951. W.R. Creighton, OTC Chairman and D.N. Gill, OTC General Manager are in the front seats on the right.
(CITY OF OTTAWA ARCHIVES CA-001685 LINGARD PHOTOGRAPHERS)

as saying he had no idea where they would run and another knew nothing about the order. Reports suggested that after coaches replaced the "E" streetcar line (BRONSON), ROCKLIFFE and BRITANNIA lines could follow suit.[83]

The Electric Railroaders' Association *Headlights* in November 1951 commented, "The OTC now has a number of trolley buses on order, delivery of which is expected this autumn. Very likely these will replace cars on the Bronson route, now handicapped by two awkward gantlets and not carrying a very heavy volume of traffic. Other routes in the capital city will continue to be operated by the present efficient electric car system." [84]

Still, all was not smooth sailing. The Board of Control held back approval to widen Kent Street so as to accommodate the poles and overhead wires, because a number of maple trees would require removal. Councillor Charlotte Whitton, a member of the Commission Board, pressured them to save 200 trees. An actual engineering estimate put the number at nearer to seventy, many of which were old and needed to be removed anyway. For the time being, Bronson Avenue was wired and the coaches were reported being finished in Montreal, though this was probably not the case as all coaches were built in Can Car's Fort William plant.[85] Finally, on June 18th, the approval was given, with much hand wringing over the 69 maples, but it was either the trees or the trolleys, said Controller Coulter.[86]

The first trolley bus arrived by Canadian Pacific Railway on June 24th at the Broad Street yard. An OTC White tow truck pulled it, resplendent in its livery of grey and black with red trim, from the end of a box car and took it to the Albert Street garage. Later, bearing fleet number 2001 and the "OTC" crest, it was proudly displayed outside the garage as the look of modern transit to come.[87]

In August of that year, Charlotte Whitton was appointed mayor to fill in for the unexpected death of Mayor Grenville Goodwin. Whitton's inaugural address referenced problems the Ottawa Transportation System faced with the city's sprawling growth and the necessity of serving sparsely-settled new areas. The OTC was also confronted with capital outlay for equipment and mounting operational costs – not an uncommon situation in the post-war period. She did not specifically mention either replacing the aging tram system or the new trolley buses as an alternative. Perhaps her concerns about public transportation was a portent of things to come, as she soon made her way *ad hoc* back onto the Commission Board, and opined her views there liberally.

To relieve traffic pressure on Sparks and Queen Streets, the city and the Federal District Commission (FDC), forerunner of the National Capital Commission, had agreed that Wellington Street could be used between Kent and O'Connor for five years as a transit route. Wellington runs directly in front of the Parliament buildings and as such was governed by the FDC as part of its ceremonial route. The downtown loop for the trolley coaches now became Kent Street north to Wellington, east on Wellington to O'Connor, then south to Laurier. The route then proceeded south on Kent to Gladstone, west to Bronson Avenue and south to the terminus. The old streetcar loop on Bronson Avenue near the Rideau Canal was filled in and graded for a bus loop designated "FDC Driveway". By September, the paving of the widened Kent Street was underway but the street poles were not yet delivered, so the ten coaches languished in the coach yard.[88]

Finally, on December 23rd 1951, the official opening of the line took place with coach number 2004 filled with dignitaries. They took apparent pride in riding their $21,819.61 new-look 48-seat coach. Resplendent in fine overcoats over suit jackets, white shirts and ties, and wearing the obligatory hat, they enjoyed the warm, silent, comfortable ride hosted by Chairman Creighton and General Manager Gill. Regular passenger service soon followed and the service was a hit.

Norman D. Wilson returned in 1952, to survey Ottawa's growing traffic and public transit problems. He noted

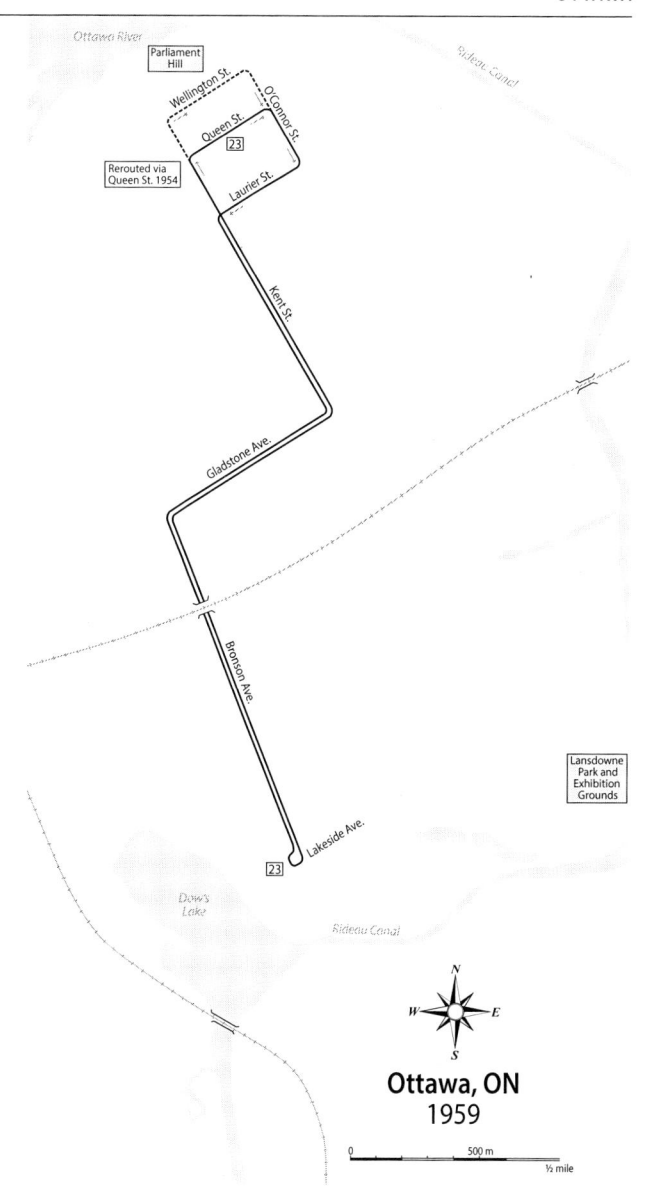

—Wire map based on OTC *Rider* route maps.

Above: On a leafy stretch of Bronson Street, at the intersection of Flora, coach 2002 silently navigates its way south on October 6th 1958.
(SCALZO COLLECTION, ILLINOIS RAILWAY MUSEUM)

that anything that impeded heavy vehicular traffic flow should be eliminated – on-street parking as well as streetcars. Replacements would be gasoline or trolley buses, and he also waxed lyrically about the possibility that trackless trolleys would be "atom powered", i.e. using nuclear-generated electricity, and so be nearly free of energy costs.

Below: Coach 2002 squeezes by a Pontiac heading south on O'Connor after it turned off Wellington, with snow slightly obscuring its rollsign. Taken probably on a test run, a few officials are riding in style inside where it is warm on December 17th 1951.
(OHIO BRASS COLLECTION, THE STRAHORN LIBRARY, ILLINOIS RAILWAY MUSEUM. LOCATION INFORMATION – BRUCE DUDLEY)

In June 1953, Hector Chaput, from the OTC's electrical Engineering Department, addressed the Westboro Kiwanis Club, and while he disclaimed that he was setting policy, he spoke in glowing terms about the merits of the trolley coach trial. In the first year of operation, savings were $100,000. He compared costs (not including depreciation) of trolley coaches at 38 cents per mile, motor buses at 48 cents per mile and streetcars from 55 to 65 cents per mile. He said that most Canadian cities found they could replace streetcars with trolley buses for what would be the cost of renewing the tram tracks. Trolley coaches carried heavier loads and were "a most desirable vehicle for routes transporting 1,000 to 4,000 people per hour." In addition, he reminded the club, the last new streetcars cost three times as much as a trolley coach. The trolley coaches were longer, wider, seated more paying passengers, had greater standing room, faster pickup and were quieter, with no fumes compared to motor buses.

The *Ottawa Journal* was not impressed with Mr. Chaput's comments. It took the position that there was nothing urgent in replacing the streetcars that had come with the city's privatization of the Ottawa Electric Railway, and they must be kept in service until the late 1960s because of the city debt incurred in their purchase. "The *Journal* thinks the OTC is too much concerned with what (if anything) will replace our trams about 1968. The *Journal* thinks its heavy propaganda in favour of trolley coaches ill-advised as the OTC has other more pressing problems." The OTC fired a return volley by placing an article in the press itemizing their experience with the BRONSON line, and that, as it was foreseen that replacement of streetcars would gradually take place, one of the most important decisions that the Commission must shortly face would be the selection of a vehicle for a new route or for a line already in existence. They followed with facts in support of the trolley. They also opined that snow conditions affected trolley coaches less than trams because of their smooth power available at all speeds, and that motorists appreciated the coach's ability to pull over to the curb when boarding passengers. Operators liked them for the greater power reserve they had, and they were bright, warm and noiseless. With this flush of success, the OTC contemplated replacing the 24-SUSSEX streetcar line and the 8-TEMPLETON bus route with trolley coaches.[79]

However, the City Board of Control reaffirmed its position: that they had the final say in any transport extension that involved interfering with city streets, such as laying tracks or erecting overhead wire, unless approved by Council. The OTC's solicitor disagreed, saying the Commission had the right to establish new trolley coach lines in any area of the city. However, since the city had the right to regulate traffic it could say where trolley coaches could not go.[90] Furthermore, the FDC nixed the idea of overhead wires cluttering the skyline on Sussex Street, which was in the process of redevelopment, complete with new bridges. *The Evening Citizen* also waded into the fray with several editorials in favour of the trolley coach, but the FDC held firm – and it held the upper hand wherever it had federal control of streets.[91] In fact every organization seemed to have an opinion about the extension of trolley coach lines. The Chambre de Commerce Française of Ottawa opposed the use of trolley coaches on the ROCKLIFFE line down Sussex and termed the coaches "obsolescing and scenery-spoilers. And moreover if the Gréber plan condemns this means of transportation, why not accept the views of those who know."[92] Alderman Charles St. Germain also voiced his opposition; he did not want trolley coaches in Sandy Hill and said he would fight any move to have the TEMPLETON bus route converted to them. He cited inadequate streets, numerous hills (that in his opinion trolley coaches could not navigate in the winter), and many beautiful trees that would be marred with the erection of trolley wires.

Many residents had petitioned him he said, opposing this recommendation arising from the 1952 Wilson report.[93] *The Evening Citizen* came out in favour of trolley coaches, asking if the public was better served without having overhead wires, but bearing the burden of more costly, less efficient gasoline buses. It opined that a conflict of authority between the OTC and the Board of Control could erupt on this question. The OTC, it said, cannot discharge its commitments if political interference brought about by local pressures prohibits a rational approach to public transit problems.[94] The editorial was an ominous portent of what was to come – the eventual killing of the trolley coach alternative in Ottawa.

In July 1954, a $750,000 Wellington Street improvement was said to be cancelled because of a dispute between the Mayor of Hull (Quebec) and the City of Ottawa. It centred on Hull Transport Ltd. getting running rights on the street once streetcar tracks were removed, as well as the erecting of trolley coach wires, and an OTC motor bus service running to Hull. Hull Mayor Caron apparently had demanded that Hull Transport get additional running rights on Wellington Street. Rather than lose some of their running rights to Hull, the OTC said it would continue to operate streetcars as well as the trolley coaches along Wellington.[95] However, by December 1954, the trolley coaches were off Wellington Street as the FDC beautification project pushed ahead with the removal of the "unsightly" overhead wires. Trolley coaches now travelled from FDC Driveway via Bronson Avenue, Gladstone, Kent and Queen to O'Connor, Laurier, Kent, Gladstone and back onto Bronson. The route was renamed BRONSON–QUEEN (23) and was supplemented during weekday peak hours with motor buses that travelled from Bell and Powell via Bell, Plymouth, LeBreton and Gladstone, Kent, Wellington, O'Connor to Sparks and then back to Bell, serving as a feeder into the trolley coach route.[96] With both the Federal District Commission and the City (personified by Mayor Whitton) firmly opposed to trolley buses, and the prospect of the antiquated streetcars years away from replacement, the now-renamed *The Ottawa Citizen* editorialized in favour of an open-minded approach to civic transportation, with the cheaper-to-maintain, faster and cleaner trolley coach to be used on well-travelled routes. Objections that they travel on fixed routes and would obstruct traffic if stalled, are invalid, the paper stated, as the trolley coaches have a fifteen-foot swing each way, and the experiences of other trolley coach-adopting cities should be noted.[97] Their opinion, though, seemed to be more of a voice crying in the wilderness of politics, both federal and municipal.

Mayor Whitton opined on trolley bus extensions in 1955, stating Ottawa would not have a trolley bus system. She was reported in *The Ottawa Citizen* to have said that high government officials had taken a stand that this type of transit system was too vulnerable in the event of war. A sneak attack on a source of electricity would put the transportation system out of service in one blow. Why a sneak attack on a bus garage was not equally troublesome did not enter into the argument. Still, by the end of 1954, Ottawa's modest 2½-mile route (one-way) had 2,141,455 revenue passengers travelling 289,044 trolley coach miles.[98] While Mayor Whitton expressed her views on transit freely, she was no longer an actual member of the Commission; that would have required an amendment to the legislation that governed the OTC which prevented any member of City Council from serving as a Commissioner.

More storm clouds were gathering, not the least of which was the OTC's precarious financial position. In a 1956 brief presented to the Royal Commission on Canada's Economic Prospects, the OTC stated there would be no electric transit by 1967. It planned to withdraw all streetcars by 1965 and the trolley coaches two years later. The number of rides per capita had dropped by nearly half in the previous nine years, and the OTC expected a further decline over the next 25 years.[99] Then, a further blow to the sole trolley coach line came with Ottawa City Council hiring in 1957, the Canadian branch of the British firm Urwick and Currie Limited to examine every aspect of the Commission. It was to look at OTC's five year plan, labour efficiency, staff and financial structure, bus and streetcar service, and passenger traffic trends. By December of 1957, a preliminary report was presented to Council which showed that OTC's five-year forecast was underestimated – Urwick, Currie Limited projected a deficit of $318,000 in 1957, growing to $2.218 million by 1961. As well as implying that current management was ineffective, it also recommended complete conversion of the existing system to all-motor buses. Ottawa's rapid annexation of communities also added fuel to the fire – the new entrants voiced strongly their opposition to overhead wires in their communities, conveniently ignoring existing telephone and hydro lines.[100]

High capital costs associated with maintaining overhead were cited by Urwick, Currie Limited, as well as the hidden costs of power stations, sub-stations and conversion equipment, distribution lines for the direct current, and the maintenance of all these, as well as stocking special equipment and parts etc. Coupling these economics with the fears of sabotage, the FDC's and residents' opposition to visual wire pollution, OTC management was eventually forced to concur with the report. The report's accusations of management incompetence were no doubt salved by newspaper editorials that supported OTC Commissioners and suggested that Ottawa City Council was lax in ignoring the OTC's pleadings over the years for more funding.[101]

May 13th 1958 found the current Mayor Nelms and Board of Control in agreement with the OTC to accept the report and scrap the remaining 96 streetcars and sell the ten trolley coaches. Conversion to an all-motor-coach system was to be implemented progressively, but quickly, to be completed by the end of 1959. After an eight-year "trial", the trolley coaches were to disappear along with the streetcars. Not that the OTC didn't like the trolleys – all the pluses were still there. It was the death of the streetcar that dragged the trolley coach down with it. Added to all this was an increasing push to beautify the city which made overhead wires of any type objectionable. Again, *The Ottawa Citizen* came out as a supporter of retaining trolley coaches, pleaded for a re-examination of the decision, and agreed with the report's recommendation to set up a traffic research department to consider not only trolley buses but also two-decker buses such as used in the United Kingdom.[102] By then, however, the die had been cast and the lone trolley coach "trial" line was shortly to become history. Also, the cost of electricity to run trolley coaches had climbed to forty per cent higher than diesel fuel. To provide power facilities and operate the coaches five days a week for the remaining life of the vehicles would cost $100,000, estimated the OTC. Furthermore, motor buses could be used on a revised routing that was more desirable and extended south as the need arose.[103]

Ottawa had the unenviable position of having been the last city in Canada to adopt the trolley coach and of having the shortest modern-era span of operation of any Canadian city – one line, three miles and eight years. There were claims the BRONSON line was chosen just because it was lightly used and the rails on the line, some of which was single-tracked, were worn out. This spurious reasoning was somehow used to justify the temporary nature of the trolley bus, but in the end none of those argument held water against the fear of foreign invasion, the sad economics of the OTC and the desire to make Ottawa into a Washington North.

On Friday May 1st 1959 at 3:25 AM the end of streetcar service in Ottawa came as a BRITANNIA tram – car No. 831 – pulled into the Cobourg Barn which it shared with the trolley coaches. The next day there was a farewell parade with majorettes and a forty-piece band, horse-tram cars and various pieces of streetcar equipment displayed, including Ottawa's famous snow sweepers.

There was however, no official last run for Ottawa's ten trolley coaches. They were quietly withdrawn from BRONSON service in June the same year, with the last coach driven by René Charbonneau entering the car barns at 3:30 AM on the 27th.[104] The units were ignominiously sold to Kitchener and Toronto to augment fleets in cities that still supported electric transit.

Footnotes:

74. *The Evening Citizen*, May 15, 1946 p. 7.
75. *The Evening Citizen*, August 24, 1946 p. 26.
76. Davis, Donald F., *A Capital Crime? The Long Death of Ottawa's Electric Railway 1947–1999*. Paper presented to the "Construire une capitale – Ottawa – Making a Capital" Conference, University of Ottawa, November 20, 1999. Published in "Ottawa Making a Capital", University of Ottawa Press, Ottawa, 2001, footnote 62. p. 381.
77. *The Evening Citizen*, August 16, 1948 p. 1.
78. *The Evening Citizen*, February 10, 1949 p. 1 & 10.

79. *The Evening Citizen*, February 17, 1949 p. 1.
80. *The Evening Citizen*, March 3, 1949 p. 14.
81. *The Evening Citizen*, April 23, 1949 p. 1.
82. Sanderson, John H., Ottawa-Carleton Regional Transit Commission – History of the Ottawa Transportation Commission, n.d. on copy received May 1977.
83. *The Evening Citizen*, February 24, 1951 p. 1.
84. Clegg, Anthony, *Ottawa Electric Railway & Ottawa Transportation Commission Trolleys in Canada's Capital* from the Electric Railroaders' Association *Headlights*, Vol. 13 No. 11, November 1951 as posted on http://www.angelfire.com/ca/TORONTO/history/Ottawa.html visited January 2013.
85. *The Evening Citizen*, June 4, 1951 p. 1.
86. *The Evening Citizen*, June 16, 1951 p. 6.
87. Watts, Dave, *Tracks, Wires, and Rubber Tires: A short history of public transportation in the Nation's Capital*, OC Transpo 2000 pp. 6-7.
88. *The Evening Citizen*, September 7, 1951 p. 3.
89. Sanderson, *Op. Cit.* pp. 23-26.
90. *The Evening Citizen*, May 26, 1953 p. 18.
91. *The Evening Citizen*, January 31, 1953 p. 34 & May 22, 1953 p. 44.
92. *The Evening Citizen*, May 1, 1953 p. 24.
93. *The Evening Citizen*, May 23, 1953 p. 4.
94. *The Evening Citizen*, May 27, 1953 p. 46.
95. *The Ottawa Citizen*, July 16, 1954 pp. 1 and 18.
96. OTC *Rider* (Ottawa Transportation Commission passenger newsletter) Vol. 3 No. 22 November 12, 1954 and No. 25 December 31, 1954.
97. *The Ottawa Citizen*, September 19, 1955 p. 40.
98. *Canadian Transportation*, June 1955 p. 338.
99. *The Ottawa Citizen*, February 29, 1956 p. 21.
100. *A Capital Crime?* pp. 365-375.
101. McKeown, Bill, *Ottawa's Streetcars*, Railfare*DC Books, Pickering ON, 2006, pp. 170, 180-1.
102. *The Ottawa Citizen*, May 17, 1958 p. 6.
103. *The Ottawa Citizen*, June 25, 1959 p. 7.
104. *The Ottawa Citizen*, June 30, 1959 p. 24.

Above: Running north-bound on Bronson just past the corner of Fifth Avenue, coach 2010 heads towards downtown on June 16th 1952. Both brick buildings in the background are still there today.
(OHIO BRASS COLLECTION, THE STRAHORN LIBRARY, ILLINOIS RAILWAY MUSEUM.
LOCATION INFORMATION – BRUCE DUDLEY/TOM GRUMLEY)

Below: October 6th 1958, and coach 2004 is southbound on Bronson Avenue near Holmwood Avenue. On this stretch of Bronson, the streetcar tracks had not yet been lifted or paved over.
(SCALZO COLLECTION, ILLINOIS RAILWAY MUSEUM)

Above: It's a blustery March 2nd 1949, as coach No. 101 is unloaded near the CPR freight offices between Amelia and Sydney Streets and Sixth and Seventh Streets. The author's memories of the yard in the late 1950s were of a small, 2-stall engine shed, an air-operated turntable and an air-operated coal bucket hoist, and of getting a "cab ride" onto and off the turntable. The coach would probably have been towed across the flat cars and on to an unloading platform/ramp at the end of the string of flat cars. (OHIO BRASS COLLECTION, THE STRAHORN LIBRARY, ILLINOIS RAILWAY MUSEUM)

Below: Exiting the Riverdale Loop with its rudimentary waiting shelter, this coach is heading back into town, probably during the summer of 1950 after the Riverdale extension opened. (OHIO BRASS COLLECTION, THE STRAHORN LIBRARY, ILLINOIS RAILWAY MUSEUM)

Cornwall (1949-1970)
Cornwall Street Railway Light & Power Co., Ltd.

By all logic this small city of about 25,000 should not have been able to support a streetcar system, much less trolley buses. But with an electric freight operation to augment the service, and an electric utility willing to provide transit service, Cornwall was the little system that could – and did.

In July of 1896, the Cornwall Electric Street Railway placed its first streetcars in service and soon after, butted heads with the town council regarding Sunday operations. So it was no surprise that when the company experienced financial difficulties less than two years later, there were no helping hands from the town, and the major bondholder – Sun Life Assurance Company – found itself owning a street railway. With the combining of the power utility that supplied the streetcars, and rail freight motor operations, the company became Cornwall Street Railway Light & Power Co., Limited, surely one of the longest urban transit names in Canada. Known more colloquially as "the insurance company's streetcars", it (CSR) operated two lines through Cornwall's incorporation as a city of 15,000 souls in 1945, and soldiered on through the early post-war period with an aging fleet of second-hand cars and increasing competition from the convenient personal automobile. The situation was somewhat complicated by the fact that CSR's first priority was, despite the order of services in their name, provision of 9200 KW peak demand power to the City of Cornwall and urban township – a customer base of 30,000. Secondarily, their mandate was providing passenger transportation for four million revenue passengers per year. Finally, they switched freight with electric locomotives – 24,000 loaded freight cars each year from three railways to industries and vice versa. Of the three though, passenger transport was far from adequate to serve a growing need.

By 1948, the writing was on the carhouse wall, and the old trams had "had their day". The only equipment options were the PCC streetcar with its attendant specialized maintenance, gasoline buses that were more maintenance-intensive and whose shorter lifespan made them more costly in the long run, and the modern trolley coach with its simpler mechanism and lower maintenance costs. Raising fares to purchase modern trams was negated by poor track, noise concerns and much single-track that would have had to be doubled. A careful study that looked at similar-sized operations such as Kitchener, showed that it made perfect sense for a company in the electricity business to continue with a form of electric transportation that so aptly suited the present and anticipated future traffic volumes.[105] But first, CSR had to take over the assets of its affiliated company Stormont Electric Light and Power Co., Ltd. on June 1st, then apply to the City and Township for a franchise which included new technology to replace the streetcars. On granting of the franchise, fifteen Can Car T-44 trolley coaches were ordered for the main line services, and the three Can Car motor buses purchased earlier were to continue as feeders to the main lines.[106]

The first three coaches arrived on December 23rd 1948, and installation of the overhead wires started shortly after.[107] A training loop was first constructed[108] and a test run was conducted with the superintendent of rolling stock, Donald Seymour at the controls. Operations commenced March 10th, running from the car barns along Cumberland to Second Street, then east to Marlborough,

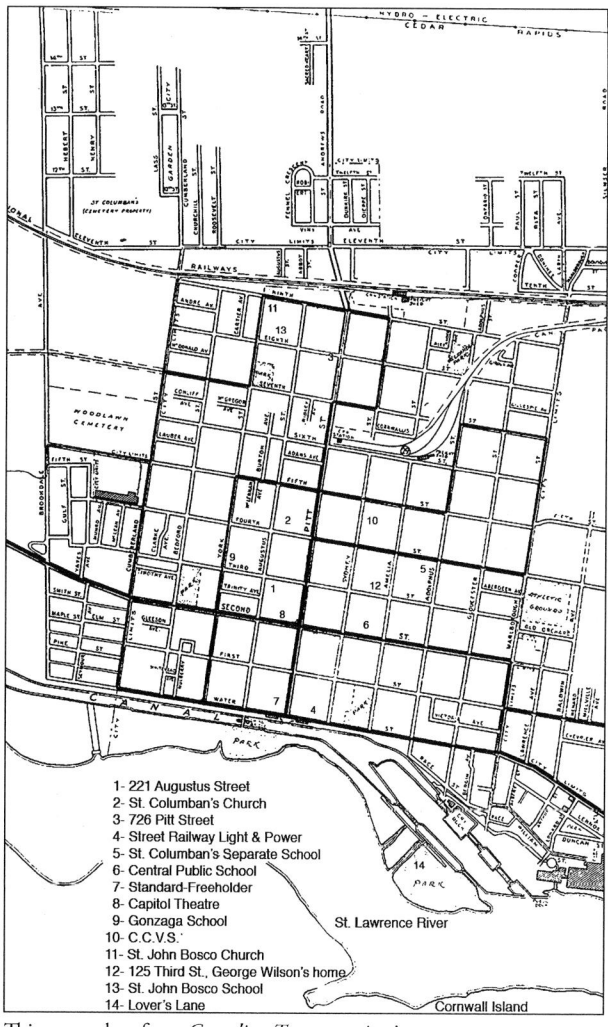

1- 221 Augustus Street
2- St. Columban's Church
3- 726 Pitt Street
4- Street Railway Light & Power
5- St. Columban's Separate School
6- Central Public School
7- Standard-Freeholder
8- Capitol Theatre
9- Gonzaga School
10- C.C.V.S.
11- St. John Bosco Church
12- 125 Third St, George Wilson's home
13- St. John Bosco School
14- Lover's Lane

This map taken from *Canadian Transportation* in summer 1949 shows the two built routes, and two planned, but never built.

Cornwall, ON 1949–1970

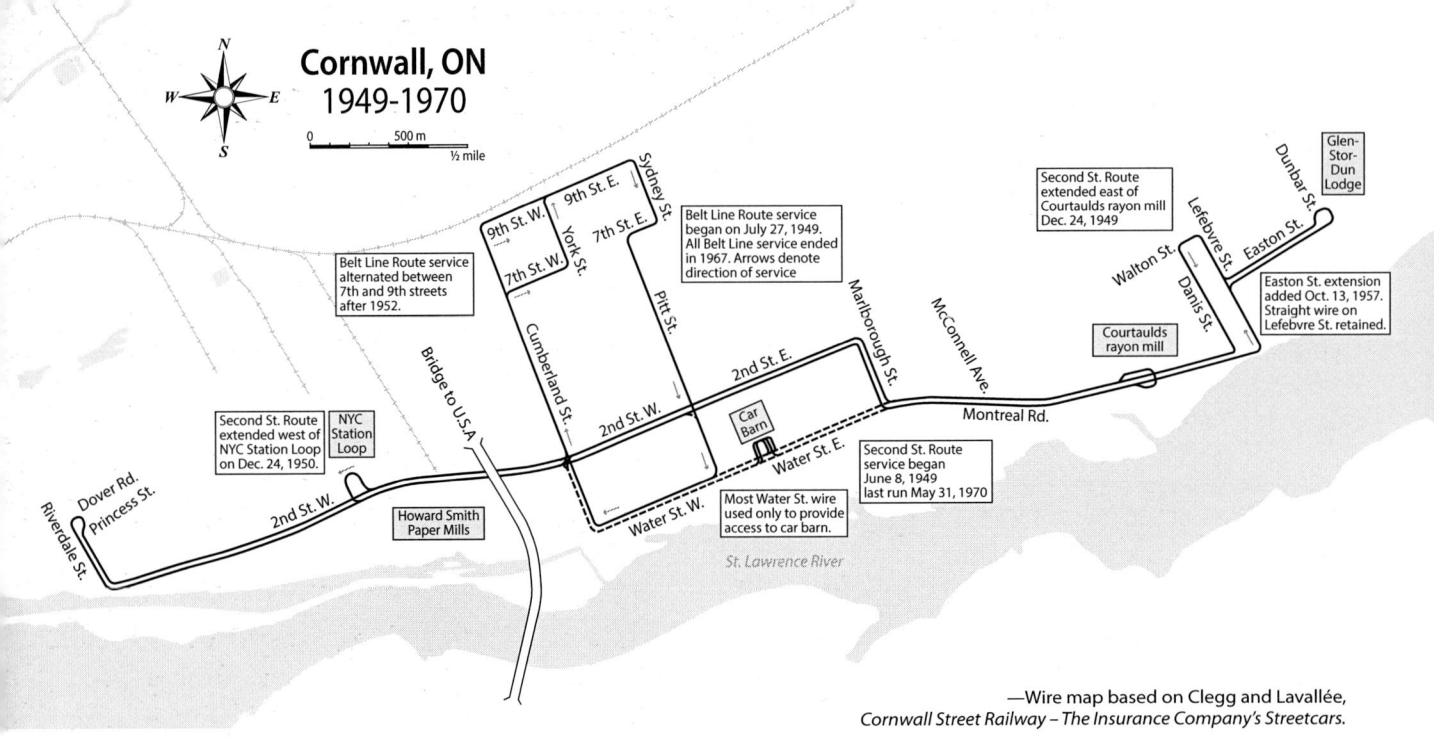

Map labels:
- Belt Line Route service alternated between 7th and 9th streets after 1952.
- Belt Line Route service began on July 27, 1949. All Belt Line service ended in 1967. Arrows denote direction of service.
- Second St. Route extended east of Courtaulds rayon mill Dec. 24, 1949
- Easton St. extension added Oct. 13, 1957. Straight wire on Lefebvre St. retained.
- Second St. Route extended west of NYC Station Loop on Dec. 24, 1950.
- NYC Station Loop
- Howard Smith Paper Mills
- Car Barn
- Second St. Route service began June 8, 1949 last run May 31, 1970
- Most Water St. wire used only to provide access to car barn.
- Courtaulds rayon mill
- Glen-Stor-Dun Lodge
- St. Lawrence River

Streets: Riverdale St., Dover Rd., Princess St., 2nd St. W., Bridge to U.S.A., Cumberland St., 2nd St. W., 9th St. W., 9th St. E., 7th St. W., 7th St. E., York St., Sydney St., Pitt St., 2nd St. E., Water St. E., Water St. W., Marlborough St., McConnell Ave., Montreal Rd., Walton St., Lefebvre St., Danis St., Easton St., Dunbar St.

—Wire map based on Clegg and Lavallée, *Cornwall Street Railway – The Insurance Company's Streetcars.*

---

south to Water and back to the barns. The local newspaper, The Cornwall *Daily Standard-Freeholder*, lauded the "manoeuverability of the huge coach", curb loading, and smooth acceleration and braking. While the changeover from streetcar to trolley coach overhead continued, there was some dispute between the City and CSR and Bell Telephone over the removing and relocating of poles. Bell contended that it should not have to bear any of the costs, while the City and the street railway felt it should be shared.[109] The issue was finally resolved by arbitration.

Official trolley bus service was inaugurated June 8th 1949 with the mayor – Aaron Horovitz – cutting the ribbon with a pair of specially engraved gold scissors. He said that the beginning of trolley coaches marked another milestone in the history of Cornwall, and that when it is complete, the city will enjoy the finest and most efficient type of urban transportation available. Then the Vice President of the company, E. R. Alexander, drove the first coach across the intersection of Pitt and Second streets. The ceremonies were then repeated in the east end at McConnell Avenue and Montreal Road, where the township reeve, J. E. U. Rouleau, officiated. Following this, officials toured the line in the new trolley coaches, and then retired to a reception and dinner at the Hotel Cornwallis where twelve speakers commended the company on its trolley coach inauguration. These included the Minister of Transportation, the Hon. Lionel Chevrier who grew up in Cornwall and was its long-time MP. Another speaker, the MPP for Stormont, John L. MacDonald, noted that people have a habit of judging a city by its transit equipment, and he was sure that people would have a favourable opinion of Cornwall in the future.[110] A one-way trip was still five cents – unchanged from 47 years earlier – but shortly after the trolley buses were introduced, on July 1st the fare was finally increased to seven cents cash or four tickets for 25 cents.[111]

This inaugural line ran from a loop at Howard Smith Paper Mills/New York Central station in the west along Second Street, south on Marlborough to Montreal Road and along it to another loop at the Courtaulds Canada rayon mill in the east. Seven weeks later, on July 27th, the trolley buses took over on the BELT LINE that ran on Water Street west from Pitt Street to Cumberland; north on Cumberland to Seventh Street; easterly on it to York Street; north on York to Ninth Street, east on Ninth to Sydney; south on Sydney for two blocks to Seventh Street; west on Seventh for a block to Pitt Street; south on Pitt to Water Street and then west on Water to Cumberland.[112] This routing was to accommodate the "working class public" that lived east of Cumberland and worked at Courtaulds rayon mill in the east, Canada Cottons (south) or Howard Smith Paper Mills in the west. July 27th 1949 was also the last day trams ran in Cornwall, with a parade of decorated streetcars and a dinner afterwards. Interestingly, the streetcar tracks were left in place, paved over and used as the return electrical circuit for the trolley coach system.[113]

There were also two other trolley coach routes in the plans. The first was a (gasoline bus) route conversion in the northwest running north from Marlborough and Fourth to Seventh, along it to Adolphus, south on Adolphus, west on Fifth to Pitt, then south to Fourth and back to Marlborough. The second was a line east of Marlborough and north of Montreal road, off Marlborough at First, east on First to a loop of McConnell/Walton/Carleton/First.[114]

There was also service wire east on Water from Pitt, past the barns to Montreal Road. While the SECOND STREET line essentially replicated the streetcar route, the BELT LINE combined the PITT STREET and the old BELT LINE carlines.

By year-end passengers carried had increased from 3,887,510 in 1948 to 4,206,882[115] and that with only half a year of the new service. Hard on that success were extensions to growing suburbs. December 24th 1949 saw the SECOND STREET line extended east from the Courtaulds loop, along Montreal Road to Lefebvre Street north to Walton, thence west to Danis and south back to Montreal Road.[116] On Saturday May 29th 1950, a new bus route was started west into Riverdale and into the wartime housing in the north, using gasoline buses temporarily for the Riverdale portion until the trolley coach wire could be installed.[117] In late December 1950, CSR announced that route would be a trolley coach line by year-end. It extended the trolley wire a mile along Second Street, up Riverdale to a loop off Riverdale between Princess and Dover Road where a waiting shelter was installed. Some of this extension was strung with the first experimental aluminum alloy grooved wire in the world.[118] Finally, on Sunday December 24th at 6:00 AM, this penultimate trolley coach extension went into service.[119] The new RIVERDALE line incorporated the north portion of the BELT LINE to Second Street, and then ran along that route to the Riverdale loop. That third route was dropped, probably as a result of a passenger survey in 1957, and west-bound riders from the BELT LINE just made a transfer.

Sometime after 1952, one-way wire was strung north along Cumberland from Seventh to Ninth and east on it to meet up with the existing (single) line at York Street. Every day and throughout the day, every second BELT LINE trolley coach went straight along Cumberland to Ninth serving "Garden City" – the area past Ninth on Cumberland (11-12-13th Streets … the CNR tracks were effectively Tenth Street) – where many Italian families lived and planted their huge gardens.[120]

Trolley coach operation was not without drama though, as on a fine April day in 1954, Garpard Martel, wearing a bulging windbreaker, boarded a SECOND STREET coach and sat down behind the driver. Under his windbreaker Mar-

The rollsign on coach 102 seems to say EAST FRONT as it navigates through the corner of Second and Cumberland on January 19th 1950. The chimney between the elm tree and the telephone poles on the left, and the digester building behind the coach are part of Howard Smith Paper Mills – one of Cornwall's largest employers. The building on the left is National Grocers. On the opposite side is the Separate School on the right of the bus. At this intersection there was wire from the car barns that got the coaches onto the SECOND STREET line going either east or west as well as the BELT LINE single set going through that intersection, and the freight railway tracks.
(OHIO BRASS COLLECTION, THE STRAHORN LIBRARY, ILLINOIS RAILWAY MUSEUM. ADDITIONAL LOCATION INFORMATION – LILY WORRALL)

tel had $3000 from cashing 56 of his workmates' cheques, which he did regularly. Shortly after he boarded, two men on the bus got up, strode down the near-empty coach to where Martel was sitting and pulled guns. They ordered the driver to stop and fired two shots right next to Martel's foot. Martel rose and tried to grab the gun, but the man punched him and began to pull the money out of his coat. Then his companion hit Martel in the head with the gun. The two felons fled and the nervous driver started the coach, but a bleeding Martel had the presence to tell the

Fare tickets from the trolley coach era in Cornwall. The children's tickets at top were purple and the adult fare, orange. Unfortunately CSRL&P Co. chose to use a motor bus illustration.
(SCHWARZKOPF COLLECTION)

Above: Why coach 104 is not in service we do not know, but it is at the northwest corner of Brennan's Corners, at Montreal Road and Marlborough, going east March 17th 1949. There once was the Roxy Movie Theatre on Montreal Road, and this rooming house has picked up the name. The building still stands today with the same brick porch, but it is no longer a rooming house.
(OHIO BRASS COLLECTION, THE STRAHORN LIBRARY, ILLINOIS RAILWAY MUSEUM. LOCATION INFORMATION – LILY WORRALL)

Below: Coach 107 is travelling east on Second Street on March 2nd 1949, just east of Pitt Street passing in front of its namesake – the brick building behind the bus was the CSR office. The St. Lawrence Power Company was located in Massena NY and had a generating plant at nearby Mille Roches ON. It sold power to the CSR, some of which it purchased from the Cedar Rapids Transmission Company in Quebec.
(OHIO BRASS COLLECTION, THE STRAHORN LIBRARY, ILLINOIS RAILWAY MUSEUM)

Right: This Ohio Brass advertisement placed in magazines in March 1954 extolled the benefits of trolley coaches in smaller communities. (OHIO BRASS COLLECTION, THE STRAHORN LIBRARY, ILLINOIS RAILWAY MUSEUM)

operator to stop the coach again. He dashed into a service station to phone the police. The driver, though jittery at having a gun to his head also, pulled into the nearby NYC terminal and also called police. The other two passengers were shaken, but safe. The bus was impounded, the bullets recovered, and the two thieves were apprehended with the cash, along with an accomplice.[121]

In late 1951, the system was able to purchase a unique Can Car T-44 trolley coach, in that it was the very first made in Canada, which had travelled across Canada as a demonstrator for five years. Although it had been modified a number of times, the windows were still the earlier sliding sash type rather than lifting as was the rest of the Cornwall fleet. Despite its travels, the coach was sound and continued to serve until the end. Some operators claimed it was the best handling and braking unit in the fleet.

The area east of Lefebvre on the SECOND STREET–COURTAULDS line had un-surfaced roads and thus was unsuitable for bus service. However, after Council agreed in July 1957 to pave Easton, wire was strung, and on Sunday, October 13th 1957, the line went as before, up Lefebvre, but then turned east along Easton, looping at Dunbar and the new Glen Stor-Dun Lodge, then back to Lefebvre and north on it.[122]

The system was not without it quirks. Part of a motor bus route paralleled the trolley coach route on Second Street … the author's father remembers one day walking down Second Street and hearing a tremendous "clap of thunder" even though it was a perfectly clear day. He turned to see a fine mess of trolley poles and broken retriever ropes, with the two operators emerging from their respective coaches, pulling on work gloves and using ungentlemanly language. It seems that one operator, usually assigned to a motor bus route, had forgotten which he was on and tried to pass a stopped trolley bus with his trolley coach. The result was not as catastrophic as it would have been if they had also brought down the overhead.

Passenger traffic was declining in the late 1950s and early '60s, so the two additional, planned trolley coach routes were postponed and then finally cancelled.[123] In addition to declining patronage, a number of incidents of power outages in the late 1950s, subsequent on- and off-negotiations to merge with electricity suppliers, not to mention a city council that was not keen on rate increases, led the CSR and its parent Sun Life to consider whether it was in the best interests of its policyholders to be in the transit business. The freight-hauling side of its operations was also suffering from worn out locomotives and a dearth of spare parts – a situation similar to the death of the streetcar twenty years earlier. However, Sun Life was not willing to sell the money-making electric power part of the company without the accompanying transit operation. While the issue surfaced from time to time, eventual inaction by the city left a status quo. A study in September 1955 by Stone & Webster recommended shortening the SECOND STREET route to turn back at the NYC Loop and running only to the Courtaulds Loop. It also recommended that to "resolve immediate operating problems facing the company," it should reduce schedules and possibly drop the BELT LINE south of Second Street; however, that would require special work for the overhead, an additional expense.[124] None of these was acted on.

By 1961, the power situation stabilized in CSR's favour, but rapid growth meant the company would be facing a power shortage forecast by 1964. The situation went on with various iterations of power suppliers until 1968, when franchises were up for renewal. The city granted the two-year extension that both Niagara Mohawk (the power supplier) and CSR asked for. Both companies felt that was the least they could maintain, and both hoped that a new city council would agree by then to purchase the CSR despite its power woes. Still, the transit section was losing money, with increased costs, decreasing passengers and wage hikes, despite another fare increase. Also, the freight division was faltering with increased truck competition. In addition, the power supplier informed CSR that it could not guarantee the company's electrical needs after 1971. Sun Life started to test the waters in Canada's Centennial Year (1967) and negotiations continued for several more years. The main sticking point was the city's unwillingness to purchase the whole package – money-losing passenger

Above: Cornwall coach 107 eastbound on Montreal Road, May 30th 1970, has just passed Baldwin Avenue. Nativity Roman Catholic Church is in the background, and beyond the trees is the Royal Hotel at the corner of McConnell Street. The IDA Drug Store is still there today as a Medical Arts pharmacy.
(SCALZO COLLECTION, ILLINOIS RAILWAY MUSEUM. PHOTO RESTORATION AND LOCATION INFORMATION – LILY WORRALL)

Below: On a fan trip over the decommissioned BELT LINE, coach 104 makes the turn off Cumberland onto Ninth Street outside the No-co-rode (Domtar) pipe plant on May 17th 1970. The electric freight line paralleled the trolley line along Cumberland to serve Domtar and on to the CNR yard.
(TED WICKSON).

and freight division as well as the profitable local electricity supplier.

By 1967, attempts were made to reduce the losses. However, worn-out trolley buses and a new shopping plaza that required transit access made the existing BELT LINE route inadequate. The decision was made to shift the line nearer the shopping centre and use diesel buses instead of trolleys.[125] The inflexibility of trolley routes was also cited as a negative as user patterns shifted.

Finally, in July 1969, CSR informed City Council that it would be getting out of the transit business when its franchise expired December 31st 1970. By June 1970, service cuts reduced runs on the remaining SECOND STREET line to four coaches on weekdays, and three slated for Sunday. The city asked for the trolley coaches to be withdrawn totally as they were well worn out and only four were in regular service anyway. On May 17th 1970, a fan trip was organized by members of the Upper Canada Railway Society (UCRS) and Ottawa-area enthusiasts over the unused BELT LINE using coach No. 104.

On Sunday, May 31st 1970, coach 100 operated by Vernon Cooke made a last west-end trip, arriving at the barns with its load of employees' families and children via Cumberland Street, pulling in at 6:00 PM, the normal end of Sunday service in this small city. Joe Meilleur with coach 111 from the east timed his entry to coincide with number 100. At 6:02, coach 106 driven by Lester Foulds pulled into the barns, coming also from the east end via the service wire on Water Street, and quietly, electric passenger service in the Seaway City came to a halt.[126] Photographs were taken, but no official ceremonies were held like they had when the trolleys took over from the trams. Some employees and transit officials made a point of witnessing the last runs, and the drivers tried to make a bit of ceremony, wearing long-haired wigs like the Father Time who had sat on the last streetcar as it went to its rest. The three last drivers were badges 1, 2 and 3 as the most senior men on the roster. After the photographs were taken, the drivers, along with some twenty others and their wives went to a social gathering nearby. The trolley's passing, was however, briefly noted in the *Daily Standard-Freeholder* with a few retrospective photos.[127] Motor buses provided the service for the next seven months, then the insurance company vacated the transit business for all time. A last-day ceremony was held in 1971 commemorating the freight service, but by then the trolley coach wires were down, and the buses sold to Toronto for cannibalization to build new Flyer trolley coaches there. An exception was the original Can Car demonstrator which was sold to an employee for use at a rural camp.[128] It was a sad, quiet end for the smallest city in Canada to operate trolley coaches.[129]

Footnotes:

105. *Canadian Transportation*, August 1949 pp. 443-446.
106. The Cornwall *Daily Standard-Freeholder*, June 6, 1949 p. 9.
107. The Cornwall *Daily Standard-Freeholder*, December 23, 1948 p. 3.
108. Linley, Bill, *Canada's Last Common Carrier*, UCRS Newsletter, June 1972 p. 93.
109. *Canadian Transportation*, April 1949 p. 206.
110. *Ibid.*
111. The Cornwall *Daily Standard-Freeholder*, June 29, 1949 p. 3.
112. The Cornwall *Daily Standard-Freeholder*, July 26, 1948 p. 3 and 9 (route map).
113. The Cornwall *Daily Standard-Freeholder*, September 14, 1949 p. 3.
114. *Canadian Transportation*, Aug. 1949 p. 443 and 444 (map).
115. Carter-Edwards, Karen, *100 Years of Service* (Cornwall Electric), p. 195.
116. Fares and dates from Carter-Edwards p. 196.
117. The Cornwall *Daily Standard-Freeholder*, May 27, 1950 p. 3 and advertisement on p. 13.
118. The Cornwall *Daily Standard-Freeholder*, December 20, 1950 p. 3.
119. The Cornwall *Daily Standard-Freeholder*, December 22, 1950 advertisement p. 8.
120. Worrall, Lily, "Postcards of Cornwall" web author, e-mail correspondence with this author August 26, 2012.
121. The Cornwall *Daily Standard-Freeholder*, April 3, 1954 p. 3 and April 5, p. 3.
122. The Cornwall *Daily Standard-Freeholder*, July 16, 1957 p. 9 and October 12, 1957 p. 7 advertisement.
123. Linley, *op. cit.*
124. CSR files in SDG Museum collection as visited July 3, 2013.
125. *Ibid.*
126. *Trolley Coach News*, #10, August 1970 p. 46.
127. The Cornwall *Daily Standard-Freeholder*, May 30, 1970 clippings from Wally Young collection.
128. Knowles, John D., correspondence with author March 30, 2010.
129. In addition to cited references, additional background information was noted from Clegg and Lavallée, Ch. 9 and 10 and Carter-Edwards, *100 Years of Service* (Cornwall Electric), Ch. 8, 9 and 11.

Below: The operators gather to bid farewell to the last Cornwall trolley coach to run after it arrived at the car barns. The gentleman with the glasses and moustache is Lester Foulds and behind him to his left is Joe Meilleur, drivers of the last and second last coaches respectively. (J.D. KNOWLES)

Above: In June 1922, the boy on the bicycle is eagerly following the new form of electric transit, the trolley coach, as it makes its way along the unpaved MOUNT PLEASANT route near Davisville Avenue.
(TTC PHOTO, WICKSON COLLECTION)

Below: This early – c1921 shot of Canadian Brill coach 20 shows the single pole with the forked collector, later replaced with conventional double poles.
(OHIO BRASS COLLECTION, THE STRAHORN LIBRARY, ILLINOIS RAILWAY MUSEUM)

Toronto (1922-1925 and 1947-1993)
Toronto Transportation Commission/ Toronto Transit Commission

A champion of electric transit, Toronto boasted all three forms: streetcars, subways and trolley coaches. In fact Toronto led the way for trolley coach rehabilitation in the 1970s and 1980s. But, somewhere along the way, the lowly, reliable trolley coach was de-wired.

Act 1:

In 1921, representatives from both the Toronto Transportation Commission and the Sandwich, Windsor & Amherstburg Railway Company viewed three competitive trackless trolley demonstration vehicles in Detroit, MI. The Windsor group was impressed enough to purchase the St. Louis Car Company demonstrator and ordered three more. Toronto was also sold, but opted for Canadian Brill vehicles with twin motor drive, with an eye to converting the MOUNT PLEASANT route from gasoline bus to trolley coach.

Backing up a little; when in 1921 the TTC became responsible for public transportation in the Mount Pleasant area, it found that local citizens expected streetcar service, much like the rest of Toronto. The "TTC" Act, passed by the Ontario Legislature June 4th 1920, made no mention of providing service other than by streetcars.

TTC management balked at the expense of laying car lines into a small serving area, however, they felt that perhaps some form of electric transit was in order. Once clarification was obtained, TTC made plans to instead introduce buses when it assumed its mandate September 1st 1921. The trolley coach had distinct advantages: reduced fuel costs over gasoline, no need to lay track, and the possibility of better headway times. Also, if ridership increased, converting the line to streetcar operation would be somewhat easier as span and feeder wires would already be in place and amortized. In addition, extending the St. Clair carline into Mount Pleasant was not possible until a bridge could be constructed on St. Clair East over the Vale of Avoca, a major ravine just east of Yonge Street.[130]

The TTC proceeded to construct trolley coach overhead from Yonge and Merton, along Merton and up Mount Pleasant to Eglinton Avenue. Each end had a wye turn, and coaches were stored in a shed until additional wire was extended along Eglinton to the car house at Yonge and Eglinton. Later the wye was replaced with a loop at Yonge and Merton.

Service was inaugurated June 19th 1922 with four Canadian Brill buses – they had Packard frames, Canadian Brill bodies and Westinghouse motors. Interestingly they were originally delivered with a single trolley pole that had a forked end with two trolley-type wheel contactors. They were later equipped with double poles, but still with trolley wheels.[131]

Mount Pleasant riders took to the new electric trackless trolley despite the hard wooden seats, solid rubber tires and the route being on unpaved roadways. Three units were used in rush hour and the service was so popular that an average of 1700 passengers rode daily. By 1925, ridership had increased to the point that full streetcar service was in order. Trolley coaches stopped running August 31st 1925 and the trams replaced them November 3rd when the St. Clair carline was extended up Mt. Pleasant Road to Eglinton. Trolley coach wire was removed and the vehicles stored off-property. In 1928 they were sold for scrap; however one escaped and was discovered at a farm museum near Cobourg in 1974 and moved to the Halton County Radial Railway museum for future restoration. As of the end of 1925, the trolley coach era in Canada was nearly over – Windsor's line was replaced with motor buses (with an eye to eventual streetcars) in 1926 – and it would be another 22 years before trolley coaches reappeared in Toronto.[132]

—Wire map based on C.H. Prentice.

Above: Canadian Brill TTC 20 makes the turn off Mount Pleasant into the Y at Eglinton Avenue.
(TTC PHOTO, JEFF MARINOFF COLLECTION)

Below: Officials inspect the Can Car demonstrator outside TTC's Lansdowne Carhouse in November 1946.
(WICKSON COLLECTION)

Right: Canada Wire and Cable Company Limited placed this ad in transportation magazines in the fall of 1947 showing off their overhead being installed for Toronto's new trolley coach lines. (PROVINCIAL ARCHIVES OF ALBERTA, SCHWARZKOPF COLLECTION)

Act 2:

"Critical examination of the operation of trolley coaches in numerous cities by Toronto Transportation Commission officials has satisfied them that the trolley coach has definite advantages over either street car or bus for certain operations; confirmed that (sic) fact that it possesses excellent ride characteristics of quietness, comfort and speed and should be made available to the citizens of Toronto." This quote from the TTC employees' publication *The Coupler* in 1946 announced the plan to reintroduce the trolley coach. In fact *The Coupler* went on to state that fifty Canadian-made coaches had been ordered for the fall of 1946.[133] Regarding the matter of "critical examination", Mr. W. F. Irwin, Research Engineer, TTC, had visited and ridden trolley coaches in Milwaukee, Chicago, Indianapolis, Cincinnati, Columbus and Cleveland, all cities of comparable size to Toronto and all of which had operated streetcars, motor buses and trolley coaches for some time – 10 to 15 years. He said "he was satisfied that trolley coaches had a very definite place in any urban transit system of a medium sized or large city." In addition, he cited the smooth ride, quiet operation, rapid acceleration and absence of fumes.[134]

Three routes were selected for conversion from streetcar to trolley coach: LANSDOWNE, ANNETTE and OSSINGTON. While LANSDOWNE replaced a car line (and was extended another ¾ of a mile), ANNETTE replaced parts of several lines including parts of the JANE and RUNNYMEDE bus lines, and the HARBORD car line. OSSINGTON would replace portions of the DOVERCOURT and HARBORD car lines and the DAVENPORT bus route.[135] All this was concentrated in the west central part of the city where several car lines had worn trackage at the ends of their routes. By re-jigging the carlines to avoid the worn track and replacing that portion of the route with trolley coaches, the Commission felt it would be money ahead and also be able to easily extend some of these routes. Mr. Irwin's estimate was a saving of $500,000 in track replacements and $200,000 in extensions if they had been streetcar lines.[136]

Pavement had to be widened on a number of streets with the TTC and the city sharing the costs. The OSSINGTON trolley coach was to run from a loop at St. Clair and Oakwood avenues south to Queen Street and east to a loop at King and Shaw streets. The LANSDOWNE run was to be from a loop at St. Clair to one at Queen, and the ANNETTE route ran east-west from a loop at Christie Street, west on Dupont and Annette, and then south on Jane to loop at Bloor Street.[137] The combined round-trip mileage of the three routes was just over twenty miles. It is interesting to note that the new trolley coach routes did not get lost in the build-up to the final planning of Canada's first rapid transit system – the Toronto subway – which had been approved by plebiscite in January 1946.[138]

The decision to introduce trolley coaches in Toronto was not for quite the same reasons as elsewhere in Canada. Post-war, the TTC had most of its streetcar fleet in reasonably good condition and it was still providing a needed service. Some lighter routes were in need of repair or expansion and it was on these lines that the Commission looked to install the trolley coach. A September 1947 advertisement by Canada Wire and Cable showed diligent TTC workers stringing "Phono-electric Trolley Wire and Weatherproof feeder cables" on May 12th. Presumably not all three trolley coach lines were yet in operation; the plan was to start with the LANSDOWNE route as it ran " … past the [Lansdowne] Division, and in addition to enabling close supervision during initial operation, it will provide a convenient route for training operators so that an adequate supply of men trained in trolley coach operation will be available for the operation of other lines as they are converted." [139]

In the meantime, a Can Car model T-44 demonstration vehicle made an appearance in Toronto on November

Text continues on page 71

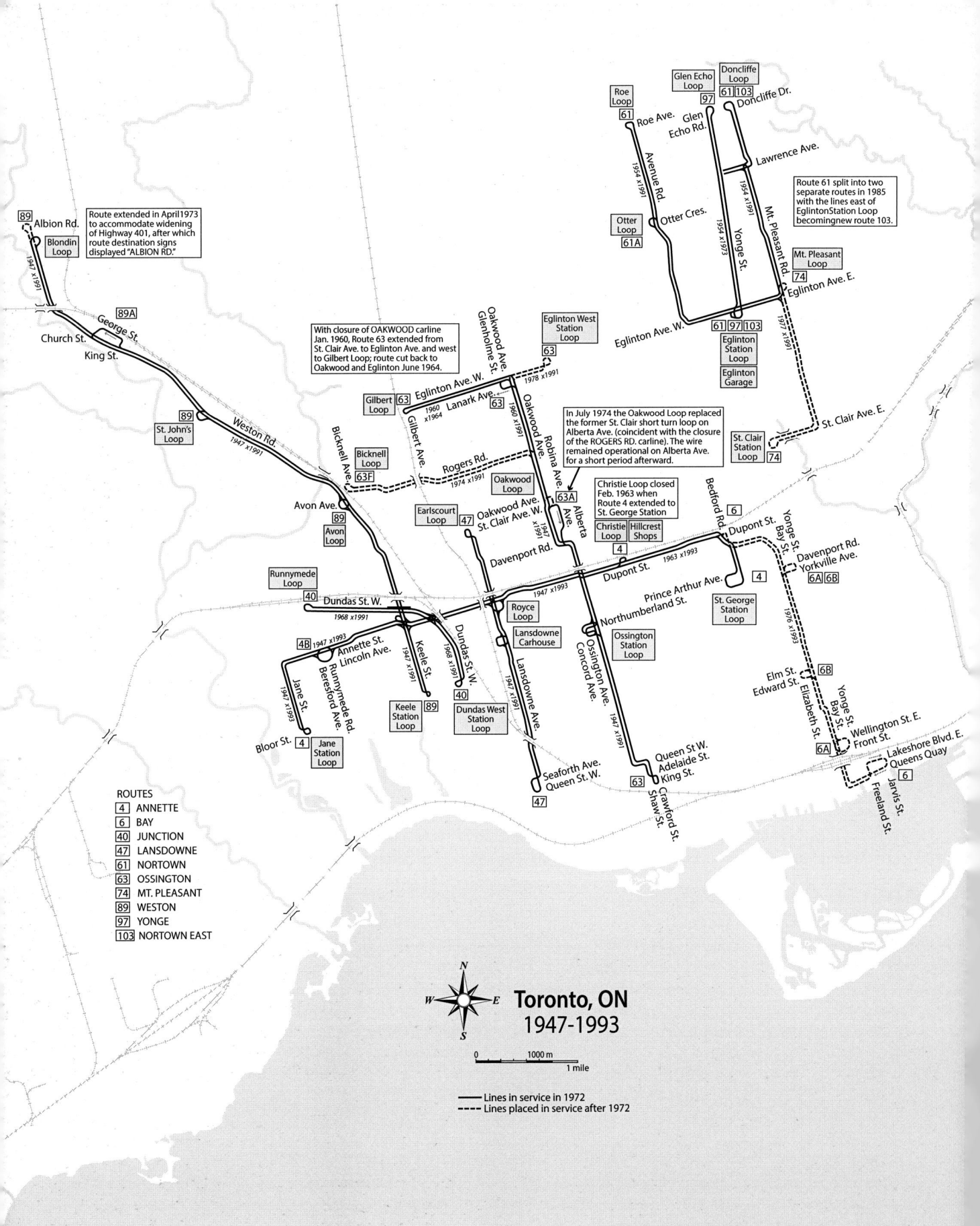

Toronto, ON 1947-1993

ROUTES
- 4 ANNETTE
- 6 BAY
- 40 JUNCTION
- 47 LANSDOWNE
- 61 NORTOWN
- 63 OSSINGTON
- 74 MT. PLEASANT
- 89 WESTON
- 97 YONGE
- 103 NORTOWN EAST

— Lines in service in 1972
---- Lines placed in service after 1972

Route extended in April 1973 to accommodate widening of Highway 401, after which route destination signs displayed "ALBION RD."

With closure of OAKWOOD carline Jan. 1960, Route 63 extended from St. Clair Ave. to Eglinton Ave. and west to Gilbert Loop; route cut back to Oakwood and Eglinton June 1964.

Route 61 split into two separate routes in 1985 with the lines east of Eglinton Station Loop becoming new route 103.

In July 1974 the Oakwood Loop replaced the former St. Clair short turn loop on Alberta Ave. (coincident with the closure of the ROGERS RD. carline). The wire remained operational on Alberta Ave. for a short period afterward.

Christie Loop closed Feb. 1963 when Route 4 extended to St. George Station.

— Wire map based on Wayne Hom (*Trolley Coach News*); T.G.J. Gascoigne; Paul Ward; Sean Marshall and others with corrections by Ted Wickson.

Above: Toronto Transportation Commission's first modern trolley coach is prepared to be unloaded at the railcar ramp in the northwest corner of TTC's Hillcrest Yard, February 12th 1947. (J.D. KNOWLES)

Below: A long way from home, BCE coach 2186 was shipped first from Can Car's plant in Fort William to Toronto to be put on display in a parking lot east of the Royal York Hotel during a Canadian Transit Association convention, June 1949. (J.D. KNOWLES)

Above: T44 coach 9024, the last of the first order, sits outside the Lansdowne carhouse waiting for service to start in a week, June 1947. (DOUG PARKER PHOTO)

Below: TTC Brill 9063 is westbound over a temporary grade crossing of the CNR Newmarket Subdivision, via Lappin and Antler, which was used for a year and a half during construction of the Dupont Street grade separation. This September 3rd 1951 view was reminiscent of many earlier grade crossings: the gates, the control tower and the myriad of overhead wires in an industrial setting. (J.D. KNOWLES)

16th 1946, went back to the Fort William plant the next month, then was recalled January 15th the next year to operate on South Lansdowne Avenue until February 17th[140] for training runs. It ran at the south end of Lansdowne Avenue where the roadway had been widened for the new trolley coach service. Since trolley wire was not yet up through the railway underpass on Lansdowne between Rideau and Dundas, operation was limited to the south end including a clockwise loop via Lansdowne, Queen, MacDonnell and Seaforth. Lansdowne carhouse emergency truck 186 towed the demo to and from its onsite training runs. To permit three-point turns at Lansdowne and Rideau, curved temporary overhead was strung for a northwest-to-westbound left turn. The backing movement was done by gravity and a short southbound forward movement made with trolley snakes to reach the beginning of the southbound wire.[141]

The first of the TTC's order of Canadian Car-Brill trolley coaches – No. 9000 – was unloaded at the Hillcrest Shops on February 12th 1947,[142] and with the subsequent arrival of more coaches, the LANSDOWNE line started regular operation June 19th.[143]

On October 6th the ANNETTE route commenced operation, followed by OSSINGTON December 8th. The original order of coaches was expanded to 85 and an additional line – WESTON – added September 15th 1948. Starting out from a loop at Annette, it ran north along Keele and Weston Road to the village of Weston and replaced a carline.[144] ANNETTE was lengthened in February 1963 from Christie Loop to St. George Station, coincident with the UNIVERSITY subway opening and the demise of the DUPONT car line. ANNETTE lasted until January 1992, but was revived with borrowed Edmonton trolley coaches as much of the access for the BAY route used Dupont Street and it made sense to run ANNETTE also as this overhead wire was being kept in shape. The final end came with the July 17th 1993 closure of the BAY route.[145]

OSSINGTON was extended northerly on January 2nd 1960 (replacing the former OAKWOOD carline) into the Township of York, and again in January 1978, when it was re-routed to terminate at Eglinton West station coincident with the opening of the Spadina Subway line.[146]

Still, the TTC did not see the trolley coach as a replacement for the streetcar even though passenger counts increased markedly on all three trolley coach routes. For instance, by using as many streetcars as possible on Yonge Street, 13,000 passengers per hour could be conveyed, while gasoline buses could only manage 4400 in one direction and trolley coaches 4800. The subway was anticipated to handle 40,000 passengers an hour.[147] So, while the trolley coach was a valuable part of the TTC network, it could not replace the venerable PCC streetcar except in a few more lightly travelled areas, or on those routes where the subway's introduction changed the passenger flow substantially. Still, when quoted by Ohio Brass for its *Traction News* magazine, TTC management said, "The trolley coach ranks next to the streetcar in its ability to provide service on medium heavy traffic lines with economy and efficiency. Public reaction has been uniformly favourable. The public appreciates the quiet, speedy, comfortable and fumeless qualities. Drivers also like trolley coaches."[148] With the advent of the subway, TTC saw the principal job of the trolley coach to feed passengers to the Eglinton terminal. YONGE was to be converted from streetcar to trolley coach from Eglinton to the city limits, and trolley coaches would replace motor buses on the LAWRENCE route as well as the EGLINTON route. Eglinton West was on the books for conversion as traffic developed. That would double trolley coach routing from the current 30.5 round trip miles. As it was, the OSSINGTON coach line was the heaviest travelled in North America with 3400 passengers per hour, mostly because it served the Massey-Harris farm equipment factory and several other large plants with a total employment of 20,000 people.[149] Certainly the TTC saw the trolley coach as a definite part of its transportation plan, moving 750 to 3000 passengers/hour squarely in-between the motor bus and the streetcar.

In 1953, the TTC saw the need to expand the popular trolley coach network and planned to create both the NORTOWN and YONGE routes by Spring of the next year. This necessitated another order of 40 coaches from Can Car, but this time they opted for the larger 48-seat T-48A model. By now, CCF-Brill (Can Car) was seeing the North American market saturated, and with trolley buses going out of fashion, this was to be the last new trolley coach order placed by the TTC. However, the Commission was able to purchase fifteen used Marmon-Herrington model TC48 coaches from Cincinnati that same year.[150]

Above: This October 1952 Ohio Brass ad features Toronto's success with six years of trolley coach operation while still planning more lines.
(OHIO BRASS COLLECTION, THE STRAHORN LIBRARY, ILLINOIS RAILWAY MUSEUM)

The NORTOWN route was the only one in Toronto not replacing any part of a streetcar line. Its genesis was in a series of feeder routes serving North Toronto using motor buses to bring passengers to heavy streetcar lines such as the YONGE route. North Toronto was too wide an area for transit users to walk to YONGE, but too narrow to support an east-west connecting line. In 1954, when the YONGE subway was completed to Eglinton, many of the routes in North Toronto were adjusted to meet the needs of riders now wanting to connect to the subway. A re-jigging of several of these feeders, and improved access to several major thoroughfares such as Avenue Road, allowed the TTC to fashion a new route – NORTOWN – that opened with trolley coaches March 7th 1954, and, along with the YONGE trolley coach line fed into the subway system. Toronto reported a trolley coach fleet that year of 149 vehicles operating over the six routes totalling 22.9 one-way miles and 3,818,254 coach miles.[151]

By 1973, the YONGE subway was extended north from Eglinton to York Mills and the NORTOWN route became more of a neighbourhood service. In April 1985, the route was split into two – NORTOWN EAST and NORTOWN WEST – each terminating at Eglinton Station, where the trolley overhead was adjusted as separate loading platforms were required. This was coincidentally the last new trolley wire strung by the TTC. However, trolley coaches were beginning to fade from the Toronto scene as infrastructure deteriorated and the trolley fleet broke down as the rebuilt

Above: In this unique shot high above the Eglinton Terminal in September 1962, one can see several Brill trolley coaches sharing the passenger load with a couple of GM products. This view looks east along Eglinton from Duplex Avenue, probably from the upper floor of a building at the northeast corner. Note the Duplex subway entrance at the lower right and the Canada Square building under construction on the upper right. The trolleys in view are on routes NORTOWN (lower) and YONGE (upper view).
(ERIC TRUSSLER/TED WICKSON COLLECTION.
LOCATION INFORMATION – TED WICKSON)

coaches were approaching twenty years of age. Both NORTOWN routes were dieselized January 5th 1992.

With the opening of the YONGE subway, the surface streetcar it replaced became redundant, but the subway ended at Eglinton while the car line had continued to Glen Echo Loop (also known as the North Toronto Terminal at the city limits). Though a stub streetcar line could have been retained for that portion, it would have been virtually isolated from the rest of the system, so the TTC converted that section to trolley coach and the YONGE route was born March 27th 1954. Almost isolated (along with NORTOWN) from the other trolley routes based at Lansdowne Division, there was non-revenue overhead to connect it with Mount Pleasant and the NORTOWN route for emergencies. The YONGE trolley operated from Glen Echo Loop to Eglinton. It served well as a connector to the subway, but in 1973, with the subway's extension to York Mills, service was abandoned on March 31st and became, notably, the first trolley bus route abandoned since the 1920s

72

Above: It's April 1971 and coach 9110 breezes along Prince Arthur just past Bedford Road on the ANNETTE route. Forty some years later with the trolley wires long gone, the author's daughter lived in the apartment building in the background while attending nearby University of Toronto. (TED WICKSON)

Below: Nothing disturbs the bucolic quiet of this Toronto neighbourhood, not even the passing of Marmon-Herrington trolley coach 9131, photographed in 1971 just months from its retirement. The coach was on a fan trip and is posed northbound on George Street in Weston on the WESTON-89A – Church/Keele Station short turn loop. It was a counter-clockwise loop: from Weston Road, east on King Street, north on George Street, west on Church Street to Weston Road and returning south to Keele Station. (TED WICKSON)

experiment. A few coaches were used April 2nd and 3rd as rush hour extras, but officials decided that traffic did not warrant even that pittance.[152] Wire and coaches from Yonge eventually found their way into the Bay Street operation in 1976.[153]

The position of YONGE and NORTOWN routes, isolated as they were from the other trolley coach lines, required a second trolley coach division operating out of the Eglinton car barn with plans to eventually link up with Lansdowne Division by means of an Eglinton West trolley line. In the meantime, if a trolley had to be transferred between divisions, it was ignominiously towed to the other maintenance facility.

Once again, the subway proved beneficial to the trolley coach and detrimental to the streetcar when the BLOOR line opened in 1966. The first phase of this subway line ran from Keele to Woodbine and removed the need for the western end of the DUNDAS carline that ran from Dundas West Station to Runnymede Road. This outer end of the streetcar line was abandoned and the JUNCTION trolley coach route inaugurated when the BLOOR–DANFORTH subway was extended May 11th 1968. JUNCTION trolleys lasted until August 3rd 1991.[154]

With all this expansion of the trolley coach network, and with no electric buses being made in North America after 1954, Toronto sourced five T-48A Canadian Car-Brills from Ottawa when its sole trolley line closed in 1959, and eight more Marmon-Herrington TC44s from Cleveland in 1963. These were needed for the extensions of the ANNETTE and OSSINGTON lines.[155]

Act 3:

By the mid-1960s, most of Toronto's trolley coaches were showing their age. With the opening of the extensions to the BLOOR–DANFORTH subway in May 1968, the surface network was restructured and the question of trolley coaches continuing to be part of the fleet was examined. The TTC decided to maintain the trolley coach, citing its advantages: capacity, acceleration and braking capabilities on all terrains, manoeuvrability and economy, and air quality. Because no new coaches had been built in North America since 1954, and European units were prohibitively expensive, the TTC approached Western Flyer Coach Ltd. to see if it was willing to test the waters for trolley coaches with a rebuild program. After all, the CGE motors and controls were still usable, as were many other components. Flyer agreed, and a program was set up to "rebuild" the CCF-Brill coaches, and to also to equip the Marmon-Herrington ones with standard parts. Accordingly, in 1970 an additional twenty-three T-44 and T-44A coaches were acquired used from Cornwall (thirteen) and Halifax (ten) for their electrical components, as those transit systems had recently been converted to diesel bus. To cover the bases though, TTC shipped two coaches as a test for possible suppliers in May 1967: one to Western Flyer in Winnipeg and another to Robin-Nodwell in England. The latter coach was not rebuilt, as Robin-Nodwell decided to pursue only motor coaches. Its contract was taken over by Leyland who planned to use a Flxible body, but when they were unable to meet timelines, the rebuild was dropped.[156] The usable parts finally returned to Toronto in November 1970.

The Flyer rebuilt coach arrived in Toronto in July 1968 as an E700 model, and was tested for a year over four routes, accumulating 27,500 miles of service. It then was sent back to Winnipeg for modifications and returned in August 1970 as an E700A. The end result was a contract with Western Flyer (subsequently renamed Flyer Industries Ltd.) to produce the chassis and body, complete with wheels, brakes, doors and suspension. TTC's Hillcrest Shop would rebuild and install the motors and electrical equipment, complete all interior finishing including seating, then complete the final painting and lettering. In all, TTC's work represented about forty per cent of the time expended for each finished vehicle. The Commission determined that a rebuilt TTC/Flyer/Can Car coach would cost $34,700 each – $4000 less than the cost of a new diesel.[157] The rebuild program started August 1970 and continued to April 1972, with 152 trolley coaches outshopped, at a cost of five million 1970 dollars. Flyer leased-back one coach (No. 9213) to tour North America as a demonstrator and it visited Edmonton, Calgary and Hamilton in Canada, as well as Boston in the United States.

The rebuilt fleet allowed the TTC to run trolley coaches exclusively, instead of supplementing rush hour service with diesels. As well, a new substation was built on Weston Road to boost capacity on that line and eliminate use of motor buses.[158] However, no new (or converted) trolley bus routes were planned for the immediate future. There was thought to convert (again) the MOUNT PLEASANT carline to trolley bus in 1973, but local opposition to removal of the streetcars put this, and all conversions except ROGERS ROAD, on hold.[159] However, the Ontario government upped its subsidy on capital expenditures to 75 per cent and, while initially it was applied by the TTC to rebuilding streetcars, it did offer the opportunity to consider converting diesel bus routes to trolley coach. Bay Street seemed a likely candidate, with some poles and feeder lines still intact from its streetcar days. In fact, a 1973 study, prompted by the OPEC oil embargo and high gas and diesel prices, offered several conversion options from diesel to trolley coach. Bay Street was the only one to come to fruition, though not for another three years. In the meantime, in February 1973, the Commission approved conversion of the ROGERS ROAD streetcar with electric coaches, pending approval from the Borough of York.[160] This was to be a branch off the OSSINGTON route going from Bicknell, east along Rogers Road to Oakwood where it joined the main route running south to King. Then, in May 1973, the BAY STREET line between Dupont and Queens Quay was approved by the Commission for conversion. One impetus for electric conversion was that Bay Street was lined with

Above: The early TTC/Flyer coaches proudly displayed their Flyer heritage as the large nameplate shows. Stainless steel bumpers were replaced with water cushion impact ones on later rebuilds. Prototype coach 9020, which later became production model 9200, as well as F.W. Woolworth Co. store on Queen at Lansdowne, are long gone. December 15th 1968. (TED WICKSON)

Below: Flyer 9317 loads passengers in September 1972 at the Glen Echo loop, at the old city limits. (TED WICKSON)

high rise office buildings, which created a canyon trapping diesel bus fumes and holding them close to the street. With over 35 of the 152 rebuilt trolley coaches idle, the time was ripe for a new route.[161] In October 1973, Toronto City Council approved the conversion in principle, in response to extensive lobbying by the public and transit advocacy groups. However, the decision was not unanimous. Alderman William Archer, coordinator of Future Yonge Street Malls angrily threatened to resign as he opined that the trolley coach would not be flexible in altering the route to direct traffic to a future mall.[162]

Service on the ROGERS ROAD–OSSINGTON route commenced July 21st 1974, replacing streetcars. The previous month the TTC gave final approval for the BAY STREET route. It was anticipated to cost $650,000, take eighteen months to complete, and use 29 coaches. Further conversions of part of the ST. CLAIR carline and MOUNT PLEASANT were also under consideration.[163] However, this was reversed in December, with the Commission voting to retain streetcars on those lines.[164]

Work on the Bay Street line continued, with end loops finalized in March 1975. Costs escalated and timelines slipped, but the route finally opened in September 1976. The line connected in the north with the ANNETTE coach line, then east on Davenport Road and south on Bay Street to Bloor. There was a short turn loop along Davenport to Yonge and back on Yorkville, and a loop at the north end along Dupont and Bedford, forming a triangle with Davenport. A second short turn loop in the south ran counter-clockwise along Front Street, up Yonge and west on Wellington to Bay and back to Front. The mainline continued down Bay to Queen's Quay, then looped clockwise via Freeland, Lakeshore and Jarvis streets. The TTC promoted the new line with advertisements touting "Because more stockbrokers are taking the bus these days, the TTC announces quieter service on Bay Street. Will the new trolleys keep their minds off the market?"[165] However, service on this newly-praised line was not to be all smooth riding.

Meanwhile, in a back-to-the-future move, the MOUNT PLEASANT streetcar line was being considered (again) for replacement with trolley coaches, because reconstruction of the former CNR Belt Line bridge (near Merton Street) would sever the carline and necessitate at least temporary diesel replacements. Track condition, replacement costs and reduced passenger traffic instead made conversion to trolley coach attractive, and in November 1976 the Commission voted it in. Conversion dragged on from an expected June 1977 date to finally open November 20th of that year. Service ran from the St. Clair subway station to the Mount Pleasant loop at Eglinton Avenue. MOUNT PLEASANT – version two – ran quietly until December 1991 when the Eglinton Garage closed its trolley coach operations, shutting down both MOUNT PLEASANT and the two NORTOWN lines.

As the TTC trolley coach network entered the end of the 1980s, the rebuilt Flyer coaches were aging, much like their predecessor CCF-Brills. Yet, a 1981 report to the TTC Board on "Possible Conversion of Diesel Bus Routes to Trolley Coach" suggested up to ten routes to be converted at a cost of $10.9 million. It would save in fuel and also remove the need to purchase twenty diesel buses by utilizing the existing trolley fleet to its fullest. However, conversion could take up to five years and would require building two new substations. A provincial subsidy of ninety per cent was also looked at. Instead, in April 1983, the TTC Board unanimously endorsed another report – this one recommending that the trolley bus should be phased out by the end of the decade when the useful life of the fleet had expired.[166] The study concluded that there were not sufficient benefits in terms of ride quality and environment to offset added costs and loss of flexibility in operation. Most trolley routes, it said, have a low level of demand, scale of operations, and joint use of diesel garage facilities resulting in inefficiencies. Differentials between diesel fuel and electricity was not thought to be significant, and since the recommendation was to phase out the trolleys, the TTC should not expand their operation, even with the provincial subsidy – which the report said would still not give any apparent savings in total expenditures. A citizen's group, Streetcars for Toronto Committee took exception to the report and approached City Council with a brief that questioned many of the TTC report's assumptions. They then went to the City Services Committee and asked them to pass a resolution asking the TTC to rescind its approval of the study, and to undertake a controlled study of diesels and trolley buses. The Committee approved this, and subsequently full City Council approved it also.[167] After much to-and-fro-ing, the Transit Commission voted unanimously on June 3rd 1986 to retain the complete trolleybus system and to eventually put in four major extensions: Avenue Road, Wellesley, Bathurst Street and Vaughan Road.

All this was well and good, but the Flyer fleet was aging and insufficient for such plans. In addition, declining revenues and subsidies gave the TTC serious concern, and replacing the trolley coach fleet wasn't possible until at least 1993, too late for most of the Flyers. Looking west, the TTC saw Edmonton, with expansion plans on hold, having a surplus of trolleys – 1980 GM-bodied, Brown Boveri electric-powered coaches with solid-state chopper controls. After testing two coaches in late 1989 and early 1990, an additional 28 buses were shipped and started operating mid-1990 on a three-year lease.

The TTC's commitment to eventually replace the Flyer fleet with new buses took a bad turn in 1991, with budget squeezes and higher operating and capital costs for electric buses. The economic downturn had hit Toronto hard and TTC ridership was in free fall. Besides, the fleet was showing its age, and the infrastructure was also wearing out. To retain trolley coach service, the TTC had to look at either rebuilding or replacing its fleet, and spending millions to upgrade aging infrastructure. The price of oil was

Above: Marmon-Herrington coach 9146 is loading at Ossington Station September 22nd 1971 on the northbound platform for route OSSINGTON-63 Eglinton/King. A recently outshopped New Flyer E700 is also loading immediately behind. (TED WICKSON)

Below: Excuse me, please. Chartered TTC Peter Witt 2424, borrowing its power from the trolley coach positive overhead wire, pauses to let Flyer trolley 9287 pass by on Shaw Street at Adelaide Street West. This trackage was required for streetcar diversions; however, trolley coaches on the OSSINGTON route usually got priority as they were in regular service on their normal routing. October 3rd 1976. (TED WICKSON)

Above: Yes it does snow in Toronto, and sometimes heavily, but the transit system soldiers on. This Flyer coach on the NORTOWN route was probably a welcome warm respite from the storm as it approaches Lawrence Avenue on a snow covered Mt. Pleasant Road on December 20th 1975. (TED WICKSON)

Below: On the ROGERS ROAD run, Flyer 9211 turns at Rogers Road and Oakwood on a summer's day in July 1974. With streetcar and trolley coach overhead, it was either visual pollution for the purist, or a glorious sight for the transit fan.
(TED WICKSON)

When TTC and Western Flyer set up partnership to develop and manufacture trolley coaches for TTC, Bill Owen, General Manager of City Transit Company of Dayton, Ohio approached TTC to have a pilot trolley coach manufactured at TTC's Hillcrest Shop. In March 1971, Bill Owen inspected the coach at Hillcrest and seemed pleased with the vehicle, although no on-street operation in Toronto was offered to him. This photo of No. 900 with boarded up rear door shows the coach (in Dayton's yellow colours) ready for shipping by rail to Ohio.

Subsequently an order of fifteen Flyer coaches was placed by City Transit to be assembled in Toronto at Hillcrest under sub contract.* But this coach was destined to be a "one off" vehicle as, in the spring of 1972, the Province of Ontario ordered the TTC to cease being a "manufacturer" of vehicles for other properties. This was because such an activity was deemed to contravene the Provincial subsidy agreement with the Commission and, as such, TTC would not qualify for subsidies or tax breaks if it produced transit vehicles for others.

Soon after this City Transit Co. was wound up and transit in Dayton became a municipal enterprise (Miami Valley Transit) and Mr. Owen retired. (Ted Wickson)

* *UCRS Newsletter*, March 1971 p. 43

also very low at that time, so the electric trolley buses had become the most expensive surface vehicles of the fleet to operate. All this and the shrinking ridership plus the advent of natural gas bus technology pushed the Commission to agree to end trolley bus service. Natural gas-powered buses promised quiet, smooth operation and reduced pollution, and the buses were marketed as ideal replacements for trolley coaches. While these improvements really were only realized if natural gas buses replaced diesels, the TTC management favoured a change in technology from electric to natural gas buses.[168] In January 1992, the TTC pulled all trolley coaches off the remaining lines trying to save $2-million towards their projected $30-million shortfall. However, the Commission was still obligated to pay for the leased Edmonton coaches, so trolley coaches were reinstated on ANNETTE and BAY in the fall of that year. It did help that the Ontario government kicked in some special funding, but when the Edmonton lease ended July 1993, ANNETTE service was withdrawn July 12th and BAY four days later. All the leased coaches but one returned to Edmonton; that coach went to Hamilton for testing there. Thus, with coach 9151 pulling into Lansdowne Garage July 17th 1993 at 1:20 AM, Toronto's long-running relationship with trolley coaches quietly ended.[169]

Footnotes:

130. Knowles, John D., correspondence with author March 30, 2010.
131. *Canadian Transportation*, September 1946 p. 506.
132. Transit Toronto web pages The First Generation ... by James Bow
    http:transit.toronto.on.ca/trolleybus/9501.shtml
    visited November 3, 2009.
133. As quoted in *Bus Transportation*, December 1946 p. 44.
134. "The Place of the Trolley Coach in Urban Transportation" symposium of the Canadian Transit Association, June 1946 pp. 35-36.
135. *Bus Transportation op. cit.*
136. CTA *op. cit.* p. 46.
137. *Canadian Transportation*, December 1945 p. 691.
138. *Canadian Transportation*, July 1946 p. 397.
139. *Bus Transportation op. cit.*
140. Transit Toronto web site The History of Toronto's Trolley Buses
    http:transit.toronto.on.ca/trolleybus/9005.shtml
    visited November 2009/August 2012.
141. Knowles, John D., correspondence with author March 30, 2010.
142. Bill Bailey notes on photo, courtesy Ted Wickson and Wally Young e-mail September 18, 2012.
143. Transit Toronto web site
    http:transit.toronto.on.ca/trolleybus/9104.shtml visited November 2009.
144. Transit Toronto web site
    http:transit.toronto.on.ca/trolleybus/9108.shtml visited November 2009.
145. Transit Toronto web site
    http:transit.toronto.on.ca/trolleybus/9102.shtml visited November 2009.
146. Transit Toronto web site
    http:transit.toronto.on.ca/trolleybus/9106.shtml visited November 2009.
147. *Canadian Transportation*, January 1952 p. 29.

148. *Ohio Brass Traction News*, Volume 24 Number 10 October 1952 p. 2.
149. *Ohio Brass Traction News*, Volume 24 Number 10 October 1952 p. 3.
150. Transit Toronto web site
    http:transit.toronto.on.ca/trolleybus/9205.shtml visited November 2009.
151. *Canadian Transportation*, June 1955 p. 339.
152. *UCRS Newsletter*, March-April 1973, p. 64.
153. Transit Toronto web site
    http:transit.toronto.on.ca/trolleybus/9109.shtml visited November 2009.
154. Transit Toronto web site
    http:transit.toronto.on.ca/trolleybus/9103.shtm visited November 2009.
155. Transit Toronto web site
    http:transit.toronto.on.ca/trolleybus/9502.shtml visited November 2009.
156. *Bus Industry*, Vol. 19 No. 71 October 2003 p. 21.
157. *UCRS Newsletter*, August/September 1969 p. 100.
158. *Trolley Coach News*, Vol. 1 #2 May 1969 p. 7.
159. *Trolley Coach News*, #19 October-December 1972 p. 122.
160. *Trolley Coach News*, #21 January-June 1973 p. 40-41.

Above: What could be a more classic Toronto pose than Flyer/TTC-built coach 9286 passing in front of Toronto City Hall, September 19th 1976. (TED WICKSON)

161. Toronto *Star*, May 23, 1973 and September 5, 1973.
162. *UCRS Newsletter*, July-August 1973 p. 124 and *The Globe and Mail*, September 25, 1973.
163. *Trolley Coach News*, #28 Vol. 6 #4 Fall 1974 p. 98.
164. *Trolley Coach News*, #33 Summer 1975 p. 59.
165. The *Sunday Sun*, September 5, 1976 p. 27.
166. *Trolley Coach News*, Summer 1982 pp. 112-114 ERRS Library.
167. *Trolley Coach News*, Summer/Fall 1984 pp. 104-108 ERRS Library.
168. Transit Toronto web site FAQ – Trolley Buses
    http://transit.toronto.on.ca/trolleybus/9003.shtml visited October 26, 2012.
169. Transit Toronto web site
    http:transit.toronto.on.ca/trolleybus/9503.shtml visited November 2009.

Above: Trolley coach 9247, operating on the new OSSINGTON-63F branch (following abandonment of the ROGERS ROAD car line days earlier), passes under the CNR overpass near Gilbert Avenue, July 21st 1974. This was when CNR still had passenger service, hence the slogan on the rail bridge. (TED WICKSON)

Below: Passing Toronto's Old City Hall, Flyer E700 rebuild (1971) No. 9304, in the new fleet livery, makes little noise proceeding up Bay Street, August 3rd 1981. (TED WICKSON)

Above: New Brill coach 101 stops in the Kitchener Junction loop, probably in March 1947. The streetcar in view (facing wrong way) is awaiting scrapping and definitely not in service. The Kitchener Junction Loop was a beehive of activity in March and April 1947 when the old streetcar fleet was being scrapped. The trolley coach overhead here was quite separate from the tram overhead, with dedicated span wires strung above or attached to the tips of bracket arms.
(OHIO BRASS COLLECTION, THE STRAHORN LIBRARY, ILLINOIS RAILWAY MUSEUM, TED WICKSON LOCATION INFORMATION)

Below: Passengers board coach 127 at the off-street loading bay in front of the Rockway Centre terminal on King Street, February 10th 1973.
(TED WICKSON)

Kitchener (1947-1973)
Kitchener Public Utilities Commission

First out of the blocks after the Second World War, Kitchener's single line soldiered on for twenty-six years with steady revenue and ridership, only to fall victim to economics and perhaps its small size.

Kitchener had plans as early as the beginning of the World War II to replace streetcars with buses, but war quotas on bus production put an end to that. As with all Canadian cities during the war years, permission to purchase new equipment had to come from the Dominion Transit Controller, and the US Office of Defense Transportation if they were transit vehicles made in America. So, in light of these restrictions, the streetcars continued to grind along Kitchener streets receiving minimal maintenance.

By 1944, with victory in sight, plans for civilian production were reactivated, and Canadian Car & Foundry's Aircraft Division retooled for bus manufacturing. That line included electric vehicles based on the successful designs of American Car & Foundry – Brill Motors. CCF or Can Car, as it was also called, established the bus division in March 1945 ... within six months, it had $11-million on the order books, and was well on its way to being the only trolley coach manufacturer and supplier in Canada.[170]

Prior to the outbreak of war, Kitchener Public Utilities Commission (PUC) was planning motorization of the K-W streetcar line, as it was called. This line ran along King Street from the southeast limits of the City of Kitchener to the northwest extremity of the adjacent Town of Waterloo (the twin "city" of Waterloo purchased its transit service from Kitchener). Despite the best efforts of the utility to meet the heavy wartime loads, the track and equipment had deteriorated to the point where replacement had become imperative. In addition, traffic congestion and the inflexibility of streetcars made the job of providing service difficult. Kitchener PUC wanted to retain passengers who had used public transit as a necessity during the war, and now that hostilities were over, it had more transportation choices.

The ability of trolley coaches to load at the curb, the fact that the PUC operated the electricity supply, and the rider appeal of a noiseless vehicle, made the choice of trolley coaches for a main line service easily justifiable. The busiest portion of King Street permitted parking on both sides of the street, and its 42-foot width gave insufficient space for vehicles to pass a streetcar stopped in the centre of the street, not a problem with curb-loading trolley coaches. The electricity costs for a trolley coach were calculated to be considerably less than fuel for a gasoline

Above: This May 1947 advertisement celebrated the trolley coach's arrival in Kitchener.
(OHIO BRASS COLLECTION, THE STRAHORN LIBRARY, ILLINOIS RAILWAY MUSEUM)

bus, and best of all from a passenger standpoint, the trolley coaches were virtually noiseless in contrast to the very noisy, aging streetcars. The fact that two of Canada's rubber companies had tire plants in Kitchener may have made the decision of going to rubber-tired vehicles more "politically practical".[171]

Kitchener, followed by Edmonton, were first off the mark with orders for Can Car, and Kitchener Public Utilities Commission received ten T-44 units in the fall of 1946. At the same time, new overhead was strung above the streetcar wire, ready to be lowered and put into use for a December 31st changeover.

However, a severe sleet storm hit on December 27th, cutting power, bringing down worn-out streetcar overhead, and coating the tracks to the point where all streetcar service ground to a halt. It wasn't sensible to restore service for the remaining four days, so the idled streetcars were pushed off the right-of-way, and the new trol-

Above: Kitchener coach 113 crosses the CNR tracks on King Street, heading for Waterloo in the early 1950s.
(ANTHONY F. KRISAK, COLLECTION OF RICHARD A. KRISAK)

Below: Trolley coach 141, signed for return trip to Waterloo, eases its way southbound through the seasonal pedestrian-transit mall on King Street in Kitchener's downtown theatre district, July 22nd 1967.
(TED WICKSON)

Kitchener, ON
1947-1973

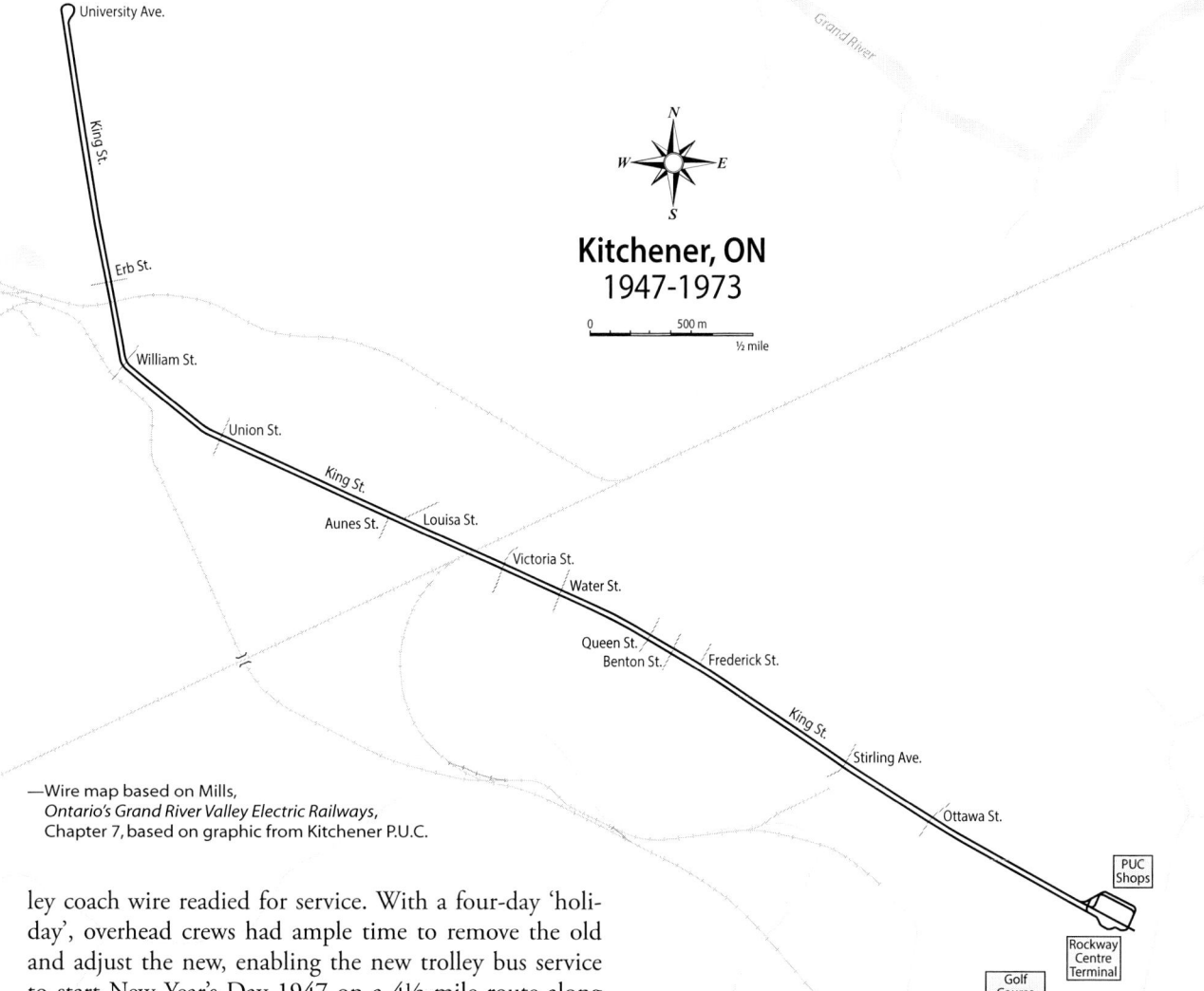

—Wire map based on Mills, *Ontario's Grand River Valley Electric Railways*, Chapter 7, based on graphic from Kitchener P.U.C.

ley coach wire readied for service. With a four-day 'holiday', overhead crews had ample time to remove the old and adjust the new, enabling the new trolley bus service to start New Year's Day 1947 on a 4½ mile route along King Street into Waterloo.[172] The line essentially followed the streetcar route with the exception of the termini: at the north end in Waterloo, it turned via an off-street loop just north of University Avenue; in the south-east, an off-street terminal was built at Rockway Centre, opposite the PUC offices and garage.

Acceptance was enthusiastic, probably due in part to a relief that the worn out streetcars were gone. An Ohio Brass advertisement of the day said "they met with such a high degree of public acceptance that, within a short time, it was necessary to order five more [coaches] to take care of the increased patronage." It went on to state that ridership had increased fifteen per cent on that line.

Those five coaches were followed by another one in 1949 and, when Ottawa closed its sole trolley coach line in June 1959, Kitchener acquired five of its bigger T-48A coaches.

All of this fleet activity was contained on the one line – KING STREET – with no extensions to the route. Not that they were not considered; James Bauer, Waterloo's mayor was quoted on retirement as saying " ... I think that the time is at hand when the King Street trolley route should be extended a considerable distance to the north on the Weber Street extension to the vicinity of the proposed intersection of Albert Street and Weber Street.

"Later on, it should be extended even further because it appears quite obvious that a new high school will have to be built in the northern part of the city perhaps as far as a mile north of the Albert-Weber intersection.

"I realize fully that there are serious technical problems involved in this proposed extension and that it would be an expensive proposition to add the necessary electrical facilities and the additional buses."[173]

However, by 1972, with 25 years of wear on the coaches, the above referred-to expense of expansion, and with no new trolley coaches being produced, Kitchener decided to retire the trolley coach fleet and replace it with diesels. This was concurrent with a restructuring of the transit operations of the PUC into a new entity, Kitchener Transit, on January 1st 1973, the outcome of a study in late 1971 that also looked at phasing out the electric buses. This study by Dr. Peter Barnard concluded that an expanded trolley coach system would cost $92,000 more than a diesel-powered system, even though new trolleys would each cost $1600 each less than a diesel bus, but $200,000 would be required to overhaul the overhead and another million to extend the line to Fairview Park Plaza in the south and to the University of Waterloo in the north. And in all probability, these extensions would require anoth-

Above: Exiting the Kitchener Mall, coach 137 passes another Canadian icon – Eaton's department store, July 11th 1968. (BILL LINLEY)

er substation.[174] This was despite the fact that for years, the PUC had reported, in trade publications, statistics favouring trolley coaches, and that revenue from the trolley coach route had helped keep the remaining system solvent. However, by 1972, the PUC was suffering a net loss despite increased ridership.[175] There was an added factor though: imminent rehabilitation of underground utilities on King Street would necessitate wire removal and probably the installation of temporary wire elsewhere.[176]

The consultant had recommended a progressive replacement of the trolleys in three stages over three years, but the PUC and city councillors concluded that an immediate replacement and restructuring would modernize the system and solve transit problems. Still, the "solution" was not without controversy. Opposition was expressed by politicians (and after the fact, by the citizenry); however the die was cast, and the trolley coaches were to go by the end of March 1973.[177]

The last runs of Kitchener trolley coaches were on March 26th 1973. As each trolley finished its morning hour rush service, it was unceremoniously replaced at the south end of the line (Rockway Centre Terminal) with a diesel bus, and then driven off to storage across the street at the PUC garage. Coach 107 had the dubious honor of bringing Kitchener's electric transit to a close. All the coaches were sold to B.C. Hydro, the overhead was taken down and sold for scrap, and the era, as Ohio Brass had advertised, of "economical, good revenue-generating, high riding appeal, and silent, speedy and safe" trolley coaches in the twin cities came to an end.

Footnotes:

170. Mills, John M., *Ontario's Grand River Valley Electric Railways* p. 175.
171. "The Place of the Trolley Coach in Urban Transportation" symposium of the Canadian Transit Association, June 1946, pp. 32-33.
172. Mills, John M., *Ibid.* pp. 163 and 174.
173. *Kitchener Waterloo Record*, January 3, 1966.
174. *Canadian Coach* Magazine, Volume VIII Number 9, September 1972 p. 11.
175. *Ibid.* Volume IX Number 1 January-February 1973 p. 12.
176. *Trolley Coach News*, #14 Vol. 3 No. 3, July-October 1971, #19, October-December 1972, and #21 January-June 1973.
177. *Canadian Coach* Magazine, Volume IX Number 3 May-June 1973 pp. 7-13.

Below: It's a fine day on July 11th 1968 as PUC Brill 105 passes well-kept residences on King Street in Kitchener. (BILL LINLEY)

Above: Splash and dash? Can Car-Brill 137, newly washed but to be retired in a few weeks, sits over the inspection pit in the Kitchener Public Utilities garage, former home of the streetcar fleet, on February 17th 1973. (TED WICKSON)

Below: So long, little fellow. One day before retirement, PUC Brill coach 137 sits in the yard ready to go while its replacement, GM diesel 731, waits patiently. Was it just coincidence that their fleet numbers were reversals? (BILL LINLEY)

Above: On a cold December 28th 1950, Brill 701 swings through an S curve in the short turn loop on route 3-CANNON at Strathearne and Roxborough with one lonely passenger. When the wiring was initially installed, the S turn was required for buses travelling westbound (coming from Reid and Dunsmure) that did not short turn. Buses going west on Roxborough would have to go through the loop (right hand turn) and then proceed north (right) on Strathearne. In the 1970s, wire was added to make the turn from west to north without going into the loop (remaining on both streets).
(OHIO BRASS COLLECTION, THE STRAHORN LIBRARY, ILLINOIS RAILWAY MUSEUM. LOCATION INFORMATION – KEVIN NICOL)

Below: HSR 702 signed CANNON–STRATHEARNE is eastbound on Cannon Street, just west of Birch Avenue. The houses in the background are still there today. The track in the foreground is part of the abandoned Birch Street private streetcar right of way (operations ended in 1951). The timeline would be sometime during the early 1950s, just after trolley buses were introduced. The fact that the street is two-way gives it a timeline before 1956, when Hamilton switched to one-way streets and the CANNON trolley buses were changed to operate eastbound on Wilson.
(ANTHONY F. KRISAK, COLLECTION OF RICHARD A. KRISAK. LOCATION INFORMATION – KEVIN NICOL)

Hamilton (1950-1992)
Hamilton Street Railway

Hamilton was the second-last Canadian city to adopt the trolley coach as part of its operating fleet. Still, it was one of the few to embrace the trolley coach's renaissance, only to succumb to the 'newest flavour' of transit environmentalism, ending the third longest continuous service in Canada.

In 1945, Hamilton ratepayers were asked to vote on acquiring the Hamilton Street Railway Company (HSR) from the Hydro-Electric Power Commission of Ontario (notably, the HSR itself dated back to 1874). The streetcar system was, as most were after WWII, worn out and outdated. A consulting engineer, Arthur Bunnell of Toronto, was retained to study the matter, and duly recommended that the system " … be transformed into one operated with trolley buses and motor buses, with the former used on heavy traffic lines and the latter on feeder and light traffic lines. … it does not make sense that electric railway cars should remain in operation in Hamilton."[178] The peculiarity of Hydro owning and operating a streetcar system came about from its acquisition of the Dominion Power and Transmission Company and subsidiaries in 1930. Following the end of Hydro's franchise with the Windsor streetcar system (SW&A) in 1934, Hamilton remained its only transportation activity, operated under the Hamilton Hydro-Electric Power Commission. However, the citizens of Hamilton felt that the acquisition price of $1¼ million on top of the costs of modernization was too rich. The alternatives were to negotiate with the Commission to continue operating the system until the 1963 franchise termination, or let a private operator buy it.

And, that is exactly what happened, when The Canada Coach Lines acquired the Hamilton Street Railway from the Hamilton Hydro Electric Power Commission in September 1946,[179] and immediately started an assessment of the streetcar lines. Tracks were in very poor condition; derailments were common, the roadbed needed extensive work as well as the paving in shared streets. Canada Coach then announced a five-year plan to eliminate streetcars and replace them with trolley coaches, diesel and gasoline buses. It took 2½ years of study to produce a plan for "one of the most modern and efficient transit services in Canada." In purchasing the trolley coaches, Hamilton became the fourteenth city in Canada to employ this type of transit vehicle, and the initial installation in Hamilton brought the number of trolley coaches in service in Canada by year-end 1950 to a total of 880.[180] *HSR Transit News*, then the take-away public flyer that HSR started publishing twice a month and put on all buses said, "Experts were brought in to advise on route planning and to forecast future needs in the way of transit facilities, and an exhaustive study of alternative types of equipment was made. Scores of questionnaires were sent out to other transportation companies all over the North American continent, so that their experience could be utilized and their mistakes studied, for lessons to be used in framing plans for Hamilton. It was finally decided that the best answer to Hamilton's transit needs lay in the use of trolley coaches." [181]

Technically, the corporation's name was The Canada Coach Lines, but shortly after the purchase of the HSR, the management of CCL decided to rearrange the corporate structure, making HSR the parent company, and CCL the subsidiary.[182]

The busy four-mile CANNON bus route was selected as the first to be converted, while other streetcar routes were

Text continues on page 92

Above: The cover of this brochure featured the new Can Car-Brill coaches soon to grace Hamilton's streets. Inside, it introduced the Cannon Street routing and extolled the new 48-seat coaches as the latest in modern transportation. (HSR/KEVIN NICOL)

89

Hamilton, ON
1969

Hamilton Harbour

CNR Station

Trolleys relocated to Park St. from Charles St. on July 12, 1970; subsequently relocated to MacNab St. by Nov. 1973.

Northern and southern sections of Wellington St. were service wire only.

Service wire only on Wentworth St. and Sanford Ave.; southbound wire on Sanford Ave. moved to Wentworth St. by Jan 1972.

Service wire only on Melrose and Gage aves., no longer shown, and replaced with loop at Beechwood Ave. by Nov. 1973.

TH&B Station

Dashed lines along King, King William and James sts. shows routing prior to introduction of one-way streets on Oct. 28, 1956.

Eastbound Cannon route moved to Wilson and Sherman sts. on Sept. 7, 1970 as a result of a one-way street implementation.

Dashed lines along Main and King sts. and Sherman Ave. shows routing prior to introduction of one-way streets on Oct. 28, 1956.

Bus Barn

Short turn loop, no longer shown by Nov. 1973.

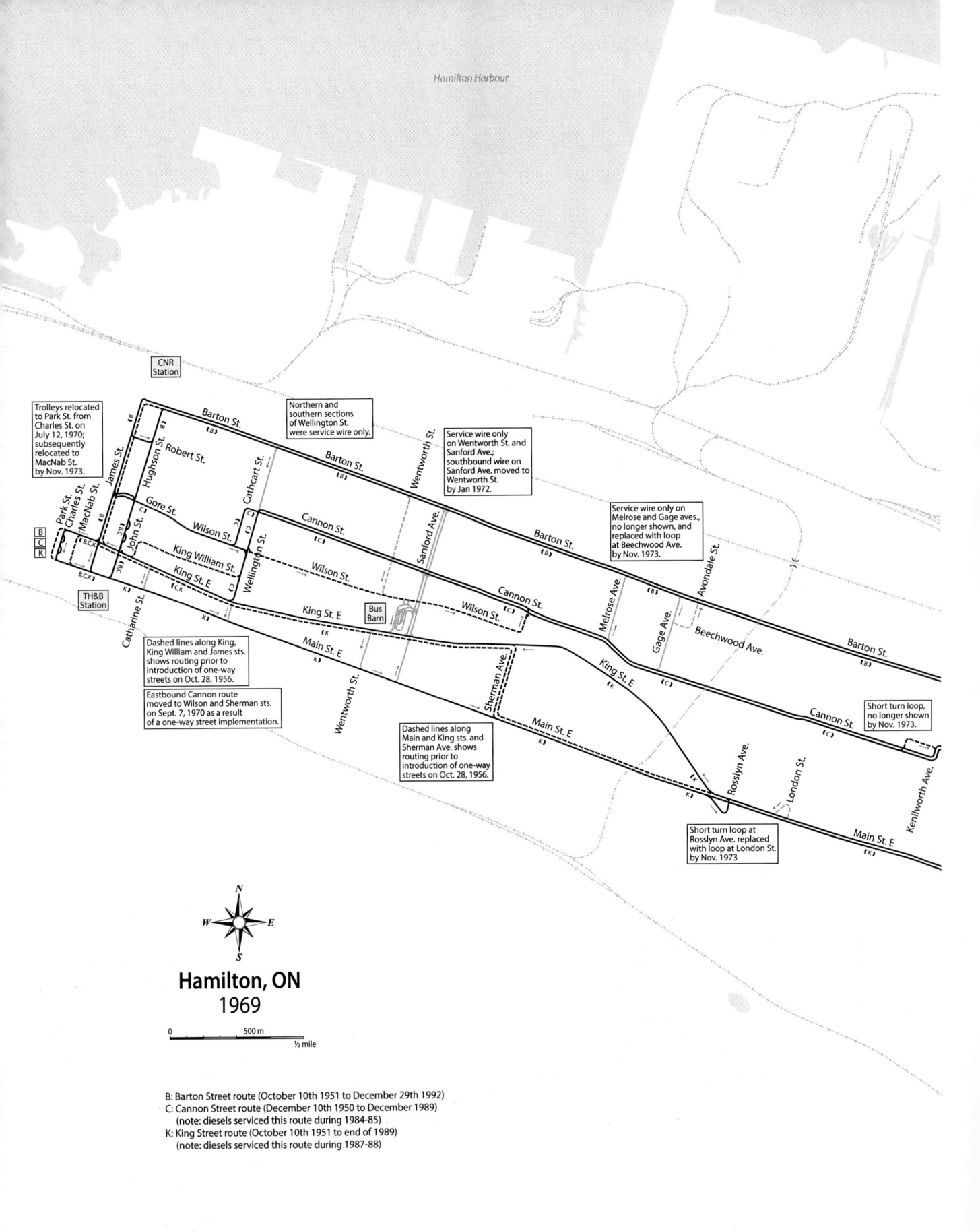

Short turn loop at Rosslyn Ave. replaced with loop at London St. by Nov. 1973.

Streets: Park St., Charles St., MacNab St., James St., Hughson St., Robert St., Gore St., John St., Wilson St., Cathcart St., Wellington St., Barton St., Cannon St., King William St., King St. E, Catharine St., Main St. E, Wentworth St., Sanford Ave., Sherman Ave., Melrose Ave., Gage Ave., Beechwood Ave., Avondale St., Rosslyn Ave., London St., Kenilworth Ave.

0   500 m
½ mile

B: Barton Street route (October 10th 1951 to December 29th 1992)
C: Cannon Street route (December 10th 1950 to December 1989)
   (note: diesels serviced this route during 1984-85)
K: King Street route (October 10th 1951 to end of 1989)
   (note: diesels serviced this route during 1987-88)

—Wire map based on maps from Tom Luton; Hamilton Transit History web page, *trolleybuses.net* web site, and from the Scalzo collection.

Lake Ontario

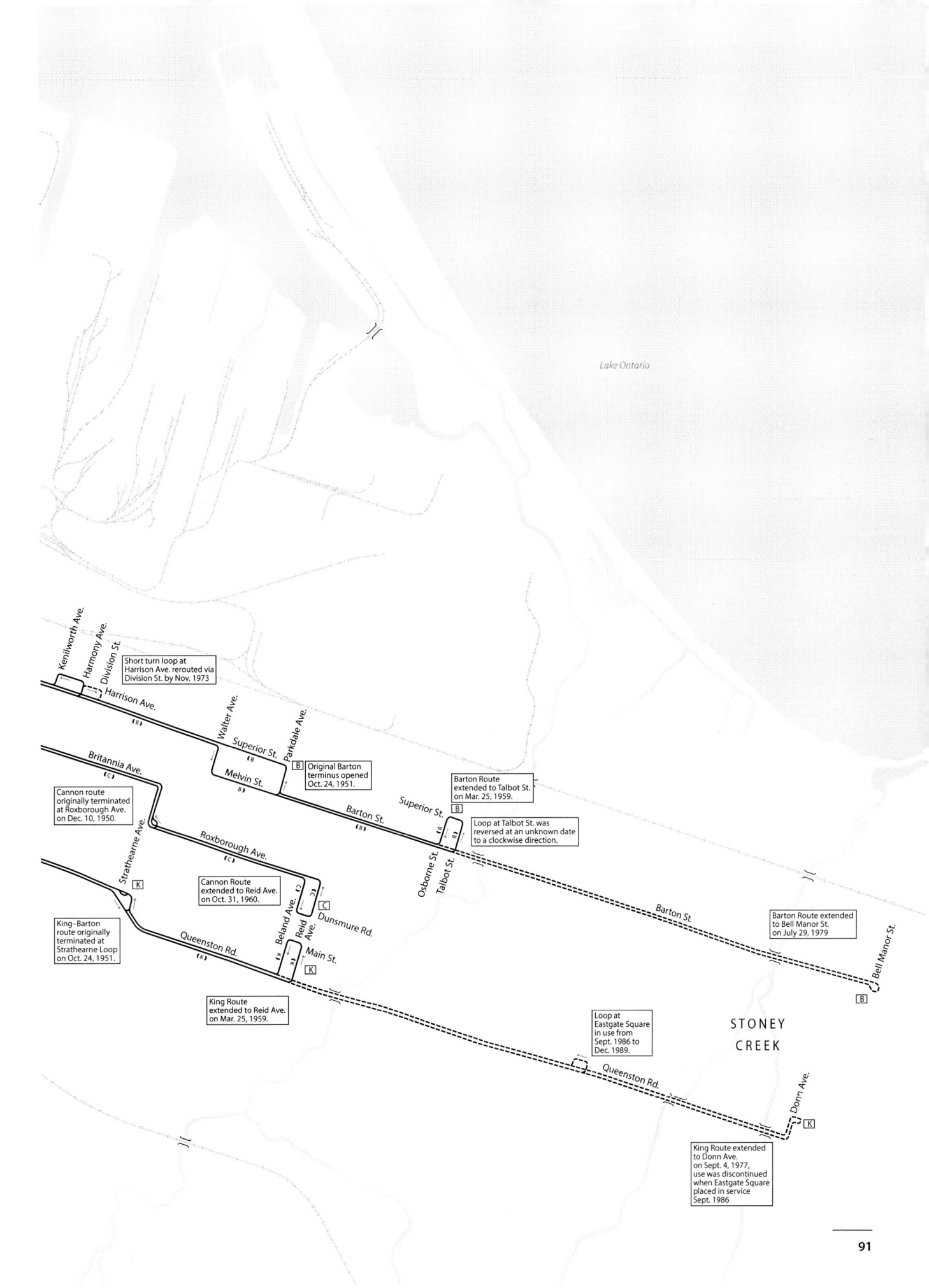

Short turn loop at Harrison Ave. rerouted via Division St. by Nov. 1973

Kenilworth Ave.
Harmony Ave.
Division St.
Harrison Ave.
Walter Ave.
Superior St.
Parkdale Ave.
Melvin St.

Original Barton terminus opened Oct. 24, 1951.

Barton Route extended to Talbot St. on Mar. 25, 1959.

Britannia Ave.
Barton St.
Superior St.
Osborne St.
Talbot St.

Cannon route originally terminated at Roxborough Ave. on Dec. 10, 1950.

Loop at Talbot St. was reversed at an unknown date to a clockwise direction.

Strathearne Ave.
Roxborough Ave.

Cannon Route extended to Reid Ave. on Oct. 31, 1960.

Beland Ave.
Reid Ave.
Dunsmure Rd.

Barton St.

Barton Route extended to Bell Manor St. on July 29, 1979

King–Barton route originally terminated at Strathearne Loop on Oct. 24, 1951.

Queenston Rd.
Main St.

Bell Manor St.

King Route extended to Reid Ave. on Mar. 25, 1959.

Loop at Eastgate Square in use from Sept. 1986 to Dec. 1989.

STONEY CREEK

Queenston Rd.

Donn Ave.

King Route extended to Donn Ave. on Sept. 4, 1977, use was discontinued when Eastgate Square placed in service Sept. 1986

91

TIRES AND WIRES

THE NEW H.S.R. TROLLEY COACH IS THE LAST WORD IN STREAMLINED TRANSPORTATION

There won't be many who will remember riding in this tram-way back in 1880 or thereabouts.

YOU only have to look at these two pictures to realize how much urban transit services have progressed since the turn of the century. The old H.S.R. tram, seating 12 persons, and drawn by one horse, is a far cry from the new streamlined H.S.R. electric trolley coach, which seats 48 persons and has 140 horsepower — and in which it is immeasurably more pleasant to travel.

Here's why you'll like the new H.S.R. Trolley Coaches:

★ **They're Quick!**
They move away swiftly and easily from a standing start and have a faster cruising speed. Reserve power permits proper speeds even on heavy grades.

★ **They're Quiet!**
Rubber tires and special body insulation minimize vibration and noise. The electric motors and controls ensure quietness — both inside and out.

★ **They're Safe!**
The body is all metal — the windows are fitted with shatterproof safety glass — and the efficient braking system ensures safe stops.

Top left: Looking toward front of spacious new coach.
Top right: Looking toward rear of new H.S.R. trolley coach.
Left: View of the operator's platform and controls.
Right: Photo of rear door (exit).

★ **They're Smooth!**
Six 12 ply balloon tires — specially designed springs — and four aeroplane-type shock absorbers help to make trolley coach travel relaxing and enjoyable.

★ **They're Convenient!**
Two doors (entrance and exit) — wide platforms — and wide aisles simplify getting on and off... and save time.

★ **They're Comfortable!**
Good lighting, good ventilation and plenty of clean, electric heat are abundantly provided in the new H.S.R. trolley coach — and you ride in real comfort on a soft upholstered seat.

Here are a few of the things which have to be done before the first trolley coach appears on Cannon Street:

★ **Overhead Structures:**
Twenty-four miles of special bronze overhead wires — dozens of special switches — hundreds of insulators and numerous new poles must be installed on Cannon Street to provide power for the new coaches. Skilled personnel and special equipment will be kept busy for many weeks.

★ **Garage Reconversion:**
Extensive alterations are being made in the H.S.R. yards and garage in order to house the electric coaches and keep them in first-class operating condition.

★ **Operator Training:**
Our operators are presently being trained in the actual handling of the new trolley coaches at other cities in Canada. When the new coaches are placed in service the operators will be thoroughly familiar with their new vehicles.

SPECIFICATIONS of the new H.S.R. Trolley Coaches

Seating Capacity	48	Tire Size	1100 x 22
Overall Length	38' 9½"	Tires	Six: 12 ply balloons
Overall Width	102"	Weight	19,500 lbs.
Overall Height	116¼"	Motor	140 H.P. 600 Volt
Wheelbase	249"	Front Door Width	32"

THE SPEEDY NEW H.S.R. TROLLEY COACHES ARE DESIGNED TO GIVE YOU THE UTMOST IN SAFETY AND COMFORT

---

modernized with motor buses. While the busy BELT LINE (KING–BARTON) might have been considered the first line needing to be changed, the heavy traffic on it would have been severely impacted during the removal of streetcar rails and repaving. HSR estimated they would need eighty motor buses to cover it while the conversion happened. Instead, HSR put trolley coaches on heavily-travelled bus routes, thus freeing up enough motor coaches to eventually convert the BELT LINE. The CANNON route was the most heavily-travelled one in the city in 1950 – 725,000 route miles and carrying 4½ million passengers[183] – and since the CANNON line was within one block of the car barns, it would only need the installation of a short length of service wire. Still, the electrical distribution system alone cost $120,000.[184]

The first trolley coach arrived April 16th 1950 and was displayed to the public at the Hamilton Industrial Fair from April 26th to 29th.[185] Operations started that December 10th, on a 4.1-mile route which ran from King and Hughson, north on Hughson to Gore, east to Wilson, on to Wellington, north to Cannon, then east to Kenilworth, north on Kenilworth to Britannia, east on Britannia to Strathearne, south to loop at Roxborough and Strathearne. It returned over the same route until Wellington, where it went south on Wellington to King William, west on King William to John, south on John to King, and then west on King to Hughson. There was also a short turn

Above: Hamilton Street Railway pulled out all the stops to introduce trolley coach service as this passenger handout tells.
(HSR/KEVIN NICOL)

loop from Kenilworth and Cannon, north on Robbins to Britannia, east on Britannia to Kenilworth, south on Kenilworth to Cannon. Passenger response was immediate, with ridership increasing and patrons indicating their approval of the noiseless, roomy electric coaches.

On April 6th 1951, all streetcar operation in Hamilton ceased, but thirty more trolley coaches were on order to operate on the KING–BARTON route, an 8.6-mile line. Overhead was estimated to cost $15,000, and a new 1250 watt mercury rectifier station was to be built in the east end to support the electrical requirements of the line.[186] On October 24th, that line was finally converted from buses to trolley coach operation,[187] "A job which experts said would take 13 months has been completed in six" *HSR Transit News* boasted to its riders.[188]

The KING–BARTON route started at the Strathearne loop at Strathearne and Main, then went west on Main to Sherman, north to King, west on King to James, north on James to Barton, then east to Walter, south to Melvin, east to Parkdale, and north on Parkdale to Barton (the terminal). The coaches then went west on Barton following the reverse routing back to Strathearne and Main. The route had two short turn loops: from Kenilworth and Barton, north on Kenilworth to Harrison, east on Harrison to Harmony, south on Harmony to Barton, west on Barton to Kenilworth; and at Delta, east on King to Rosslyn, north on Rosslyn to Main, west on Main to King.

Wire also ran along Sanford between the two routes to access the Wentworth garage at Sanford via Wilson and King streets. The trolley coaches had arrived in a new paint scheme of bright cream and red, and as of the end of streetcar service, all HSR vehicles were painted in the same colours.[189]

To achieve this modernization of Hamilton's transit, "the H.S.R.'s engineers and line crews were working double shifts all summer. In all, they have strung some 40 miles of trolley wire, weighing over 40 tons, together with nearly 12 miles of guy wire, weighing six tons, to support the main wires. Some 250 Western cedar poles, each 35 feet long, were brought from British Columbia, together with 65 steel poles for use in the downtown area where heavy intersections require greater strength. Over 14 tons of feeder cable have been laid to carry power into the overhead wires. This type of cable alone, if laid out in one length, would stretch from Hamilton to Dundas. Over ten tons of electrical fittings have been incorporated in the overhead wires, making the switching of vehicles on turns and loops completely automatic. All that a bus operator has to do is to press a button as he approaches the switch, and it clicks into place automatically, in the same way as railway switches are operated by remote control. A single unit of this equipment alone weighs 225 pounds, and costs no less than $500"[190] wrote *HSR Transit News*

Above: HSR Brill 739 crosses on King Street (travelling westbound) while No. 730 waits on James Street (travelling southbound) for a quartet of shoppers to cross before proceeding around the curve and following No. 739 on a snowless January 20th 1973.
(TED WICKSON. LOCATION INFORMATION – KEVIN NICOL)

glowingly. At a cost of $1½ million plus the $80,000 substation, HSR finally fulfilled the pledge it made when The Canada Coach Lines purchased it – to completely convert from streetcars to buses.

Within six months, system ridership rose by 8.2 per cent; ridership on the CANNON route had risen 4.3 per cent in a similar time period.[191]

On March 25th 1959, the KING–BARTON route was extended beyond Parkdale, east on Barton, north on Talbot, west on Superior, south on Osborne and back west on Barton. Barton became Superior Street at Walter, then jogged at Walter south and resumed the Barton name. In the late 1960s there was street reconstruction in the area that resulted in the renaming and realignment of some streets, so that portion of Barton was renamed Melvin, and Superior east of Walter was renamed to Barton. When the roads were renamed or reconstructed, the new Barton Street was also built with a small bridge over the Red Hill Creek. It was at this time that the left turn from Talbot northbound to westbound Barton was restricted, forcing trolley coaches to reverse the loop via Talbot, Superior/Barton and Melvin. Instead of going counter-clockwise, it now went clockwise.

At the same time as the above extension (March 25th 1959), the King/Main leg of the KING–BARTON line was

93

Above: TTC Flyer 9213 on loan passes HSR 738 on the CANNON route in East Hamilton, March 25th 1972. (TED WICKSON)

Below: First day, first new trolley coach. November 29th 1972 and coach 751 is hailed as it proceeds during the opening ceremonies … and the Grey Cup Festival is in full swing. (TED WICKSON COLLECTION)

extended east from Main and Strathearne along Queenston Road to Reid, then looping via Reid-Main-Beland.[192]

In May 1959, the Hamilton Street Railway was put up for sale (along with The Canada Coach Lines) and, after Ontario Legislature approval in March the next year, the city purchased HSR/Canada Coach Lines, administering it under a transit commission confirmed by council in October 1960.[193]

On October 31st 1960, the CANNON terminal in the east was extended from Strathearne at Roxborough, along Roxborough to a loop at Beland, Dunsmure Road and Reid Avenue.[194] At the same time the KING–BARTON route was split into two lines: KING, and BARTON. Service was removed from James Street South between King and Main streets, and both operated downtown on King to Charles servicing the new City Hall.

By 1969, however, the trolley's future looked a bit bleak. While proximity to the Niagara Falls electric generating stations meant that operating costs were less than a diesel bus, "At the moment, we have been unsuccessful in finding anyone who is marketing an up-to-date and modern trolley coach and the question of replacements looks doubtful." stated General Manager Frank Cooke. "If the situation remains unchanged, these lines, of course, will be changed over to diesel operation as and when the trolley coaches are scrapped individually. As the fleet shrinks we will always maintain a line as either fully provided with diesels or fully equipped with trolleys, and as there are not sufficient trolleys left to equip the remaining of the three routes, all will [then] be abandoned." [195]

However, looking back to October 28th 1956, the introduction of one-way vehicle traffic for downtown did not delete trolley coach routes as happened in so many other cities. A later conversion on September 7th 1970 resulted in the removal of eastbound overhead on Cathcart and Cannon streets as far east as Sherman Avenue, as well as wiring installed on Wilson Street and Sherman Avenue North. All overhead was removed from Kenilworth and Britannia avenues as far as Barons Avenue and re-erected on the new Cannon Street extension. Southbound overhead was removed from Sanford Avenue North and re-erected on Wentworth Street North. All this construction was required to accommodate the change-over of Cannon-Wilson, Sanford-Wentworth, and Birch-Sherman to one-way traffic pairs. Electric trolley operation resumed on September 7th.[196]

Not that the veteran Brill coaches ran without incident. On January 6th 1970, a four-ton truck loaded with stone chips rammed an HSR coach and flipped it on its side. Its stone load shattered the trolley coach windows and buried passengers. Several passengers were injured and unit 732 had to be rebuilt with parts from another unfortunate coach that had tangled with a car and lost. Coach 732 had one more life left at retirement, as it became the only preserved HSR Brill, going to the Halton County Radial Railway museum in Milton, ON.

The trolleys were relocated to Park Street (between King and Main) from Charles Street on July 12th 1970 due to the construction of the Hamilton Place Theatre Auditorium.

Through all of these changes, HSR continued to use its aging CCF-Brill trolley coaches. However, by 1970, Toronto had undertaken a replacement trolley coach program in cooperation with Flyer Industries, and Hamilton was very interested as it followed the progress of the first dozen or so TTC coaches in operation.[197] In March 1972, a Flyer demonstrator coach (TTC 9213) arrived in Hamilton for trials, and HSR followed through with an order for forty of the new E700A model coaches. The Brill trolleys were to be retired, with the exception of seven (later to become ten) of the units.[198]

The first of the new buses began to arrive in late 1972 and into the next year. They were painted in a yellow-with-black stripes scheme, emulating the colours of the local CFL (Canadian Football League) football team, the Tiger Cats. In concert with the arrival of the new buses, the consulting firm of De Leuw, Cather & Co., in mid-1973 recommended extensions of all three east-west routes past Red Hill Creek to minimize transfers needed with diesel bus feeders.

HSR bought Thunder Bay coaches for parts to be used in the Flyers, and also bought special work from the now-dismantled Kitchener system to facilitate this. Downtown, a new transit terminal on MacNab Street opened on July 26th 1973, and HSR added a short stretch of wire on MacNab between King and East Main streets, replacing that on Park Street.[199]

The KING line was designated as the first to be extended, and work started in 1974.[200] The town of Stoney Creek asked that the line be extended easterly into its territory. However, negotiations for the end point delayed the project. In the meantime, plans went forward for an extension to the BARTON route eastward.[201] In February 1977, a Regional Transit Commission took over the HSR as part of the newly created Regional Municipality of Hamilton-Wentworth.

Finally, on September 4th 1977, the Stoney Creek extension of the KING route came into effect with a new fully-automatic substation.[202] That extension ran from the former loop at Reid Avenue and Queenston Road to a new loop at Donn and Queenston Road, replacing the KING stub diesel bus which had operated to Gray's Road.[203] In addition, HSR ordered sixteen of the latest Flyer Industries E800 trolley coaches to replace the remaining Canadian Car-Brills, and to cover the BARTON extension due to open the next year. On July 29th 1979, trolley coaches began operating through service on the new Barton Street East overhead extension from Talbot Street to a new loop at Bell Manor Street, replacing a stub bus.[204]

In 1984, nearly a decade after the Flyer coaches arrived, a report suggested phasing out the trolleys in 1993, and a consultant's report in 1986 recommended the scrapping of all 56, by now aging, trolleys. Public opposition to this plan convinced both the City Transportation and Environment Committee and other regional transportation services to keep them. However, the KING route kept operating sporadically. While they were removed in the summer of 1987, Barton construction in 1988 returned trolleys to service on King up to the end of 1989.[205] Meanwhile, despite the writing seeming to be on the wall, the CANNON and BARTON lines soldiered on.

Nevertheless, the trolley system seemed to atrophy. During the summer of 1984, route 3 (CANNON) was dieselized due to road construction, and HSR proposed making this permanent, but public protest put an end to that idea. However, all trolley lines were diesel-operated on weekends because the trolley garage was closed. Contrary to the attrition, in a beautification project on King Street, span wires were replaced with attractive poles and bracket arms. By early 1985, the road works on the CANNON line were complete, but the diesels stayed on.[206] At some point after that, HSR resumed trolley service sporadically through to December 1990.[207]

In 1988, staff recommended a $1.32-million refit program to put auxiliary engines in sixteen of the coaches. Since the new transit garage would not have overhead wire, the discontinuance of trolley coach service was again considered. Regional Council agreed, and with that, trolley coach service on the CANNON route ended in December 1989 when HSR operations were moved to the new bus garage. This left only the BARTON route under wire.

In 1989, Council approved a $24-million, three-year plan to upgrade the trolley buses, but reopened the debate in 1990, and public opinion was again expressed in the trolley's favour. HSR then commissioned a study that, while not recommending eliminating trolley coach service, concluded it was the most expensive option.[208]

In January 1992, new natural-gas fueled (CNG) buses started running in Hamilton, but Regional Council renewed its commitment to trolley buses as well as the CNG vehicles. However, things took a U-turn in December of that year when HSR announced that the provincial licences for the remaining fifteen trolley coaches would not be renewed and they would be taken off the streets for two years until new equipment could be sourced. This was not to be the case. The remaining BARTON route only retained its trolley coaches until Tuesday, December 29th 1992. The buses were stored pending a decision to keep or permanently scrap electric transit, but their condition deteriorated rapidly as they were stored outside. It probably did not help that in 1993, Toronto ditched its trolley fleet, and Hamilton felt left out in the cold vis-à-vis any nearby trolley coach operator. Meanwhile, HSR staff was directed to look at buying second-hand trolleys from Edmonton to revitalize the system (as Toronto had done, renting the BBC/GM coaches as stop-gap measure in 1990), but on February 21st 1994, Hamilton-Wentworth Transportation Services Committee rejected buying or even renting used trolleys. Regional Council voted March 1st against trolley buses and in favour of natural-gas buses, and any hope of reviving the trolley coach era in Hamilton came to an inglorious end.[209] Interestingly, most of the first generation CNG buses had been retired by 2007,[210] having lasted half as long as their electric compatriots.[211]

Footnotes:

178. *Canadian Transportation*, December 1945 p. 684
   Provincial Archives of Alberta, APRA Collection 75-11 box 5.
179. *HSR Transit News* Vol. 2, No. 38, October 15, 1951, courtesy Kevin Nicol, HSR.
180. *Canadian Transportation*, June 1951 p. 326
   Provincial Archives of Alberta, APRA Collection 75-11 box 5.
181. *HSR Transit News* Vol. 1, No. 4, May 15, 1950, courtesy Kevin Nicol, HSR.
182. Luton, Tom, Hamilton Transit History web page
   http://hamiltontransithistory.alotspace.com/CCL.html
   visited February 6, 2013.
183. *Canadian Transportation*, June 1952 p. 333.
184. *HSR Transit News* Vol. 1, No. 5 June 1, 1950, courtesy Kevin Nicol, HSR.
185. *The Hamilton Spectator*, October 17, 1950.
186. *Ibid*. p. 328.
187. *HSR Transit News* Vol. 2, No. 36, September 15, 1951, courtesy Kevin Nicol, HSR and *Hamilton Spectator*, October 23, 1951.
188. *HSR Transit News* Vol. 2, No. 38, October 15, 1951, courtesy Kevin Nicol, HSR.
189. *Canadian Transportation*, June 1951 Op. Cit. p. 327.
190. *Op. Cit. Transit News*, September 15, 1951.
191. Miller, William, web page on The Hamilton Street Railway Company – Trolley Coach Operations (routes, dates and ridership)
   http://www.trainweb.org/elso/hsr-tc.htm
   visited April 2008.
192. Luton, Tom, personal correspondence with the author February 10, 2013; *HSR Transit News* Vol. 7 No. 158 April 29, 1959, and *HSR Route 1 History 1960-1993*, both courtesy Kevin Nicol, HSR, and personal e-mails Kevin Nicol to author February 15, 2013.
193. *Industrial Hamilton: A Trail to the Future – Hamilton Street Railway*, Hamilton Public Library as stored in the Library and Archives Canada Electronic Collection
   http://epe.lac-bac.gc.ca/100/205/301/ic/cdc/industrial/hsr-history.htm
   visited again February 2013.
194. *HSR Route 3 History 1960-1987*, courtesy Kevin Nicol, HSR.
195. *Trolley Coach News*, December 1969 Vol. One, #6 p. 48.
196. *HSR Route 3 History 1960-1987* courtesy Kevin Nicol, HSR.
197. *Trolley Coach News*, August 1970 Vol. 2 #4 p. 67.
198. *The Hamilton Spectator*, March 23, 1972 p. 12.
199. Luton, Tom, personal correspondence with author, February 10, 2013.
200. *Trolley Coach News*, #28 Fall 1974 Vol. 6 #4 p. 93.
201. *Trolley Coach News*, #38 Winter 76/77 p. 28.
202. *Transit Canada*, May-June 1976 Vol. XII #3 p. 9 (substation).
203. Annual report summaries of the HSR supplied by Tom Luton February 10, 2013.
204. *Ibid*.
205. Kevin Nicol, email correspondence April 25, 2018.
206. *Trolley Coach News*, #60 Spring-Summer 1985 p. 60 ERRS Library.
207. Kevin Nicol, email correspondence April 25, 2018.
208. Hamilton Public Library,
   Industrial Hamilton: A Trail to the Future – Hamilton Street Railway
   http://cpc.lac-bac.gc.ca/100/205/301/ic/cdc/industrial/hsr-history.htm
   taken from Library and Archives Canada.
209. *Ibid*.
210. Luton, Tom personal correspondence with author, February 2013.
211. Hyslop Jr., Andy, *DEWIRED How Hamilton Lost Their Electric Trolleybuses* as posted on Citizens' Transportation Coalition web site
   http://www.ctchouston.org/forums/viewtopic.php?t=1776
   visited November 2009.

Above: Hamilton Street Railway 785, a Flyer E700, is westbound on Barton Street at Division Street on September 15th 1989. The coach is passing the Serbian Eastern Orthodox Church, a local landmark. (J.D. KNOWLES)

Below: Just-delivered Flyer E800 No. 7805 sits beside E700 No. 787 in the HSR's Wentworth Street coach yard on November 10th 1978. There were definite differences in the coachwork between the two Flyer series down to the shapes of the windows and the roofline, and the E800 also sat lower for improved accessibility. (TED WICKSON)

Above: An early photo of a Windsor St. Louis coach, probably the Detroit demonstrator.
(OHIO BRASS COLLECTION, THE STRAHORN LIBRARY, ILLINOIS RAILWAY MUSEUM)

Below: Windsor Coach No. 1 (probably the demonstrator) goes through the turn on the LINCOLN ROAD run.
(OHIO BRASS COLLECTION, THE STRAHORN LIBRARY, ILLINOIS RAILWAY MUSEUM)

Windsor (1922-1926)
Sandwich, Windsor & Amherstburg Railway – Hydro Electric Railway, Essex Division

The first to adopt the trolley coach, Windsor was a transit contradiction, in that it was the centre of a vibrant motor bus industry.

From 1901 through to 1920, Windsor's streetcar system was incongruously under American ownership, as the Detroit United Railway owned the Sandwich, Windsor & Amherstburg Railway. However, in January 1920, the Hydro-Electric Commission of Ontario, on behalf of the City of Windsor, purchased the SW&A and operated it as the Hydro-Electric Railways, Essex Division – Essex being the county in which most of the operations were centred.

Hydro promptly scrapped all the obsolete, derelict Windsor streetcar stock and replaced it with new trams, then two years later embarked on a plan of expansion to bring service into developing areas of Windsor. This was to be accomplished using trolley coaches until passenger demand justified the expense of building track for streetcar lines. Three such feeder routes were identified: Lincoln Road, Erie Street, and Bruce Avenue which was never built.

This was a brave step for Hydro. There were only a few trolley bus operations in the US and none in Canada. The trackless trolley was in its infancy, but Detroit had a demonstration line promoted by the streetcar and trolley bus builder, the St. Louis Car Company, so a visit was in order to see how the trolley bus operation worked. It must have been an impressive demonstration because Hydro ordered four trolley buses, sufficient to provide service on the first two proposed lines, presumably with two buses on each route. The new St. Louis trackless trolleys seated 29 passengers, and were powered by a pair of 25 HP, 600-volt Westinghouse motors. Mahogany was used for the interior woodwork, while polished, lacquered bronze was utilized for the window and door fittings. Like many electric vehicles of that era, they cruised at one of two preset speeds. One of the coaches in that order was the demonstration vehicle that had impressed both Windsor and Toronto officials in Detroit.

The first route extended 1.6 miles along Lincoln Road in the suburb of Walkerville from the streetcar connection at Wyandotte Street to an outer terminus and another streetcar connection at Tecumseh Road. Service commenced May 4th 1922, earning it the title of first trolley coach operation in Canada. Passengers transferring from trolley coach to streetcar and vice versa obtained a special transfer, for which they were charged one cent.

Overhead construction then shifted to the second route, ERIE STREET, which opened on September 22nd of the same year. Again starting from a streetcar connection at the corner of Ouelette and Erie, it ran along Erie, then around Langois, Ottawa, Gladstone, Giles Boulevard and back to Langois – a 1.25-mile run.

The BRUCE AVENUE line was planned by Hydro Electric to start at Sandwich and Ferry streets, running on McDougall, Wyandotte, Bruce Avenue and Grove streets; however, this never came to pass.

From the start, the LINCOLN and ERIE street routes were never intended as permanent installations, but rather as a stop-gap measure to provide fast economical transit in a growing area until it was feasible to build a full-fledged streetcar line. The thought was that, when the time came, the overhead would be dismantled, and then re-erected in another growing suburb of Windsor to power the moved rolling stock. The theory was sound and Toronto followed

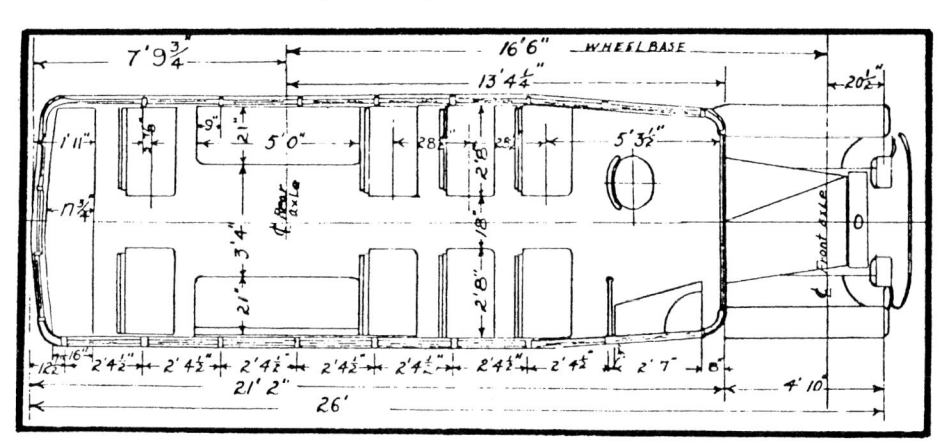

This floor plan from *Canadian Railway and Marine World* shows how the Windsor St. Louis trolley coaches were laid out.
(BERNIE DROUILLARD COLLECTION)

Above: This 1925 photo shows the Windsor Hydro Electric Railway carbarn on London Street with two of the trolley coaches (Number 1 at the left and number 3 beside it) stored outside. Bernie Drouilllard guesses from the snow around the coaches that this was after the Erie Street trolley coach route was converted to streetcars and that these two coaches were stored surplus to Lincoln Street needs.
(*WINDSOR STAR* PHOTO, BERNIE DROUILLARD COLLECTION)

suit, immediately, opening the MOUNT PLEASANT trolley bus line weeks after Windsor's LINCOLN ROAD – and they also replaced it with a streetcar extension in 1925.

Rapid growth in this area of Windsor predicated that the trolley bus service was soon inadequate to handle passenger loads, and operations on the ERIE line were suspended in the latter part of 1923 to make way for a double-track extension of streetcar service. Within the space of one year after that, revenues on this line, which from trolley coaches had amounted to approximately $740 a month, increased to $9500 a month using the streetcars. That no doubt doomed any chances of trolley coaches surviving as independent lines, and this was probably a wise decision, given the low passenger capacity of the coaches vis-à-vis a streetcar. The LINCOLN ROAD line continued to operate into 1925 using all four trolley coaches, but maintenance costs on the trackless trolleys were found to be higher than streetcars, though still lower than gasoline buses. However, the disadvantages of the trolley coach, namely interruption to service if the electric supply was compromised, inflexibility of route and the cost of erecting and maintaining overhead, pushed the servicing of lightly-travelled routes in favour of motor buses, while trams were still preferred for the heavily-travelled routes. In May 1926, LINCOLN ROAD trolley coaches were retired, and motor buses replaced them, with an eye to an eventual extension of the streetcar line.[212]

And so, in four short years, Canada's first trolley coach adventure was over. It would be a decade before dual wires spanned any Canadian city street again – but when they did, the trolley coach came back in full force with improved efficiency, and loads comparable to the (by then aging) tram networks. Sadly, Canada's first city to have trolley coaches never got back on that bandwagon – maybe having motor buses built right in town had a little to do with that.

An interesting footnote: in 1930, the Ontario Legislature passed an act (re)creating the Sandwich, Windsor & Amherstburg Railway as a corporation. Then, on mid-

Windsor, ON 1922-1926

Bruce Ave. route was only planned and never built

Erie St. route ran Sept. 22, 1922 until late 1923

Lincoln Rd. route ran May 5, 1922 until May 1926

—Wire map based on Drouillard, Bernard W., *Transit in Windsor*, p. 21.

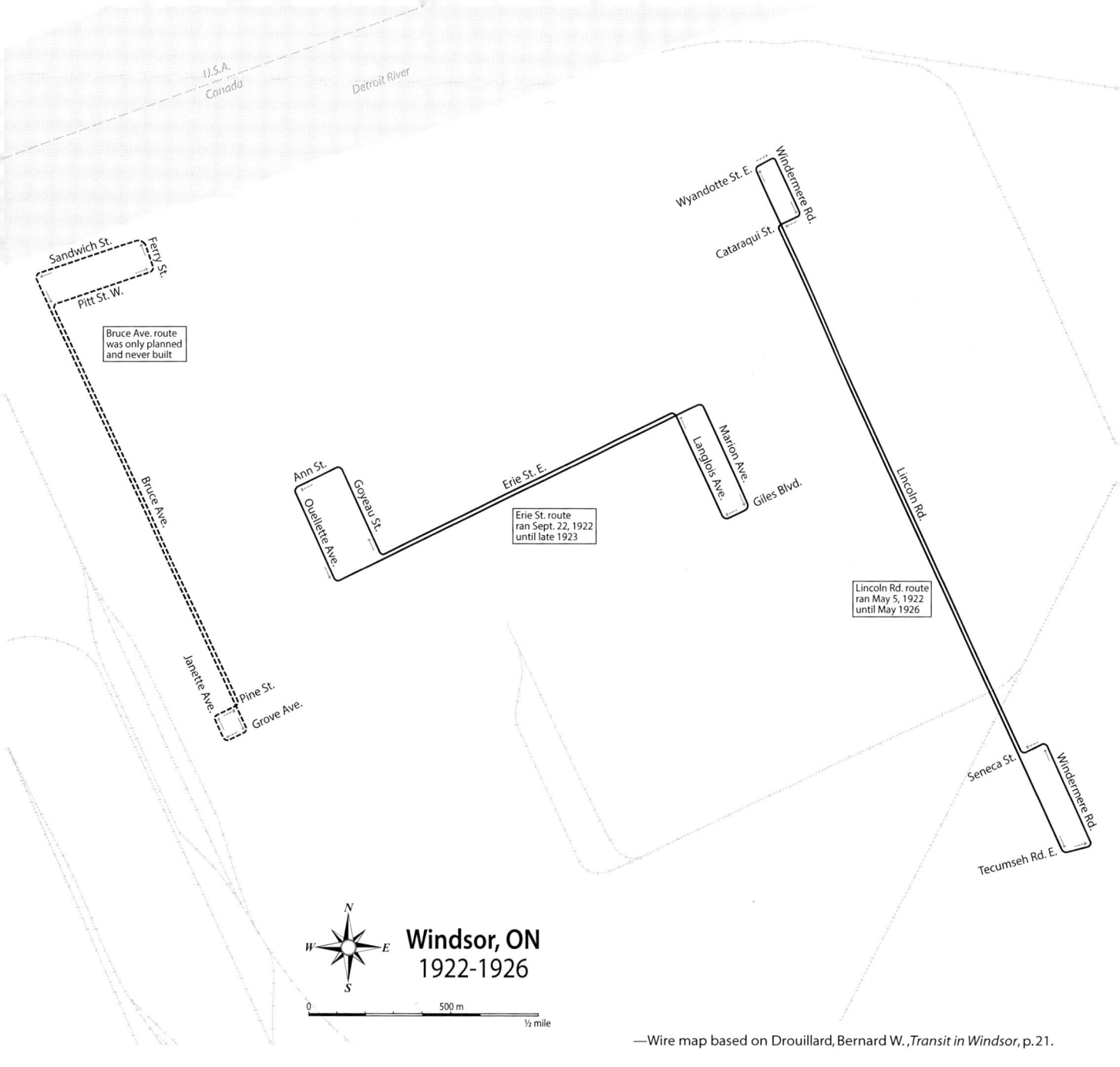

night, September 22nd 1934, Hydro Electric terminated its operating agreement with the SW&A Railway Company. There was little advance warning of this action, and the company suddenly found itself in dire straits with few cash reserves and steadily increasing annual losses. In the fall of 1937, S. E. Gorman, Chairman of the Board of Directors, Sandwich, Windsor & Amherstburg Railway Co. stated in a report to the Ontario Premier that the property's equipment was worn out, and recommended the use of trolley coaches for all except the less travelled routes. He stated that the trolley coach had lower maintenance and operating costs than a motor bus, could maintain faster schedules in traffic, and was smoother in operation. He added that since both the province and the municipalities were in the electricity business, they would profit from the use of it by electric buses. Further he suggested that with funds on hand, they buy enough trolley coaches to equip the cross town routes first, with other routes added as time and money permitted.[213] However, the Ontario Municipal Board appointed W. H. Furlong to succeed Gorman as Chairman, and when he assumed his post in February 1938, he opted for an all-bus, Ford-built system. Conversion from streetcars to buses started that year and proceeded rapidly: within fourteen months, the transit system had been completely motorized.

Footnotes:

212. The majority of this chapter is based on: Drouillard, Bernard W., "Transit in Windsor," *Bus Industry* Vol. 9, #2, April/May/June 1982, pp. 16-38. Permission to use it and a copy was kindly supplied by Bernie to this author and augmented with e-mail notes and illustrations from Bernie. Material on the City of Windsor's web site is also taken from Drouillard's article.
213. *Canadian Transportation*, September 1937 pp. 443-445.

Above: Passing in front of Chapples, formerly The Grain Exchange building, Fort William coach 47 urges us to take the bus and avoid the hassles of driving.
(PETER COX PHOTO COURTESY DAVID WYATT)

Below: Fort William Brill 42 is southbound on Syndicate, having just turned from Victoria passing Fort William's iconic Chapples Department Store (the newer building) on October 14th 1949.
(OHIO BRASS COLLECTION, THE STRAHORN LIBRARY, ILLINOIS RAILWAY MUSEUM)

Port Arthur–Fort William/ Thunder Bay (1947-1972)
Port Arthur PUC and Fort William Transit / Thunder Bay Transit

Two city systems operating separately, then jointly, then separately, then jointly again in one merged city, made trolley operations interesting. However, the equipment didn't have far to travel from the manufacturer – CCF-Brill was just "down the street".

Perhaps in order to better understand the back-and-forth machinations of transit in The Lakehead, we need to step back and look at a little history of the two cities. A silver-mining boom in the Port Arthur area ended mining in the late 1800s, wiping out much of their economy. Adding to that blow, Canadian Pacific Railway decided to build grain elevators and rail yards in nearby Fort William. With little business and workers moving nearer to the jobs, Port Arthur decided to build a streetcar line to take advantage of Fort William's booming economy, much to that town's displeasure. And so, in 1892, Port Arthur began operating Canada's first municipally-owned street railway, serving both towns. However, in 1907, when Port Arthur and Fort William became cities, the Ontario Railway and Municipal Board forced Port Arthur to sell the street railway section located in Fort William to that city, which took over operation on December 31st 1908. After that, each city ran its own streetcar system – the Port Arthur Civic Railway and the Fort William Street Railway. In 1913, Port Arthur added two belt lines to the MAIN LINE service, but Fort William only operated the MAIN LINE, intercity tram line, connecting with Port Arthur cars at the city limits. This joint-then-separated transit system(s) set the stage for operations – at times strained – throughout the Lakehead cities' transit history until amalgamation into the city of Thunder Bay in 1970. However, the systems could and did interconnect; the intercity streetcar line ran as an interlined service, that is to say, each city's cars ran to the end of the other city's line and vice versa.

Like most Canadian streetcar systems during WWII, both cities' systems were worn out and in bad shape. The fact that the Fort William plant of Canadian Car & Foundry was looking to acquire a licence from ACF-Brill to manufacture trolley buses no doubt made that transit alternative attractive. In July 1942, a joint meeting of the Fort William City Council Public Utilities Committee and the Port Arthur Public Utilities Commission consisted of considerable discussion on the possibility of establishing trolley coach service on the main route connecting the two cities. While they realized that nothing could be done during the war, the thought was that after the war's termination, they should consider introducing trackless vehicles, and to that end, they considered striking a permanent committee to study the matter.[214]

By 1946, both utilities were seriously considering the trolley coach as a streetcar replacement. In August 1946, Port Arthur acquired the first of fourteen Can Car 36-passenger gasoline buses and discontinued tram operations on the ARTHUR STREET line. At the same time, it renamed its system "Port Arthur Transit". In December, gasoline buses took over the MAIN LINE intercity car line.[215] On December 10th 1946, a rapid transit intercity gasoline bus service started operating with a fixed fare and a "no transfers from other utilities' conveyances will be accepted in either city"[216] policy. The rapid transit bus service was intended to operate until the new trolley buses arrived, but intercity rivalry bubbled to the surface from time to time, especially in the matter of intercity transit. An article in the Port Arthur *News-Chronicle* quoted one alderman from Fort William trying to avert the accusation that the manager of the street railway was opposed to trolley coaches running on the MAIN LINE (the intercity route).[217]

However, by early 1947, Fort William had placed an order for eight trolley coaches along with twelve gasoline buses with Can Car, which was to be completed by August. The route was set to travel along Fort William Road to Simpson Street and follow the tram route to Victoria, Syndicate, Walsh, Sprague to Brock, south on Ford to Frederica.[218] The end loop was along Frederica to Stanley, south to Gore and back along it to James, then north on it to Frederica. The coach barn was off Walsh near Franklin. In May, a proposal was raised to drop the Syndicate leg in favour of Franklin–Walsh–Sprague–Brock which would serve more residences, but it met with fierce opposition. Several groups, including a number of industries, presented a case to have the original (streetcar) route retained to pass nearer their plants along Syndicate Avenue South. That routing stayed.

Port Arthur also ordered eight coaches, later adding two more to be delivered in 1947. In Port Arthur, the MAIN LINE route ran on Fort William Road–Algoma–St. Paul–Cumberland and then looped via Grenville–Lillian–Leslie–Arundel–Hodder and back onto Cumberland. Port Arthur's garage loop was off Cumberland via Wolseley–Front (the garage)–Van Horne to Cumberland. Two of the Port Arthur trolley buses were to be assigned to a

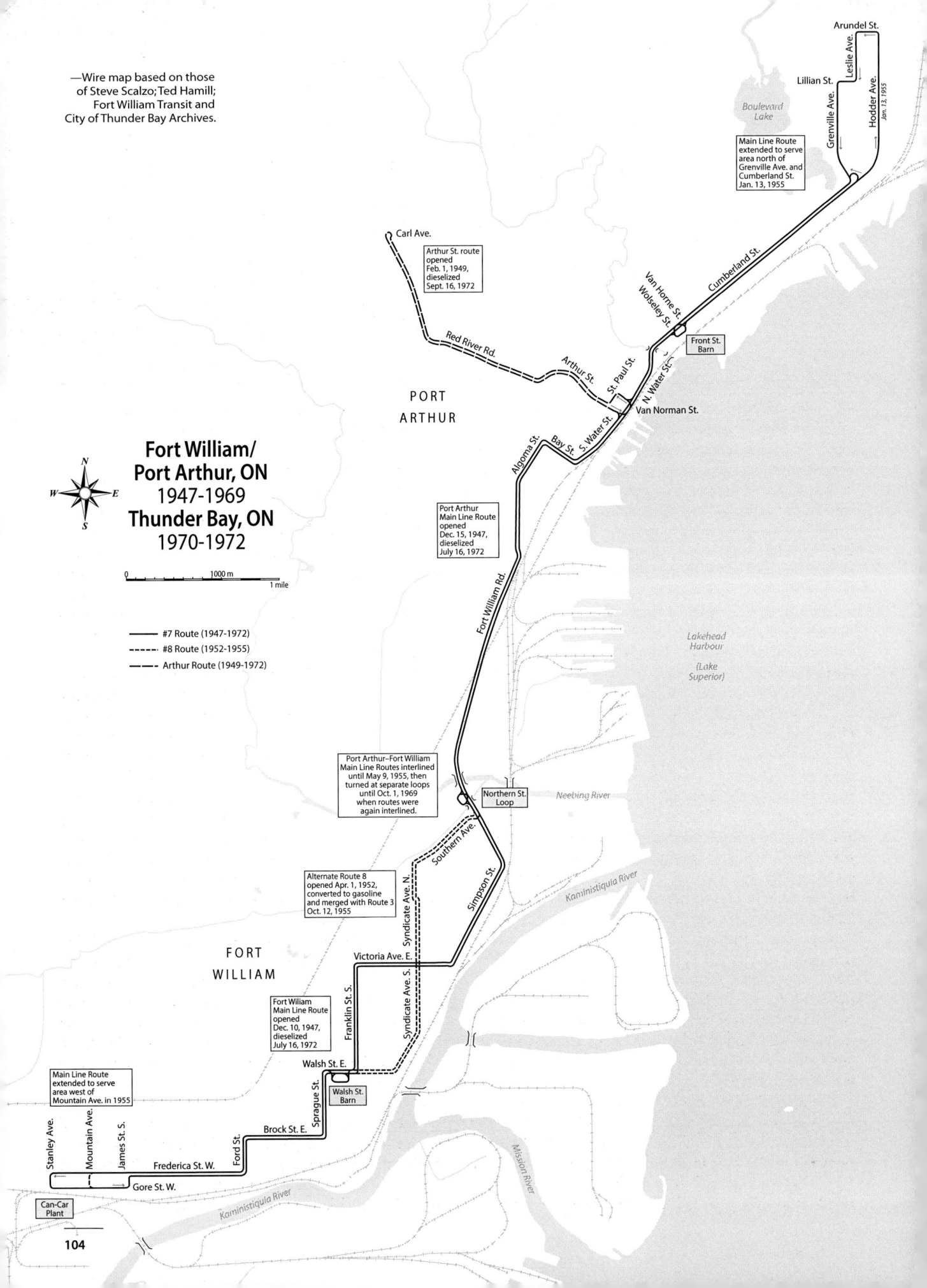

—Wire map based on those of Steve Scalzo; Ted Hamill; Fort William Transit and City of Thunder Bay Archives.

Fort William/ Port Arthur, ON 1947-1969 Thunder Bay, ON 1970-1972

0   1000 m
1 mile

——— #7 Route (1947-1972)
- - - - #8 Route (1952-1955)
— — — Arthur Route (1949-1972)

Main Line Route extended to serve area north of Grenville Ave. and Cumberland St. Jan. 13, 1955

Arundel St.
Leslie Ave.
Lillian St.
Grenville Ave.
Hodder Ave.
Jan. 13, 1955

Boulevard Lake

Carl Ave.

Arthur St. route opened Feb. 1, 1949, dieselized Sept. 16, 1972

Red River Rd.
Arthur St.
St. Paul St.
Van Horne St.
Wolseley St.
Cumberland St.
N. Water St.
Van Norman St.

Front St. Barn

PORT ARTHUR

Algoma St.
Bay St.
S. Water St.

Port Arthur Main Line Route opened Dec. 15, 1947, dieselized July 16, 1972

Fort William Rd.

Lakehead Harbour (Lake Superior)

Port Arthur–Fort William Main Line Routes interlined until May 9, 1955, then turned at separate loops until Oct. 1, 1969 when routes were again interlined.

Northern St. Loop

Neebing River

Southern Ave.
Simpson St.
Syndicate Ave. N.

Alternate Route 8 opened Apr. 1, 1952, converted to gasoline and merged with Route 3 Oct. 12, 1955

Kaministiquia River

Victoria Ave. E.
Syndicate Ave. S.
Franklin St. S.

FORT WILLIAM

Fort William Main Line Route opened Dec. 10, 1947, dieselized July 16, 1972

Walsh St. E.
Walsh St. Barn

Main Line Route extended to serve area west of Mountain Ave. in 1955

Stanley Ave.
Mountain Ave.
James St. S.
Ford St.
Sprague St.
Brock St. E.
Frederica St. W.
Gore St. W.

Can-Car Plant

Kaministiquia River
Mission River

104

Above: Southbound in Fort William territory, Port Arthur PUC 204 travels a lonely landscape in June 1964.
(G.M. ANDERSEN PHOTO, KRAMBLES-PETERSON ARCHIVE)

second route called ARTHUR STREET, which ran from a loop at Cumberland – the east/west MAIN LINE route – along Arthur onto Red River Road to a terminal at Carl, connecting downtown with a residential area in the north.[219] This route did not begin service, however, until February 1st 1949.[220]

However, more trouble was brewing. In June 1947, Port Arthur Mayor C.W. Cox laid into the Utilities Commission, threatening to withhold payment for the coaches because he did not believe a trolley coach system was suitable for Port Arthur. Not only were they too expensive, he fumed, the route was all wrong and the gasoline bus was cheaper and more flexible. The mayor demanded that a motion to move control of transit to Council be speeded up. Instead, it was withdrawn when he went out to take a phone call, spurring more threats when he returned. He blustered that no North American city of less than 50,000 had implemented trolley coach service, quoting late night tram ridership as an indication of how little, he thought, the coaches would be used, and claimed a motorcycle would be adequate. He then threatened to withhold funds and hold up paving. The Utilities Commissioner diplomatically said that "it is most unfair of you to come in here and tell the commission what equipment they are going to buy and tell us where to run the buses". The mayor retorted that someone had to tell them. When reminded that he had signed an agreement in January, the mayor claimed he had new cost figures from a Fort William alderman that were much higher, and produced them. These were immediately refuted by the Commissioner. The verbal battle continued until the Mayor put on his hat and, as he left, said, "you can do what the ___ ___ you want, but I tell you right now I'm not going to let a bunch like you handle city affairs this way."[221]

Things must have cooled down as, in July, Port Arthur Commissioner R.B. Chandler reported that Fort William Road would be used and the Fort William Public Utilities Commission was in agreement. Still, the terminus in Fort William continued to be up for debate, with Mountain Avenue (today called Mountdale) now the end point, and the Stanley Frederica/James (old streetcar) loop abandoned. More petitions for the latter to be the terminus and more meetings continued through July and August.[222]

Canadian Car expressed concern in April that the removal of electric railway overhead wires on Montreal Street, in preparation for the new trolley buses, would remove their source of DC power that they used under arrangement with the city to power their trolley coach test loop in the plant. They were assured that that the feeder cable would remain.[223]

On October 16th 1947, the last tram pulled in to the Fort William barns. However, the trolley buses were not an immediate replacement, as they were not expected to be delivered for about six more weeks and overhead work still remained to be done. Gasoline buses were to fill in until then. An interesting side note on the Fort William trams' last run was that the "fare" was cash or cans of food collected in aid of Britain's wartime shortages.[224] Wire-stringing continued through November and finally, the two cities agreed to officially open trolley coach service on December 15th 1947. (Streetcars continued to run in Port Arthur on another line – the NORTH BELT LOOP – until February 15th 1948.)

But, Fort William beat Port Arthur to the punch implementing regular service at 7:30 AM Wednesday December 10th. Service was limited to that city in that it ran from Southern Avenue to the Mountain-Gore terminus in the west end using four trolley coaches. In addition, for the first time, Sunday service was to be started that week. When full interlined service between the two cities was in operation, five buses from each would operate. Aldermen broke off from their meeting to take a ride on the new buses, and take on a few regular passengers that were allowed to ride free to the city boundary. The Port Arthur Public Utilities Commission said it hoped that the full MAIN LINE service would start Saturday, with official ceremonies on the following Monday, and it was starting trial runs the next day (Thursday) December 11th. The PUC wanted the new coaches in service as soon as possible, as Christmas shopping ridership was putting a strain on the gasoline buses.

The official opening ceremony on December 15th had both mayors – Garfield Anderson and Charles Cox – cut a ribbon at the boundary at 11:30 AM. They then retired to the Royal Edward Hotel for lunch, along with aldermen from the respective municipalities, representatives from Canadian Car, Ohio Brass (maker of overhead fittings) and Canada Wire and Cable.[225] After lunch and a toast to the King, messages of congratulation were read, and both mayors addressed the assembly, followed by officials from Can Car and Canada Wire and Cable, as well as the heads of the utilities.[226] With this auspicious ceremony and luncheon, the Lakehead became "the 21st Canadian community to adopt the trackless trolley".[227] How they arrived at this figure is uncertain.

The interlined route between the two cities, called MAIN LINE, had some unique operating practices on it. The route ran from the far west end of Fort William (almost at the Can Car plant) to the far east end of Port Arthur, passing through the downtowns of both cities, a round trip of 20.5 miles. There was an undeveloped area between the two cities, with the boundary between them actually at the west end of this vacant area, right where the populated area of Fort William ended. This area made a convenient virtual boundary slightly inside of Port Arthur. As a coach stopped at the boundary, the driver took a fare box belonging to the other city and walked down the aisle, collecting another fare. That fare box then went on the stand at the front door until a similar exchange coming back in the other direction.[228] Each property operated five coaches, the ten coaches providing a ten-minute headway and the round trip taking one hour and forty minutes.[229] As traffic increased, each transit operator put seven T-44s on the route, increasing to eight each during rush hours.

From 1947 through to at least 1949, Canadian Car test coaches were being run through both cities. For example, in 1948 a T-44 coach was run on the MAIN LINE from June 7th to August 5th and then returned to Can Car. In all probability, this coach was the demonstrator T-44 with upgrades or improvements to be tried out, or to see how it had fared in demonstration service.

In the fall of 1948, Port Arthur Main Line coaches' route destination signs were altered to read MAIN LINE instead of "Port Arthur" and "Fort William", so as to be consistent with the Fort William coach signage.[230] Erection of the overhead current distribution system for the ARTHUR STREET trolley coach line in Port Arthur commenced May 1948, and full operation began in February 1949.

A June 1951 survey of the Owl Service on the intercity route (trips operating between 1:30 AM and 4:30 AM) showed that revenue on the Fort William side was all of $5.11 per day, and only $3.77 in Port Arthur. Since the trolleys cost 27 cents per vehicle mile to operate, and the passenger revenue worked out to 14.1 cents per mile, it was obvious that, although it was a handy service, it was not paying, by a long shot.[231]

On January 19th 1951, the Ontario Municipal Board approved the City of Fort William's proposal to convert an existing line using gasoline buses into one using trolley coaches. The route was to run on South Franklin from Walsh to Victoria Avenue, Victoria from Franklin to Syndicate, north to Southern, and along Southern from Syndicate to Simpson. "We consider that our electric trolleys give us a substantial net revenue while the gasoline buses lose amounts that more than offset this gain," said Alderman K. Gordon Carson, chairman of the Public Utilities Committee. It was proposed that alternating buses presently travelling along the MAIN LINE over each loop would provide a twenty-minute headway in the downtown area. Local merchants were less than thrilled at the reduced service on the MAIN LINE, but the transit agreement had stated that a twenty-minute service was acceptable.[232] In February 1951, Fort William contracted for additional material to wire the Franklin–Victoria–North Syndicate–Southern extension.[233] Fort William Transit (now a department of the City) also ordered two more trolley coaches from Can Car. Although Canadian Car was now only making the larger 48-passenger buses, the city got them at little additional cost over the T-44s. Interestingly, these T-48s were produced nearly two years after Can Car introduced the revised model T-48A. The only difference between the two was the frame, which was aluminum in the T-48 and steel in the A version. Perhaps CC&F had two aluminum frames still around and offered to make two buses at a reduced price for the hometown operator.[234]

Delays in securing the steel poles delayed the extension opening date. Finally, in September 1951, Northern Electric advised the city that their supply of the steel poles would be shipped by boat at the end of the month. Besides shortages of steel, getting supply boats near the end of the shipping season was cited as a problem.[235] The south portion of the overhead wire was finished by December 13th, and additional service was announced "south on Franklin Street and Victoria Avenue via Simpson Street and the intercity boundary, with return to the bus terminal and on to west Fort William during the afternoons on weekdays, and with extended service on Saturdays." The service was to start Friday (December 14th) for the convenience of Christmas shoppers. Work was progressing, the *Times Journal* reported, on the new trolley line on North Syndicate and Southern avenues.[236]

April 1st 1952 saw the inauguration of the alternate routing of the MAIN LINE from the Walsh Street Depot to the boundary. What was originally approved as one new route was rationalized as two routes, each using parts of the new wire. This change added ROUTE #8 which ran parallel to the old #7 until Walsh and Franklin. Here the #8 took the existing wire along Walsh and up South Syndicate, then crossing Victoria where the street became North

Below: Port Arthur coach 210 is about to enter the exchange loop and let passengers transfer to the waiting Fort William coach in the background.
(BILL VOLKMER COLLECTION)

Below: This Port Arthur coach is turning south from Van Norman onto St. Paul street, October 13th 1949. Note the new Chrysler products parked behind it.
(OHIO BRASS COLLECTION, THE STRAHORN LIBRARY, ILLINOIS RAILWAY MUSEUM. LOCATION INFORMATION – TED HAMILL)

Above: Not trusting that newfangled electric transit, the old reliable horse and cart crosses the railway tracks on Fort William Road just south of 11th Avenue in Port Arthur on a June day in 1964.
(G.M. ANDERSEN PHOTO, KRAMBLES-PETERSON ARCHIVE.
LOCATION INFORMATION – JOHN DAY AND MARK WALTON)

Syndicate on new wire to Southern, and east to Simpson, rejoining the old ROUTE #7 to Port Arthur. ROUTE #7 now ran as before until Franklin, where it turned north on new wire to Victoria, east on it to Simpson where it utilized the existing wire, continuing to the boundary and into Port Arthur.[237] The new ROUTE #8 made the MAIN LINE accessible to many more residents, which was what had been argued in 1946 when the original routing was disputed. The South Syndicate route had been chosen originally as it was the old streetcar route. However, with the city growing west it made sense to extend the trolley route west also. ROUTE #1 (a gasoline bus route) was discontinued, as most of its area was now served by trolley coaches (ROUTE #7).[238] Both routes were called MAIN LINE and at night, ROUTE #7 coaches had amber front lights, while those on ROUTE #8 used green ones.[239] With each route running every twenty minutes alternating, this gave service at the Boundary equivalent to a ten-minute headway. Extra trolleys ran from the depot with ten-minute service via Franklin, Victoria and Simpson, connecting there with northbound trolleys during peak hours. However, by June, Port Arthur asked for twelve-minute service on the MAIN LINE and Fort William PUC concurred. Not only did this save on coach miles, it reduced the number of vehicles needed from five to four – a considerable saving.[240]

In January 1952, the issue of a rapid bus service arose again. Although it had been tried out in late 1946 and had met with public approval, it had been discontinued. Now, it was suggested by Port Arthur Council, to serve a growing population along the May–Memorial artery. The two transit systems were urged to give it serious consideration, especially since some school children along that route had to walk over a mile. This would have been a gasoline bus service running from the centres of the two cities, and with limited stops.[241]

In 1954, passenger volume was not meeting expectations, so Fort William Council directed Transit to terminate the #8 trolley bus route at the depot on Walsh instead of going on to the Westfort Loop, and to establish a thirty-minute headway on April 1st 1954. This was presumably to avoid the duplication with the #7 routing, and improve service while cutting costs. Even so, on Saturdays the #8 still ran to Mountain.[242]

Meanwhile, intercity trouble was brewing. On October 5th 1954, the *Times-Journal* headline screamed "Pt. Arthur buses to stop operating in Ft. William". A resolution was passed at the Port Arthur PUC meeting citing the cut as part of an economy program the transit system was inaugurating to curtail revenue losses. While the announcement seemed to have caught Fort William officials off guard, they were assured that it would not happen until a passenger shelter was constructed, and not until the New Year. PUC Manager E. A. Vigras said that though the mainline trolleys operated in both cities over 5.2 miles, in Fort William, the business section was three times longer and "we have more work to do there." In other words, the Port Arthur coaches were carrying more passengers in Fort William but not getting the revenue (presumably these were passengers travelling entirely within Fort William and not crossing the boundary). The PUC had to effect economies, since even a fare increase could not wipe out a projected $90,000 deficit.[243] In an April 14th 1955 meeting, the Fort William Public Utilities Commission concurred, setting a date of May 9th to short-turn their buses. A $3700 shelter was to be constructed at the boundary, with Fort William agreeing to pay $1300 of it,[244] and a double loop was constructed at the boundary so the buses never left their owner's city. It was not a decision that pleased many. The Fort William Chamber of Commerce appealed to Port Arthur to reconsider the service cut, but the Port Arthur PUC replied they had taken a long, hard look at this, and that the decision was only arrived at after a long and careful consideration.[245]

Passengers now had to walk across the loop (and pay another fare on the other bus) in order to complete their journey. This became a major inconvenience, especially in winter, and by late 1955, passengers were already complaining about the inadequacy of the passenger shelter and the service. It would seem that there was not always a waiting bus at the transfer point, and though each city paid half of the shelter's cost, it apparently had no roof or walls.[246] While patrons on both sides of the boundary complained, Port Arthur blamed Fort William for the inadequate shelter, but Fort William placed the blame for the entire situation squarely on Port Arthur, as it was their decision initially to terminate the interlining, leaving Fort William with no choice but to do likewise.[247] An attempt was made on February 18th 1956 to arrive at a resolution, with a joint meeting of mayors and transit officials and aldermen.[248]

Perhaps now that there could be no argument that coaches ran a longer route in one city or the other, on April 12th 1955, Fort William Council directed Transit to "proceed with the extension of the present westerly route to Stanley Avenue."[249] This extended the Fort William terminus east along Frederica from Mountain to Stanley, south to Gore, along it to James, and north on James back to Frederica. This had been the original streetcar loop that residents had lobbied for when trolley coach service first started, but was not put into effect then as it would have made the Fort William routing longer than that in Port Arthur.

Meanwhile in May 1955, Port Arthur moved ahead to secure a debenture to electrify the Current River subdivision transit service with trolley coaches. It was to run from Grenville and North Cumberland, east on Cumberland to Hodder, Hodder to Arundel, Leslie Avenue and Lillian to Grenvillle, then back to Cumberland and Granville. This was to dispense with the transfer from mainline trolley coaches to gasoline buses and it was hoped this, along with the short turning of the MAIN LINE, would help get the transit system out of the red.[250] The opening of the extension was celebrated at the Port Arthur PUC's inaugural meeting (after an election) on the evening of January 12th, when officials took a spin around the new route. Regular service commenced the next morning.[251]

On October 12th 1955, Fort William Council approved a two-month transit routing trial that combined the #8 trolley route with the gasoline bus ROUTE #3. That in effect withdrew trolley service on the #8. The new combined route ran from Walsh and Syndicate to Southern, on to Pacific, and then followed the rest of the #3 routing. Along with more frequent service, this was an attempt to cut Fort William's transit losses.[252] Trolley coaches still ran on Sundays on the old ROUTE #8. By early November, this re-routing (and others) plus a fare increase had improved revenues by 17.4 per cent.

At her inauguration in January 1956, Port Arthur Mayor Eunice Wishart proposed that services on the two transit systems be reunited. Still, tempers ran high in Fort William Council meetings, where some thought members should just mind their own city's business, while others vehemently objected to a "wall around the city" attitude. In February 1956, Port Arthur's Transit Department Manager S.L. Bishop wrote a detailed report on a joint study with the manager of Fort William's system and the respective transit commissions, on the advisability of re-opening joint service. They agreed that joint service would be of benefit to patrons riding across the boundary and should result in increased patronage. However, they noted that the intercity traffic was around ten per cent of total patronage, and also that other patrons on other routes had to walk from one bus to another. In addition, both transit systems noted that service reliability had improved since they split, but resuming an interlined service would increase delays and hamper the respective systems' ability to compensate for them. Again the issue of unequal distances in the two cities was raised; with the Current River extension opened in Port Arthur, though it was just under a mile and a half each way, over a day it amounted to nearly 67 miles of equipment operation – a sizable amount of extra wear over the course of a year. While Fort William thought they should then be compensated for the extra mileage, Port Arthur countered that they too experienced extra wear while in Fort William territory. With fewer Port Arthur coaches available per day, their buses assigned to route #7 had to handle well over 700,000 more passengers in Fort William than in Port Arthur. Port Arthur also carried twice as many boundary passengers as did Fort William. Altogether, the prospect of interlined service was not an easy one to negotiate. Further, Bishop felt that, while it imposed some inconvenience on through passengers, the split (transfer) arrangement now resulted in better, more accurate schedules in both cities.[253] The issue was raised in March at a joint meeting of the two utilities, with the same arguments aired, though finally, a joint resolution was passed proposing a three-month trial be held starting April 1st. The motion had then to be endorsed by both city councils, but unfortunately, this did not happen, as it was obvious that support from the Port Arthur Utilities representatives was lukewarm, and they declined to vote.[254] At their meeting March 13th, the Port Arthur PUC again rejected any reconciliation or even a three-month trial – with only the mayor voting for the motion.[255]

In January 1957, Cincinnati Transit wrote Fort William Transit offering any of their forty surplus used trolley coaches of varying ages and makes, including Twin, Marmon-Herrington, St. Louis and Pullman. One suspects they wrote a number of properties using trolley coaches, but Fort William was not interested in expanding either their lines or their fleet.[256]

Several more transit interchange meetings were held, and in March of 1956, when members of both utilities, mayors and aldermen met for a third time, they finally passed a resolution to again interline the services. Still, even then this was not unanimous, as two Port Arthur commissioners declined to vote.[257] Again the argument was that more revenue went to Fort William than was due. Port Arthur Mayor Wishart accused Port Arthur Utilities of putting revenue ahead of service. Ed Vigras, manager of Port Arthur Utilities, countered that service was better for both sides since the split. Fort William Mayor Badani left, pessimistic that any solution was imminent; he even suggested it may go to a public plebiscite, since the resolution had to be endorsed by both city councils, and the Port Arthur commissioners were still clearly against any change.

His pessimism was warranted, as service wasn't reintegrated until over a decade later, on October 1st 1969.[258] Concurrent with this breakthrough was a single thoroughfare and a central depot for more efficient service. Fort William Transit Manager Syd Bishop was instrumental in making these changes, working with his counterpart in Port Arthur, Manager Ed Vigras[259] who, it would seem, had by now come around. Fort William ROUTE #7 coaches were signed INTERCITY on the way out and WESTFORT on the return trip.[260]

This resumption of intercity service was predicated on the impending merger of the cities of Port Arthur and Fort William into the city of Thunder Bay on January 1st 1970. Both the Port Arthur Public Utilities Commission and Fort William Transit delegated transit responsibilities to the newly-formed Thunder Bay Transit. At the time of amalgamation, the view was expressed that the coaches might be replaced with something more flexible, but there was opposition to this from some city councilors, who cited higher diesel bus maintenance costs and air pollution issues.[261] However, there were reports that the two 1913 Fort William DC generators were on their last legs,[262] and that operating cost was also an issue.

Amalgamation also brought a uniform paint scheme: cream with a green belt rail and bumpers and gold lettering. At least two Port Arthur units, Nos. 210 and 216, were redone in the new cream and green scheme.[263] For Fort William buses, this was their third livery: originally they were orange on the bottom, with cream above the belt rail and on the roof, dipping in the front to a V at the bumper. Port Arthur trolleys were always dark red below the belt rail, with cream on top and on the roof. In the late 1960s, the Fort William buses were completely light cream with a small maroon belt line and blue, red or chrome bumpers, with no logo, only a bus number. This paint scheme was used on Fort William buses before resumption of the interlined service, when they still turned at the Simpson and Northern loop.

An interesting side note: in March 1961, the local Fort William radio station CKPR 5-8-0 AM/FM entered into an agreement with the city to install Electrohome Custom transistorized radio sets into each bus, fixed at the 580 frequency and connected to two speakers, one at the rear and one half-way down the bus. These radios were controlled by the operator, who could turn them on or off and also adjust the volume. At first, the radios were in five to ten buses and later, since the experiment was deemed a success, more were added. The arrangement ran for three years, and was extended at least another three years. It seems that Port Arthur was also approached for a similar arrangement and implemented it. The radio station claimed that a similar system in Brandon increased ridership 7.76 per cent.[264]

The trolley coach system trundled along until January 1971, when Council commissioned a study by Kates, Peat, Marwick & Company to assess operating and capital costs of trolley versus diesel operation. Several scenarios were presented, including a reduced trolley (coach) system and a hypothetical new trolley bus route. The issue of diesel bus versus automobile pollution was used to presumably support more diesel buses. Operating costs were compared, as was service flexibility and availability of parts and equipment. In that last section, the report referred to the Western Flyer rebuild program being carried out by the TTC in Toronto, but noted that Flyer would only engage in new trolley bus manufacturing if and when a viable market emerged. Finally the report discussed fleet standardization and, given that operating savings only amounted to 2.2 per cent of the annual system's costs, warned that new trolley coaches would cost double that of a diesel. Furthermore, it stated that a reduced system did not offer any savings, pollution was deemed to be insignificant, and that the trolley coach system be scrapped to give the transit service operating flexibility, parts availability and standardization.[265]

Following tabling of the report, in January 1972, council voted eleven to three in favour. It did amend the report's recommendation that the system be completely replaced starting in September, and voted to do half in 1972 and half in 1973. Despite the Ontario Provincial Government's program of paying a subsidy for overhead and garages, there were the additional costs of continuing to maintain the operation of trolleys when the Current River Bridge needed renovation, necessitating the wires to be moved, and so the die was cast. The plan was to convert the ARTHUR STREET line as well as the northern portion of the MAIN LINE in 1972, and the remaining southern part of the MAIN LINE in 1973. This would allow routings to be adjusted in the North Ward and older coaches to be retired in August of 1972.²⁶⁶

However, life happens while you are making plans, so the saying goes, and the June 2nd demise of a DC generator in Fort William at the Walsh Street substation hurried the abandonment.²⁶⁷ So, as soon as enough diesel buses arrived, the entire MAIN LINE was converted on July 16th 1972.²⁶⁸ The ARTHUR STREET line lingered a bit longer, and

Above: Fort William 41 sits in the loop with Port Arthur 210 waiting behind. It looks like the passenger transfer has taken place and the Fort William operator is completing his paperwork before pulling out. The infamous shelter looks adequate for a June 1966 day, but not for a winter's night. (COLIN K. HATCHER)

Below: Fort William coach 42 traverses Victoria Avenue just past Syndicate in August of 1966 on the intercity run. The Chapples building in the background was once The Grain Exchange. (BILL VOLKMER COLLECTION)

the last trolley coach ran Saturday September 16th[269] of that year. The demise of the trolley coach went unheralded, overshadowed by the Transit Parade held with bands, majorettes and seven of the new diesels.[270] At about the same time the parade was starting, Driver Len Edwardson made the last run driving (Port Arthur) unit 214. As he passed through his Weston neighbourhood, he paused outside his home where his wife snapped a photo of him behind the wheel of a still-red and cream Port Arthur bus. He then he drove it to the Southside barn and into Thunder Bay history.[271]

The twenty units were sold to Hamilton for parts and were scrapped and salvaged in Thunder Bay, ironically the place where they had first been built in Canadian Car's Fort William factory.

Footnotes:

214. *Canadian Transportation*, July 1942.
215. *Canadian Transportation*, June 1948 p. 329 and Wikipedia Thunder Bay Transit.
    http://en.wikipedia.org/wiki/Thunder_Bay_Transit
    quoting Port Arthur News-Chronicle August 1 and 13, 1946 visited October 21, 2010.
216. Fort William *Times-Journal*, December 5, 1946 pp. 1 and 14.
217. Port Arthur *News-Chronicle*, Wednesday January 30, 1946.
218. *Times-Journal*, March 26, 1947 p. 1.
219. Peter Cox personal e-mail to author July 16, 2012 and Scalzo wire map.
220. Thunder Bay Archives file 4251-09 "Report on Second Year of Trolley Coach Operation" D.A. Kemp to R.B. Chandler.
221. *Times-Journal*, June 13, 1947, pp. 1 and 10.
222. *Times-Journal*, July 18, 1947 p. 1 and August 13, 1947.
223. Thunder Bay Archives file 216-11.
224. *Times-Journal*, October 17, 1947 p. 1.
225. *Times-Journal*, December 10, 1947 pp. 1 and 2.
226. Thunder Bay Archives file 216-11.
227. *Times-Journal*, November 28, 1947 p. 1.
228. Cox, *op. cit.* and *Canadian Transportation*, August 1952 p. 456.
229. *Canadian Transportation*, June 1948 p. 329.
230. Thunder Bay Archives file 4251-09.
231. *Times-Journal*, June 21, 1951 p. 2.
232. *Times-Journal*, January 19, 1951 p. 1.
233. *Times-Journal*, February 14, 1951 p. 5.
234. Cox, *op. cit.*
235. Thunder Bay Archives file 0580-07 Letter Northern Electric Lakehead Branch Mac McEwan Manager to A.V. Steele Manager Fort William Transit, September 24, 1951.
236. *Times-Journal*, December 13, 1951 p. 3.
237. *Times-Journal*, advertisement for New Bus Routes March 29, 1952 p. 12.
238. *Times-Journal*, January 30, 1952 p. 16.
239. *Times-Journal*, Bus Routes *Op. Cit.*
240. Thunder Bay Archives file 0580-02 Letter from A.V. Steele, Manager Transit Department to Public Utilities Committee, June 5, 1952 and Council approval June 11, 1952.
241. *Times-Journal*, January 22, 1951 p. 16.
242. Thunder Bay Archives file 0508-02 Transit Bus Routes.
243. *Times-Journal*, October 5, 1954 p. 1.
244. *Times-Journal*, April 15, 1955 p. 1.
245. *Times-Journal*, April 20, 1955 p. 2.
246. *Times-Journal*, December 6, 1955 p. 1.
247. *Times-Journal*, December 8, 1955 p. 1.
248. *Times-Journal*, February 11, 1955 p. 1.
249. Thunder Bay Archives file 0508-02 Correspondence from City Clerk to A.V. Steele, Transit Manager April 13, 1955.
250. *Times-Journal*, May 13, 1955 p. 3.
251. *Times-Journal*, January 12, 1956 p. 3.
252. *Times-Journal*, October 12, 1955 pp. 1 and 5.
253. Thunder Bay Archives file 1078-10.
254. *Times-Journal*, March 2, 1956 p. 1.
255. *Times-Journal*, March 14, 1956 p. 17.
256. Thunder Bay Archives file 0508-07 Cincinnati Transit to Mayor H. Badanal January 4, 1957.
257. *Times-Journal*, March 2, 1956 p. 1.
258. Rollsign Gallery.
259. Letter from E.I. Poole, Manager, Thunder Bay Transit to Thunder Bay Mayor Walter Assef, May 26, 1975.
260. Tom's Trolleybus web site – various dated Fort William photos.
261. *Trolley Coach News*, Vol. 2 #4 issue #10 August 1970 p. 69.
262. *Times-Journal*, Lon Patterson Reports June 7, 1972 p. 12.
263. *Trolley Coach News*, #19 October-December 1972 p. 121 and Vol. 6 #5 issue #29 Winter 1974 pp. 131-132 and photo of No. 210 from Ted Hamill.
264. Thunder Bay Archives File 0508-08 various correspondence.
265. NATTA Special Bulletin No. 4, May 1972 – a reprint of the Kates, Peat, Marwick & Company report.
266. *Canadian Coach*, June 1972 p. 3.
267. *Times-Journal*, June 2, 1972 p. 1.
268. *Chronicle-Journal*, July 7, 1972 p. 13 and July 15, 1972 p. 13.
269. *Chronicle-Journal*, September 7, 1972 p. 17.
270. *Chronicle-Journal*, September 15, 1972 p. 3.
271. As quoted on the Canadian Public Transit Discussion Board, Feb. 13, 2007
    http://www.cptdb.ca/index.php?showtopic=1761
    Original source unknown visited February 4, 2008.
272. *Ibid.*
273. Thunder Bay *Chronicle-Journal*, June 29, 2012 and various e-mails between the author and Ted Hamill August 2012.

CODA: In 2002, members of the Amalgamated Transit Union approached Thunder Bay Transit for help in acquiring two Brill trolley buses from a private Vancouver-area storage/collection, to cosmetically restore them to Port Arthur and Fort William liveries. Although these buses were originally delivered to Saskatoon, then sold to B.C. Hydro for service in Vancouver, they did well as Fort William/Port Arthur stand-ins, and of course, they were back in the very territory they were made in. Finding spare parts was an adventure with the bus driver members rebuilding doors and scouting over 300 miles of roads to find and install original steering wheels, treadle gates, windows, seats, lights and gauges, to name a few increasingly rare components.[272] The buses were put on display in 2012 at the Bombardier (formerly Can Car) plant for its 100th anniversary.[273] The city will store the restored Brill buses in the main transit garage as long as the Thunder Bay Historical Transportation Committee continues in its efforts to build a transit museum.

Opposite Top: Forward to June 27th 1969: the transfer point at the Port Arthur Fort William boundary looks the same, but the shelter has definitely improved since 1966. In practice, most service was through-routed, with pooling of coaches from both systems.
(T.V. THOMPSON/TED WICKSON COLLECTION)

Opposit Middle: Fort William coach 46 makes the turn into the Fredrica/Stanley/Gore loop in June 1964 as it prepares to go northbound on the intercity run.
(G.M. ANDERSEN PHOTO, KRAMBLES-PETERSON ARCHIVE)

Opposite Bottom: On single wire around the loop at the end of the Port Arthur line, coach 204 goes about its silent business in August 1964. (G.M. ANDERSEN PHOTO, KRAMBLES-PETERSON ARCHIVE)

113

Above: Mack No. 1516, with rollsigns newly installed, sits in front of the Mack plant in Allentown, PA in 1938.
(JEFF MARINOFF COLLECTION)

Below: In October 1938, unit 1502 is being given a trial run at the Mack plant prior to being shipped to Winnipeg.
(JEFF MARINOFF COLLECTION)

Winnipeg (1938-1970)
Winnipeg Electric Co. / Greater Winnipeg Transit Commission / Metro Winnipeg Transit

The first to adopt the trackless trolley in western Canada, Winnipeg could also boast of having the prototype Canadian trolley bus, a varied fleet of American and Canadian coaches, severe winters and devastating floods. Ironically, it had an extensive system of electric transit that was terminated just when a new trolley bus supplier arose within its own city.

In a March 1931 report to the Municipal and Public Utility Board of the Province of Manitoba regarding "Public Transportation Services in Greater Winnipeg", its authors commented that the trolley bus had been used by transportation systems of British and other European cities for the past twenty years, ... and that over 200 of them were then in use in America. It recommended that twelve trackless trolleys be purchased during 1931 for service on Sherbrook-Portage to Logan, Logan-Arlington to Main, Ellice and Westminster. Furthermore they recommended that as soon as the Salter Street road extension was completed in 1932, an additional thirteen coaches be purchased for service thereon.[274] The first twelve 40-passenger coaches were estimated to cost $228,000 and infrastructure $45,000.[275]

However, given the economic conditions of the depression years, and the new technology of the trolley coach of the day, the Winnipeg Electric Co. (WEC) decided the economics were just not there. It wasn't until 1938 – seven years later – that this dream of modern trackless transportation was finally realized in Winnipeg. Serendipitously, it was another street construction that predicated the move.

The reconstruction of Sargent Avenue would incur streetcar track work expenditures of $275,000 in addition to re-paving most of the right-of-way/street, so the company felt that this was an opportune time to study the feasibility of trackless trolley operation in Winnipeg's infamous climate. The aging condition of the existing trams no doubt hastened this decision. Mr. C.H. Dahl, Manager of Transportation, Winnipeg Electric Company, was quoted as saying, "When that good amount of money was expended, we would have a good set of tracks but from the passengers' standpoint, there would be no particular improvement because the same old streetcars would be operating. We felt it was important to make an impression on the passengers and concluded new vehicles were far more important than new tracks. We figured we could take up our tracks, restore the pavement to good condition, and equip the route with trolley coaches and the necessary overhead at an expenditure which would not exceed the cost of replacing the tracks."[276]

WEC was certainly a groundbreaker in western Canada in this respect. Aside from the early Windsor and Toronto experiments and Montreal's trolley buses a year earlier (1937), no other Canadian city had ventured into these waters. An added complication was that, as a private operator, WEC had to negotiate with the City for any changes to the transportation network, but the City finally agreed that the company could operate trolley buses instead of streetcars on the 2½-mile SARGENT AVENUE run. So in May of 1938, six Mack CR3S coaches which could carry forty passengers each were ordered. Late summer turned into fall as the trolley coach overhead was converted, tracks in the carhouse converted for coach servicing, and specialwork installed. The trick was that throughout this work streetcar service had to continue. WEC ingeniously dropped the streetcar wire by a foot, then erected the trolley bus wires above it, raising the span wires while drooping the actual streetcar running wire and using the spans to carry both wires. This permitted the trolley buses to begin using their wire immediately on start up, allowing the streetcar wire to be removed after conversion without interruption of trolley coach service.

Late night and early morning training commenced for a number of operators until the morning of November 21st 1938, when the first trolley coach in western Canada pulled away from Garry Street and Portage Avenue. The operation was an immediate success; by 1939, net returns on the line had climbed from negligible to a fourteen times increase. Considering that the coaches started operating in Winnipeg's notorious winter, operation exceeded expectations.

With that immediate response in increased ridership, and given that the trolleys ran on the identical line that the streetcars had, and that there was no bleed in ridership from adjacent routes, the City, seeing a good thing, granted permission for a second line on Notre Dame Avenue to commence in late 1939.[277] To service this line, an additional nine Mack coaches were ordered in May 1939, with service to commence December 18th. Buses along this route served many wartime industries so it was no surprise that more coaches were needed in a short time. But, this was wartime and coaches were hard to come by as many manufacturers were switching to building tanks and oth-

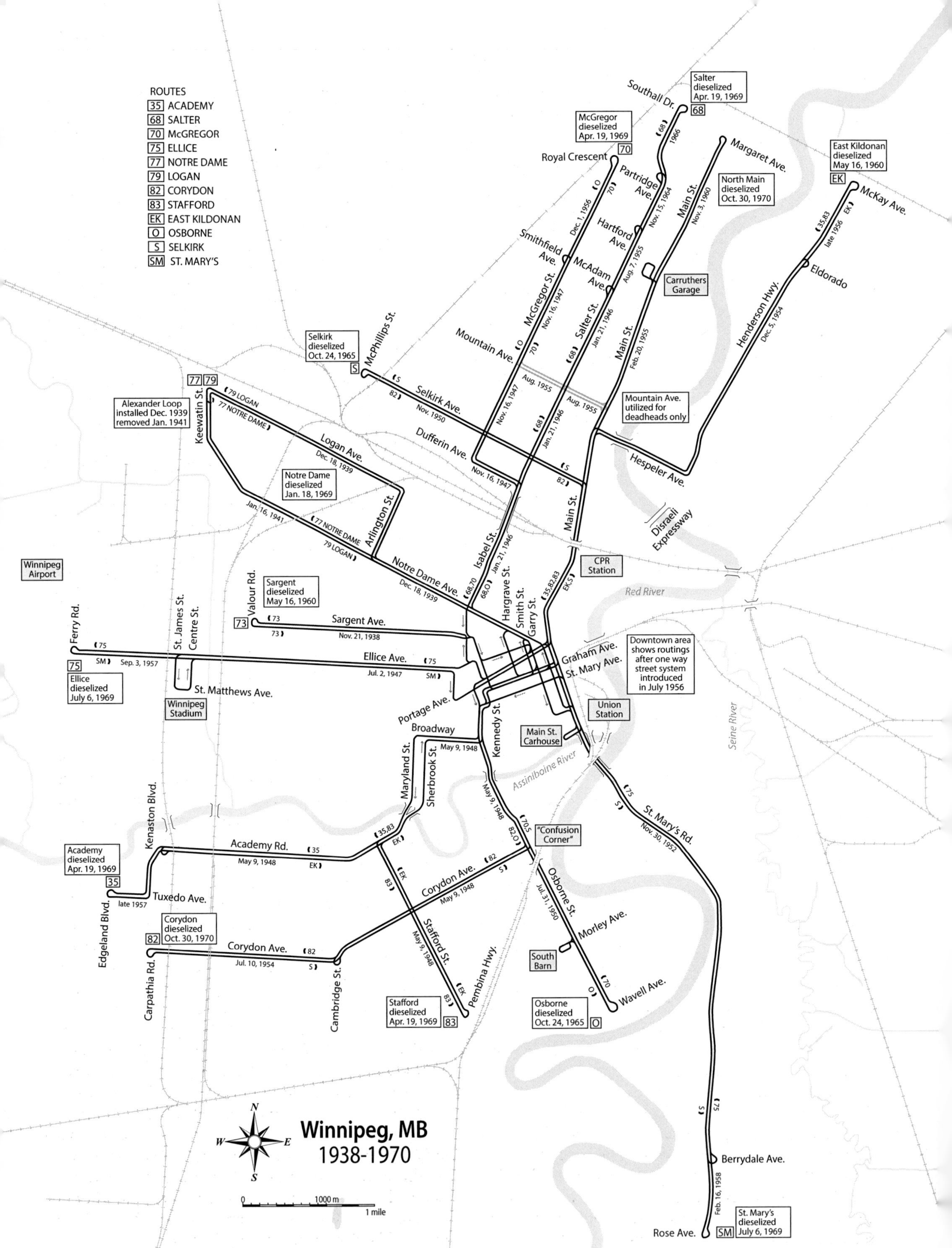

—Wire map after Baker, *Winnipeg's Electric Transit*, Chapter 9.

er military vehicles. Fortunately, the Wilkes-Barre Railway Corp. had an order being fulfilled by Mack, and agreed to divert one CR3 coach now being finished and take its replacement later. It was already painted in the Wilkes-Barre livery and, again because of war restrictions, stayed that way in Winnipeg service until 1946. War restrictions could sometimes be flexible, though, so wire was procured which permitted an extension downtown on Smith from Ellice to Notre Dame, then on Notre Dame from Smith to Arlington; along Arlington to Logan; up Logan to Keewatin; and along Keewatin to the old streetcar loop at Alexander. Loops were moved and routes adjusted, but the demand for the new trolley coaches continued. By 1942, trolley coaches ran on three routes: NOTRE DAME, route 77 from Notre Dame and Portage, via Portage, Smith, Notre Dame to Keewatin and Logan and return via Logan; LOGAN, route 79 also from Notre Dame and Portage via Portage, Smith, Notre Dame, Arlington, Logan to Keewatin and return via Notre Dame; and SARGENT, route 73 from Notre Dame and Portage via Portage, Smith, Ellice, Kennedy, Sargent to Valour Road and return.[278]

In a report to *Canadian Transportation* magazine on their trolley coach successes, WEC showed they had only modest net revenue up to 1939, less than one per cent, but after trolley coaches were introduced, revenue climbed to between thirteen and eighteen per cent. Further, there had been no fare increases and no additional route miles vis-a-vis the streetcar service on the lines reported.[279] Based on this success, more coaches were needed.

Above: With additions and a second line being planned, Ohio Brass pointed out how trolley coaches had come through Winnipeg's notorious winters with flying colours in 1939. (OHIO BRASS COLLECTION, THE STRAHORN LIBRARY, ILLINOIS RAILWAY MUSEUM)

WEC now turned to a hometown supplier, Motor Coach Industries in Winnipeg, and asked them to produce a prototype coach based on the Mack. In February 1942 it was delivered, and pronounced a success. This unique coach continued to operate as late as 1957.[280] However, just as it was delivered, bus production at MCI ceased in favour of war needs, and no more local-built coaches were produced. The wartime Canadian Transit Controller did allow WEC to purchase five more coaches from Mack, which was still able to supply some bus company units. Although that order was for 44-passenger coaches, in January 1943 they received standard forty-seat coaches, presumably as this was what was available due to wartime production.[281] These Mack buses were of the same construction as the three ordered by Edmonton, and with their arrival, the trolley coach fleet stood at 22. This, however, concluded Mack's involvement with Winnipeg, and when, by 1944, needs again dictated an expansion of the fleet, Pullman-Standard was contracted to produce eight 44CX coaches at $22,000 each. Material and sub-assembly delays pushed the delivery of these coaches to October 1945. In anticipation of their arrival, wire was strung on a new route, coincidentally one that was recommended in 1931 – SALTER STREET. This line opened January 21st 1946.

In this General Electric ad from May 1947, the advantages of the modern trolley coach were touted in terms of increased passengers and decreased costs. GE supplied motors and controllers for most of the trolley coaches built in North America, though some of Winnipeg's Macks, the MCI coach and the Pullmans, used Westinghouse components.
(OHIO BRASS COLLECTION, THE STRAHORN LIBRARY, ILLINOIS RAILWAY MUSEUM)

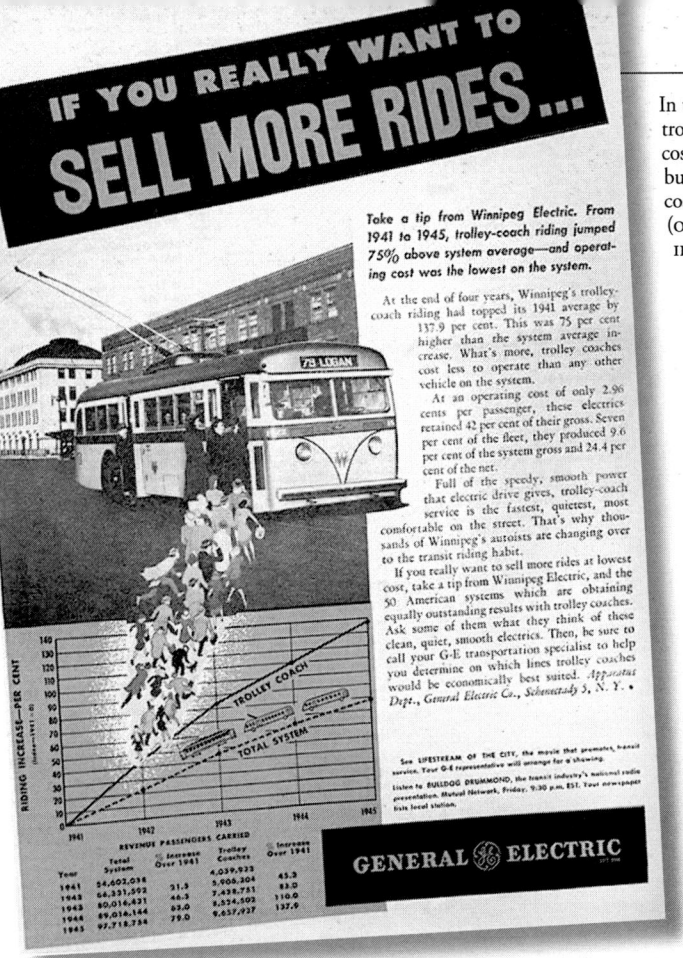

Edmonton city commissioners paid a visit to WEC on February 17th 1945, and commented that "public reaction is excellent, in fact the new coaches are something that the people are inclined to brag about.... The public prefers trolley buses to all other forms of transportation." [282]

WEC did consider operating the remaining streetcar routes with PCC streetcars, but decided the success of the trolley coach routes made a conversion of those car lines a sensible choice instead. In fact, Winnipeg was often highlighted in articles and advertising promoting trolley coaches. The *Vancouver News-Herald*, in May 1943, ran a picture/caption article, a 1946 Imperial Oil bulletin on Lubrication of Trolley Buses illustrated a Winnipeg Mack bus, the September 1946 issue of *Canadian Transportation* covering the Canadian Transit Association meeting in Winnipeg pictured Winnipeg trolleys, and Canadian General Electric also featured Winnipeg coaches in a 1945 advertisement.[283]

By 1946, Canadian Car & Foundry in Fort William was starting to produce the Brill trolley bus, and WEC saw these superior to American coaches as they included typical Canadian modifications such as extra insulation, bigger heaters and more weather-resistant windows and doors. Thirteen T-44 coaches were ordered and delivered in April 1947. On July 2nd, trolley coaches replaced motor buses on ELLICE, and on November 17th, the same happened for McGREGOR. To relieve traffic problems in the downtown area, construction of a loop was started on Vaughan from Isbister Place to Graham, along it to Smith, then along Smith to connect with the wire at Portage Avenue. More coaches were delivered: six in January 1948, one in February, and nine in March. These were for the former STAFFORD and ACADEMY ROAD car lines, and on May 9th trolley coaches took over those two routes. Completion of the downtown loop saw wire run on Kennedy from Ellice to Graham, on Notre Dame and Fort from Ellice to Graham and completing it on Graham from Fort to Smith. Routes were rationalized: SARGENT was combined with STAFFORD–ACADEMY, while SALTER coaches were taken off Ellice and routed on Graham.

More trolley coaches rolled into the WEC shops; two in October and another pair in December. Streetcars had disappeared from the CORYDON line June 20th 1948, with motor buses temporarily replacing them while overhead was strung and the roads re-paved. On September 10th 1949, the new coaches started operating on CORYDON. With the addition of the CORYDON route to several others already using Graham, this placed a strain on that street, and subsequently that year a few trolley coach routes were moved over to Portage, necessitating some additional overhead. December 1949 saw the arrival of ten CCF-Brill T-48 coaches with their larger capacity and double-loading front doors.

Winnipeg is noted for its nasty winter weather, but the 1950 one was especially severe. Record snowfall and extreme temperatures tested the transit system to its fullest, with the trolley coaches having to cope with the most arctic of conditions. The cold snapped overhead and on occasion broke poles; snow and high winds made life generally miserable. As if that weren't enough, the second week of April brought a sudden spring, with temperatures into the 30s Fahrenheit and a repeat of the infamous flooding of the Red and Assiniboine rivers experienced in 1948. The Maryland Bridge over the Assiniboine carried three trolley bus routes, and it was sandbagged to stop the river from encroaching onto the roadway – but to no avail. By early May, service was abandoned over the bridge.

It got worse, though. The Main carhouse was close to the Main Street Bridge – also spanning the Assiniboine. It became apparent that it too would lose the battle with the river, so all materials and coaches were withdrawn to St. Mary Avenue just one day before the water inundated the carhouse site to a depth of two feet. Nevertheless, equipment maintenance had to continue, carried out on St. Mary Avenue in the open, and under less than ideal weather conditions. The damage to the car barns was even more devastating. Mud covered everything, electrical wiring had to be completely replaced, and inspection pits

Above: Built like a tank! Brill 1608 on the Sargent route passes a Sherman M4A2 tank – advertising the new James Mason movie at the Garrick movie theatre – southbound on Garry Street, while the bus in the background turns right from eastbound Ellice Avenue onto Garry, November 6th 1951.
(OHIO BRASS COLLECTION, THE STRAHORN LIBRARY, ILLINOIS RAILWAY MUSEUM. LOCATION INFORMATION – MARK WALTON AND DAVE WYATT)

pumped. Finally, by the end of May, life, for trolley coaches at least, returned to normal.

OSBORNE streetcars were discontinued in June 1948 and, after wire was strung, trolley coaches took over July 31st. In November 1950, trolleys succeeded trams on SELKIRK. To service these changes, three orders were placed for T-48As; seven in October, twenty-one in November and a final two in December. Some routes were combined, others split to make the most of the new arrivals.

An interesting sidelight was the introduction of a public address system on Winnipeg trolley coaches in January of 1951. This was a first for Canadian urban transit vehicles and was installed on all 134 trolley coaches. It was designed to "produce volume and clarity when the operator is calling the names of streets and transfer points and giving other necessary directions to transit riders." This was thought to be an added inducement to ride the trolley coaches, and was publicized with pamphlets and bus notices. It also alleviated the perennial problem of standees bunching at the front, leaving empty seats at the rear, as passengers "cannot fail to heed the quiet yet completely audible voice above them urging them to 'move along please.' This should cause rejoicing among those who have been left out in the cold because the centre aisle of a trolley bus is blocked." [284]

Change was still in the air in 1952 as trolley buses took over the ST. MARY's route on November 30th, but by far

Below: Mack 1526 is a bit patched and rusted, but still ready for a hard day's work. This unit was in the second Mack order of 1939 and posed June 12th 1954.
(EDMONTON RADIAL RAILWAY SOCIETY, FONDS LESLIE CORNESS)

Above: Greater Winnipeg Transit Commission Brill coach 1600 advertises the virtues of taking public transit on June 9th 1954. The venerable Brill trolley coaches still had another sixteen years of useful life ahead.
(EDMONTON RADIAL RAILWAY SOCIETY, FONDS LESLIE CORNESS)

Below: Two coaches, no waiting. June of 1964 and the Brills are showing their age as they wait in the loop at the south end of the Osborne route at Wavell. While the front coach is a Canadian product, the rear one is a US-made ACF-Brill. Today this is an empty lot on Wavell Avenue at Montgomery Street. The loop was probably removed when Osborne Street was rebuilt to accommodate the approaches to the new St. Vital Bridge which opened October 24th 1965, and also when Montgomery Street was built. The gentleman supporting the telephone post isn't catching a bus; he too is photographing the coaches and is the travelling companion of the photographer.
(G.M. ANDERSEN PHOTO, KRAMBLES-PETERSON ARCHIVE.
LOCATION IDENTIFICATION – DAVID WYATT.)

the biggest change occurred on May 29th 1953, as private operation of Winnipeg's transit system ceased and it became The Greater Winnipeg Transit Commission, chaired by the former president of the Winnipeg Electric Company. This came about because the WEC did not want to operate the transit system any longer, so a referendum was conducted in March 1953, with only the electorate in the city proper eligible to vote. The citizens approved the takeover, and with this public ownership came ambitious plans to even further modernize the system, extending trolley coach routes and converting streetcar lines. This was realized the next year, with numerous wire-stringing of trolley coach extensions, and the abandonment and conversion of the EAST KILDONAN streetcar line December 5th 1954. All of this activity necessitated a dedicated facility for the trolley buses, so, in February 1955, a new garage at Main and Carruthers was opened. More extensions followed and it soon became apparent that still more buses were needed. Unfortunately, by 1956, no new trolley coaches were being manufactured either in Canada or the United States. Can Car in Thunder Bay had ended production with a delivery of T-48s to Edmonton in 1954, and Marmon-Herrington essentially ceased manufacturing of trolley coaches in 1955. No one would commence production for an order of less than 150 units! However, used coaches were plentiful as various properties in both countries grew weary of the trolley coach and were dieselizing on the excuse of desiring one standard form of public transportation. Winnipeg profited with the purchase of eighteen Pullman 44CX units from Providence, RI, and ten ACF-Brill T-46s from Flint, MI. These arrived in late 1956 and were found to be relatively new; the Pullmans were eight years old and the ACF-Brills five. Still, the Commission rebuilt them extensively, and with their introduction into the fleet the total number of trolley coaches stood at 162.

Trolley coach extensions had necessitated purchasing more vehicles, and now the new buses made more extensions possible in 1957. The future looked rosy for the trolley coach, yet, on May 15th 1960, the SARGENT route, the first one put into service in 1938, was dieselized. The advent of the Disraeli Expressway spelled the end of trolley buses to EAST KILDONAN May 16th of 1960, and with these two route abandonments, the Mack buses went first into storage, and then to scrapping. However, the overhead was salvaged and used for extensions, along with route modifications.

The provincial government introduced a Greater Winnipeg Area Administration Act in 1960, changing the Commission into a Transit Department of the Metropolitan Corporation of Greater Winnipeg, commonly called Metro Transit. While trolley coaches continued to serve Winnipeg riders, this was an opportunity for the system to be evaluated. Overhead clutter was cited as a detriment to downtown upgrading, along with the non-availability of new coaches and the aging of the fleet. Projections for expanded operation of the transit system, plus the cost of electricity were cited against continuing to extend trolley coach operation. Curiously, since power was purchased on a flat rate system, the cost per coach was the same no matter how many coaches ran. One might think this was a plus, but as coaches aged and fewer ran, the cost per coach rose, again cited as a mitigating factor against the trolley bus. This led to the inevitable conclusion to convert trolley coach routes to diesel as circumstances would allow over the next few years. Still, Metro extended SALTER to Southhall Drive on November 15th 1964. Counter to that, however, bridge construction across the Red River led to the end of trolley coach service on OSBORNE October 24th of that year.

During the 1960s, while Metro Winnipeg Transit was reducing the trolley bus fleet, Winnipeg City Council asked

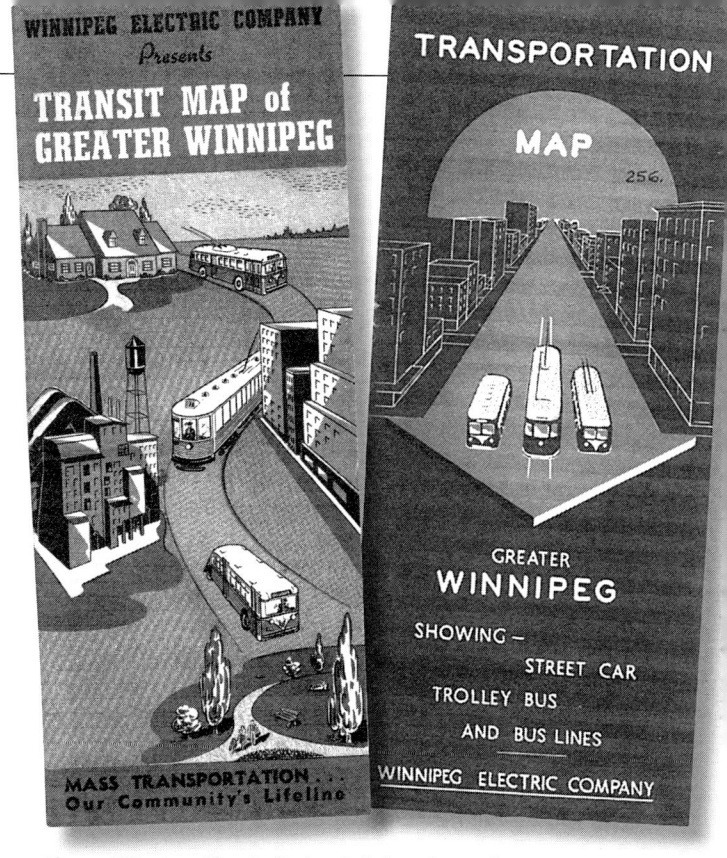

Above: Winnipeg Electric displayed all three forms of public transit vehicles on these 1940s transit maps. The right one is dated July 1st 1940; the left one has a message inside from President W.H. Carter who took over in 1940. (WALLY YOUNG COLLECTION)

Metro to stop the phase-out. City Council was unanimous in urging Metro to wait until the Manitoba Clean Environment Commission prepared a report on pollution for the provincial government. Council hoped the Commission would do something about diesel buses which "contribute materially to air pollution". They also referred to the 1969 contract from the TTC for Western Flyer Coach of Fort Garry to rebuild Toronto's trolley coaches – right in Metro's back yard, so to speak. Mayor Juba expressed surprise that Metro claimed it had to phase out the trolley coaches, then sold fifteen of them to Edmonton for $1000 for parts and replaced them with $25,000 diesels. Metro ignored these concerns.[285]

If the winter of 1950 was bad, that of 1965-66 was worse. A major blizzard on Friday, March 4th blocked streets, and trolley coaches began to stall. Winds up to 68 MPH added to the toll, and by 11 AM all bus operations ceased and the vehicles were recalled where possible. The storm was so intense, drivers could not be rescued from their stranded trolley coaches, so power was kept on to at least provide heat and light – if they could keep the poles on the wires. It took the remainder of the weekend to tow units in, then clean and dry them out for Monday service.

Some wire was removed, but the fleet stayed stable throughout Centennial Year and 1968. The following year saw two routes converted to diesel, NOTRE DAME (January 18th) and ACADEMY (April 19th), and the ACF-Brill buses scrapped. By 1969, weekend service was diesel, thus sav-

TIRES AND WIRES

WHY YOU PROFIT MOST WITH THE TROLLEY COACH

[1945 General Electric advertisement]

CANADIAN GENERAL ELECTRIC CO. LIMITED

Above: This 1945 General Electric advertisement, though missing a little at the fold, featured a Winnipeg Mack trolley coach equipped of course, with GE motors and controllers.
(PROVINCIAL ARCHIVES OF ALBERTA, SCHWARZKOPF COLLECTION)

ing money by closing the power substation and not having wire crews on hand. More construction, this time on the Salter Street Viaduct, provided an excuse to remove wire, dieselize two routes – SALTER and McGREGOR April 19th, and also parts of two others – STAFFORD April 19th and ELLICE July 6th. Routes were adjusted, surplus coaches sold to Edmonton, and all buses moved to Carruthers garage. Another route, ST. MARY'S was withdrawn on July 6th. Then the final blow was delivered in the fall of 1970.

The agreement for power with Winnipeg Hydro expired at the end of October 1970. By now, trolley coaches only operated weekdays, and sufficient diesels were available to replace them permanently, so it was determined that trolley coach service was to be terminated Friday, October 30th, one day ahead of the expiration of the power agreement.

A last run was planned, with coach 1768 cleaned up and run as a free trip. It was so well received that another coach was added, No. 1774, which also conveyed appreciative riders. John Baker recounts in *Winnipeg's Electric Transit* riding the last revenue trip, and the final power cut. For the first time in 63 years, no 600-volt DC power was being sent over trolley wires into Winnipeg's streets – not

Above: The one, the only. Homegrown trolley coach 1532, the only modern pre-WWII Canadian coach built (by MCI) sits in the sun at the Winnipeg Electric coach yard.
(DAVE'S RAILPIX)

for the late lamented streetcars nor for their successors, the trolley coaches. An era of electric transit in the prairie gateway city had ended – an inglorious footnote to Manitoba's centennial as a province.

A faint glimmer of hope was raised in 1976, when Manitoba's provincial NDP government, under Premier Ed Schreyer, agreed to aid Winnipeg City Council in investigating the possibility of reintroducing trolley coaches in the interest of promoting the use of electricity versus the rising cost of diesel fuel. It was pointed out – again

— that Flyer Industries, then owned by the Manitoba Development Corp. and the only trolley bus manufacturer in North America, was located in Winnipeg.[286] But it was just that, a glimmer that died, just as the original trolley coaches had that October day six years before.[287]

Footnotes:

274. Wilson, Bunnell, & Borgstrom, Limited, Consulting Engineers report, March 4, 1931 Volume I, p. 29 –Provincial Archives of Alberta file 75-11.
275. *Ibid.* p. 53.
276. "The Place of the Trolley Coach in Urban Transportation" Canadian Transit Association symposium, June 12, 1946 p. 10.
277. "Winnipeg Electric Co. Report on 1939 Operations" *Canadian Transportation*, September 1940 – Provincial Archives of Alberta file 75-11.
278. Transit Map of Greater Winnipeg, Winnipeg Electric Company, January 1, 1942 W. Young collection.
279. *Canadian Transportation*, "Trolley Coaches in Winnipeg" no date, assumed to be late 1943 or early 1944.
280. *Canadian Transportation*, June 1957 p. 77.
281. *Canadian Transportation*, July 1942.
282. Edmonton City Archives, City Commissioners files A73-52 Box 151, 1945.
283. All materials quoted are from the collection of the author.
284. *Canadian Transportation*, June 1951 pp. 333-334.
285. http://uwto.org/trib/transit_1969keeptrolleybuses.html and *The Winnipeg Tribune*, December 2, 1969.
286. *Transit Canada*, Vol. XII #2 May-June 1976.
287. Except where otherwise footnoted, information in this chapter is drawn from: Baker *Winnipeg's Electric Transit* Chapter 9.

Above: The name has changed to Greater Winnipeg Transit Commission, but it's the same old Mack trolley coach. Part of the original 1938 order, unit 1502 sits off-wire with a 1947 Brill No. 1650 peeking out behind. Note the early form of side advertising.
(EDMONTON RADIAL RAILWAY SOCIETY, FONDS LESLIE CORNESS)

Below: Winnipeg Electric Mack coaches 1534 and 1518 sit with fellow Macks on a fall day at the Main Carhouse. The iconic Fort Garry Hotel is in the background.
(EDMONTON RADIAL RAILWAY SOCIETY, FONDS LESLIE CORNESS)

Winnipeg, October 30th 1970: Last Trolley Bus

ADDENDUM: Mark Walton, Editor, Transit News Canada from 1982-1990 recounts his teen years with Winnipeg trolley buses and specifically the official last run. Although it duplicates a little of the main text, it is included here in its entirety as an exclusive recollection for this book.

I lived in Winnipeg from March 17th 1967 to August 24th 1973. When my family arrived there, most of the trolley bus routes were still operating, and so were most of the vehicles. Only the pre-war and World War II era Macks and Pullmans, and the single MCI prototype No. 1532, had been retired and scrapped. All the CCF-Brills were still in service, plus the last eighteen Pullmans (ex-Providence, Rhode Island), and the ten ACF-Brill T-46s (I much later dubbed those "Cosmopolitans", because they served in all three North American countries. They were built for Flint, Michigan; Winnipeg later sold all but one of them to Mexico City). During my first three years there, things changed quickly, and not for the better.

Through 1967 and 1968, word was around that trolley buses were on their way out. In late 1968 and early 1969, the then-Metro Transit received its first 65 Western Flyer D700 diesel buses, after a year-long trial with prototype No. 700 (later 666). Those were soon followed by eighty D700As, then still more (around 240 by 1973). Their stated purpose was to replace the trolley buses; replace them they did.

Weekend trolley bus service was discontinued in February 1969, and weekday evening service in July 1970. In a series of major route changes in April 1969, the trolley bus system was reduced to only two routes: Corydon-North Main and Ellice–St. Mary's. The latter went diesel in July 1969, leaving only Corydon-North Main running for the last sixteen months. The fleet was reduced to the ten T-48s and thirty T-48As, fleet numbers 1728-1806 even, built in 1949 and 1950. In the fall of 1969, there was a political controversy over the phase-out of trolley buses. A good part of it was over Western Flyer's recently-won contract to build 150 new trolley bus shells for Toronto, so why would Winnipeg not be doing the same? Metro Transit's power agreement with Winnipeg Hydro expired October 31st 1970, a Saturday; so Friday, October 30th was the last day of trolley bus operation.

That day, nationally, Canada was still in the grip of the FLQ kidnap-murder crisis in Montreal, with the War Measures Act in force across Canada. Manitoba had just celebrated its Centennial as a province, and I was in Grade 11 at Kelvin High School, and had turned 16 just four days earlier. At about 6:30 PM, I hopped a Flyer diesel at Kenaston Loop, headed for Corydon and Osborne, where I would board the duly identified "Last Trolley Bus". I was not interested in any substitutes. Near River Heights Library at Brock Street, my bus passed westbound trolley bus No. 1752. The driver asked me: "Why don't you take that one, that's a trolley bus?" I told him: "It's not the last trolley bus! That one will have a big lighted sign on it saying so!"

At Corydon and Osborne, a sizable crowd was waiting, including a pair of mechanics with their service truck that carried an extra pair of trolley poles on the outside; and a couple whose first date had been riding the last streetcar fifteen years earlier (September 19th, 1955). The temperature was just under 3°C, with wind from the north at 30 km/h, for a wind chill of -3°C. After a while, No. 1752 turned north from Corydon onto Osborne; it was the last trolley bus in regular revenue service. Unknown to me at the time, John E. Baker was aboard; in 1982 he wrote the book *Winnipeg's Electric Transit* in which he recounted the trip, and much of the detailed history. Sadly, I never met John; he died in 2000.

About five minutes later came the moment I was waiting for: I saw the lights of one, then two, tow trucks emerging from the railway underpass just south of Corydon. The first one was towing 1774, shanghaied almost at the last minute to be the Last Trolley Bus Section 1. Right behind came the second truck with 1768, the Last Trolley Bus, with the illuminated sign on the front, as promised (there was no time to make another one for 1774; so it had a paper sign). Both had been towed from the Fort Rouge Transit Base, opened only the year before (also in fall 1969, the old Main Carhouse at Main and Assiniboine which had housed trolley coaches was demolished to make way for Bonnycastle Park). There were no trolley wires on Osborne south of Corydon, so both buses had to be towed to the overhead at Corydon.

The minute the tow trucks stopped, the waiting mechanics raised the trolley poles to the wires. On contact, the inside lights went on, the illuminated sign on the front of 1768 lit up, and the air compressors started pumping up enough air pressure to open the doors. While the tow trucks were uncoupled and driven away, people lined up to board; I of course headed straight for 1768. The driver was an old-timer wearing cap badge Number 12; he held his hand over the farebox, announcing that the trip was free. I sat near the front, beside a supervisor named Marshall. On the rear bench seat sat Transit brass, including General Manager Roy Church. While both 1774 and 1768 carried a lot of people, getting on and off all along the route, the actual run was ironically uneventful – not even a dewirement to mar the occasion. The route was north on Osborne and Memorial Blvd., east along Portage, then north on Main to Carruthers (North Main) Garage. As we neared the garage, Roy Church came to the front of the bus. He made a short speech saying there were "misconceptions" about the end of trolley bus service, particularly in relation to air pollution, then becoming as hot a topic as it is today.

Eventually No. 1768 turned off Main onto Carruthers, where Mr. Church and other brass posed in front of No. 1768 for some pictures. I stayed inside with the driver; both of us are clearly shown inside the picture, which appeared in Transit's Public Service News flyer about a month later. A D700A was waiting in front of the garage to take people back downtown; I ignored it and hung around for a while longer. After I got off, 1768 pulled away under its own power for the last time, around the yard at the back of the garage. After a while, I looked inside the garage, and saw a tractor pushing 1768, with its poles now hooked down, into a parking bay. I had heard about a group that went down to Winnipeg Hydro's Mill Street Substation to watch the power being killed for the last time. I was not part of that group, but John Baker was; he described it in his book.

Above: In the dying days of trolley coach operation in Winnipeg, June 1970, Brill No. 1742 takes a time out at "Confusion Corner". This (in)famous crossing was where McMillan Avenue, Donald Street, Corydon Avenue, Osborne Street, and Pembina Highway all converged, and where coaches took a time point for their departure times. (BILL LINLEY. LOCATION INFORMATION – MARK WALTON)

Below: It's June of 1970 at Confusion Corner. Unit 1802 looks ready to retire and hand over the duties to that upstart Flyer diesel tailing him. (BILL LINLEY)

Above: Regina trolley coach 100 signed for 13ᵀᴴ AVE. WEST is turning from a westbound trip along 11th Avenue south onto Albert Street, September 11th 1947.
(OHIO BRASS COLLECTION, THE STRAHORN LIBRARY, ILLINOIS RAILWAY MUSEUM. LOCATION INFORMATION – COLIN HATCHER)

Below: Coach 102 signed for BROAD NORTH is turning from an eastbound trip along 11th Avenue north onto Broad Street on September 11th 1947.
(OHIO BRASS COLLECTION, THE STRAHORN LIBRARY, ILLINOIS RAILWAY MUSEUM. LOCATION INFORMATION – COLIN HATCHER)

Regina (1947-1966)
Regina Municipal Railway / Regina Transit System

While Regina entered the trolley coach era literally in a baptism of fire, it had the dubious distinction of being the first in Canada to exit.

At the end of the Second World War, Regina, like many other cities, was faced with the growing problem of an aging street railway system and a growing population. City Council had formed a Post War Reconstruction Committee, and, as part of its mandate, a plan was produced for the Regina Municipal Railway.

This plan, unveiled on September 18th 1944, called for the complete abandonment of the streetcar system and its replacement with trolley coaches. Like many other properties, not only was the rolling stock worn out (which could have been replaced with the PCC car), but the track was also. The trolley coach also had the appeal of being easier to maintain using the same shops as the trams. Gasoline buses, with their limited passenger capacity, were suitable only for feeder routes and would have required new shops.

Like many municipalities, the report took some time to be accepted and come to fruition. Through 1946, the streetcars trudged along, becoming more and more shabby, but staying in safe condition thanks to diligent maintenance. Ten trolley coaches were ordered from CCF in Fort William and were due to arrive in the fall of 1947, taking some of the strain off the remaining streetcar fleet.

P. G. McAra assumed the post of Superintendent in 1947, and was immediately faced with the conversion of the streetcar system to rubber tires. Ten more coaches were ordered, and ROUTE 3 (BLUE LINE) was partially abandoned August 4th 1947, with gasoline buses providing an interim service while streetcar overhead was removed and trolley bus wire strung. Trolley coaches commenced operating September 6th on the portion from the Edward Street loop to Albert Street, and then north to the car barn loop, taking over all of ROUTE 3 later that month.

ROUTE 2 was next when, almost a year later (August 8th 1948), that tram route fell silent – again in stages – until September, when rubber tires and overhead dual wires replaced the aging streetcars. With two lines now fully converted to trolley coaches, the remaining tram lines could be better serviced by the remaining streetcar fleet, allowing an orderly replacement over the next few years.

Then disaster struck. On the morning of January 23rd 1949, a fire broke out at the Regina car shop. It was the worst of times since Sunday morning service meant that few transit vehicles were out and a minimal crew was in the shop. Bitter temperatures and winds didn't help. When it was over, seventeen of the 23 trolley coaches, including the first coach No. 109, were destroyed, along with nine gasoline buses and nine streetcars. Three of the trolley buses were brand new, never having run in revenue service, still stored awaiting conversion of routes 4 and 5, scheduled for later that year.

But Regina is resilient. Service was re-jigged, buses rented from other entities, and the remaining streetcars concentrated on ROUTE 1. Rush orders were placed with Can Car, and other cities in Canada willingly gave up their place in the production run. Trolley coaches began to arrive within days from Fort William so that the two routes could be run with a reasonable service.

A previous order for ten trolley coaches had been placed, and this too speeded up deliveries. It also helped that the surviving trolley coaches were relatively new, and could be pressed into longer service schedules without needing heavy maintenance. Still, the streetcars gamely pressed on, being serviced outdoors in biting cold, and breaking down with no replacement parts available. The tram system was by necessity cut back, and to add to the streetcar's diminishing role, the entire operation was re-named Regina Transit System on September 5th 1950. Four days later the last tram ran, and the 38 trolley coaches (thirty T-44s and eight T-48s) along with sixteen gasoline buses ruled in Regina,[288] the "Home of the Mounties"*.

The trolley coaches ran on essentially the same routes as did the streetcars – four lines running spoke-like from the city centre to the four corners of Regina.[289] These were ROUTE 1 DEWDNEY WEST–COLLEGE AVENUE EAST, ROUTE 2 PARLIAMENT BUILDING–EASTVIEW/WINNIPEG NORTH, ROUTE 3 13TH AVE. WEST/BROAD NORTH, and ROUTE 4 PASQUA NORTH–VICTORIA EAST. Some extensions to this basic system occurred. The PARLIAMENT BUILDINGS terminal was extended south on Albert Street to 25th Avenue, west along 25th Avenue to Argyle Road, north to Hill Avenue and east back out to Albert Street. At that time, the south leg of the route became known as ALBERT SOUTH. Curiously, a year or two before that line was abandoned, it had been extended further south on Albert Street to Parliament Avenue, west to Retallack Street and north to 25th Avenue, where it joined the existing wire, then continued north on Argyle Road. In 1954, Regina ordered a fleet of new GM diesel buses allowing it to establish some new routes, among them the BROADWAY EAST/4TH AVENUE WEST line. That alteration in routes resulted in the COLLEGE AVENUE EAST trolley coach leg being extended east to College Avenue and Abbott Road. It also resulted in the

---
*The Training Depot for new recruits of the Royal Canadian Mounted Police is located in Regina, hence the unofficial moniker "Home of the Mounties".

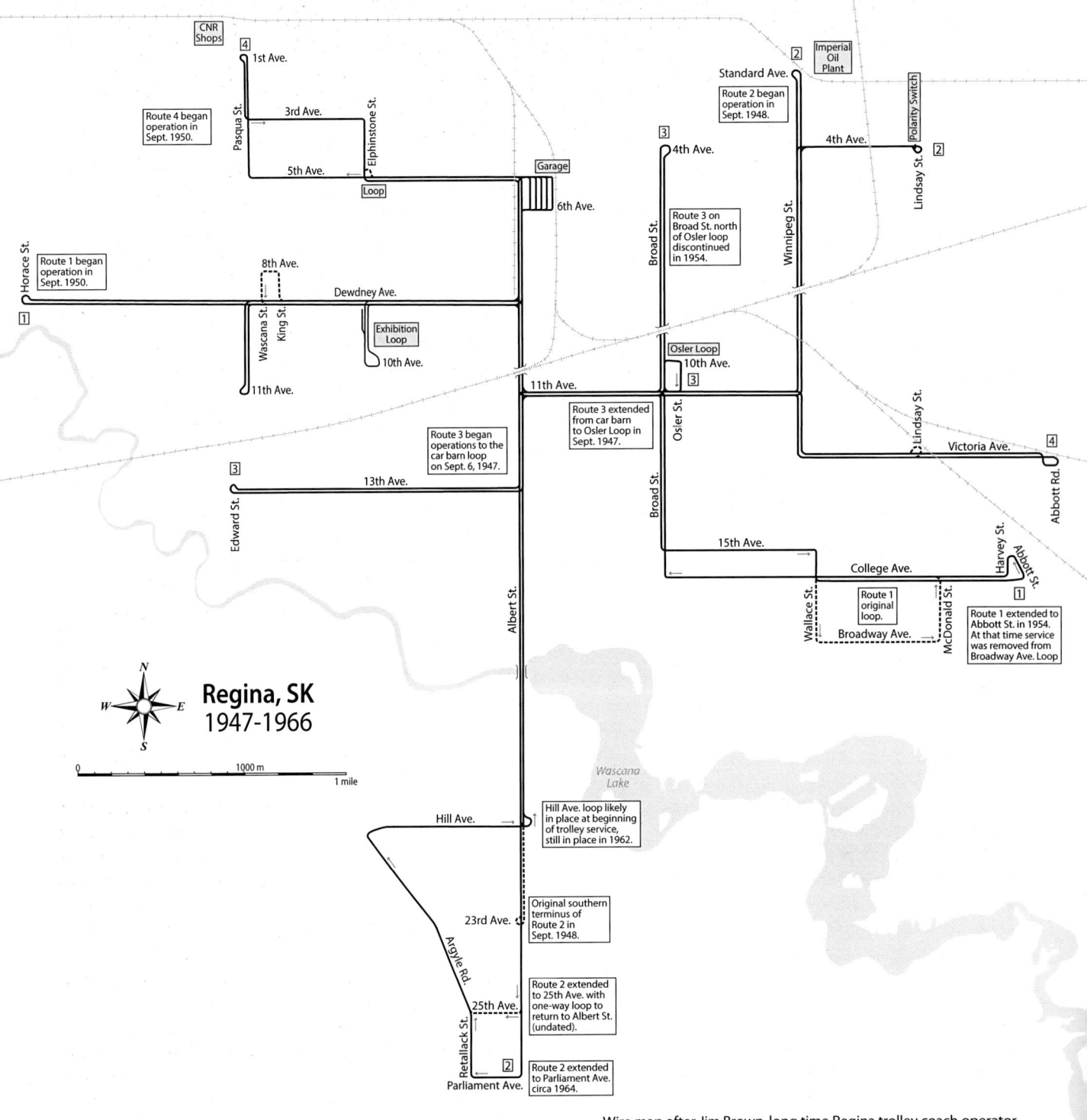

abandonment of trolley coach service on the Broad North leg. The 13TH AVE. WEST trolley coaches travelled into the downtown area, turning back on a loop via a left turn off 11th Avenue onto Broad Street, a right onto 10th Avenue, then south onto Osler Street, and then west again onto 11th Avenue. At the end of 1954, the system's 38 coaches operated on sixteen miles of one-way route, totalling 1,314,470 coach miles and carrying 12,100,929 revenue passengers.[290] An oddity was that Regina had centre pole construction for the streetcar overhead on many streets, and found that the existing bracket arms could not accommodate the negative (return) wire for trolley coaches on the curb side of the arm while maintaining the positive wire in its place for streetcar running. The solution was to put the negative wire on the inside of the positive and reverse the polarity of the trolley motors in that section, using the operator's reversing switch (effectively an electrical reverse gear) in the coach. Care had to be taken where the polarity on the overhead reversed, to avoid damage to the traction motor.[291]

In those early years, Regina used an old gasoline bus that had poles mounted on the roof to travel the lines

128

Above: Two coaches, no waiting? Regina Municipal Railway 128 is signed PARL'M'T BLDGS while 137 says PASQUA NORTH. Both are stopped on 11th Avenue between Rose and Hamilton Streets.
(EDMONTON RADIAL RAILWAY SOCIETY, FONDS LESLIE CORNESS)

Right: It's fuzzy, the result of a hand-held camera in a dark garage, but this may be the only record of Regina's unique trolley wire de-icing (motor) bus.
(EDMONTON RADIAL RAILWAY SOCIETY, FONDS LESLIE CORNESS)

after a frosty night to clear the hoar frost off the lines before regular service began.[292]

Little else changed, even as the system celebrated its Golden Jubilee in 1961. By then, diesel buses had taken over from gasoline ones, but the trolley coaches soldiered on. In that year, the Regina system had nine basic routes with #1 through #4 the only trolley coach lines. An editorial in *The Leader-Post* complimented the " … considerate, kindly bus and trolley drivers … " and commented that "whether or not the city should switch entirely in the next few months, or years, from trolleys to diesels, one thing is certain, the Regina transit system … is capable of continuing to do a maximum fine job … ".[293]

In February 1962, Council recommended that a transit survey be undertaken by a consultant. The trolley coaches had between 400,000 and 450,000 miles on them, the electrical substations dated from 1911 and 1947, a legacy from the streetcar days, and much of the infrastructure – poles and feeder wires – had deteriorated. In fact, in March of that year, one of the vacuum power convertors blew and another lost vacuum, resulting in a power loss that necessitated a temporary electric fleet reduction with substitution by motor buses.[294] The survey must have spelled the death knell for the trolleys, for Regina, like other Canadian cities at that time, had few options. No transit supplier was making trolley coaches, and though the trolley's electrics could be rewound and refurbished, after nearly twenty years of service, the coachwork and frames were certainly at a point where they needed serious remediation, at a cost probably nearing that of a new (motor) bus. A 1964 article in *The Leader-Post* cited RTS' report to Council, noting that "During September, the city's aging trolley buses continue to be replaced." In fact, the #2 route was temporarily assigned motor buses, with a view to making the change permanent later in the fall.[295]

By August 1965, the news stated that conversion to diesel buses would be completed by March of the next year. In fact, only three lines were left under trolleys, and ROUTE 1 DEWDNEY WEST–COLLEGE AVE. EAST line was slated for dieselization that October. That would have left only ROUTE 3 – 13TH AVENUE WEST and ROUTE 5 – PASQUA NORTH–VICTORIA EAST operating.

Of the original 38 coaches, only 19 remained.[296] There were some route changes in November of that year to allow for a possible closing of the Alberta Street subway. There also was a contingency plan to dieselize the PASQUA NORTH route in such an eventuality, but despite the earlier report, all three routes continued to operate as trolley coach lines right up to the end.[297]

As it was, trolley coach service continued just into March, as the last revenue service day for trolley coaches in Regina was Saturday March 5th 1966.[298] Assistant

129

WINNIPEG NORTH
REGINA MUNICIPAL RAILWAY
142

WINNIPEG NORTH
REGINA MUNICIPAL RAILWAY
143

Esther's
REGINA MUNICIPAL RAILWAY
146
146

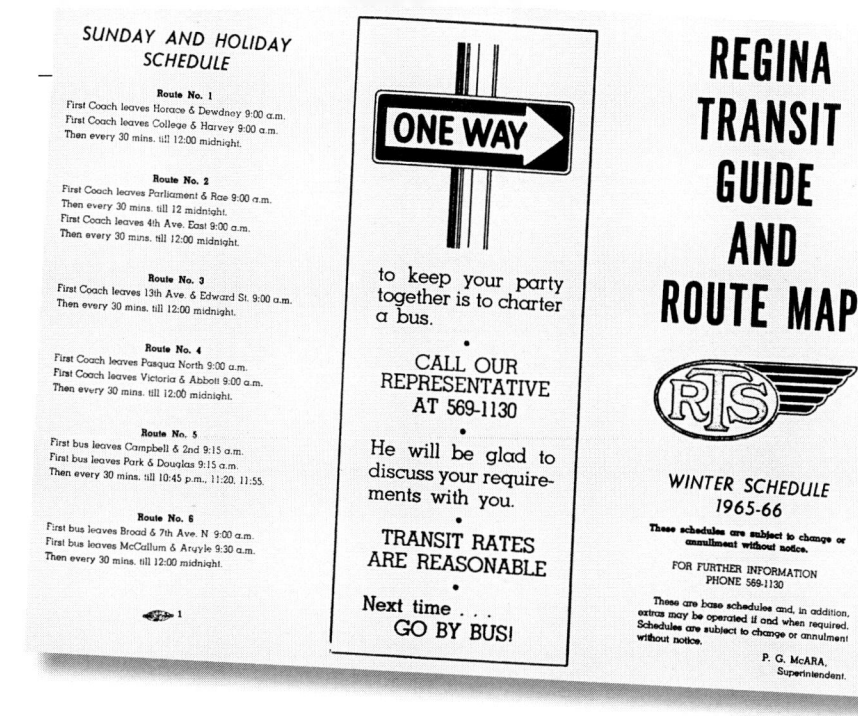

Left: This 1965-66 public timetable differentiated between (trolley) coaches and (motor) buses in the Sunday and Holiday schedule to the left. (COLIN HATCHER COLLECTION)

gural streetcars in Regina 55 years before.[300]

The coaches proceeded directly back to the garage where the official reception took place. At that ceremony, Mayor Henry Baker commented that Regina was the first in Canada to complete conversion from trolleys to diesels. He elaborated on the high cost of electricity compared with diesel fuel, discontinuance of coach manufacture, parts unavailability, and the versatility of diesels over trolleys.[301]

General Manager Wally Atkinson felt that a suitable ceremony was in order to officially retire the trolleys, and approached Council. Monday March 7th was fixed as the date, and the power kept on.

The final official last run operated with three trolley coaches numbers 135, 150 operated by Jim Brown, whose father was an early motorman on the streetcars, and 130 running in that order. The other two operators were L. Lucyk and G. H. McAdoo. Trolley coach 130 was the only one decked out in "last run" livery, with those words across the front and tears painted under the "eyes" headlamps. Upon leaving the garage, they travelled in convoy south on Albert Street, west on 11th Avenue to Broad Street where they turned on the downtown loop via Broad Street, 10th Avenue and Osler Street to 11th Avenue again proceeding eastbound past City Hall (then located between Rose and Hamilton streets). They stopped immediately east of Scarth Street where they picked up the invited guests and Mr. John Johnson, who was the first fare-paying passenger on a trolleybus in Regina when the system opened.[299] Then General Manager P. G. McAra slid into the driver's seat, many thought for a photo op. However, to the surprise of the invited guests, McAra took the controls, and drove the coach on its final run. It was fitting he did that, since his father had operated one of the inau-

Ten of the better trolleys were sold to Edmonton, ostensibly for parts, but were instead put into service there, replacing the more ancient Pullmans.[302] Unit 130 – the last-run coach – was saved and stored, but later scrapped. Two additional coaches were saved: No. 147, to be part of the Regina Transit collection, and No. 154.

While being the first to scrap their trolley buses might not be something to brag about today, Regina was proud of having achieved a "modern" transit system, but the trolleys were not entirely forgotten. In a reminiscing article, Fred Otway Sr., who had helped start streetcar service by stringing overhead, and had watched with anticipation the maiden voyage of the trolley buses (for which he had again strung overhead) said that "he believes that there will never be another piece of transportation equipment like the trolley coach. 'They were silent, fast, smokeless and odourless, and warm in winter.' But he agreed the city had no choice in the matter because of costs and the vanishing supply of parts."[303] Prophetic words heard many times in many cities, for many years after the first abandonment of a trolley coach system in post-war Canada.

Opposite Top: Regina Brill 142 signed WINNIPEG NORTH makes light work of the snow-covered streets.
(EDMONTON RADIAL RAILWAY SOCIETY, FONDS LESLIE CORNESS)

Opposite Middle: Clean, warm and ready to go, Regina Municipal Railway coach 143's operator is readying his paperwork before setting out on the WINNIPEG NORTH route.
(EDMONTON RADIAL RAILWAY SOCIETY, FONDS LESLIE CORNESS)

Opposite Bottom: Making its turn off 11th Avenue onto Albert Street South, coach 146 is signed 13TH AVE. WEST on Route 3. Judging from the cars parked, this was taken in either 1947 or 1948, before the fire of January 1949.
(EDMONTON RADIAL RAILWAY SOCIETY, FONDS LESLIE CORNESS)

Footnotes:

288. Hatcher, Colin, *Saskatchewan's Pioneer Streetcars*.
289. *Bus and Truck Transport*, May, 1951 p. 37.
290. *Canadian Transportation*, June 1955 pp. 338-9.
291. CAT Proceedings June, 1948 p. 92.
292. Hatcher, Colin, personal e-mail to author, October 10, 2012.
293. *The Leader-Post*, Regina, August 3, 1961.
294. *Ibid.* March 13, 1962.
295. *Ibid.* no date probably 1964 (Hatcher collection).
296. *Ibid.* August 13, 1965.
297. Hatcher, Colin, personal correspondence to author, September 2010.
298. Hatcher, Colin, personal email to author, January 6, 2013.
299. *Ibid.*
300. *The Leader-Post*, Regina, March 7, 1966.
301. *Ibid.*
302. Hatcher, October 10, 2012 *op. cit.*
303. *The Leader-Post*, Regina, April 2, 1966.

Above: Coach 134 on ROUTE 4 navigates a half grand union interchange turning from its southbound run on Albert Street eastbound into 11th Avenue. Trolley coach 125 on ROUTE 1 is parked facing northbound on Albert Street having just turned off 11th Avenue. (COLIN K. HATCHER)

Regina Transit System Trolley Coach Destination Curtains

13TH AVE. WEST
PASQUA NORTH
DEWDNEY WEST
EXHIBITION
CAR HOUSE
BROAD & 11TH
VICTORIA EAST
COLLEGE AVE. E.
EASTVIEW
ALBERT SOUTH
BROAD NORTH
PARL'M'T BLDGS
WINNIPEG NORTH
STADIUM
5TH & ELPHINSTONE
COLLEGE & WALLACE
ALBERT & 11TH

Coach 148
EXHIBITION GRDS
Coaches 147 and 149
COLLEGE AVE. EAST

Above: These destinations, taken by Colin Hatcher from his photographs, are what would have appeared on Regina trolley coach rollsigns, but not by any means in the order they appeared on the curtain.

Above: A little girl hops off coach 133 under the watchful eye of the Regina Transit operator. Even though it is March 4th 1966, there is still enough cold and snow to ensure she will be running straight home from the loop at Edwards and 13th Avenue. (COLIN K. HATCHER)

Below: July 1975 and RTS 147 sits in the Exhibition Loop at Elphinstone Street West and 10th Avenue. In the background are the spires of Holy Rosary Church, a landmark in Regina. The Exhibition Loop was only used during Regina's Provincial Exhibition days. (COLIN K. HATCHER)

Above: Say it with flowers. A sad goodby as the last run of the last coach turns onto the carhouse wire. The "operator" is General Manager P. G. McAra who took the wheel for the last few miles. (COLIN K. HATCHER)

Below: Not the end of the line. Though their service in Regina ended on these flat cars, captured on March 8th 1966, RTS 137 and 141 were destined for Edmonton to start a new life there as ETS 129 and 128 respectively, where they ran well into the late 1970s. (COLIN K. HATCHER)

Above: Saskatoon trolley coaches 161 and 151 are northbound on 2nd Avenue approaching the HBC Building at 23rd Street, November 1st 1951. The HBC Building was originally the J.F. Cairns Store. The HBC Building is now the 2nd Avenue Lofts. The building behind trolley coach 161 is the King George Hotel.
(OHIO BRASS COLLECTION, THE STRAHORN LIBRARY, ILLINOIS RAILWAY MUSEUM. LOCATION INFORMATION – COLIN HATCHER)

Below: A blustery winter's day and passengers are boarding streetcar 201 while trolley coach 158 passes on Route 3 signed 7TH AVENUE – AVENUE H at 2nd Avenue and 21st Street.
(EDMONTON RADIAL RAILWAY SOCIETY, FONDS LESLIE CORNESS)

Saskatoon (1948-1974)
Saskatoon Municipal Railway / Saskatoon Transit System

The City of Bridges joined the rush to trolley buses in the late 1940s, offering enviable service for a city of only 130,000: ten-minute headway along shady streets, long, one-way loops and three routes serving a wide area.

George Archibald pondered the future of Saskatoon's post-war transit system. As Transit Commissioner for over thirty years, Archibald had guided the system through two world wars and the public's increasing love affair with the motor car. He had been appointed in 1915 for a two-month trial that would eventually stretch to 33 of the Municipal Railway's 39 years, but now was the time for some serious rethinking of this northern Saskatchewan city's public transit.

It was a typical post-WWII dilemma. Track and streetcars were worn out from the outcome of the wartime "keep them running" austerity. Equipment was hard to replace, though some trams purchased on their abandonment from other cities had useful life in them. But this was 1946: modern times demanded modern transit solutions. The old streetcars were drafty, rattled and creaked, and occupied street centres, an increasing concern with the rise in automobile traffic.

The new motor buses had limited passenger capacity, fine for outlying areas and lightly travelled routes, but not for the city centre. Trolley coaches had by now proven themselves in Edmonton, Winnipeg, and out east in Montreal. They provided a smoother ride and could pull over to the curb to load passengers from the sidewalks, a safer alternative and one that did not impede car and truck traffic. The same electrical expertise now in use for streetcars would carry over, meaning there was little re-training required of maintenance crews and only a little required for operators.

Archibald's plan called for thirty new trolley coaches and twelve motor buses from 1946 to 1951, with conversion beginning the next year (1947). Circumstances dictated that motor buses operate first to replace the single-truck streetcars, and these then be replaced by trolley coaches. The plan was adopted and the motor buses procured. Eight 44-passenger Brill trolley coaches at $18,500 each were ordered in 1947 from Canadian Car, but then, unfortunately, Archibald suffered a stroke in March of that year and died unexpectedly. His assistant replaced him briefly, but due to ill health was succeeded by Commissioner Burt Scharfe, who continued to steer Archibald's planned conversions.

The first shipment of Can Car trolley coaches arrived October 4th 1948. Training of operators followed in November, with some of the Saskatoon operators sent to Regina first, for training on that city's trolley coaches. Finally, on November 22nd, regular service commenced on the AVENUE H–7TH AVENUE line. Streetcars had vacated this route in October of 1947, with motor buses filling in temporarily.

The following year, on September 25th, trolley buses replaced streetcars on the Pleasant Hill to city centre part of the PLEASANT HILL–EXHIBITION line. Two more coaches arrived in November 1949 to augment the increased route mileage.

August 15th 1949 saw the transit system change its name from Saskatoon Municipal Railway to Saskatoon Transit System, to better reflect its multi-modes of transportation. In 1950, transit board members mused about only a partial conversion to trolley coaches as a solution to the cost of the newly-acquired vehicles, since some of their second-hand streetcars still had useful life in them. However, the writing on the bus barn wall told them that inevitably, trams were not the way to go, and instead they ordered four more CCF coaches – 48-passenger, double-door units at $24,116 each. Tenders were called to convert the remainder of the PLEASANT HILL–EXHIBITION line and that work was finished later in 1950.

Next up was the conversion of the MAYFAIR–UNIVERSITY car line. To service this line, sixteen more T-48 coaches were ordered in February of 1951 at a cost of $23,341. This acquisition brought the trolley bus fleet to an impressive thirty units. With the MAYFAIR–UNIVERSITY line slated for conversion, streetcars in Saskatoon would no longer clang, creak and sway their way down the city's pleasant streets. November 10th 1951 saw the last run, with the "traditional" sad face painted on the last tram. The parade was delayed due to a flat tire on the trolley coach; perhaps the tram had a last laugh. The next day, coincidentally Remembrance Day, trolley coaches completed the conversion Archibald had drawn up six years earlier – on schedule. The total cost was $1,592,319 – a considerable sum for a small transit system – but Saskatoon residents now had a modern, efficient system to look forward to. A few more tweaks remained. Since streetcars and trolley coaches operated side-by-side in the three years of conversion, passengers boarded both trams and trolley coaches in the middle of the street. Now that the streetcars were a memory, safer curb loading was possible with the quiet, sleek trolley buses as soon as the overhead could be moved. In fact, some people said that because the trolley coaches were so quiet, they were a traffic hazard. Another minor improvement was the addition of route numbers to

150
150

BALDWIN
HOTEL
SASKATOON
HOUSE LTD
153
153
GRINDERS

CO. LTD.
EXHIBITION
172
172

the three routes: MAYFAIR–UNIVERSITY became ROUTE 1 ... PLEASANT HILL–EXHIBITION, ROUTE 2 ... and AVENUE H–7TH AVENUE was renamed ROUTE 3.

A number of terminals changed when trolley coaches were introduced and some routes realigned. Of note, the Pleasant Hill terminal was eventually extended along 20th Street from Avenue S to Avenue W, and further moved in 1965 along 20th Street to Winnipeg Avenue, then along it to 18th Street, thence on Ottawa to 20th Street. The Exhibition terminal was also moved nearer the main gate. In the 1960s, the AVENUE H line was also revised.

Trolley coach routing shrank in 1964 when College Drive underwent extensive rebuilding, resulting in their removal from that end of the MAYFAIR–UNIVERSITY line. The next year they looped around Victoria School, and in May the overhead was removed from 12th Street and Dufferin to the University terminal. Construction of the Idylwyld Freeway forced the trolleys to move from 9th to 8th Street between Broadway and Lorne.

The 1960s saw major redevelopment in downtown Saskatoon resulting from the relocation of the CNR tracks and station to the southwest of the city. This allowed the joining up of 20th and 22nd streets, and ROUTE 3 trolleys were rerouted from 19th to 20th Street between Idylwyld and 1st Street in late 1965. In 1967, again because of street mergers, ROUTE 2 trolleys were relocated from Idylwyld to 1st between 20th and 23rd streets. That same year the AVENUE H portion of ROUTE 3 was renamed to RIVERSDALE.

However, the removal of the UNIVERSITY trolleys was a portent of things to come. While all these re-routings were going on, in 1967 Urwick, Currie Limited was retained by the transit board as consultants to study the whole transit system. Given this firm's findings in other cities where they had been retained, it came as no surprise that they recommended trolley coaches be replaced with diesels. A number

Opposite Top: Saskatoon Municipal Railway Brill coach 150 trails a streetcar on 2nd Avenue. Note the use of a common positive overhead wire.
(EDMONTON RADIAL RAILWAY SOCIETY, FONDS LESLIE CORNESS)

Opposite Middle: Saskatoon Brill 153, signed AVENUE H – 7TH AVENUE, tracks along 2nd Avenue. Note the centre street bracket arms holding the trolley coach overhead.
(EDMONTON RADIAL RAILWAY SOCIETY, FONDS LESLIE CORNESS)

Opposite Bottom: Now known as Saskatoon Transit System, trolley coach 172's operator gets on with a hot coffee, navigating the mud and slush of a prairie winter.
(EDMONTON RADIAL RAILWAY SOCIETY, FONDS LESLIE CORNESS)

Above: It's lonely turning the loop at Rupert at Alexandria as 176 gets ready to return on the #3 – 7TH AVENUE line in June 1964.
(G.M. ANDERSEN PHOTO, KRAMBLES-PETERSON ARCHIVE)

of route changes were also suggested, and the transit board agreed to all of them.

More diesels buses were added to the city's fleet, so by 1971, twelve trolleys were retired for parts. The Pleasant Hill to City Centre loop was dieselized in 1972, and since buses were already operating on the University portion of that line, the complete line became motorized and was called PLEASANT HILL–UNIVERSITY.

With the arrival of the STS order of eight GM diesel buses, the RIVERSDALE–7TH AVE. ROUTE 3 was converted in November 1973 [304] and six trolleys were sold to Vancouver. The remaining ROUTE 1 (MAYFAIR–EXHIBITION) was to be discontinued in December, but the shipment of Flyer diesel buses was delayed due to a shortage of essential components. Finally, with the delivery of six of the ten Flyer buses, on May 10th 1974 the last trolley, No. 174 ran from the Exhibition grounds at 6:50 PM Friday, and the poles were pulled down for the last time in the transit garage, thus ending a 26-year trolley bus run in the City of Bridges.[305]

There does not seem to have been any official last run or farewell, but then there were only three routes and thirty buses – not an overwhelming force. Still, after 26 years of yeoman service, one wonders at their quiet exit. The remaining trolley coaches were sold – again to Vancouver, where they went immediately into service, and the remaining overhead went to Edmonton (the ROUTE 3 overhead was sold along with the coaches to Vancouver).[306] Some questioned the wisdom of electric transit leaving Saskatoon when the oil crisis of the 1970s hit, but were reminded by transit officials that the lines had served old, established areas of the city with no passenger growth. That, and the expense of new coaches, wire and poles was deemed prohibitive. So ended an era, and with it, George Archibald's grand plan. Today, Saskatoon still continues to provide excellent transit service, albeit without the singing of trolley poles on wire on a crisp prairie evening.[307]

Footnotes:

304. *Saskatoon Star-Phoenix*, December 12, 1973 p. 3 and May 9, 1974 p. 4.
305. *Saskatoon Star-Phoenix*, May 9, 1974 p. 4.
306. *Saskatoon Star-Phoenix*, December 12, 1973 p. 3.
307. Except as noted, the above is sourced from Wayman, *Saskatoon's Electric Transit*, Chapter 8, with additional material from NAATA *Trolley Coach News* #14 Vol. 3, Number 3, July-October 1971.

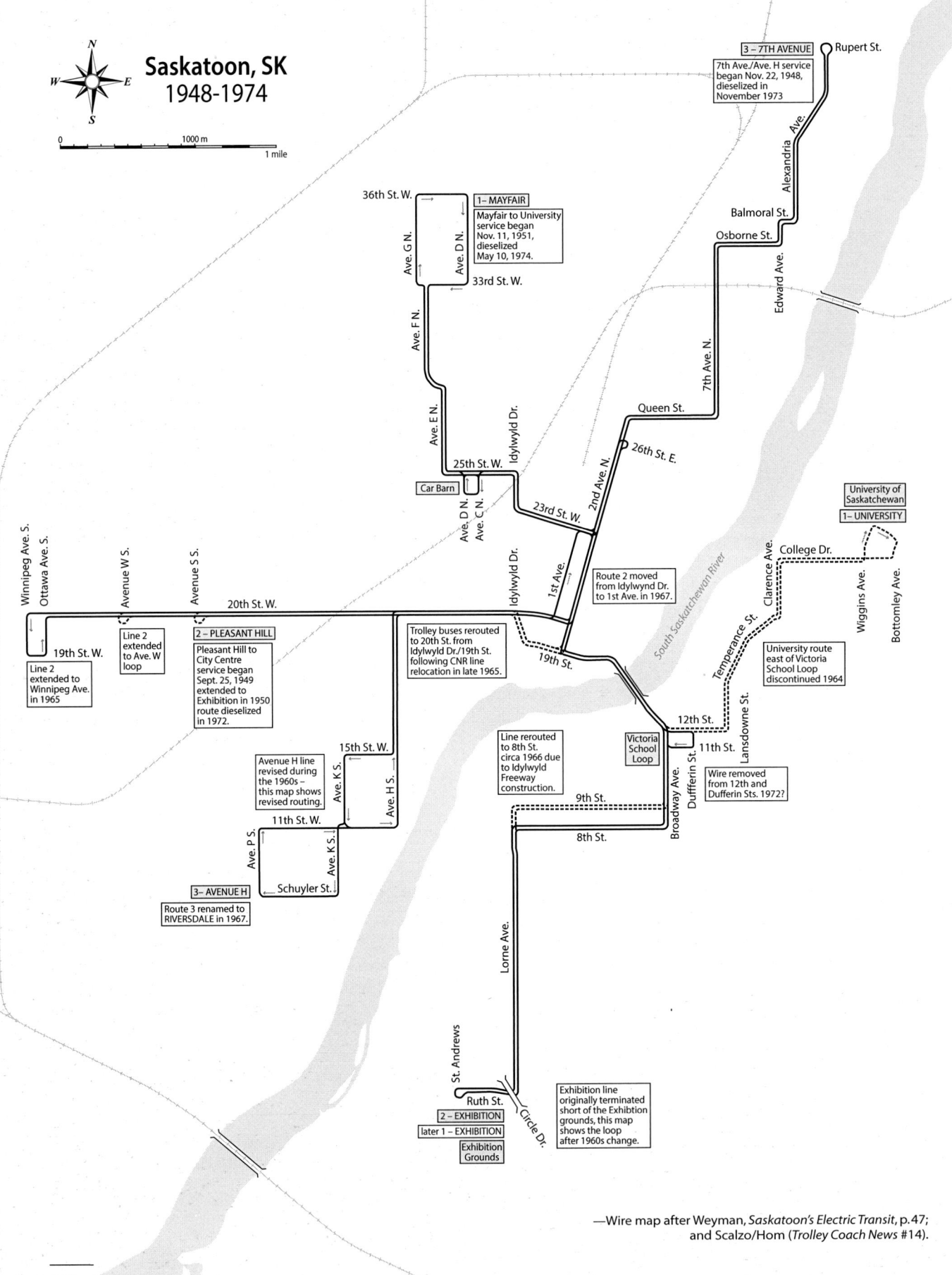

Saskatoon, SK
1948–1974

3 – 7TH AVENUE
7th Ave./Ave. H service began Nov. 22, 1948, dieselized in November 1973

1 – MAYFAIR
Mayfair to University service began Nov. 11, 1951, dieselized May 10, 1974.

1 – UNIVERSITY
University of Saskatchewan

University route east of Victoria School Loop discontinued 1964

Route 2 moved from Idylwyld Dr. to 1st Ave. in 1967.

Trolley buses rerouted to 20th St. from Idylwyld Dr./19th St. following CNR line relocation in late 1965.

2 – PLEASANT HILL
Pleasant Hill to City Centre service began Sept. 25, 1949, extended to Exhibition in 1950, route dieselized in 1972.

Line 2 extended to Winnipeg Ave. in 1965

Line 2 extended to Ave. W loop

Avenue H line revised during the 1960s – this map shows revised routing.

3 – AVENUE H
Route 3 renamed to RIVERSDALE in 1967.

Line rerouted to 8th St. circa 1966 due to Idylwyld Freeway construction.

Victoria School Loop

Wire removed from 12th and Dufferin Sts. 1972?

2 – EXHIBITION
later **1 – EXHIBITION**
Exhibition Grounds

Exhibition line originally terminated short of the Exhibition grounds, this map shows the loop after 1960s change.

—Wire map after Weyman, *Saskatoon's Electric Transit*, p. 47; and Scalzo/Hom (*Trolley Coach News* #14).

138

Above: STS 170, a CCF-Brill T-48A built in 1951 pulls away from the stop as another coach takes on passengers in the busy shopping district on 2nd Avenue near 21st Street, June 27th 1973. Coach 170 survived abandonment of trolley service to resurface as a Vancouver Transit vehicle. (TED WICKSON)

Below: Showing off its stuff, Saskatoon Transit System 170 is inbound on the EXHIBITION route June 27th 1973, making the turn from Lorne Avenue to 8th Street. (TED WICKSON)

Above: One of the first English trolley coaches, A.E.C. unit 103 travels on the centre street wire westbound down Jasper Avenue approaching 100 Avenue on a snowy day in 1939. Judging from the snow beside the tracks, the trolley hot wire was common to both streetcars and coaches using that part of Jasper Avenue.
(PROVINCIAL ARCHIVES OF ALBERTA BL260.4, A. BLYTH COLLECTION)

Below: Probably now only used for overload or emergency/shortage service, Edmonton's first trolley coach A.E.C./E.E.C. coach 101 was captured in the ETS yard on a pleasant summer's day.
(PETER COX PHOTO COURTESY DAVID WYATT)

Edmonton (1939-2009)
Edmonton Radial Railway / Edmonton Transit System (ETS) / Edmonton Transit (ET)

One of the first to enter and the second-last system left, Edmonton hung on into the 21st century to be the longest-lived continuous trolley bus service in Canada, but the trolley's uniqueness finally failed against politics, questionable economics, and the onslaught of diesel buses.

The clang of streetcar bells and the screech of wheels on the rails drifted through the window on a warm summer day in 1938. The sounds were a constant reminder to two men seated at a table, of decisions that had to be made.

Thomas Ferrier, Edmonton Radial Railway Superintendent, and City Commissioner Robert J. Gibb looked at the material spread out in front of them, material gathered on a recent trip across Canada and the US to attend a transit convention in Quebec City. The brochures and notes were grouped into three subjects: streetcars, motor buses and the new electric bus or trolley bus. The Edmonton streetcar system was in bad shape and something had to be done. Would they rehabilitate the lines, extend them and replace the aging fleet with the new PCC car? Were motor buses, with their smaller capacity but increased mobility, the answer? Or was the hybrid-electric bus the best solution? It used the existing technology and investment in electric transit, but didn't rely on costly rails. It had a larger carrying capacity than the motor bus, but a limited mobility to manoeuvre around obstacles. Finally, roadways could be paved more economically if the rails were removed.

But the public liked the trams. There had been a great outcry when the subway under the CNR tracks crossing 97 Street was constructed. Plans had included the removal of the streetcar tracks, but the ERR had been forced to replace them when construction was complete. If it tried to introduce the same kind of rubber-tired vehicles as were running in Montreal and were soon to be operating in Winnipeg, would it get the same opposition even though the new vehicles were smoother and quieter than the streetcars?

Questions went back and forth for hours. The advantages and disadvantages of each vehicle were carefully weighed. A consultant's report the previous April had strongly recommended that the street railway system be replaced by trolley buses on a gradual basis. City Council had tabled that report and asked the Commissioners and the Superintendent to forward their recommendations as a basis for a decision.

After much deliberation, Ferrier and Gibb arrived at a decision. They would recommend to the City Council that an experimental route be strung with double-overhead wires to accommodate new trolley coaches. This experiment could relieve a troublesome situation on Scona Hill where the track shifted in the unpaved roadway during every rain. It would retire some of the worst downtown track, that on 95 Street, and hopefully provide a fast, quiet and clean service that the public would accept. If all went well, Edmonton would be, by early 1939, the third Canadian city to use the modern trolley coach.

Let us review the steps that led up to this decision. As early as 1930, Edmonton Radial Railway had been receiving literature on trolley coaches. Information had also been solicited on motor buses and some companies had even sent demonstrator vehicles. The main drawback of the motor bus, however, was its small size, typically 25 to 29 seats capacity. By 1937, the transit situation had become critical, with the tram system limping along. Due to the steep inclines on either side of the North Saskatchewan River, one streetcar crossing was limited to a very circuitous route down the slopes and over the Low Level Bridge. A trolley coach could climb the steep hills more directly and shorten this route considerably. The 1937 report on the Street Railway recommended that, for 1938, either trolley or motor buses be used between the (Cromdale) car barns and Whyte Avenue via 95 Street and McDougall Hill. This report favoured trolley buses over the motor buses, but left the decision open.[308] When trolley coach suppliers became aware of this report through the papers, they rushed to forward literature favouring their particular products.

At a City Council meeting on February 28th 1938, a motion was passed to retain Wilson & Bunnell, engineering consultants of Toronto, to make a report on the state of the transit system in Edmonton, with attendant recommendations.[309] They subsequently accepted this offer and dispatched Norman Wilson to Edmonton to study the situation.

The street railway in the meantime queried Portland, Oregon for information on its trolley bus system, influenced, no doubt, by the fact that conditions there were similar to Edmonton's. A trolley coach network in Montreal had started to function, using English-built buses, and its progress was also being carefully followed.

Wilson tendered his report to Council on April 30th 1938. He recommended against further street railway extensions; instead, a trolley coach system should be started to "ultimately eliminate streetcar service". The first route he proposed was to extend from Whyte Avenue and 104 Street via 99 Street and McDougall Hill to a downtown loop via 100 Street, 102 Avenue, 102 Street and Jasper Avenue, thence by 95 Street, 111 Avenue and 86 Street to 115 Avenue at 85 Street. Six buses were to service this route. Since Edmonton's weather and terrain conditions were not the same as Montreal's, he suggested that if British-built buses were chosen, they should be specially designed for Edmonton's severe weather conditions.[310]

In his report, Wilson referred specifically to British buses, although there were several US trolley bus builders active at this time. He felt that the British had more experience building trolley coaches as they were supplying, besides the many networks in the UK, other British Empire countries as well. In addition, there were no tariff barriers when importing from within the Empire, whereas US-built buses would be subject to duty and tax. Loyalty to the Mother Country had economic advantages as well as emotional ones.

Following the tendering of this report, Superintendent Ferrier and Commissioner Gibb headed across Canada to the Canadian Transit Association's convention at Quebec City. This afforded them the opportunity of visiting, along the way, the Winnipeg transit system which was preparing to put trolley coaches into operation; Associated Electric Co. of Montreal, agents for the Associated Equipment Co. of England (trolley coach manufacturers); Ohio Brass Co., (makers of overhead fittings); Wilson & Bunnell; and the Montreal Tramways' trolley coach operation. They also toured trolley bus installations in Milwaukee and Duluth as well as the Pullman and Ford bus manufacturing plants, and the General Electric Company's traction motor manufacturing facility in Chicago.

As a result of their observations during this trip, Commissioner Gibb submitted their report on June 20th recommending the installation of a trolley bus line. Some cost figures presented showed the anticipated economies of this conversion; the city would save $17,000 each year on mileage alone using the trolleys. Moreover, the trolleys would not need a new garage: their motors were immune to cold weather starting problems, and these buses could be stored outside if need be. Gibb and Ferrier had been especially impressed with the smooth ride of Montreal's English Electric three-axle buses, and recommended that similar equipment be considered.[311] However, City Council wanted more time to consider this proposal and deferred its decision for the time being.

Early in July, Commissioner Gibb appeared before Council, again stating that, judging from answers to enquiries made to other transit companies, electric trolley coaches were definitely past the experimental stage. Finally, on July 13th 1938, Edmonton City Council passed the recommendation of the City Commissioners regarding Street Railway Rehabilitation, which included the installation and operation of a trolley coach route. Council upheld the consultants' recommendation that British manufacturers should be favoured with the bid.

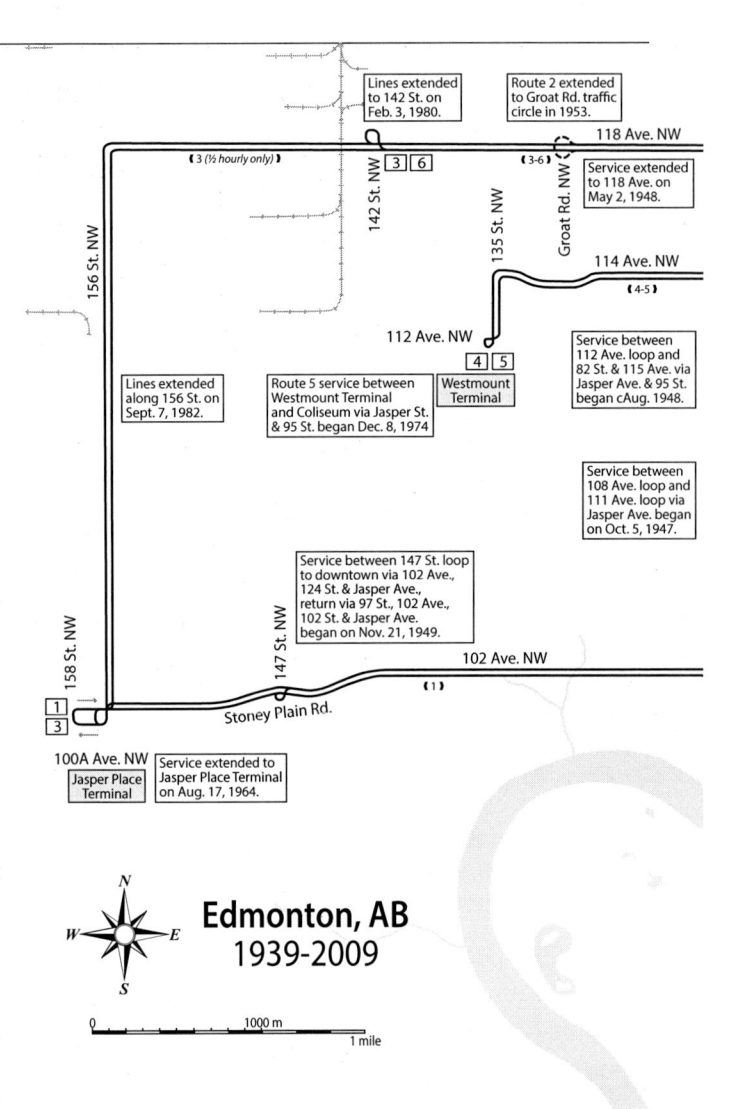

Tenders were called for six 38- to 44-passenger buses. They were to have the ability to negotiate a gradient of 9.8 per cent maximum on a 133-foot radius at 22 MPH up the north hill, and 30 MPH up the south hill. The buses were to handle a peak load of eighty people and have an average speed of 12 MPH with seven stops per mile. An unusual feature specified was equipment to discharge coarse sand by air pressure in front of each driving wheel and, as well, in an emergency, to discharge it behind these wheels. The low speed points were to be controlled by the motorman to facilitate starting on ice. There were three brakes specified: regenerative, emergency and air. Storm sashes were required on the windows to cope with Edmonton's notorious winter cold. This practice continued right up until the end of the Brill trolleys. The buses were to have a centre exit for one-man operation as opposed to the British practice of rear exits and two-man operation. The recommendation added a wise warning that "the attention of British manufacturers is drawn to the fact that the drive is on the opposite side from English practice".

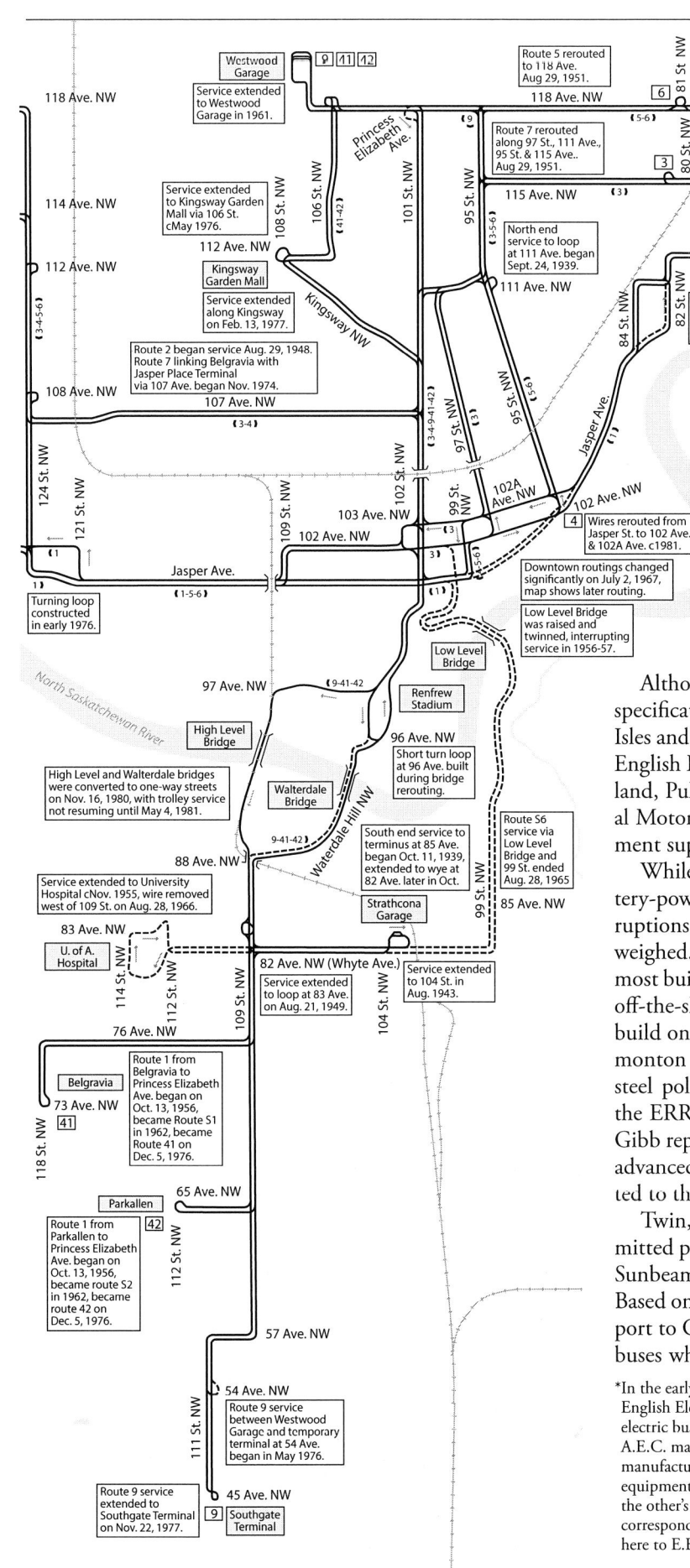

EDMONTON

—Wire map based on Hatcher and Schwarzkopf, *Edmonton's Electric Transit*.

Although Council favoured British manufacturers, this specification was sent to fifteen firms in both the British Isles and the United States. Notable among them were: the English Electric Company (E.E.C.)*, Sunbeam, Guy, Leyland, Pullman, Ransomme Simms, Canadian Car, General Motors, St. Louis Car and Mack. Two electrical equipment suppliers were also included.[312]

While the bids were being solicited, details such as battery-powered manoeuvring capability during power interruptions and the advantages of three axles over two were weighed. The Brill Company, at that time one of the foremost builders of trolley buses in the US, replied offering an off-the-shelf bus, likely feeling that it was uneconomical to build only six buses to the special requirements of the Edmonton specification. After the bids had been awarded for steel poles, overhead and fittings, General Motors asked the ERR to reconsider using motor buses. Commissioner Gibb replied that planning for trolley coach operation had advanced to the point where Edmonton was fully committed to that mode.

Twin, Pullman, Brill, GM, St. Louis and Mack all submitted proposals and the UK firms of Ransomme, Karrier, Sunbeam, E.E.C./A.E.C. and Leyland also presented bids. Based on these tenders, the Commissioners tabled their report to Council. "The American firms make only two axle buses while British manufacturers turn out both two and

*In the early 1930s, the Associated Equipment Co. Ltd. (A.E.C.) and the English Electric Co. Ltd., (E.E.C.) foremost manufacturers of gasoline and electric buses respectively, collaborated in producing a line of trolley coaches. A.E.C. manufactured the chassis and components, while the bus bodies were manufactured (usually by a subcontractor) by E.E.C., as was the electrical equipment and motors. A.E.C. and E.E.C. are often referred to by one or the other's name, and the names have been wrongly used interchangeably in correspondence. The bus crests carried both companies' names. Reference here to E.E.C. implies the consortium of E.E.C./A.E.C.

143

Above: These two advertisements placed in the newspapers by Edmonton's Street Railway Department invited transit riders to try out the new trolley coaches and let the department know how they liked them.
(PROVINCIAL ARCHIVES OF ALBERTA, SCHWARZKOPF COLLECTION)

three axle jobs. Supt. Ferrier, as a result of his visit to United States points and Montreal was of the definite opinion that the three axle job gives better riding quality … . In view of their recommendation we finally eliminated all bids except those of the English Electric Company and the Leyland Company … . However in view of the fact that both Mr. Ferrier and Mr. Watson have actually examined the English Electric Company's buses in Montreal, your Commissioners agree with them in recommending that the bid … for English Electric buses be accepted at a price of $17,053.00 per bus." This price was for an E.E.C. body as there were several body options by other suppliers.[313] On October 11th 1938, Council passed the recommendation "That if the Leyland Company can advance delivery date satisfactory to Commissioners and provided the English Electric Company will undertake to put in a stock on consignment to be paid for as the parts are put into the buses – and provided satisfactory arrangements can be made by Commissioner Gibb for a uniform body by both firms – we award a contract for three English Electric and three Leyland buses."[314]

Additional features requested on the E.E.C. buses were resistance heaters, 38-passenger capacity, extra heaters and insulation, and Ohio Brass (US) trolley pole retrievers, as well as battery-powered manoeuvring and a 115 HP traction motor. The battery-powered manoeuvring capability was specified only for the E.E.C. buses and was to be sufficient to be able to get them off the railway tracks on the Low Level Bridge. The Leyland buses were to have 135 HP motors and Ohio Brass harps and shoes. All buses were to have Park Royal bodies. E.E.C. had quoted on this body option at a higher price, but presumably it accepted the change at the bid price.

After the contract had been awarded, some consideration was given by Council to purchasing an additional bus, but a decision on this was delayed until service had begun, when the need for extra buses could be evaluated. If a proposal to extend the passenger-carrying route to 82 Street along the car barns wire was to be put into effect, then more than one additional bus would be required.

Arrangements for procuring and constructing the overhead line concluded early in 1939. The Northern Electric Co. and Canadian General Electric provided the wire; the contract for erecting it went to McGregor Telephone & Power Co. Ltd. In April of that year, Commissioner Gibb somewhat prophetically expressed the hope in a letter that "Mr. Hitler wouldn't start something before their buses were shipped".[315] In May he told the *Edmonton Journal* that Britain's rearmament race had caused a delay of at least two months, setting the arrival date back from July or early August to September or October.[316] Finally, on June 28th, E.E.C. informed the City that it would ship its three buses on the ss *Lochkatrine* bound for Vancouver. Shipping restrictions at the time, however, delayed loading, and space on another ship was procured.

On September 4th 1939, a German submarine torpedoed the passenger vessel RMS *Athenia*, Montreal-bound from Great Britain. This action, a scant seven hours after Britain had declared war on Germany, killed six and sent 1400 persons into lifeboats after the torpedo struck without warning.[317] Edmonton's Leyland buses were supposed to have been loaded on this vessel, but fate intervened and space had been found for two of them on another ship, the ss *Beaverford*, leaving on August 25th for Eastern Canada. This area of entry was considered a quicker passage, and E.E.C. had also revised its shipping plans, having sent its buses, as well as the remaining Leyland bus on September

1st and 3rd to Montreal. Edmonton Radial Railway wasn't the only entity grateful for this turn of events. An irate passenger was informed on sailing day that his space on the *Athenia* had already been taken and that he would have to take the next ship. This author's father calmed down when he read the next day of the ship's fate, and he cheerfully accepted the later, but safer, crossing to Canada. Had things worked out differently, Edmonton's first trolley coaches and the writer of this account might not have arrived.

On Tuesday, September 12th, buses 101 and 102 arrived by train in Edmonton. Two more were in Montreal being unloaded, and the third pair was expected to dock soon "unless the boat carrying them has been torpedoed" said the *Edmonton Journal*.[318] The second shipment of buses had the distinction of carrying Edmonton's first trolley bus passengers. Two hoboes named Hughie and Walter had taken a ride in bus 103 from Toronto to Edmonton, where they apparently had a speedy and forced evacuation, leaving behind half a loaf of bread and a pound of bologna. They had the audacity, or perhaps the good grace, to write to Mr. Ferrier from "Jungles Ltd.", the transient settlement near the Calder railway yards, to thank him for the shelter. They apologized for not asking his permission for the ride, and asked for the return of their food. Mr. Ferrier insisted to the press that the letter was genuine, saying he had found the food in the coach, but had given it to children playing nearby.[319]

On September 22nd and 23rd, trial runs were made with the new trolleys on the North Side* under the newly-completed wiring. The northern terminus was the loop

*Although not official names, Edmontonians referred to communities as being on the *North Side* or *South Side* of the North Saskatchewan River. For clarity, we've capitalized those informal regions.

Above: Operator Joe Caswell poses beside Leyland coach 104 outside his home on 115 Avenue near 89 Street on the single overhead line between Cromdale and the 115 Avenue and 95 Street loop. The dog belonged to Joe and the photo was taken by his wife c1942. (EDMONTON RADIAL RAILWAY SOCIETY, J. CASWELL & A.R. KERR)

at 95 Street and 111 Avenue. The remainder of the overhead was service-only wire. The south-side wire was to be completed a week later.[320] On Sunday, September 24th, the north-side service was officially placed in operation with three buses[321] and the public was encouraged to "take a ride and see how you like them". The regular fare, ten cents cash or five tickets for a quarter, applied even for this first day. The *South Edmonton Weekly News*,[322] the *Edmonton Journal*[323] and *The Bulletin* all heralded this start of a fifteen-year program of modernization of the street railway system. This program was to cost $1.5 million and involved purchasing a total of 45 trolley buses.

Public response showed a wholehearted acceptance of the new buses; the motormen, James Billingsley and Thomas McWhirter, twenty-year tram veterans, and four younger men, Harry Humpish, Gordon Murray, Lionel Fouracre and Edward Hillary, were kept busy all day Sunday. All six drivers said that they liked the new buses better than the trams.[324]

By mid-October, partial paving on the South Side was completed[325] and on October 11th, the buses started running over the Low Level Bridge to a terminus at 99 Street and 85 Avenue. Paving on 99 Street as far as Whyte Avenue was to be completed by the weekend, and the buses were then to run via 99 Street to Whyte Avenue and 104 Street, where they were to be turned.[326]

Within a week, ridership pushed the system to its peak capacity, so on October 18th, Mr. Ferrier asked Council

145

for more buses. In the meantime, the route was terminated at 99 Street and Whyte Avenue until traffic conditions on Whyte could be studied more carefully. A wye had been built at this intersection and was used to turn the buses.

The new service was not without problems. There was a heavy snowfall on October 23rd so some delays were experienced before adequate cindering of the hills kept the buses moving. Another delay occurred when a CNR locomotive, unable to get a grip on the icy rails on the Low Level Bridge, stalled and blocked traffic.

The headway of this route had been doubled over that of the trams and, as a result, the number of passengers carried also doubled. Still, ridership over the route increased dramatically and motor buses were needed in the peak hours to help.[327] By early November, Council asked both of the bus suppliers to quote on two more coaches as "patronage had exceeded expectations". At this time the two portions of the line were treated as two separate routes, probably to allow better balancing of passenger flow from and to the South Side. On November 27th, the purchase of three more vehicles was approved, one for each route and one spare, for a total cost of $54,000. These were to be ordered from Britain, again because of the higher tariff costs on buses from the US. Even though delivery time from Great Britain was longer, it was argued that the savings realized and the contribution to the war effort made this a wise decision.[328] This decision was to be regretted often during the next months.

The order was split, one bus to Leyland and two to E.E.C.. Heavier springs, improved (non-dragging) brakes, traffic-turn-indicators, better dust protection for the equipment and passengers, and stronger rear bumpers, better able to withstand the frequent impacts of Edmonton's errant drivers, were specified.[329] On December 13th, E.E.C. regretfully informed the city that, due to the war, it had been instructed by the British Government to discontinue the manufacturing of buses. Accordingly its order was transferred to Leyland. As the year closed and the war clouds darkened, Council optimistically asked for estimates to be prepared for several trolley coach extensions.

Early in 1940, several more estimates were prepared for proposed routes, as well as for lifting of the BONNIE DOON streetcar stub from 99 Street to the originally-proposed trolley terminus at 104 Street. City engineers were also looking at replacing the streetcar line over the High Level Bridge with trolley coaches, on either the upper or lower deck, to serve a belt line running along 109 Street.

It had been suggested that trolley coach service be extended through Norwood from 111 Avenue and 95 Street via 111 Avenue east to 91 Street, north to 115 Avenue, east over what was currently service wire to 85 Street and the Fort Trail. This was as recommended in the original Wilson & Bunnell report. This line, however, was never built, but service from 95 Street and 111 Avenue to a loop at 115 Avenue and 82 Street was eventually put into effect in January 1946, probably along the former service wire.

In the meantime, small design problems in the first order of buses were being rectified, and turn-indicators were being installed to lessen the occurrence of impacts with Edmonton motorists. Ridership increased 25 per cent due to the new buses, and, at peak hours, was estimated to have increased by 50 to 100 per cent. In June, the city asked ACF-Brill (Chicago) if there were two trolley buses available for delivery in November. Brill would have been happy to supply them, but investigation showed that there would be a ten per cent duty imposed; therefore, the City reluctantly decided to wait for the British coaches to arrive and risk possibly impaired winter service. Commissioner Gibb all the while was pushing the British Trade Commissioner to speed up the shipment of the Leyland buses. Steel shortages and quotas in Great Britain were delaying the fabrication of the chassis – and, in a time of intense shortages, the manufacturer was reluctant to have the bodies or motors fabricated until the whole bus could be assembled. Edmonton argued that special consideration should be given this order because it not only supplied much needed foreign exchange to Britain, but also the route the buses were to be used on served Canadian war industries. Volumes of correspondence were exchanged between Edmonton and the British Trade Commissioner in Vancouver, and between Vancouver and England, but all to no avail. The quota systems were so complex and restrictive that any pleas fell on deaf or at least immovable ears.[330] The best that Leyland was able to do was offer some 80 HP diesel buses built for Canton and undeliverable due to the hostilities. They were very anxious to get rid of them, but Edmonton felt that they were underpowered for climbing the hills, and gasoline rationing would render them useless. Moreover, they would have no value at the war's conclusion. By the end of 1941, Leyland advised that the trolley bus chassis were finally completed. Early in 1942, Edmonton's new Leyland trolley buses were still only partly fabricated in England. A considerable exchange of letters ensued and the City retained a consulting engineer in England to supervise Leyland's progress and to push where necessary.

The first of these Leyland buses was finally shipped in June 1942, arriving in Edmonton by the end of July. But the troubles were not over. The second bus was broken into en route, and despite careful supervision by the Associated Equipment Co. of Montreal during the unloading, the third bus had some of its panels damaged. This added one more delay to a frustrating wait, but finally all three coaches were safely housed in the Cromdale barns. These units, numbered 107-109, were supposed to be used to augment service on the 95 ST:111 AV line, but were instead used on the South Side 99 ST:82 AV line. Leyland regretfully informed the city that this shipment of export buses was the last it would be allowed to produce for the duration of the war. A curious fact was that all the Leyland buses lacked a builder's crest. This omission might have gone unnoticed except that in July, Leyland shipped

Right: Edmonton's 1943 Pullman Standard order of trolley coaches prompted this advertisement in transit publications. Today the only surviving Pullman trolley coach in Canada is No. 113 (actually No. 116) in the Edmonton Transit historical collection. (OHIO BRASS COLLECTION, THE STRAHORN LIBRARY, ILLINOIS RAILWAY MUSEUM)

twelve crests to Edmonton and asked that two be affixed to each of its last export order of buses. These were, in fact, the last overseas-manufactured trolley coaches shipped to Canada by any builder.

In August 1941, the Canadian government had established the position of Transit Controller in the Department of Munitions and Supply, a post which was responsible for the administration of urban and interurban transportation vehicles. Indirectly, as shortages of tires, gasoline and equipment increased, it became responsible for all civilian vehicles. Local committees assessed the needs of the community and requested vehicles or service accordingly. All purchases of equipment were placed by the Controller, and equipment was allotted on a need basis by him. A thorough 1941 study of transit needs and timely delivery of equipment led to the majority of Canadian orders being filled in the United States, before the US War Production Board terminated export production in July 1942. The Transit Controller issued orders forbidding the operation of charter buses except as a direct contribution to the war effort. Interurban bus lines were consolidated, terminated or shortened to maximize utilization of available resources. Few vehicles were scrapped and most modernization programs were shelved. Taxis were restricted, and so eventually were private cars, except where pooled to drive workers to war industries. Even then, the riders were assigned by the Controller's Office. All this placed a severe load on public transit systems. Even with staggered work hours and advertising imploring the housewife to shop in off-peak hours, the buses and trams were packed. The far-sightedness of the Board in allowing early bus purchases resulted in more new vehicles being available to transit systems than might otherwise have been the case. Nonetheless, every request for additional vehicles involved a fight to convince the board that Edmonton's need was greater than another city's. George S. Gray, the Controller, had an excellent relationship with Edmonton, one that helped propel Edmonton, after the war, into the front ranks of Canadian transit systems and established it as a leader in trolley and motor bus networks.[331]

In May 1942, the Transit Controller approved a tentative Edmonton order for three more trolley buses, to be the same as those ordered by Winnipeg. These were to be 40-seat Mack buses built in the US. Meanwhile, service was suffering because of the supplemental diesel buses' inability to handle McDougall Hill. Accordingly, trolley coach service was withdrawn from the 95 Street extension to 115 AV : 82 ST, and the more-powerful electric buses were used instead on the 99 ST : 82 AV route.

On May 21st 1942, the order for Mack buses was confirmed by the Transit Controller. The order was allowed only because Winnipeg had already ordered some Macks and the Edmonton order could be tacked on.[332] The Mack order dragged through an expected December delivery date and then a January one. Finally, on February 10th 1943, the buses arrived and were placed in service the following week on the 95 ST : 111 AV route.[333]

Ridership had mounted steadily with 2,463,071 riders in February 1943, compared with 1,762,490 for the same period in 1942. The arrival of the three Mack buses permitted increased service on the Low Level route and enabled the English coaches to be overhauled, a much-needed chore. The E.E.C. vehicles were giving the city problems due to severe passenger overloading, thus straining the smaller motors. The situation would have been graver, however, had Edmonton accepted the standard 80 HP motors on these coaches instead of specifying heavier ones.

The 95 Street extension to 115 Avenue and 82 Street was probably not re-opened when the Macks arrived since the number of vehicles in service was still inadequate. Immediately on receipt of the Mack units the City asked the Transit Controller for permission to order three more. However, the US Department of Defense Transportation curtailed production of Mack buses and the order was denied. It was suggested that Edmonton try instead to get Pullman trolleys. In August 1943, an order to the Pullman Standard Car Co. of Worcester, MA for eight 44-seat trolley buses at a cost of $21,000 each was approved by the Dominion Transit Controller.[334] Completion of this order would give Edmonton one of the largest fleets of electric buses in Canada and would release six streetcars for other service. Trolley coach service was to be extended to 104 Street and 82 Avenue on the South Side, probably using the original loop proposed by Wilson & Bunnell. On 115 Avenue, an extension through to the Exhibition Grounds was proposed. The Pullman buses were scheduled to arrive in December;[335] however, fabrication did not commence immediately as a shortage of axles delayed the start of construction until the following April.

Optimism replaced pessimism in the latter part of 1943. In October, City Council approved planning for the post-war modernization of the transit system. Extension of trolley coach service to Highlands was recommended, as well as the conversion of the South Side tram loop. The new trolley coach belt line would tap the existing line on Whyte Avenue, running along Whyte to 109 Street; it would return to the North Side via the High Level Bridge to Jasper, and link with the existing route at 102 Street. The run over the High Level was proposed to be on the top deck, then occupied by streetcars, using steel plate decking and substantial concrete wheel guards acting like a guideway.[336]

In February 1944, the City requested eight additional trolley buses to help keep up with the increasing demand, but this request was turned down by the Transit Controller in April of that year. This decision was reversed in May[337] and the order confirmed in June.[338] The English buses were showing signs of wear, and the war prevented a good supply of spare parts from being available.

The public liked the Mack buses better than the English ones, and the feeling was that the Street Railway Department should stay with North American coaches when the conflict was over. In late summer 1944, the first eight Pullman buses, ordered in August 1943, finally arrived. They were immediately put into service, probably on August 12th 1944, as tram service on Whyte Avenue from 99 Street to 104 Street ceased that day. At the same time, the terminus was finally extended to the originally-proposed location at 104 Street.

The service was still badly pressed; the Street Railway Department asked later that month for an additional two trolleys, and indicated that the system might need as many as four more. In January 1945, the Transit Controller, Mr. Gray, wrote a confidential letter to Commissioner Gibb in which he revealed that Canadian Car & Foundry (CCF) was planning to produce, under licence, the ACF (American Car & Foundry) Brill trolley coach. He offered Edmonton the choice of either two more Pullmans or two ACF-Brills. Gray stated he hoped to be able to get the opinion of one of Canada's most progressive transit operations on the proposed Canadian trolley coach. He also asked that the ERR keep the streetcars running on 114 (Spruce) Avenue until the spring when he could then get eight more Pullman buses for Edmonton.[339] In a later official letter, he asked if the City would like to try the new ACF-Brill trolley buses. Commissioner Gibb replied that they would like to have the American Brills instead of Pullmans because of the many favourable reports they had heard about them.[340]

On March 16th 1945, ACF submitted a quote for two Standard 1945 Model TC-44 trolley buses, complete except for the tires, at US$13,650 each net. The tires were excluded due to high tariffs on rubber goods, so would instead be bought locally. This quote was less than the list price of $14,600, but the order had been tacked-on to a US order with the saving passed on to Edmonton. The buses were to feature aluminum sheathing, sloped front windshields, a centre control cabinet and protected control rods, a feature needed in Edmonton's severe weather and not found on any previous buses.[341]

The order was duly placed through Canadian Car & Foundry Co. Ltd. for two ACF-Brill trolley coaches to be delivered in the spring of 1946. CCF also advised the City that it expected to start manufacture of the Brill trolley coach under licence in 1946. In March 1945, CCF announced officially the signing of an agreement to build the ACF-Brill buses under the name "Canadian Car-Brill". This trademark was to grace nearly all Canadian trolley coaches from that time until 1954, when CCF ceased trolley coach production.[342] The City stated that it would definitely buy Canadian-made trolley coaches when they became available, but it still asked for two additional Pullmans to add to the eight expected in May.[343] This request was turned down by the Transit Controller's office on the grounds that Edmonton had been favoured in the past, and many cities were worse off.[344]

CCF promised to start production of coaches in the third or fourth quarter of 1946. Selling price was estimated to be $15,500 each. Given the import duties on any US-made buses, this would save between $4000 and $5000 per unit. The City accordingly placed a tentative $50,000 order for twenty coaches for 1946 delivery.[345]

The planning for a trolley bus route over the High Level Bridge went ahead, but there was considerable public fear expressed about the possibility of a bus going off the deck and plunging 150 feet to the river below. On the other hand, the public also objected to the concept of using the lower deck for fear of dewired trolleys fouling up traffic. Public opinion favoured some form of transit across the bridge, however, and the Street Railway Department was hard put to plan around these conflicting preferences. In February 1946, a growing concern by the public about the safety of the High Level route forced the Commissioners to seek re-approval of the decision made by them the previous August to go ahead with the High Level plan. Council showed their confidence in the Commissioners by reaffirming this decision.[346]

A concerned citizen of the Walterdale area asked the City in a letter if the public would be better served by hav-

Edmontonians flock to trolley coaches

They respond to year-round reliability, quietness, and smoothness — boosting revenue more than three times above average system increase

During one of Canada's toughest snow storms, Edmonton's powerful trolley-coach fleet outlasted every type of vehicle on the street—both public and private.

It's performance like this—year-round reliability in all kinds of weather—that's causing Edmontonians to flock to trolley coaches. A substantial upswing in Edmonton's trolley-coach riding habit forcibly demonstrates the high passenger appeal of these electrics. Since 1942 total system riding has increased only 17.8 per cent.

Yet, on a representative trolley-coach route, riding has increased 76.3 per cent—*more than four times the increase for the system.*

Availability High, Maintenance Low

Each trolley coach is carrying about 33,913 passengers per month; the system average load per vehicle is 26,925. Yet trolley-coach maintenance cost is considerably lower than the system average!

Trolley coaches take heavy loads in their stride because they're big, fast, and electrically powered. Electric drive, with its few wearing parts, keeps maintenance cost down, pushes availability up. Electrics need no elaborate garage facilities—in fact, they can be stored outdoors throughout the year. Their unlimited power reserve assures fast, smooth riding no matter what the weather.

Everybody Likes Them

Trolley-coach performance in Edmonton offers a striking example of the tried-and-true popularity of trolley coaches in more than 50 American cities. Passengers like these electrics because they're fast, smooth-riding, and maneuverable—they pull up to the curb to load and unload passengers. People along the route like them because they can hardly hear a trolley coach go by. City officials like them because trolley coaches minimize traffic bottlenecks—they use street space so efficiently. Transit men like them because they're the ideal vehicles for holding on to present high revenues when all riding gets back to normal.

You can effect the greatest good for the greatest number, and get a head start on automobile competition, by making the trolley coach a basic unit in your postwar fleet. For early call on delivery of new trolley coaches, schedule your orders now.

Packing power and smoothness into their service, Edmonton's trolley coaches recently outlasted every type of vehicle on the street during a severe snowstorm. Operators and city officials alike are greatly pleased with this high standard of year-round reliability.

The steady increase in Edmonton's trolley-coach riding habit strongly indicates public preference for these clean, quiet, smooth-riding electrics. That's why Edmonton Street Railway intends to convert most of its old streetcar lines to trolley coaches.

GE ELECTRIC TRANSIT EQUIPMENT

CANADIAN GENERAL ELECTRIC CO. LIMITED
Sydney • Halifax • St. John • Quebec • Sherbrooke • Montreal • Ottawa • Toronto • New Liskeard • Hamilton • St. Catharines • Sudbury • London • Windsor • Fort William • Winnipeg • Regina • Saskatoon • Lethbridge • Edmonton • Calgary • Trail • Kelowna • Vancouver • Victoria

---

ing the proposed High Level route go instead over the 105 Street Bridge. This would serve residents who had no service instead of those who already had, in her opinion, adequate service.[347] In his reply the Commissioner stated that the High Level Bridge route was the best to serve the needs of the public, as a 105 Street route would antagonize the west-end residents and Provincial Government employees.[348] Council concurred with the Commissioner, but the public-spirited citizen was prophetically right. Some time, however, was to pass before this was borne out.

Pullman sent word that delivery of its buses would be delayed till mid-June. In mid-July 1945, with still no sign of the Pullman buses, Commissioner Gibbs' patience was wearing thin. He complained to the Transit Controller that he was most anxious to get the buses by September. Pullman promised delivery early in July, then late in July or early August. Pullman finally promised partial shipments through the month of August.

The Commissioners had recommended to the Transportation Committee that a new HIGHLANDS trolley coach line replace the remains of the WHITE carline. This was a secondary streetcar line with long stretches of single open track. Where track was embedded in pavement, it was in very bad condition. Reconstruction would have cost over $230,000. New pavement could also be laid when the open track was lifted, giving a new roadway into the area. While not a heavy residential area, it was growing,

Above: In 1945, General Electric highlighted Edmonton's four fold ridership increase with trolley coach routes versus the overall system ridership. The right hand sketch shows Pullman 114 northbound on Scona Hill heading for the Low Level Bridge. The left top photo is of a Pullman and the bottom Mack 111 on Jasper eastbound.
(PROVINCIAL ARCHIVES OF ALBERTA; SCHWARZKOPF COLLECTION)

and the trolley coach line would also serve the Exhibition Grounds, and Borden Park, with its zoo and open swimming pool as well as a hockey arena.[349] The trolley coaches could be run downtown, they suggested, in an opposite direction to the LOW LEVEL BRIDGE and 95 ST : 111 AV routes. The buses would go west on Jasper, north on 102 Street, east on 102 Avenue, and south on 100 Street to avoid congestion at Jasper Avenue and 101 Street, then continue from there along Jasper to 112 Avenue and 61 Street. This meant doubling the overhead in the downtown loop, but the new set of wires could be installed on the existing overhead spans at a cost of only $7000. Council concurred.[350]

On July 22nd 1945, the WHITE (HIGHLANDS) car line ceased operation. In the meantime, rapid progress was being made on the new trolley wire along this route.[351] Trolley coaches replaced the trams in September, after the open track along Borden Park was lifted and the street paved. The route ran from an off-street loop at 112 Avenue and 61 Street, via 112 Avenue, 82 Street and Jasper Avenue to the downtown loop, where it followed the existing single wire in the same direction as the other routes, and not on the double wire as recommended.[352]

On September 30th 1945, oversight of transit by the Transit Controller was withdrawn. This allowed the City to place whatever bus orders it felt necessary to meet its post-war expansion plans. To fill 1946 requirements for trolley coaches, bids were requested from Pullman, Twin, Mack, Motor Coach Industries (Winnipeg), and Canadian Car & Foundry (CCF) for twenty 44-seat coaches.[353] CCF bid $15,500,[354] Mack was not ready for production,[355] Twin wasn't sure about re-entering the field[356] and Pullman felt that it couldn't compete with tax and duty on imports.[357] Its poor delivery on the last order probably didn't help. MCI, which had built one Mack-type trolley bus as a prototype for Winnipeg, bid $19,660 – and so ended its chance of being a second Canadian trolley coach manufacturer.[358]

Accordingly, on October 10th 1945, a firm order was placed with CCF for 22 trolley coaches[359] to be manufactured in Fort William. In a letter to Twin Coach, which was now promising the imminent arrival of "the best trolley bus ever,"[360] and in another to Mack,[361] the City said that they could risk waiting no longer. This removed the last US contenders from Edmonton's market; it was CCF all the way. Even with a rise in price of the ACF-Brills to be delivered in November,[362] from $13,776 to $14,465, the City still felt that the Can Car-Brill bus was the way to go. Another Canadian venture, Hayes Manufacturing Co. Ltd. of Vancouver, belatedly offered a 100 per cent Canadian-built trolley coach, but Edmonton's order had already been awarded by Council.

The City's enthusiasm for trolley coaches was somewhat ambivalent at times. The Canadian Department of Transport, when it wanted to lower the height of streetlights and poles at the airport on Kingsway Avenue, asked about the mode of transit to be used in the future on this route. The City Engineer specified diesel buses but the Commissioner said that trolleys would be used. DOT took its chances and lowered the light standards. The Commissioner's proposed trolley bus subway along Kingsway never materialized, but statistics bore out the popularity of the trolley coach routes elsewhere. 1945 ended with the Street Railway Department again planning many ambitious trolley routes.

In January 1946, the 95 Street extension to 115 Street and 82 Avenue was recommended for the third time. Also planned was an extension of the trolley route west on Jasper from 101 Street to 124 Street, then north on 124 Street, with turning loops at 112 and 118 Avenues. Another route was to be established on 107 Avenue from 101 Street and Jasper, north on 101 Street, west on 107 Avenue, south on 124 Street, east on Jasper, with the same route in reverse.[363] This line was not, however, run as a separate route as proposed, but was, as we shall see, absorbed into an existing route.

On March 20th 1946, 25 more trolley coaches were ordered from Canadian Car for delivery in the third and fourth quarters of 1947.[364] Special service during the Exhibition was advertised that year. Ten-minute service from the centre of the city to the Main Gate via "the most direct route from 102nd and Jasper" was provided by the quiet, fast trolley coaches.[365]

Changes were made in the trolley overhead in March of 1947, from the streetcar wire that was being used at that time, probably to the grooved wire that characterizes trolley coach operation today. During this conversion, the practice of centre-street running was changed in favour of curb-side running.[366] The centre-street bracket arm poles that had been installed for streetcar overhead were removed on Jasper from 109 to 124 streets as they were replaced with curbside poles and span wire. The streetcar rails were also removed on 124 Street from 102 to 107 avenues and the track allowance paved. Paving was continued to 108 Avenue where the turning loop for the trolley coaches was constructed.

Buses 153 through 177 were delivered in September 1947.[367] Twenty-two Brills had been received in January and February with twelve of those immediately put into service; the rest were held until paving programs were complete.[368]

The new west-end extension went into operation Sunday, October 5th, with twenty trolley coaches serving a route from 111 Avenue and 95 Street, south on that street to Jasper Avenue, then west to 124 Street, north to 108 Avenue and return. Introduction of this new trolley coach service replaced streetcar service on Jasper Avenue west of 109 Street.[369]

An *Edmonton Journal* headline of October 4th 1947 read "Trolley buses take on route numbers". These were shown in an outside holder at the right rear of the bus. Officials felt that the front roller names were sufficient without numbers. The west end line linked with the 95 ST : 111 AV line became ROUTE 5; HIGHLANDS ROUTE 2 and the LOW LEVEL BRIDGE line became ROUTE 6. The English buses were delivered with route indicator windows in the front, but they weren't used in the beginning. The Pullmans and Brills did not have separate route number windows, so the outside signs were necessary.[370] By March 1947, the three A.E.C. trolleys were operating only occasionally, but were scheduled for regular service in the summer after extensive overhauling.[371]

Ten more Can Car-Brill T-44 trolley coaches were ordered in March 1948, bringing the total fleet up to 78.[372] By late April of that year, overhead had been strung on 124 Street to 118 Avenue. On Sunday May 2nd, service on the ROUTE 5 line was extended on 124 Street from 108 Avenue to 118 Avenue, except for rush hours when extras turned short at the 112 Avenue loop. RED AND GREEN streetcars westbound on 107 Avenue wyed at 107 Avenue and 124 Street, and then left this point operating over the same route to the South Side as before. A stub service operated into Calder from 124 Street and 118 Avenue.[373]

Streetcar service on 114 (Spruce) Avenue and also on

Above: Two Pullman trolley coaches meet at the intersection of Jasper Avenue and 100 Street. The first coach from Highlands is making the turn from its westbound trip along Jasper Avenue north onto 100 Street leading into the Downtown Loop. It appears the coach poles have "split the switch", that is, one has made the turn, the other followed the streetcar (shared) wire going straight through. The operator has stopped and will get out to re-wire the errant pole. Once that is done, it will make a passenger stop around the corner. The closer trolley coach is on the Low Level Bridge line and is travelling north across Jasper Avenue on 100 Street. Both trolley coaches will go around the Downtown Loop and return to Jasper Avenue, running east from 102 Street. The imposing Imperial Bank of Canada building no longer occupies this site.

(OHIO BRASS COLLECTION, THE STRAHORN LIBRARY, ILLINOIS RAILWAY MUSEUM. LOCATION INFORMATION – COLIN HATCHER)

Below: Probably shortly after introduction, Pullman coach No. 113 – the first of the order – has just come out of 102 Street which formed part of the Downtown Loop and is heading east on Jasper Avenue toward 101 Street. The trolley coach line is in the centre of Jasper Avenue sharing the wire with the streetcars.
(OHIO BRASS COLLECTION, THE STRAHORN LIBRARY, ILLINOIS RAILWAY MUSEUM. LOCATION INFORMATION – COLIN HATCHER)

Above: Pullman trolley coach 128 is working up McDougall Hill from the Low Level Bridge to turn onto 100 Street at the top of the hill. Note the CNR (Edmonton Yukon & Pacific) tracks leading away from the Low Level Bridge which is out of sight behind the photographer. The Alberta Legislature building dome can be seen in the background.
(OHIO BRASS COLLECTION, THE STRAHORN LIBRARY, ILLINOIS RAILWAY MUSEUM.
LOCATION INFORMATION – COLIN HATCHER)

Below: Trolley coach 120 has just turned off 103 Street (today's Gateway Blvd.) from the Strathcona loop and is proceeding east on Whyte Avenue at the CPR crossing north of the CPR South Edmonton station, where it makes the obligatory stop to check for oncoming trains. Note the wire guards to catch the trolley poles if they should come dewired so the coach could still safely make it clear of the crossing. The Western Hardware Building with the glass cupola on top still stands, as does the Princess Theatre identified by its sign. The grain elevator is long gone.
(OHIO BRASS COLLECTION, THE STRAHORN LIBRARY, ILLINOIS RAILWAY MUSEUM.
LOCATION INFORMATION – COLIN HATCHER)

101 Street was discontinued on Sunday, August 29th. As recommended for the third and final time in January 1946, ROUTE 5 was extended to serve 115 Avenue. It ran as follows: from 82 Street and 115 Avenue west on 115 Avenue to 95 Street, south on 95 Street to Jasper Avenue, west on Jasper to 124 Street, north on 124 Street to 112 Avenue and return. Extra coaches were operated from 111 Avenue and 95 Street to 108 Avenue and 124 Street only. ROUTE 2 was also extended to run to 118 Avenue and 124 Street as follows: from 61 Street and 112 Avenue, west on 112 Avenue to 82 Street, south to Jasper Avenue, west to 101 Street, north to 107 Avenue, west to 124 Street, north to 118 Avenue and return. This routing finally used the 107 Avenue section that was proposed as a separate route in 1946 but was never used as such. The sign carried on the westbound leg was 118TH AVE. & 124 ST. and, on the eastbound run, HIGHLANDS.[374]

On January 23rd 1949, a disastrous fire in Regina destroyed the car barns of the Regina Transit System. Included in the loss were many new CCF-Brill trolley coaches stored there awaiting the conversion of the Regina street railway system to trolley coach; many of these had never seen service. The fire so crippled the Regina system that Edmonton's Mayor H. D. Ainlay sent a telegram offering to lend six of Edmonton's trolley coaches.[375] This offer was graciously declined, but Edmonton, which had nine buses on order, waived its place in the CCF order schedule so that Regina could get its desperately-needed vehicles more quickly. (Several other Canadian systems did likewise.) Because of this, the three A.E.C. and six Leyland coaches were given a reprieve from scrapping and were used as short haul peak-hour extras. To reduce the maintenance problems associated with the twin rear axles, one set of the dual axle drives was removed.[376]

Norman D. Wilson returned to Edmonton in 1949 to give a report on the future of the (now named) Edmonton Transit System. He expressed the opinion that the 115 Avenue trolley line, which had been originally strung as a necessity to reach the carhouse, should be abandoned in favour of a north/south line on 95 Street. To solve immediate problems, Council approved an extension of the 115 Avenue trolley coach line west to 102 Street, south on that street to Kingsway Avenue and to 101 Street. This was to overcome duplication of service on 95 Street and bring mainline service into the growing area north of the Royal Alexandra Hospital. This line was, however, never built. The ultimate extension of this proposed 101 Street line south was to be via a descent to the 105 Street bridge and up Walterdale Hill to 109 Street and 82 (and eventually 72) Avenue. This was planned to be in effect before the High Level Bridge could be closed for reconstruction.[377] Extension of trolley coach service over the former 102 AVENUE and BONNIE DOON car lines was also approved. A problem with the proposed 102 Avenue line was that it would provide service to an urban area outside the city limits, the Town of Jasper Place. The city fathers felt that for a self-sustaining transit system, no discrimination should be made regarding provision of transit services to suburban residents within the city limits, so they recommended that the line terminate at the city limits either by an around-the-block loop (149 Street and 103 Avenue) or by an off-street loop. It was further suggested that looping arrangements be made at 123 Street to permit the 102 Avenue line to be operated as a stub service at off-peak hours. Overhead was also to be constructed permitting trolley coaches to be routed to and from the carhouse from the 102 Avenue line via 107 Avenue and 115 Avenue, without having to go through downtown. This was approved in principle, except for the western terminus of the 102 Avenue line which was to be considered further.[378]

Projected Bonnie Doon trolley coaches were to operate via 109 Street and 82 Avenue to provide a cross-town service on 82 Avenue. The line was to follow the same route as the tram line did, except that it would loop downtown or be temporarily linked to the 101 Street–118 Avenue line via 101A Avenue. The question was raised of having the line go up a new road near Connors Road instead of up the hill in Cloverdale. The Cloverdale route was, however, agreed upon.[379] The Bonnie Doon extension was not built, as, in 1951, the feasibility of this cross-town service on Whyte Avenue was discounted due to the great length of this branch, compared with the King Edward Park (99 Street) branch. It was felt that this would result in irregular service over the common route to the North Side.[380]

Some further studies were suggested in 1949 on downtown loops and crosstown service,[381] a change from CALDER streetcars to trolley coaches, and extensions to the ROUTE 5 and ROUTE 2 trolley routes.[382] Council could only agree to locate the 102 Avenue loop of the west-end line on the south side of that avenue between 147 and 148 streets.[383]

In May, Brill buses 188 through 192 were ordered, with delivery for late November and early December.[384] A noticeable change in these and subsequent orders was that the side windows lifted in a manner similar to a house window, instead of the lower sash sliding as it did on the previous models. Improvements in control cables and operating parts were also introduced at this time to better cope with winter icing conditions.

On August 21st 1949, streetcar service on Whyte Avenue ceased and was replaced by trolley coaches. ROUTE 6 trolley coaches continued west of 104 Street along Whyte to 109 Street, where they looped off-street at 83 Avenue to connect with the streetcars. Motor buses served the extension until paving was completed[385] at the end of August when the trolleys then took over.[386] On November 13th, the 102 Avenue west-end motor bus service was converted to trolley coach as ROUTE 7. The route was from the off-street loop at 102 Avenue and 147 Street, downtown via 102 Avenue, 124 Street and Jasper Avenue. Return was by way of 97 Street, 102 Avenue, 102 Street and then via Jasper and as above.[387]

Above: Edmonton Street Railway issued transfers specifically for use on trolley coaches. The left transfer was red and was for the North Side trolley bus route while the right one was white or cream one and was for the South Side route.
(EDMONTON RADIAL RAILWAY SOCIETY; FONDS LESLIE CORNESS)

This new west-end service called for additional power. Late delivery of equipment to increase the capacity of the west-end power substation in 1950 led to a severe drain on power resources early that year. This necessitated spacing of trolleys and trams during the rush hours and corresponding service impairment.[388]

In 1951, the final conversion from street railway to bus operation was outlined. The premise in 1939 had been for a basic electric coach network with feeder motor buses. The war and the attendant material restrictions that continued afterward had given rise to transit operating deficits. Over this period, Edmonton had expanded rapidly, putting an additional strain on the system. However, the trolley coach was still the most economical vehicle to operate; next came the streetcar, and last, the motor coach.[389]

For example, in January 1951, streetcar and motor bus operations lost $16,401, while the trolleys made $13,262 profit. Cost of running a trolley coach was 46.1 cents per mile while it earned 51.05 cents per mile. Motor buses cost 55.1 cents per mile and earned only 42.03 cents per mile. Streetcars cost 62.8 cents per mile and earned 61.2 cents per mile. In the light of these figures, the original policy of using the trolleys on the main routes was upheld.[390]

A new $500,000 South Side Strathcona ("Scona") garage was opened in July 1951, and trolley coach servicing for the buses used on the South Side runs was moved there from the Cromdale Barns. The Pullmans, used mostly on the South Side ROUTE 6 were based out of Scona garage as were their replacement Brills, which were acquired second-hand from Regina in 1966.

A money bylaw to provide funds for conversion of the upper deck of the High Level Bridge to a four-lane street had been defeated in the previous November's election. This was a blow to the High Level trolley coach belt line proposals. However, an alternative north/south route was urgently needed, and while the planning went ahead, a motor bus shuttle was instituted across the lower deck.

Ritchie service was started directly to the North Side with gasoline buses but conversion to trolleys was forecast. New housing around the shopping centre in Belgravia demanded bus service. Again, motor buses were to be used, with eventual replacement by trolleys.[391]

Routes 2, 5, 6 and 7 were suggested for restructuring in a report by the consulting firm of Stevenson Kellogg. It was also felt that the use of a downtown loop on a regular basis should be eliminated.[392] One alternative suggestion was to move it so it ran north on 100 Street to 102 Avenue, east to 97 Street, north on it to 111 Avenue, thence by 95 Street to 118 Avenue, then east to 80 Street and return.[393]

The trolley coach, soon to be the only electric transit in Edmonton, had brushed up its service on August 29th with a switch in routes. "It will be noticed" the *Edmonton Journal* said, "that the east end of the Number 5 Route which formerly went from 95th St. and 115th Ave. to 82nd St. and 115th Ave. has been re-routed to go up 95th St. to 118th Ave. and along 118th Ave. to 80th St. The Number 7 Route which at present is looped downtown will service 97th St. and 115 Ave. from 95th St. to 82nd St."[394] This route ran in the northeast, north from Jasper Avenue on 97 Street to 111 Avenue, east on it to 95 Street, north on 95 Street to 115 Avenue, and along it to 82 Street.

On September 2nd 1951, the last streetcar ran on Edmonton streets, with the trams becoming just a nostalgic memory.[395] Where the steel wheel on steel rail had jostled and swayed with its clickety-clack, now there was just the muffled whine of trolley coach motors as they moved deftly in and out of traffic. The public was enthralled with the coaches' quietness and comfort. But the tram had died prematurely, and the 'Seventies would see its rebirth.

After over a decade of hard service, the last of the English-built buses were retired and scrapped. There was an attempt to sell them in June to the Montreal's transit system, which had the first post-World War I trolley network.[396] Although Montreal Tramways had pioneered the Canadian use of English buses, it wasn't interested in them now. Leyland trolley coach No. 104 had been equipped with a streetcar air whistle at one time in its life, and its scrapping ended many an innocent citizen's bewilderment at hearing a tram coming along trackless pavement.

In 1952, a study was undertaken on the cost possibility of operation by trolley coaches on a 105 Street bridge route. When the new Bellamy Hill road was paved in the spring, a more direct motor bus route from Westwood to Parkallen and Belgravia was instituted. The motor bus route prior to this time detoured west to 109 Street and then back east on Jasper. This resulted in low ridership, but the Hill route was expected to increase passenger loads to the point where electrification was economical. This route would allow a decrease in running time from 82 Avenue and 109 Street to 101 Street and Jasper Avenue, to twelve minutes from the 21 minutes that a trolley coach would take over the High Level Bridge. This, along with the adverse public reaction over the years, sounded the death knell for the High Level Bridge trolley coach proposal.[397]

During 1952, Edmonton ordered four T-48A Brill trolley coaches. These larger buses seated 48 passengers and were equipped with independently opening, double-width, front doors. These could be opened separately or together to facilitate passenger loading and unloading, while minimizing the amount of cold air entering in the winter.[398] In 1953, the only expansion of the trolley network was on ROUTE 2. It was extended in the west end to the Groat Road traffic circle along 118 Avenue.[399]

In August 1954, Council approved the purchase, at a cost of $24,706 each, of six more T-48A trolley coaches.[400] This was the last order for such vehicles, as in that year Canadian Car ceased production of trolley coaches, ending a remarkable manufacturing career in this electric vehicle field.[401] These larger buses were purchased to meet a steady increase in passenger traffic which had not been budgeted for. Fortunately, funds were made available from reserves.[402]

In 1954, the original span of the Low Level Bridge was raised and a new span built beside it. After both spans opened, the north span was only used for northbound travel and the new span for southbound traffic.[403] The ROUTE 6 trolley overhead was altered accordingly. In that same year, ETS pioneered the use of fiberglass panels on buses by installing curved panels at the rear, between the back wheels, and at the front, from the door to the opposite wheel, to minimize wear on these exposed parts. These were made in its own shops.[404]

In 1955, Parkallen residents fought the battle of the petitions for and against a trolley coach route on 65 Avenue. The "cons" were against the sight of poles along their tree-lined street, however they were outnumbered 512 to 45.[405] The next year, the original 1951 proposal for Belgravia was implemented, with that part of the motor bus line moved from 72 Avenue to 76 Avenue and south on 118 Street to loop at 73 Street. This was in preparation for the final electrification stage of this line which served both Parkallen and Belgravia.[406] ROUTE 6 was extended on the south-side to the University Hospital, looping via 82 Avenue, 114 Street, 83 Avenue, 112 Street and return via 82 Avenue eastbound. This was announced on November 27th 1955 and went into service shortly afterwards when wire stringing was complete.[407]

On October 13th 1956, ROUTE 1 was changed from propane buses* to trolleys. It went north on 101 Street to 118 Avenue; the motor bus section from there to 122 Avenue was dropped and covered by other routes. Trolley wires had been installed on 76 Avenue in Belgravia and 65 Avenue in Parkallen, and a roundabout constructed to connect Princess Elizabeth Avenue, 101 Street and 118 Avenue at the north end of the route. The switch from propane to trolley was a matter of economics since electricity was cheaper. This completed the long-range plan of electrifying this Bellamy Hill/105 Street bridge route as patronage increased. Availability of coaches, however, was a concern because the extension had cost $25,000 per mile over four miles.[408]

"Patrons are advised that during the next few weeks they will not see the familiar trolley coaches on this (the No. 6) route. Construction work at the north end of the Low Level Bridge requires the substitution by motor buses. Schedules and service will remain the same." This advertisement in the October 13th 1956 *Edmonton Journal* was unduly optimistic – the construction of traffic interchanges at both ends of the bridge continued until November 17th 1957, when service was finally restored.[409]

In 1958, the transit system celebrated its fiftieth anniversary. The operation covered 57½ miles of trolley overhead using 93 trolley coaches, as well as 106 gasoline, diesel and propane motor buses, cruising over 116 miles of routes. Total assets were nearly $4 million, with a staff of 456 drivers, inspectors and maintenance men. Transportation was being provided to 34,137,948 passengers over 5,616,641 miles a year on a 10¢ fare. Trolley service was seen by Superintendent MacDonald as being too expensive at $30,000 a wire-mile for overhead in residential areas, but it still held sway in the heavily-travelled core.[410] Even as late as 1961, however, with the increasing use of motor buses, statistics still showed that the trolleys turned in $527,000 revenue over expenses. Motor buses ran up a deficit of $785,404 that same year.[411]

With the completion of the new Westwood Garage in 1961, service wire was extended along 118 Avenue west from 101 Street to a loop at the garage at 106 Street. North Side trolley coach servicing and storage was then transferred from Cromdale to Westwood.

On January 1st 1962, the Town of Beverly (pop. 6000) was amalgamated with the City of Edmonton. Any argument against extension of a trolley route into this suburban area no longer held, and Beverly residents demanded better transit service.[412] On September 2nd of that year, the South Side routes were improved with the splitting of trolley ROUTE 1 into two. All South Side routes were

*Propane had been introduced as an economical fuel several years previously.

given letter/number designations. Thus, ROUTE 6 became ROUTE S6, while ROUTE 1 became ROUTE S1 to BELGRAVIA and ROUTE S2 to PARKALLEN.[413]

Late in 1962, the city purchased ten used T-44 Brill trolleys from Vancouver at $2500 each. These twelve- and thirteen-year old vehicles were to be used as spares to replace, in part, the Macks that had been scrapped that year.[414] An *Edmonton Journal* cartoon showed one of the newly-acquired Vancouver buses pulling up to a stop and discharging a cargo of water and fish from the front doors, presumably left over from its Vancouver days.[415]

Since Can Car (CCF) had stopped producing trolleys nearly five years previously, the supply of electric vehicles had become scarce. Several cities had abandoned them due to electricity costs being higher than diesel fuel. However, with its city-owned power utility, Edmonton had been sheltered from this effect. In March 1963, it was recommended that the HIGHLANDS (ROUTE 2) line be extended east in Beverly from 61 Street and 112 Avenue to 50 Street and 118 Avenue.[416] On June 30th, this was put into effect, extending the route east on 112 Avenue to 53 Street, then north to 118 Avenue, east to 50 Street, south on 112 Avenue and return.[417]

In 1964, the trolley system both grew and shrank. In May, Council approved a budget that included $80,000 for a trolley extension to the Town of Jasper Place (pop. 35,000) which was to be amalgamated into the City on August 17th.[418] This was followed by a retrenchment. Power demands exceeded the supply, and due to the high peak-hour ridership on the S6, this route was slated for dieselization. There was also the prospect of considerable roadway changes in that area, so more overhead moves would be expensive. This route had the oldest buses on it, the Pullmans, and the wire over the old Low Level Bridge was worn out. Nonetheless, this stretch of wire had to be replaced to keep the system going for the balance of 1964, even while two or three of the seven coaches were replaced by the experimental motor buses then under test. The remaining Pullman trolleys were scheduled for removal in mid-1965. However, Superintendent MacDonald was optimistic that the motors from the scrapped trolleys could be used in other bus bodies such as the Japanese Nissan and the British-built Daimler designs then under test.[419]

On August 17th 1964, on schedule, service was started into Jasper Place, now a part of Edmonton. This line, ROUTE 7, beginning at 115 Avenue and 82 Street, had looped at the old western city limits between 147 and 148 Streets and Stony Plain Road. It now was extended via Stony Plain Road to 157 Street where a terminal had been constructed. This was called by one source at that time, "the last trolley bus extension in Canada and perhaps in North America."[420]

By the year's end, concern was mounting that the agitation in Calgary to scrap electric transit there would have repercussions in Edmonton. Superintendent MacDonald came out strongly, stating that Edmonton had no intention of scrapping its fleet of 100 trolleys. Their advantages, including their non-polluting capability, made them a viable transportation form. Peak electricity costs that were troubling Calgary were no problem in Edmonton.[421]

On Saturday, August 28th 1965, the last trolleys were removed from the S6 LOW LEVEL BRIDGE route – Edmonton's first trolley coach line falling victim to the relentless onslaught of the diesel bus.[422] Despite MacDonald's statement, some called this line's termination the start of a phasing-out of the trolley bus network. Trolleys were the most efficient bus that the transit system had, but the lack of a bus builder and the disadvantage of being tied to a relatively fixed route were cited as reasons for their gradual disappearance.

Though the Pullmans were the oldest trolleys in the fleet, their passing from the scene was a disappointment to many operators. They were extremely comfortable buses, with excellent heating and a wide driver's compartment that could comfortably fit the most portly operator. Beneath the operator's window was a wide shelf on which one could leave lunches and coffee cups. However this convenience proved a discomfort to operator Dave Fillion one day on the S6 run. The bus had stopped at one end of the Low Level Bridge single span, waiting for the light that controlled traffic flow to change. It was a warm summer day and many of the bus windows, including the operator's, were open. Dave was eating his lunch when he suddenly noticed that his tomato sandwich was soggy. As he pondered the supposed effect of an over-ripe tomato on untoasted bread, a very irate passenger was coming rapidly up the aisle with a damp shirt front demanding at the top of his lungs "what is the transit company going to do about it?" The explanation suddenly became apparent as Dave noticed in his rear view mirror an open cattle truck passing the end of the bus going the opposite way with one cow's tail lifted. The hapless driver could only think of the standard response for any vehicle encounter, "Did you get the number of that cow, sir?"[423]

By 1966, the fleet was down to 82 coaches, the year built ranging from 1946 (six vehicles) to 1954. The Pullmans, Macks and the ACF-Brills, as well as some of the early CCF-Brills, had gone to the scrapyard. The trolley fleet rose to 92 with the purchase of some second-hand units from Regina in March 1966, when that system abandoned its electric buses.

These buses were repainted in a new colour scheme, with a brighter red, and white instead of cream for the roof. Most existing units were also repainted in this scheme.

That same month, city crews started removing the wires on 100 Street from Jasper to 102 Avenue, down MacDougall Hill over the Low Level Bridge, and up Scona Hill to Whyte and west on Whyte to 103 Street. This removed the last reminders of Edmonton's first trolley coach line, 27 years after it had begun operating. Wire was also slated to come down on the University Hospital extension from

109 Street to 114 Street, along 83 Avenue to 112 Street, and south to Whyte Avenue.[424]

With the changing of several downtown streets to one-way, trolley routes were restructured on July 2nd 1967. Two sections of wire were strung downtown; a single westbound line from 97 Street to 101 Street along 102A Avenue for short-turning buses, and a single line west from 101 Street along 103 Avenue to 102 Street, then south on 102 to Jasper. A second section ran along 102 Avenue from 102 Street to 97 Street. The trolley routes were rearranged and renumbered at this time. Routes 2 and 7 were dropped. The new ROUTE 3 went from 115 Avenue and 82 Street to Groat Road and 118 Avenue. When going eastbound, it ran south on 101 Street, west on 103 Avenue, south on 102 Street, east on 102 Avenue to 97 Street and north on it. Morning and afternoon extras worked the west end of this line, and were numbered ROUTE 4, looping east on 102A Avenue, south on 97 Street, west on Jasper Avenue, and north on 101 Street. There were no changes in ROUTE 5, but the north terminus of the S1/S2 was moved from the 118 Avenue and 101 Street circle, along the former service wire, to a loop at 106 Street and 118 Avenue at the south end of Westwood Garage.[425]

The future looked bleak, but the system held on until the Seventies dawned. Pollution became a popular topic, and the environment was being "saved" all over North America. Edmonton, with its fume-free buses, committed itself to prolonging the system. Fifteen trolley coaches were purchased from Winnipeg in 1969 to be cannibalized for parts.[426] The system continued to hang on by its teeth.

However, the trolleys' sun was rising in the east. In 1970, the Toronto Transit Commission purchased 151 new bus chassis and bodies to make into new trolleys by installing the indestructible motors from the old Brills. The bus skeletons were to be supplied by Western Flyer

Above: Skipping in anticipation of Daddy arriving on the next bus, the little girl is not as interested in Pullman 121 in its last days in June 1964 at the 101 Street and 118 Avenue loop on the S2 route.
(G.M. ANDERSEN PHOTO, KRAMBLES-PETERSON ARCHIVE)

Industries in Winnipeg. The Toronto rebuild had been "in the works" with Flyer since 1967, and Edmonton watched the progress of the Toronto experiment anxiously. Maintenance costs on the old trolleys had climbed past that of diesel buses, but "fuel" was still a cent a mile and depreciation costs by now were nil. The costs of wire extensions had risen from $30,000 per mile in the 1950s when the last extension had been made, to $60,000. Importing equipment from Europe was ruled out as too expensive. Toronto was probably the only transit system with extensive-enough shops to undertake the rebuild job itself, since it also maintained Canada's only streetcar fleet in the same facility. Cities other than Toronto would have to order the trolleys factory-built, and until there was sufficient volume, the cost of the Flyer trolley coach was deemed uneconomical.[427] The remaining systems were in Vancouver, Toronto and Hamilton, with the Calgary network dying a slow death.

In September 1971, MacDonald was appointed City Transportation Director, retaining his position as Superintendent of ETS. He had joined the organization in 1946 and had overseen the gradual replacement of streetcars by trolley coaches. He continued the conversion of the trolley coach network after he replaced Thomas Ferrier as ETS Superintendent in 1951.[428] Now he was watching to see if it would experience a rebirth.

The trolleys' supposed salvation arrived in Edmonton on January 6th 1972. A Toronto Transit Commission/Flyer-built trolley coach (TTC No. 9213), looking much like a GMC "new look" diesel in appearance, ran on the

Above: ACF-Brill 129 on the s1 run is northbound on 109 Street (Edmonton South Side) making the turn to go down Walterdale Hill on a winter's day March 21st 1965.
(PETER COX COLLECTION, CANADIAN TRANSIT HERITAGE FOUNDATION. LOCATION INFORMATION – COLIN HATCHER)

101 Street route on a trial basis. This trolley bus, on a tour of several western Canadian and US cities, was the first built in North America in thirteen years, and the first in Canada in eighteen. Toronto was committed to replacing its 152 trolley coach fleet entirely with 152 new Flyers, and Edmonton's 92 Brill trolley coaches were in no better shape.[429] In 1973, the balance of trolley operations was transferred from Scona to Westwood garage, and all but one of the trolley wires through the Scona garage were removed.

By 1973, Toronto had taken delivery of 152 Flyer trolley coaches, and Hamilton had some also. A factory-built trolley was now an economic reality so Edmonton ordered 37, the start of a planned replacement that would see 75 new trolleys in the next two years.[430] Western Flyer was now known as Flyer Industries, and the Manitoba government, through the Manitoba Development Corporation, had taken a controlling interest in it. Several US transit systems were looking seriously at the new trolley and helped boost support for it.[431] In December 1973, Robert R. Clark, an Edmonton Transit supervisor, wrote a report "Comparison of Trolley and Diesel Buses", recommending the existing routes be continued and fully utilized, that vehicles and overhead be upgraded, and extensions made where the volume of traffic warranted.[432]

The first shipment of 25, E800 Flyer coaches was due in February 1974, to be followed in June by the remaining twelve.[433] In August, Edmonton ordered twenty more coaches worth $1.1-million for delivery in September 1975, and seventeen coaches worth another $1.1 million for September 1976.[434] By December 1974, only one unit (No. 213) had been delivered, and the remaining 24 were five months overdue.[435] Technical problems with the controller on bus 213 kept it from being put into service for a time. Flyer was also in the midst of a disastrous strike that was to delay further the balance of Edmonton's order for new coaches.[436]

In the fall of 1974, ETS purchased twenty of Calgary's trolleys for parts as they were too rundown to rehabilitate. It also acquired motors, poles, controllers and line hardware from the now-defunct Calgary system.[437]

In May 1975, there were four Flyers in Edmonton, and by July, the Flyer contingent was up to eight. Delivery problems, as well as many mechanical and electrical problems with the buses, prompted ETS to ask for a full financial analysis of maintaining or phasing out the trolley coaches. Another factor against the electric buses was increased power costs due to rising natural gas prices, which fueled the electricity generation facilities. In addition to labour problems, Flyer was having trouble meeting its promised dates due to sub-suppliers' late deliveries. There were problems with electrical components burning up when the power polarity was changed. Flyer revised its polarity-sensitive components. Other problems surfaced, such as the bus heaters drawing so much power that they tripped the power switches in the overhead. The design of the rear spoiler (to hold optional air conditioning) caught the retriever ropes when the poles swung out on a far reach. ETS modified the rear of the buses as each required shopping.

Three more Flyers had arrived, but shortly after settlement of the long strike, the plant had shut down again for summer vacation. Edmonton was becoming discouraged about the trolley's salvation to the point of requesting another trolley coach feasibility study be undertaken by an independent firm regarding retention of the system.[438]

In November, a new ROUTE 7 – linking Belgravia with Jasper Place via 107th Avenue – was constructed, extending wire along 107 Avenue from 124 Street to 156 Street and thence south to the Jasper Place terminal.[439] On December 8th 1974, an extension from 124 Street west on 114 Avenue through to the new Westmount transit terminal was opened to trolleys.[440] A unique feature of this line was the one-block private right-of-way running through the parking lot of the Charles Camsell Hospital. This avoided the buses having to make a jog around the Hospital. No doubt the silent running of the trolleys was a plus factor in obtaining permission to run a bus route directly behind a hospital. The line passed through a residential area, and again the trolleys' features helped in winning over the homeowners to having a bus route run past their doors. The line looped behind the Westmount Shopping Centre, giving passengers immediate access to it. This wire was used by the new ROUTE 5 that ran from Westmount Terminal via 114 Avenue to 124 Street, south on it to Jasper Avenue, east on Jasper to 95 Street, north to 118 Avenue and along that to the eastern terminus. At least one truck driver was surprised by this addition when he drove his oversize load through the new overhead as he went down Groat Road during a Friday rush hour. By then, 37 Flyer coaches were on ETS property, but the Brills were still kept in service as much as possible. Other routings were a peak hour ROUTE 4 from Downtown, north on 124th Street to the terminus of ROUTE 3 on 118 Avenue and Groat Road/St. Albert Trail. The routes actually looped around the Groat Road roundabout, terminating on 118 Avenue just east of the loop.

In late spring 1975, Jasper Avenue was closed from 102 Street to 100 Street during the construction of the new Light Rail Transit line.[441] At first, buses only were allowed. The trolleys ran on temporary overhead suspended from wooden centre-street poles. Finally, on June 8th, all traffic was banned, so all eastbound trolley routes detoured around the site by going north on 102 Street over a new stretch of wire to 102 Avenue and then to 97 Street. Westbound buses travelled via 97 Street, 102A Avenue and 102 Street. The north/south wire on 101 Street was left intact as it crossed Jasper for the S1/S2 buses.[442] Service was restored on Jasper Avenue in September.

In September 1975, a start was made on extending the 109 Street overhead through to the new Southgate Transit Centre, initially located at 111 Street and 54 Avenue. This would allow the new ROUTE 9 to be electrified. This route initially began service with diesels on November 9th 1975, offering fifteen-minute service between Southgate and 118 Avenue and 101 Street. At that same time the north terminus of the S2 route was moved south to 109 Street and 83 Avenue, operating on a half-hour service. The S2 ran only during the peak hours through downtown to the Northern Alberta Institute of Technology (NAIT). For a time before this, there was a controversy over the routing of ROUTE 9 through the residential section of the Pleasantview area near Southgate. Eventually the trolleys won, and the line was extended south on 109 Street from 65 Avenue to 57 Avenue, west to 111 Street and south to the temporary terminal at 54 Avenue.[443] By the year's end, wire was strung and construction of a new power substation was well underway.[444] On February 1st 1976, the north terminus of ROUTE 9 was extended to loop at Westwood garage. At the same time, poles were being erected down 106 Street south past NAIT, to enter the new Kingsway Garden Mall from 106 Street and loop there. This was the first time that a shopping plaza had allotted space for a transit terminal in the actual mall area for shoppers' convenience.[445]

By April 1976, feeder cable was strung for the SOUTHGATE ROUTE 9 extension and the substation completed.[446] In May 1976, regular trolley bus service began on ROUTE 9. The NAIT/Kingsway Mall extension was also completed as the north part of the S1.[447] A turning loop was also constructed on 121 Street and 102 Avenue west to 124 Street for the western terminus of an eventual electrified #2 route. Equipment shortages and overhead changes stalled this conversion.[448] On February 1st 1976, ROUTE 4 was changed to run to Westmount transit terminal instead of to Groat Road and 118 Avenue. A new ROUTE 6 was introduced to run from Groat Road and 118 Avenue to 81 Street and 118 Avenue along ROUTE 5. ROUTE 4 and ROUTE 6 were peak-hour-only services.[449]

All Flyer buses as received had been painted in the Edmonton Transit System colours of white and red. In 1976, the word "System" was dropped from the name, with an ultramodern new logo and a blue, white and yellow paint scheme adopted. Since all Flyer trolleys had been fabricated and painted before the change, only those damaged in use were repainted. Bus No. 232 was the first one dressed up in this new finery.[450]

In September 1976, poles were erected on Kingsway Avenue from 108 Street to 101 Street in anticipation of an extension to the S1 and S2 from the Kingsway Mall to 101 Street.[451]

Another era passed on December 5th 1976, when the old letter/number route designations were replaced with numerals only. The only trolley routes affected were the S1 ROUTE 41 and S2 ROUTE 42. In the first part of 1978, all transit buses were equipped with new roller signs to give a consistency to the fleet for the Commonwealth Games.

The extension along Kingsway Avenue came into service on February 13th 1977. It ran from 101 Street to 108 Street, where it turned north and joined the loop in the Kingsway Shopping Mall. At this time, the north leg of ROUTE 42 was reinstated, allowing Parkallen residents all-day through-service to downtown and NAIT. Both ROUTE 41 and ROUTE 42 looped through the Westwood loop, (106A Street and 118 Avenue) and then ran via 106

Street to 112 Avenue through the shopping mall to 108 Street, and thence south to Kingsway, 101 Street, Bellamy Hill, 105 Street bridge, Walterdale Hill, 109 Street. At 76 Avenue, ROUTE 41 ran west on it to 118 Street and south to 73 Avenue. The ROUTE 42 line continued down 109 Street to 65 Avenue and west on it to 112 Street.[452] On November 22nd 1977, the temporary terminus at the south end of ROUTE 9 was moved from 54 Avenue to a permanent transit centre in the Southgate Shopping Mall.

The Kingsway Mall loop was rearranged in April 1978, so that the through wire path was straightened. The loop was broken so that coaches could not turn back at the mall and go north unless there was a wire jump. The remainder of the loop was retained in case ROUTE 18 should be electrified. Late in 1978, ROUTE 1 was rewired to pass by the Stadium LRT station. This involved a jog up 84 Street from Jasper to 111 Avenue, and east on it to join the old wire at 82 Street. The existing outbound wire was retained for short-turning use. In that case, outbound buses would proceed past the new switch at 84 Street, along the old wire, and turn into the station at 111 Avenue, so that all inbound buses were facing the same way. The change in routing, however, only took effect in the summer of 1979.

Old age took its toll of the Brills, however. Every two months, one was taken out of service and pensioned off. Some were stripped for parts to keep healthier sister units going. Many were stored and patched so as to be serviceable for the two weeks of the Commonwealth Games, when all available vehicles would be needed. A small but vocal public noticed the attrition and kept asking about the state of electric transit in Edmonton. With the advent of the Light Rail Transit System, the logic of maintaining electric surface transit became stronger, but the fleet still dwindled.

What was to become of the oldest continuously-running trolley coach network in Canada? The unhappy experiences with the new Flyer trolleys forced the City to commission another evaluation of the advisability of continuing with electric buses. A report by Hu Harries and Associates supported the viability of trolley coaches – but the question remained: whence will they come? The Brills' day had passed; they lasted longer than most motor buses, but even these venerable war horses would have to be put out to pasture eventually. These questions were put by an *Edmonton Journal* reporter to E.V. Miller, Edmonton Transit's General Manager, early in 1978. Miller cited the difficulties they had experienced in finding suitable replacements, and the fact that the old Brills were falling apart. The possibility of a joint purchase with Vancouver in order to lower the vehicle price was being investigated. Mr. Miller stated that not only was there money budgeted for new trolleys, but wire improvements were being planned as well. Edmonton Transit, he said, has a firm intention to continue to provide trolley bus service.[453]

Would Edmontonians be able to stand a few years hence on an early frosty winter's morning and hear the stillness broken only by the hiss of carbon shoes on wire and the "clickity-clack" of the poles passing through the switches? Would the only sound as the bus pulls away from the stop be a soft whine from the motor and the thump of the compressor, or would the stillness be broken by a diesel's growl? Certainly the sound wouldn't be that of a Brill, for on November 19th 1978, the last of the breed ran on a special farewell trip. ET bus 202, the last T-48 Brill produced in Canada, was chartered by the Alberta Pioneer Railway Association, and sent with much publicity on a grand tour under most of the city's overhead. Harry Venecamp negotiated the bus through numerous pieces of special overhead and posed the bus for the many picture stops. At the conclusion of the trip, coach 202 joined 191 – an example of an unaltered T-44 Brill still in the cream roof and red sides paint scheme – and Pullman 113 as part of the Edmonton Transit historical collection. But perhaps the best news was confided to this author by Mr. Miller during the pre-trip press session, that at least fifty trolleys would be purchased for delivery over the next two years. These coaches would replace the Brills and build the fleet back up to its previous strength. This information was publicly confirmed on the day of the trip and warmly received by the assembled trolley coach supporters.

This was a first step in the right direction, but things seemed to move slowly. It wasn't until the summer of 1979 that the next extension took place. In conjunction with reconstruction of Groat Road and 118 Avenue traffic circle, routes 3 and 6 were extended to an off-street loop at 142 Street and 118 Avenue. Work progressed throughout the summer and into the new year. Service started on February 3rd 1980. Older style overhead was replaced with state-of-the art K&M (Kummler+Matter) equipment, and power switches in the lines were replaced with radio controlled switches. Further extensions were planned to Northgate, Abbotsfield, and West Jasper Place (West Edmonton Mall). In addition, tenders for one hundred new trolleys were called in the winter of 1979, with delivery to commence in 1981. Despite concerns over a sole-source supplier, and the delays delivering the Flyer E800 order, the competitive process took a more comfortable turn with the announcement in 1975 that General Motors of Canada would produce trolley coaches in its London plant. They had already bid on a Vancouver order and on one for Philadelphia. Edmonton bet on GM, and the order was placed with a consortium of Brown Boveri (electrics) and GM (chassis and body) in August 1980 that would bring the trolley coach fleet up to 137, the largest ever.

Extensive changes also took place in the Edmonton trolley coach scene during the years between the retirement of the CCF-Brills and the arrival of the Brown Boveri coaches. Some of these were brought about by the planned redirection of roadway traffic, resulting in the need to alter bus routes. Others were necessitated by major construction projects. Finally, some changes came about due to the extension of the trolley coach network to areas never before served by electric transit vehicles.

Above: The sun is setting on a crisp January day in 1977 and venerable T-44 coach 191 is seeing its last days on ROUTE 9 southbound on 109 Street at 84 Avenue. The only T-44 still in its as-delivered configuration (original tail lights etc.), No. 191 was saved from the wrecker to become part of the ETS historical fleet. Unfortunately, vandalism during storage doomed its survival.
(TOM SCHWARZKOPF)

In an effort to maximize the use of existing roadways, the City of Edmonton instituted an extensive system of one-way streets approaching the High Level Bridge and Walterdale Bridge over the North Saskatchewan River. This was called Project Uni. The project affected north-south trolley coach routes. The High Level Bridge connecting 109 Street across the river became one way southbound and the Walterdale Bridge (105 Street bridge) became one way northbound. New wire for southbound coaches was strung from the foot of Bellamy Hill at 97 Avenue, west to 109 Street, and then across the traffic deck of the High Level Bridge, to connect again with the existing southbound wire on 109 Street at 88 Avenue. Subsequently, southbound trolley coach overhead was removed from Walterdale Hill, Walterdale Bridge, the 105 Street traffic circle, and 104 Street to 96 Avenue.

Project Uni went into effect on November 16th 1980. It was May 4th 1981, however, before South Side bus routes 9, 41 and 42 were again electrified. The stringing of trolley coach overhead across the traffic deck of the High Level Bridge with its low clearances posed some difficulties, but these were overcome. The wires were suspended from a corrugated panel fixed to the bridge members and running the full length of the bridge. The panel was slightly wider than the wire track and served to prevent the trolley poles from flailing up against the cross members of the bridge should the poles become de-wired. Coincident with this new overhead construction, a short-turn loop at the Renfrew Park Baseball Stadium (now called Telus Field) was built. The former southbound wire from Bellamy Hill across 97 Avenue to 104 Street was left in place as far as 96 Avenue. From this point, the wire was extended one block east on 96 Avenue to connect with the northbound line at Rossdale Road where the Renfrew Stadium was located.

During the summer of 1980, Jasper Avenue was closed from 99 Street to 96 Street to allow construction of the Edmonton Convention Centre (now called Shaw Conference Centre). This necessitated the rerouting of all transit services in this area. Since trolley coach overhead was not in place on the detour routes, diesel buses were assigned to routes 1, 5 and 6. Effective with this rerouting, trolley coach operation in Edmonton was restricted for a period of almost one year to occasional deployment on ROUTE 3. Trolley coach assignment to this route was possible as, effective December 23rd 1979, it operated on 102A Avenue between 97 and 101 Streets, where overhead was already in place.

Two further closures of sections of Jasper Avenue resulted in additional rerouting of transit services. The first detour took effect on October 26th 1980, when Jasper Avenue from 106 Street to 109 Street was closed to allow work on the extension of the underground LRT stations. The second stage of the LRT construction detour became effective March 1st 1981, when Jasper Avenue was closed to all transit traffic from 102 Street to 109 Street. Most of these transit services were rerouted to 102 Avenue.

Above: Well past its retirement, Pullman 113 (nee 116) is taken on a fan trip November 2nd 1975. Here it is passing through private right-of-way behind the Charles Camsell Hospital. This was the only fan trip on the only surviving Pullman coach on probably the only trolley coach private right-of-way in Canada. (TOM SCHWARZKOPF)

During the period when trolley coach operations were severely restricted, considerable work was undertaken to prepare for the delivery of the 100 new Brown Boveri trolley coaches. Westwood shop was extended with the overhead line in and around the shop completely rebuilt. Edmonton Power crews were also busy installing new overhead wire in the downtown area. The first of these new installations involved an eastbound extension of the overhead on 102 Avenue from 97 Street through to the intersection of 95 Street and Jasper Avenue, to connect with northbound wire on 95 Street and eastbound wire on Jasper Avenue. The existing westbound wire on Jasper Avenue was routed into 102A Avenue and extended west along 102A Avenue to connect with existing wire at 97 Street. Wire was also installed on both sides of 102 Avenue from 102 Street to 109 Street, and south on 109 Street to Jasper Avenue. Completion of this work enabled Edmonton Transit to assign trolley coaches to the detoured ROUTE 6. Westbound buses on this route detoured via 102A Avenue, from 95 to 102 Street, south to 102 Avenue, then west into a contra-flow bus lane on 102 Avenue (that avenue is one way eastbound) to 109 Street and south to Jasper Avenue, where they continued their westbound trip. The eastbound ROUTE 6 buses detoured off Jasper Avenue at 109 Street, travelling north to 102 Avenue, then running east to 95 Street, where they turned north to pick up their regular route again.

Once the LRT construction advanced far enough to allow the re-opening of Jasper Avenue, most transit services returned to that thoroughfare in two stages. During the first phase, while transit traffic was still very light on Jasper Avenue, the overhead line was replaced on both sides of the avenue between 102 Street and 109 Street. New wire was installed north on 99 Street from Jasper Avenue to existing wire on 102 Avenue, affording an eastbound connection onto 102 Avenue. For westbound service, the line was extended north on 99 Street to connect with the 102A Avenue line, enabling westbound trolleys to branch off the 102A Avenue line and run south on 99 Street to Jasper Avenue.

The existing trolley overhead wire was removed along 102 Avenue from 128 Street at the entrance to the Royal Alberta Museum to 156 Street. The traction poles that supported the trolley wires along this stretch were removed and replaced with larger, heavier poles, and two sets of new trolley overhead wires were installed in each direction. One set was for regular trolley service on ROUTE 1, while the second set was to allow for the electrification of ROUTE 10, which ran express along this stretch. New traction poles were installed along 97 Street toward Northgate, but overhead wire was not erected there at that time.[454]

By April 25th 1982, all of these installations were completed, and effective with that date, most transit services were restored to Jasper Avenue, with the exception of the three block Convention Centre detour. Since new overhead wire was constructed along the detour route, trolley coaches began to appear again on routes 1 and 5 for the first time in almost two years. With the return of ROUTE 6 to Jasper Avenue, the new line on 102 Avenue from 102 Street to 109 Street, and on 109 Street from 102 Avenue to Jasper Avenue, became surplus to any regular service. It remained intact, however, as an alternative route in case of an emergency, offering the flexibility necessary to maintain an efficient service in the downtown area. The de-

In July 1981 Edmonton Transit aired out its historical fleet (Pullman 113, Brill T-44 No. 148 and T-48 No. 202) to offer sightseeing tours through old Strathcona and over the High Level and Low Level bridges to and from the City Centre. (SCHWARZKOPF COLLECTION)

livery of most of the new Brown Boveri trolley coaches, combined with the installation of the previously described overhead wire, enabled Edmonton Transit to assign trolley coaches to all of the routes formerly served by that mode.

A major extension of trolley overhead line in the west-end from the ROUTE 3 terminal at 118 Avenue and 142 Street, enabled coaches on that route to extend their trips west on 118 Avenue to 156 Street and south on 156 Street to the Jasper Place terminal at Stony Plain Road. Since ROUTE 3 trolley coaches shared this terminal with the ROUTE 1 coaches, overhead wiring in the terminal area was extended and extensively upgraded to accommodate the intended electrification of two additional bus routes using the terminal. The terminal was therefore laid out to handle a total of four trolley coach routes. Most of the new overhead in Edmonton was suspended with European K&M fastenings, but most of the turnouts, except for a few new electric ones, were of the Ohio Brass design. The Jasper Place terminal area, however, used the European suspension and turnouts exclusively. One ROUTE 3 bus operated over this new extension every half-hour, while fifteen-minute base and ten-minute peak hour services were maintained on the balance of the route.

Service on the extension commenced on Sunday, September 5th 1982. Due to Edmonton Transit's practice of serving all routes with diesel buses on Saturdays, Sundays and holidays, the first revenue trolley coach operation was delayed until Tuesday, September 7th 1982, right after Labour Day. ROUTE 3 and ROUTE 4 service also returned to Jasper Avenue effective September 5th 1982, after an absence of almost three years. Westbound trips operated via 102A Avenue, west to 99 Street, south to Jasper Avenue, then west to 101 Street, where they turned north to continue along their former routes. Also effective September 5th 1982, westbound ROUTE 1 trips travelled along Jasper Avenue to 121 Street only. Here they turned north to 102 Avenue, then proceeded west to the Jasper Place terminal. This change eliminated the left turn at the busy intersection of 124 Street and 102 Avenue. All other trolley coaches continued west on Jasper Avenue, past 121 Street to 124 Street, then turned north onto 124 Street. The overhead at 124 Street and 102 Avenue was altered to accommodate the route change.

The Brown Boveri trolley coaches were built by General Motors, not in London, but at Ste. Thérèse, Quebec to T6H 5307N specifications. GM also designed the roof reinforcement to support the trolley pole assembly. The coaches seated 42 passengers. Single cross-seats along the left side made for a wide aisle, providing free movement of passengers when entering or leaving the coach on the heavily-travelled main line routes to which these coaches were assigned. The completed bodies were shipped to Edmonton on railway flatcars during the closing months of 1981 and throughout 1982. Final installation of the Brown Boveri chopper control electrical equipment was carried out by Bennett & Emmott Ltd. in Edmonton. The chopper control reduced maintenance and energy consumption, as well as offering extremely smooth starting and braking. Powerful dynamic brakes reduced the need to use air brakes, resulting in increased brake lining life. A transistorized converter supplied the low voltage system and charged the batteries. The heating system ensured passenger comfort during those occasions when Edmonton temperatures dip as low as minus 40 degrees on either the Celsius or Fahrenheit scales. Passenger safety was enhanced by the double-insulation of all systems connected to the line.

The prototype coach number 100 underwent extensive testing on city streets before being placed in revenue service. On November 10th 1981, coach 100 was officially accepted by Edmonton Transit and began regular operations on November 19th. By mid-January 1982, several of the new coaches were operating in regular service. Soon the Brown Boveri coaches greatly outnumbered the 37 Flyer coaches which had held a three-year monopoly on trolley coach assignments in Edmonton since the November 1978 retirement of the Brill coaches.

In September of 1982, all runs on all trolley routes were filled by trolley coaches – but only for a day, as power supply problems kept much of the city's new $21-million trolley fleet off the streets. There was a risk that if three or four buses were in the same section of trolley overhead, an overload could result, said Ed Kyte, general manager of Edmonton Power, and there are other phases of operation where a similar result can occur. Over the next few weeks, the number of BBC trolleys on the road gradually increased, but a significant number of the scheduled trolley trips continued to be filled by diesel buses.

By September 1983, trolley service had begun on a revised ROUTE 2 running from the Oliver loop at 124 Street and 102 Avenue via Jasper Avenue, 84 Street, 111 Avenue, 82 Street, 112 Avenue, to the Highlands loop at 53 Street, 118 Avenue and 112 Street. Four-tracking of the overhead on Stony Plain Road and 102 Avenue was completed from 156 Street to 128 Street, but was still unused. Plans were in place for an extension of ROUTE 9 north from 101 Street, east on 118 Avenue to 97 Street, north to the Northgate loop at 135 Avenue.[455]

By 1984, a drop in transit ridership and an economic recession resulted in City Council looking for economies, and it decided that Transit had 100 surplus vehicles. Edmonton Transit, which had been an independent department, became a part of the Transportation and Streets Department, resulting in an increased focus on roadways and a lesser focus on transit.

Then, a 1985 report recommended that the city maintain an equivalent-sized fleet of diesel buses solely for the purpose of providing emergency back-up for use in instances of power outages or construction, a recommendation that was adopted by ET despite the fact that no other trolley coach system maintained such a back-up fleet. Although much of this report was not given much credence, Council did cancel all of the planned trolley extensions, and as a result, Transit had an immediate surplus of trolley coaches: forty almost-new BBC trolleys, and 37 Flyer coaches that were just over 10 years old. This meant that the express wire to Jasper Place would never see revenue service, and the Northgate extension would never be completed. It was suggested that the surplus trolley coaches be sold to other transit properties. Accordingly, the 37 Flyer trolleys were sold to Mexico City. A buyer could not be found for the forty BBCs.

In 1988, the City commenced negotiations with the Toronto Transit Commission (TTC) to lease or sell up to forty trolley coaches, with an option for a further lease of twenty units to the end of 1991. The end result of these negotiations was that the TTC leased forty surplus BBC trolleys for three years starting in 1990.

In 1993, there was another lengthy review of the trolley service. Following this, City Council agreed to a "proactive upgrade program", which meant that the trolley infrastructure would be upgraded, and a better, ongoing maintenance plan implemented to improve the condition of the overhead. Council also directed "that the Transportation Department, Edmonton Transit, Edmonton Power and the Public Works Department be instructed to make maximum use of the trolleybus and trolley wire system presently in place". Things seemed to be looking up for trolley coach service.

The lease of the forty Edmonton trolleys to the TTC expired in July 1993, and the buses were returned to Edmonton, but instead of being put into service, were inexplicably placed in storage. Rick Millican, General Manager of Transportation stated that it would be more difficult to keep trolleys on the road in Edmonton as the $720,000 annual revenue from the lease had been used to maintain and upgrade the overhead lines. In an attempt to save costs, it was proposed that all South Side trolley routes be dieselized. The proposal included combining trolley ROUTE 9 with diesel ROUTE 29, and extending service to Northgate. City Council agreed to a four-month test to compare the cost of running trolleys on South Side routes 41 and 42 with the cost of running diesels on ROUTE 9. A report comparing the costs was never prepared, and diesel buses continued to run permanently on ROUTE 9. As a result of strong opposition from residents of Belgravia and Parkallen districts, Council directed that trolley service continue on routes 41 and 42. With trolley service now discontinued on ROUTE 9, it meant that the number of trolley buses in daily service was reduced, and the overhead wiring from 65 Avenue to Southgate was no longer being used at all, seemingly the exact opposite of City Council's directive to make maximum use of the trolley coaches and trolley wire system in place.

In May 1994, trolley routes 1 and 2 were merged to form a combined ROUTE 1, which ran between Jasper Place and Highlands.

In 1997, Edmonton Transit commenced a program called Horizon 2000, which called for an overall restructuring of public transit throughout the City. ROUTE 1, which had been a trolley route, was extended to Clareview in the northeast and Grant MacEwan College downtown, but without additional overhead, it became a permanent diesel route. From that point on, trolley overhead to Highlands was never used again, although it did remain in place, again the opposite of Council's directive to maximize trolley use. Trolley routes 41 and 42, which ran from NAIT to Belgravia and Parkallen respectively, were discontinued. Trolley ROUTE 7, which had run from Jasper Place to the downtown Rossdale loop via 156 Street and 107 Avenue, was extended south along the portion of the former ROUTE 41 into Belgravia. A new trolley ROUTE 133, was created, and followed the same route as ROUTE 7, except that it continued along what had been the southern portion of ROUTE 42 into Parkallen. This ROUTE 133, however, ran during peak hours only, Monday through Friday. Only routes 3 (Cromdale to Jasper Place) and 5 (Westmount to Coliseum) remained intact and unchanged. ROUTE 5 was supplemented during peak hours by a short turn version of the route running from Downtown to Westmount called ROUTE 135. Another new trolley route created at this time was ROUTE 120, which replaced the western portion of the former route 1 to Jasper Place. This route ran during daytime and evening hours from Jasper Place, along Stony Plain Road, 102 Avenue, and Jasper Avenue to down-

Above: Coach 174 sits at the NAIT terminal on a February 1977 afternoon waiting for a sister Brill to leave. The venerable coaches were showing their age, but kept in service in anticipation of heavy passenger traffic for the August 1978 Commonwealth Games as advertised by the rear window sticker.
(TOM SCHWARZKOPF)

town, terminating at Stadium Station. A final new trolley route replaced the northern portion of routes 41 and 42, running from NAIT through downtown to the Rossdale loop. This route, 131, was to run only during peak hours and only during the portion of the year that NAIT was in session. However, it attracted few passengers and was discontinued after less than one year. The end result of these changes to the trolley routes was that scheduled peak hour vehicle requirements dropped to 38 from 44. Many scheduled trolley trips were still being serviced by diesel buses, and trolley coaches continued to be a rare sight on weekends.

Increased overall transit ridership resulted in some trolley service improvements. During 1998, service on ROUTE 135 was expanded from peak hours only to daytime service from 7:00 AM to 6:00 PM weekdays. To alleviate frequent overcrowding on diesel ROUTE 9, a short turn version of the route was created in 1998, running between the Rossdale loop and NAIT via Kingsway Avenue. This route was serviced by two trolleys running weekdays between 7:00 AM and 5:00 PM. As well, one morning trolley trip was added on ROUTE 9 between Southgate and NAIT.

In April 1998, the contract for maintenance of the trolley overhead with Edmonton Power (EPCOR) was renewed for a further ten years. In the year 2000, a new trolley substation was built in Rossdale at a cost in excess of $2 million.

In 1999, plans were announced to increase service on the short turn ROUTE 9 by adding two additional trolley coaches, but this was never implemented. However, on September 25th, sixty years and a day after the first trolley coach ran on Edmonton's streets, ETS threw a Trolley Party. They recreated an historic bus stop on 102 Avenue just east of the Provincial Museum of Alberta, where they unveiled a trolley coach commemorative plaque. Then from noon until 4:00 PM, there were rides on two historic and one modern trolley for 1939 fares (10 cents adult; 5 cents child). The historic buses were units 148, a 1949 T-44 Brill, and 202, a 1954 T-48A Brill, and a modern bus, a 1982 BBC. In addition, Pullman No. 113 was displayed, and rides circled a loop from 124 Street to 147 Street along 102 Avenue. A slide show ran at the Museum, and trolley bus souvenirs were sold. Aside from getting the historic bus' build dates wrong in the promotion, it was a truly a festive occasion. This had been preceded with a picture of historic Leyland No. 106 on the Spring Summer Ride Guide noting 60 Years of Trolley Service.[456]

But even with all this trolley coach hoopla, the arrival of articulated diesel buses in 2001 for service on ROUTE 9 resulted in cutbacks to the trolley service. First, the start time for the trolley-operated short turn route was moved up to 11:00 AM, and the end time moved to 4:00 PM. In 2006, trolley service on the route was cut back to only one bus. A number of citizens observed that trolley service had been deteriorating and that replacement with diesel buses was ever more frequent. At the encouragement of former Alberta Environment Network (AEN) Executive Director Barry Breau, a group of these citizens gathered in the facilities of AEN in 2001 and formed The Edmonton Trolley Coalition. Early members included a former City councillor, a retired ETS supervisor of transit planning, several university professors, and representatives from three community organizations. As the decline of the trolley system became increasingly evident, the organization experienced

165

an influx of concerned citizens from all areas of the city, including trolley drivers and other transit personnel, and representatives from community leagues where the trolleys operated. In 2003, Citizens for Better Transit, a general transit advocacy group, was also drawn into the issue.

In 2003, evening and Sunday service was discontinued on ROUTE 120. At the same time, midday and Saturday service was interlined with ROUTE 3. In late 2003, as part of the annual budget review for 2004, City Council asked city administration to look for ways to cut $18 million from the budget without cutting services. The City's Mobile Equipment Services Department undertook a review of the costs of operating the trolley coach fleet, and engaged consultants Booz Allen Hamilton (BAH) to review the City's trolley operations. Their report was released in January of 2004, and was met with immediate criticism. The report stated that the price of diesel fuel was stable and would remain so for the foreseeable future. In fact, the price had been increasing steadily for several years, and the increases were sometimes so steep that transit administration had to request additional funds from the city, partway through a budget cycle. The report also compared the cost of maintaining 23-year-old trolley coaches with an average for the diesel fleet, the better part of which was less than six years old. On the other hand, the report did point out that utilization of the trolley network had declined over the past few years, and stated that in recent years, it had been operating at 45 to 70 per cent utilization. A representative of BAH described this performance as being "below industry standards". The report did not make any recommendation regarding whether or not the trolley system should be retained, but did state that the city could save $19.83 million over six years if trolley service was eliminated and replaced with diesel buses.

On March 9th 2004, City Administration prepared a report "Future Trolley Operations In Edmonton" which recommended that Edmonton's trolley coach operation be discontinued in 2004, with the trolley fleet and infrastructure declared surplus and disposed of. The report stated that this would result in savings of $43.2 million over the next ten years. On March 16th, the Transportation and Public Works Committee (TPW) of City Council directed Administration to consult on the future of trolley operations with the community, as well as appropriate bodies such as the ETS Advisory Board and the Edmonton Federation of Community Leagues. The firm Marcom Works was engaged to conduct the public consultations. There were three components to the public consultation. One was a telephone survey of randomly selected citizens, the second was a customer survey of individuals randomly selected at transit centres, and the third was two advertised public meetings with interested participants. The telephone participants were read a background paper with a seemingly anti-trolley bias "to assist their understanding of the issues", and then were then asked a series of questions. The transit customer participants were given the background paper to read, then asked the same survey questions.

The public meetings were moderated by an external facilitator from Marcom Works. Attendees were given the background paper, and presentations were made by the Manager of Edmonton Transit, a member of The Edmonton Trolley Coalition, and a member of Citizens for Better Transit. The facilitator then directed questions from attendees to the three presenters. Questionnaires, similar to those used in the previous two surveys, were distributed at the close of the meetings. Results of the surveys were as follows:

a) Telephone survey: 48% agreed with the recommendation to discontinue trolleys, 37% disagreed, and 15% had no opinion.
b) ET customers: 58% agreed with the recommendation to discontinue trolleys, 30% disagreed, and 12% had no opinion.
c) Public meetings: 15% agreed with recommendation to discontinue trolleys, 76% disagreed, and 9% had no opinion.

At the June 22nd 2004 Transportation and Public Works Committee meeting, a Non-Statutory Public Hearing was held. Twenty-two citizens of Edmonton made presentations in support of continuing trolley operations. A representative from Booz Allen Hamilton presented their report, indicating that the city could save $19.83-million if trolley service was eliminated and replaced with diesel buses. City Administration presented their report, recommending that trolley service be ended immediately, and stated that this would result in savings of $43.2-million.

At the July 27th 2004 City Council meeting, motions were made and carried that:

1. Edmonton Transit continue to operate trolleys until 2008.
2. Administration arrange to have a demonstration of low-floor trolley and hybrid buses to be utilized within the system for information gathering.
3. Expansion of the trolley fleet to Northgate be considered in the 2006 budget.
4. A report be provided to Council in 2008 regarding continuation of trolleys based on
   • service levels
   • environmental concerns in light of the demonstration of low-floor trolley and hybrid buses, and other options.
5. Administration continue to look at ways to maximize the cost-benefit of trolleys.

During discussion of motion 5, City Manager Al Mauer was asked what could be done to achieve this. A suggestion was made that the trolley system could (again) be expanded to Highlands, and he responded "we've got to look at the whole thing … of adding to it, there is (sic) lines that are there right now that aren't used … the other is to look

Above: Old trolleys never die, they just go south to a warmer clime. November 6th 1978 finds retired Edmonton Flyer trolley coaches on flat cars at the South Edmonton yards, bound for Mexico and a new life. (COLIN K. HATCHER)

at the possibility in the construction season of staging our construction different and so on … the decision has been made, and we will maximize use."

A Transit News Release issued on July 29th 2004 contained a Manager's Message stating "We will continue to operate trolley buses as we do today until 2008. There are no changes planned to the existing routes and schedules where trolley buses run", seemingly in contradiction to his statements to Council. Media reports following Council's decision quoted City Administration as stating that $60.7 million could be saved by ending trolley service, however that figure had not been mentioned in Administration's presentations to City Council.

In 2006, a newly-elected City Councillor initiated a strong push to end trolley service, but was unsuccessful, and funding was instead approved to refurbish 25 trolley buses. However, trolley service was suspended on ROUTE 7 to facilitate LRT construction and though set to return in 2008, it did not. City Council decided that it would be too costly to extend trolley service to Northgate.

In 2007, overhead wiring to Southgate Transit Centre along 111 Street from 57 Avenue was removed, ending the sole morning trolley trip on ROUTE 9. Eighteen vehicles had been refurbished by June 2007 when the program was suspended and no further refurbishment took place.

In April 2007, the City engaged R.A. Malatest & Associates Ltd. to survey passengers riding on ETS trolley buses. Participants were given a survey form to complete, and asked to drop it in a box near the exit of the bus. Survey results were:

1. 35% of respondents agreed they ride a particular route because it is a trolleybus, 65% neither disagreed nor agreed.
2. 16% would not ride routes 3, 5, and 9 if a regular bus was substituted for a trolleybus, 84% neither agreed nor disagreed.
3. 49% of respondents agreed that they preferred trolley buses over other types of buses, 51% neither agreed nor disagreed.

After the unsuccessful attempt to end trolley service in 2006, administrators began to act on the testing of hybrids, new trolleys and diesels, as required of them in the 2004 City Council decision. Arrangements were made for the purchase of six diesel-hybrid buses from two different manufacturers, and a single new low-floor trolley coach was leased from Vancouver for a period of one year. It arrived on June 19th 2007, but did not enter service until September 4th, wasting almost three months of the trial period. Booz Allen Hamilton was called back to update their 2004 report, and Dr. David Checkel, a University of Alberta professor with a background in internal combustion engines, was engaged to produce a second report. Leger Marketing was engaged to survey citizens, bus users, operators and maintenance staff, and relevant stakeholder groups for their opinions on future bus purchases.

The hybrid buses were put into service sporting large signs promoting the hybrid technology both inside and outside the vehicles, proclaiming them as "clean diesel". The leased trolley, however, did not have any promotional signage. During the comparison of the three modes, at no point did the various test buses run on the same route under the same service conditions. The hybrids were housed in a suburban garage, and they were assigned to long-haul diesel ROUTE 8. During the month of February 2008, at which time Leger Marketing was surveying users on ROUTE 5, the hybrids were moved to ROUTE 5. During that month, no trolley buses, not even the leased Vancouver trolley, were run on that route. Noise tests for the diesels and hybrids took place at the Namao army base air field, far from the city in an open field, where the sound could dissipate in the open air. Trolley noise testing took place on an urban street near a rail level crossing with several buildings nearby to amplify any low noise levels that the trolley might produce.

Trolley coaches, like light rail, run on fixed infrastructure that has a relatively fixed annual maintenance cost.

167

Above: Wearing the fleet number of a retired Brill, BBC 191 swings through a leafy residential neighbourhood with barely a sound on the Belgravia run in 1985.
(TED WICKSON)

If many trolley coaches run, then the portion of the per-km cost of operation related to infrastructure maintenance will be low, but if few trolleys run, then their per-km cost will appear very high. The 2004 Council motion had specifically called for service levels to be included in a review of trolleys. However, at the time of the review, there was a peak assignment of 24 trolleys running on a system designed to run 100 trolleys. These buses were providing only rush hour and midday tripper service. Thus, in the 2008 reports, all cost assumptions were based on a trolley system operating at one quarter of its designed capacity.

In April 2008, the leased Vancouver trolley coach was returned after less than seven months of testing on Edmonton streets. The operators who drove it were never asked for their opinion. Unfortunately, during the testing, the bus ran only on weekdays, only on ROUTE 5 and its short turn version, ROUTE 135. Early in 2008, trolley service on the short turn ROUTE 9 ended, replaced by diesel buses.

On April 18th 2008, the last trolley coach ran on ROUTE 5. After that, the overhead wires were removed on a portion of 118 Avenue for a street beautification project. They were never returned.

On June 10th 2008, a Non-Statutory Public Hearing on the future of trolleys was held in City Council chambers. Twenty-six members of the public spoke in favour of retaining the trolley system, a large number considering that most issues in Edmonton bring out only a few speakers. In his presentation, hired consultant Dr. Checkel stated that the City could save $110-million by replacing the trolleys with diesel buses, or $100 million by replacing the trolleys with hybrid buses. The Booz Allen Hamilton report stated that replacing the trolleys with diesel buses would save the City $130-million, and replacing trolleys with hybrids would save $122-million. City Administration claimed there would be a $99.7-million saving by replacing trolleys with hybrids. While the end result savings figures looked fairly similar, there was considerable variation in how they were arrived at. For example, a comparison of some costs per bus km:

Costs/Report	Checkel	BAH	Vancouver 2000*
General bus maintenance	$0.86	$0.34	$0.46
Power cost	$0.31	$0.14	$0.15
Overhead maintenance	$1.75	$2.46	$0.28

*Vancouver figures were from a year 2000 report, and reflected costs of operating older trolleys. They were shown for comparison only. A similar breakdown of figures used by City Administration was not available. There were other inconsistencies evident throughout the reports.

Leger Marketing also made a presentation at the Public Hearing, however the results of their survey were considered to be of little value. According to Marc Tremblay, vice president of Leger Marketing, their survey compared modern diesel buses, hybrid buses, and 28 year-old trolley coaches. No comparison was made with the leased Vancouver trolley.

On June 18th 2008, City Council met, and a following motion was tabled that:

1. the trolley system be phased out in 2009 and 2010.
2. the purchase of 47 new hybrid buses, to be received in 2010, be approved, with funding identified in the 2009-2011 capital budget process.
3. the decommissioning of the remaining trolley infrastructure in 2010 be approved.

The final debate over the future of Edmonton trolleys started with a plea by Transportation General Manager Bob Boutilier who said "Every dollar you spend on trolleys is money that's not being spent on other transit service and other transit technology." Transit officials had recommended eliminating trolleys by 2010 and buying 47 new hybrid buses. Trolley supporters said the system should be retained and expanded, disputing the figures used in the reports, and arguing Edmonton needed alternative sources of power for its transit fleet because oil is becoming scarce.

Councillor Jane Batty said, "If we're really that passionate about the environment … then in my opinion we have to support the motions that are in front of us. Trolley buses need to be eliminated, … ."[457] Apparently, in her opinion, hybrid diesel-electric buses were better for the environment than all-electric trolley buses.

But University of Alberta engineering professor David Checkel, the author of one report, accused his critics of taking a nostalgic approach that didn't reflect the improvements in modern buses.

"It's a combination of a whole lot of improbable things to make trolleys look attractive," he said. "I would rather see us spend money to put more buses on the streets so we can get more cars off the road."[458]

The vote was 7-6, with the majority of councillors accepting reports indicating the move would save $100 million over the next eighteen years, enabling the City to expand the transit system.

By the fall of 2008, the hybrid buses, the perceived wave of the future, were running into problems. Despite ads on the buses claiming fuel savings of 35%, only a 10% reduction had been realized. That, coupled with reliability issues, the high purchase price and the lack of significant emission reductions resulted in City Council deciding to replace the hybrid order with standard diesel buses. Two of the hybrids proved to be so unreliable that they were removed from service early in 2009. They would ultimately go back to the manufacturer, be gutted, and turned into conventional diesel buses.

A decision was made to end trolley service in May 2009 instead of 2010 to shave $756,000 from the 2009 budget.

"Anyway, only 24 of Edmonton's 37 trolleys, which date from 1982, are still in active service," said Dennis Nowicki, Edmonton Transit's director of community relations.[459]

Funding for removal of the overhead wires was budgeted for three years, starting in 2009. Due to budget constraints, in the fall of 2008, City Council approved a motion not to fund the first scheduled year of wire removal, but despite this motion, wire started vanishing late in 2008, and continued in earnest into 2009. Repeated attempts by the Edmonton Trolley Coalition and Citizens for Better Transit to determine how this overhead removal was being paid for, if funding had indeed been withdrawn, were to no avail. Soon, all wire not directly used for the remaining trolley operation had been removed.

Trolley service on ROUTE 133 was scheduled to end on April 24th 2009, but a watermain break and sinkhole on April 2nd resulted instead on it ending that very day.

Friday, May 1st 2009 was scheduled to be the last day of trolley service in Edmonton. Councillor Don Iveson, who wanted to retain the vehicles, was still unhappy. "The outcome was prejudged and that remains a great disappointment to me as an elected official, that a case was brought to us with a predetermined conclusion." The Councillor said the city administration didn't propose cheaper ways to operate trolleys, such as putting more vehicles along less than the 127 km of wire now being maintained. "This sad failure is why trolley supporters, including a number of us on Council, will mourn the decommissioning of this remarkable aspect of Edmonton history" he blogged.[460]

The only routes still being serviced by trolleys were 3, 135, and 120. Routes 135 and 120 ran only until 6:00 PM, and although there had been seven trolley routes, the only one still running full time was #3, between the Jasper Place Transit Centre and the Cromdale loop at 115 Avenue and 82 Street. The last ROUTE 3 trolley returned to Westwood garage at approximately 1:00 AM the following morning, May 2nd.

Senior administrators didn't want a ceremony to mark the end of nearly seventy years of trolley service in Edmonton, but after pressure from the Edmonton Trolley Coalition and Citizens for Better Transit, Charles Stolte, Manager of Transit, organized a ceremony of sorts by running trolleys on ROUTE 3 on Saturday May 2nd 2009. Service began at 5:29 AM between Jasper Place Transit Centre (100 Avenue and 156 Street) and the Cromdale loop. The last complete trip on a regular BBC trolley left Jasper Place at 2:30 PM, returning at 4:30 PM. Regular fares applied! A special charter on a vintage red-and-cream Brill trolley (T-48 No. 202) provided free service on the route from 1:45-3:45 PM. The final trip, driven by operator Ernie Bastide, carried special guests including trolley-supporting councillors Hayter and Iveson, from downtown to Cromdale, arriving at the Westwood Garage as "the last Edmonton trolleybus" at 5:00 PM.[461]

By Monday, May 4th 2009, all overhead wiring was removed from Westwood garage and power to remaining

Above: Coach 158 painted with an unique environmental message passes under the China gate leading to Edmonton's China Town, 102 Avenue and 97 Street. This was a charter run for the Edmonton Radial Railway Society on March 13th 1994.
(COLIN K. HATCHER)

overhead was turned off. Edmonton Transit planned to keep one of the vehicles for its historical display while one went to the Reynolds-Alberta Museum in Wetaskiwin. One BBC was sold to the TRAMS transit historical group in Vancouver, one to the Seashore Trolley Museum (Kennebunkport, ME), one to the Illinois Railway Museum, one to The Trolleybus Museum in Sandtoft, UK (billed as Home to the Word's Largest Trolleybus Collection), and two went to Dayton, OH. Fifteen months later, all traces of the 87-mile overhead system, which had been valued at $116-million by the City's Asset Management Department, had vanished, a full year ahead of schedule. Over $6-million was expended to remove the wires, which were sold as scrap for $250,000. Just two years later, service on some of the most heavily used former trolley routes had already been reduced, suggesting that fewer people were now riding those lines, and no satisfactory account of what happened to the claimed $100-million in savings was ever produced.

After closure of the trolley system, 28 BBC trolleys were sold to Plovdiv, Bulgaria for $2500 each. Upon their arrival in Bulgaria, government customs officials stated that the buses were worth much more than $2500, and assessed customs duties accordingly. The duties were not paid, and at last report the buses were going to be sold by the government for scrap. All in all, the final sad ending to the longest continuous trolley coach service in Canada.

Footnotes:

This account is extracted from *Edmonton's Electric Transit*, Colin K. Hatcher and Tom Schwarzkopf, Railfare Enterprises Limited, Toronto, ON, 1983 – Chpts. 15-17 authored by Tom Schwarzkopf – and Appendix D Trolley Extensions from 1981-82 by Colin K. Hatcher. Complete information from September 1982 to closure was written by Brian Tucker, Edmonton with edits and additional sources provided by Tom Schwarzkopf.

308. City of Edmonton Archives City Commissioners Files, A 73-52 Box 151, Report on Edmonton Street Railway and Recommendations for 1938 Program, December 22, 1937.
309. *Ibid.* Minutes of Edmonton City Council, February 28, 1938.
310. *Ibid.* Report of Wilson & Bunnell, April 30, 1938.
311. *Ibid.* "Report on Street Railway Improvements" by Commissioner R.J. Gibb to City Council, June 20, 1938, pp. 3 and 4.
312. *Ibid.* Copy of call for tenders for 6, 38 to 44 passenger trolley buses for the City of Edmonton, July 21, 1938.
313. *Ibid.* Recommendation of Commissioners to Council, October 11, 1938.
314. *Ibid.*, Council's decision, October 11, 1938.
315. *Ibid.*, Letter from Commissioner R.J. Gibb to R.D. Parsons, J.G. Brill Co., Chicago, April 19, 1939.
316. *Edmonton Journal*, May 19, 1939.
317. *Ibid.*, September 4, 1939, and subsequent accounts.
318. *Edmonton Bulletin*, September 12, 1939, p. 1.
319. *Edmonton Journal*, September 21, 1939.
320. *Edmonton Bulletin*, September 20, 1939, p. 1.
321. *Edmonton Journal*, September 23, 1939, p. 18.
322. *South Edmonton Weekly News*, September 21, 1939, pp. 1 and 2.
323. *Edmonton Journal*, September 23, 1939, p. 15.
324. *Ibid.*, –September 25, 1939.
    –*Edmonton Bulletin*, September 25, 1939, p. 1.
325. *Edmonton Journal*, October 4, 1939, p. 9.
326. *Ibid.*, October 11, 1939, p. 10.
327. *Edmonton Bulletin*, October 24, 1939, pp. 1 and 16.
328. Commissioners, *Op. Cit.* Council Minutes, November 27, 1939, Item 10.
329. *Ibid.*, Letter from Commissioner R.J. Gibb to C.R. Garnett, Gorman's Ltd., December 8, 1938.

330. *Ibid.*, –Letter from R.J. Gibb to S.L. Wilson Goode,
H.M. Trade Commissioner, Vancouver, October 24, 1940.
–Reply to above, October 26, 1940.
–Letter from R.C. Humphry, Leyland, Toronto, to
Commissioner R.J. Gibb, October 4, 1940, re: Canton buses.
–Subsequent correspondence through balance of 1940.
331. *Canadian Transportation*, January 1948, pp. 32-35.
332. City of Edmonton Archives, City Commissioners Files,
Transit Controller G.S. Gray to Commissioner R.J. Gibb, May 21, 1942.
333. –*Edmonton Bulletin*, February 10, 1943.
–*Ibid.*, February 15, 1943.
334. Commissioners, *Op. Cit.* Telegram from Commissioner R.J. Gibb
to Controller G.S. Gray, August 3, 1943.
335. *Edmonton Bulletin*, *Op. Cit.*, August 16, 1943.
336. *Ibid.*, –September 14, 1943, p. 1.
–October 5, 1943, p. 16.
–October 13, 1943.
337. Commissioners, *Op. Cit.* Letter from Controller G.S. Gray
to Commissioner R.J. Gibb, May 29, 1944.
338. *Ibid.*, Decision of Council, June 12, 1944.
339. Commissioners, *Op. Cit.*, G.S. Gray to R.J. Gibb, January 9, 1945.
340. *Ibid.*, R.J. Gibb to G.S. Gray, January 17, 1945.
341. *Ibid.*, ACF-Brill Motor Co. Philadelphia, to R.J. Gibb, March 16, 1945.
342. *Ibid.*, Letter from ACF-Brill Motor Co., Philadelphia,
to R.J. Gibb, March 16, 1945.
343. *Edmonton Bulletin*, *Op. Cit.*, March 6, 1945.
344. Commissioners, *Op. Cit.*, Letter from G.S. Gray to R.J. Gibb,
April 2, 1945.
345. *Ibid.*, Canadian Car-Brill, Toronto, Ontario to R.J. Gibb, July 24, 1945.
346. *Ibid.*, Minutes of City Council, February 1, 1946
(reaffirming decision of August 13, 1945, pp. 230 to 232).
347. *Ibid.*, Letter from Winnifred Audley to Mayor J. Fry, February 23, 1945.
348. *Ibid.*, Reply to Miss Audley from R.J. Gibb, February 27, 1945.
349. "The Trolley Coach", a symposium held during the 41st Annual Meeting
– Canadian Transit Association, June 12, 1946, from a talk by Thomas
Ferrier, Superintendent, Edmonton Radial Railway, pp. 17-24.
350. Commissioners, *Op. Cit.*, Recommendations, R.J. Gibb
to Transportation Committee, May 10, 1945.
351. *Edmonton Bulletin*, July 20, 1945, p. 15.
352. Provincial Archives of Alberta, Collection 75-11 Box II,
Carbon of Newspaper ad copy.
353. Commissioners, *Op. Cit.*, Copy of requests for bids, August 20, 1945.
354. *Ibid.*, Reply to tentative order for Edmonton, from
Canadian Car & Foundry-Brill, Toronto, August 13, 1945.
355. *Ibid.*, Reply to bid from Mack Trucks of Canada, Toronto,
August 20, 1945.
356. *Ibid.*, Reply to bid from Twin Coach, Kent, OH, August 23, 1945.
357. *Ibid.*, Reply to bid from Pullman-Standard, Chicago, August 28, 1945.
358. *Ibid.*, Reply to bid from MCI (Motor Coach Industries), Winnipeg,
August 23, 1945.
359. –*Ibid.* City Council Minutes, re: Transportation Committee Report
No. 6, Section 2 dated September 29, concurred on October 9, 1945.
–Letter from R.J. Gibb to E.J. Cosford, Sales Manager,
Canadian Car & Foundry Ltd., Toronto, Ontario, October 10, 1945.
360. *Ibid.*, Letter from R.J. Gibb to Twin Coach, October 10, 1945.
361. *Ibid.*, Letter from R.J. Gibb to Mack Trucks of Canada,
October 10, 1945.
362. *Ibid.*, Letter from W.J. Beatty ACF-Brill, Philadelphia to R.J. Gibb,
October 4, 1945.
363. Commissioners, *Op. Cit.*, City Council Minutes, February 18, 1946.
364. *Ibid.*, Memo from R.J. Gibb to Superintendent T. Ferrier,
March 20, 1946.
365. Archives, *Op. Cit.*, Carbon copies of newspaper ad copy used in 1946,
1949, 1950 and 1951.
366. Commissioners, *Op. Cit.*, Memo, D.B. Menzies Commissioner,
to Chief Constable R. Jennings, City Police, re: bus route changes,
March 27, 1947.
367. Edmonton Transit, Telegrams from CCF-Brill to Superintendent
T. Ferrier, re: shipments of units T44-47-5176 through T44-47-5193,
September 4 to 17, 1947.

368. *Ibid.*, Telegrams, re: shipments of units T44-47-5023 through
T44-47-5044, January 8 to February 6, 1947.
Ibid., Letter to R.R. Mills, District Manager, Canadian Ohio Brass Co.
Ltd., Niagara Falls, Ontario, from Superintendent T. Ferrier, July 31,
1947.
369. *Edmonton Journal*, October 4, 1947 and Archives carbon
of newspaper ad copy.
370. *Ibid.*, p. 1.
371. Transit, *Op. Cit.*, Letter from Assistant Superintendent D.L. MacDonald
to Associated Equipment Co. of Canada, March 15, 1948.
372. *Ibid.*, Letter to E.J. Cosford, Sales Manager, Canadian Car & Foundry
Ltd., Toronto, from Assistant Superintendent D.L. MacDonald,
April 2, 1948.
373. *Edmonton Bulletin*, May 1, 1948, p. 2, and Archives carbon of
newspaper ad copy.
374. *Edmonton Journal*, August 28, 1948 and Archives carbon
of newspaper ad copy.
375. Commissioners, *op. cit.*, Telegram from Mayor H.D. Ainley (Edmonton)
to Mayor Garnet Menzies (Regina), January 24, 1949.
376. Transit, *op. cit.*, Letter from D.L. MacDonald, Assistant Superintendent
ERR, to D.J. Monroe, Superintendent Equipment, Montreal Tramways,
January 27, 1949.
377. Commissioners, *Op. Cit.*, Recommendations of Commissioners,
re: Report of N.D. Wilson, part B reference pp. 22 and 23 of Wilson
Report. Recommendation (1).
378. *Loc. Cit.*, Recommendation (2).
379. *Loc. Cit.*, Recommendation (3).
380. *Ibid.*, Report "1951 – Final Conversion from Street Railway
to Coach Operation", p. 2.
381. Recommendations, *op. cit.*, Recommendation (6).
382. Commissioners, *Op. Cit.*, Proposed 1948 Conversion,
April 26, 1948, Item 3.
383. *Ibid.*, Council Minutes, July 11, 1949.
384. Transit, *op. cit.*, Letter to A.E. Jennings, Assistant Sales Manager,
Bus Division Canadian Car, Montreal, from D.L. MacDonald,
Assistant Superintendent, May 12, 1949.
385. *Edmonton Journal*, August 20, 1949, p. 1, and
Archives carbon of ad copy.
386. *Ibid.*, August 29, 1949.
387. Archives, *op. cit.*, carbon of ad copy dated November 12, 1949.
388. *Edmonton Journal*, January 27, 1950.
389. Commissioners, *op. cit.*, Report "Edmonton Transit System
Streetcar Conversion Program – 1951 – Final Conversion from
Street Railway to Coach Operation", March 1951.
390. *Edmonton Journal*, March 12, 1951.
391. *Ibid.*, January 18, 1951, p. 1.
392. Commissioners Report 1951, *Loc. Cit.*
393. Commissioners, *op. cit.*, Council Minutes,
C.R. No. 16 Item 8, April 9, 1951.
394. *Edmonton Journal*, August 29, 1951.
395. Dated photograph, N. Corness collection.
396. Edmonton Transit to R.E. Fielder, G.M. Truck & Coach Div.,
Pontiac, MI., from T. Ferrier, June 22, 1951.
397. City Archives, *op. cit.*, undated clipping probably Spring 1952.
"Study Busline to South Side for Conversion to Trolleys."
398. *Trolley Coach News, Trolley Bus Bulletin No. 105*, and
Edmonton Transit Garage Records.
399. Route Map, Edmonton Transit dated September 1953.
400. Commissioners, *op. cit.*, City Council Minutes,
Commissioners Report No. 24, Item 10, August 9, 1954.
Note of concurrence dated August 9, 1954.
401. *Edmonton Journal*, March 28, 1966.
402. *Edmonton Journal*, August 9, 1954.
403. City Archives, *Edmonton Journal* clipping only dated 1954,
"Both Bridges Open But Cars Using One."
404. *Ibid.*, October 18, 1954.
405. Commissioners, *op. cit.*, petitions by 512 Parkallen residents in favour of
and 45 objecting to trolley poles on 65th Avenue, May 19, 1955.
406. Edmonton Transit, paper "History of Route Extensions and Systems
Expansion", no date – c1958, p. 3.

Trolleybus Souvenirs

To commemorate the 60th Anniversary of the Trolleybus in Edmonton, we've produced a few very nice limited edition souvenirs.

The trolleybus calendar contains 16 months of spectacular photos of historical and current trolleybuses on Edmonton streets. Cost is $10.

The lapel pins have an image of a cream and red historic Brill trolleybus and are available for $3.

The t-shirts are a pale yellow with a logo similar to the lapel pin and come in two sizes - child is $10 and adult (M, L, XL, XXL) is $15.

All items will be on sale on site at the 60th Anniversary celebrations, September 25. After the celebrations, calendars and lapel pins will be available at the Citizen Action Centre in City Hall. The ETS Customer Information Office in Churchill LRT Station will sell all three items.

Quick Commute Downtown

Commuting Downtown by bus may be easier and faster than you think. We've got two super-express routes from Heritage Mall and West Edmonton Mall that will get you to work, in most cases, as quickly as by car. West end and southside residents who neither need nor can afford the woes and costs of Downtown parking can try these routes to the heart of the city.

Route #47 is a weekday peak service running non-stop to Downtown from Heritage Mall along Calgary Trail. Park for free at Heritage and ride worry free to work.

Route #100 is an all-day super express route that travels from West Edmonton Mall to Downtown with no stops until it gets to 111 Street. After that, it stops at all the bus stops along the route into the Downtown.

"In Transit" is published for customers of ETS by the Customer Services Section, 11904 - 154 Street, Edmonton, Alberta T5V 1J2
www.gov.edmonton.ab.ca/transit

It's a Trolley Party!

Our trolleybus service turns 60 this year and we're having a party to celebrate. You're invited!

The party is planned for Saturday, September 25 because it was September 24, 1939 that Edmonton's trolleybuses first went into service.

We've recreated an historic bus stop on 102 Avenue just east of The Provincial Museum of Alberta (12845 - 102 Avenue). That's where we're starting the celebrations, with an official ceremony featuring the unveiling of a trolleybus commemorative plaque.

From noon to 4 p.m., we've organized public rides on two historical and one current trolleybus. For the outrageous cost of 10 cents per adult and 5 cents per child (1939 fares), you'll be able to hop on a 1948 Brill, 1953 Brill or a 1982 BBC trolleybus and ride a circle loop from 124 Street to 147 Street along 102 Avenue. There's also a 1944 Pullman trolleybus on display.

We also have historical trolleybus slide shows by Douglas Cowan, a noted trolleybus supporter and historian, at the Museum Theatre during the afternoon.

Trolleybus souvenirs include a 16 month commemorative calendar, lapel pin and T-shirt.

Commemorating 60 years of trolleybus service in Edmonton 1939 - 1999

This plaque is located on the route of the Centre Loop, Edmonton's original downtown trolleybus terminus, in use from 1939 to 1965. The Centre Loop ran counterclockwise via 100 Street, 102 Avenue, 102 Street and along Jasper Avenue.

Left and Above: In 1999, Edmonton Transit System celebrated the 60th anniversary of trolley coach service with Leyland 106 on the Ride Guide cover, a Trolley Party with souvenirs and T-shirts, and a commemorative plaque – all for the longest running trolley coach system in Canada. Ten years later the trolley coach system had vanished from Edmonton streets. (RIDE GUIDE AND PARTY: SCHWARZKOPF COLLECTION; PLAQUE: TROLLEYBUSES.NET)

---

407. *Loc. Cit.*
408. *Edmonton Journal*, October 13, 1956.
409. –*Ibid.*, October 13, 1956 (advertisement).
    –Commissioners, Memorandum from D.L. MacDonald to City Commissioners, etc., November 15, 1957.
410. *Edmonton Journal, Loc. Cit.*, March 4, 1958.
411. *Ibid.*, March 28, 1962.
412. Edmonton Transit, paper "History of Trolley Coach Route Installations, Extensions, Removals", no date c.1965, p. 2.
413. Edmonton Transit System "New Improved ETS South Side Routes Effective September 2, 1962" (Schedule).
414. Commissioners, *Op. Cit.*, Memo from D.B. Menzies, Commissioner, to D.L. McDonald, Superintendent Transit System, November 7, 1962.
415. *Edmonton Journal*, Editorial Cartoon, November 1962.
416. Commissioners, *op. cit.*, Letter from W. Robertson, Director Operations, Edmonton Transit to Commissioner D.B. Menzies, March 7, 1963, and *Edmonton Journal*, November 8, 1962.
417. Transit, History of Trolley Coach, *Loc. Cit.*, p. 2.
418. *Edmonton Journal, op. cit.*, May 12, 1964.
419. Commissioners, *op. cit.* – Memo from D.L. McDonald to C.Z. Managhan, Supervisor Electrical Distribution System and W.D. Kirland, Supervisor Power Plant, Edmonton Power, May 14, 1964.
    –Memo from D.L. McDonald to D.B. Menzies, Commissioner, June 2, 1964.
420. CRHA *Rattler* (Canadian Railroad Historical Association – Rocky Mountain Branch), September 12, 1964, p. 3.
421. *Edmonton Journal*, December 21, 1964, p. 34.
422. *Ibid.*, August 27, 1965, p. 22.
423. Personal recollections of D. Fillion as related by his son-in-law, R. Rynerson.
424. *Edmonton Journal*, March 28, 1966.
425. *Ibid.*, June 30, 1967, p. 23.
426. *Trolley Coach News*, No. 10, August 1970, p. 57.
427. *Edmonton Journal*, August 14, 1970.
428. Edmonton Transit, List of Superintendents of the ETS.
429. *Edmonton Journal*, January 7, 1972, p. 22.
    Loc. Cit., October 18, 1972.
430. *Ibid.*, October 12, 1973.
431. *Edmonton Journal*, November 3, 1973, p. 30.
432. *NATTA Special Bulletin No. 9*, April 1975, reprinting Report #1 November 1973
433. *Ibid.*, August 9, 1974.
434. *Ibid.*, October 25, 1974.
435. *Ibid.*, December 7, 1974, p. 8.
436. *Ibid.*, August 1, 1975, p. 7.
437. *Edmonton Journal*, August 1, 1975, p. 7.
438. *Transit Canada* magazine, September-October 1975 Vol. XI No. 5, p. 13.
439. *Trolley Coach News*, #28 Vol. 6 #4 Fall 1974 p. 91.
440. Personal observations by author.
441. Personal observations, Schwarzkopf and Hatcher.
442. *Edmonton Journal*, June 5, 1975, p. 21.
443. Alberta Pioneer Railway Association (APRA) *Marker*, September 1975, p. 7.
444. *Ibid.*, October 1975, p. 4.
445. *Ibid.*, November-December 1975, p. 13.
446. *Ibid.*, April 1976, pp. 46-47.
447. *Ibid.*, June 1976, p. 71.
448. *Ibid.*, September 1976, p. 102.
449. *Edmonton Journal*, January 31, 1976.
450. Personal observations by author.
451. Personal observations by author.
452. *Edmonton Journal*, February 8, 1977, p. 29.
453. *Edmonton Journal*, February 22, 1978, Section B, first page.
454. Brian Tucker.
455. *Trolley Coach News*, #56 Summer/Fall 1983 pp. 13-14.
456. *In Transit*, September 1999 Customer Publication of Edmonton Transit System (ETS) author's collection.
457. "City council votes to scrap trolley buses", Gordon Kent, edmontonjournal.com, June 18, 2008.
458. *Ibid.*
459. "Edmonton trolleys parked for good on Saturday" Gordon Kent, edmontonjournal.com, May 1, 2009.
460. "Trolleys' last stop on road to oblivion. Supporters mourn decommissioning of fleet" Gordon Kent, *Edmonton Journal*, May 2, 2009 p. B3.
461. Gordon Kent, edmontonjournal.com, May 2, 2009 and Andrea Sands, *Edmonton Journal*, May 3, 2009 p. A5.

Above: It was a sunny, but still chilly March day in 1994 when BBC coach 134 passed by Alex Taylor School on Jasper Avenue at 94 Street. (COLIN K. HATCHER)

Below: The Vancouver Eskimos!? On loan to Edmonton from Vancouver for evaluation, New Flyer E40LFR is westbound on 114 Avenue near the St. Albert Trail (just after exiting the Charles Camsell Hospital private right-of-way), showing its support for the Edmonton football team in September 2007. Alas, this was not to be the new face of trolley coaches in Edmonton as all service was terminated less than two years later. (TERRY DEJONG)

Above: It looks like the gallant operator of coach 462 has just helped the lady navigate the grass and mud of the stop and is returning to take his private charter back to town on October 25th 1949.
(OHIO BRASS COLLECTION, THE STRAHORN LIBRARY, ILLINOIS RAILWAY MUSEUM)

Below: Ex-Baltimore ACF-Brill 2178 now as CTS 491 sits in the sun in front of Eaton's heading north on 4th Street SW just north of the 8th Avenue SW intersection.
(OHIO BRASS COLLECTION, THE STRAHORN LIBRARY, ILLINOIS RAILWAY MUSEUM. LOCATION INFORMATION – COLIN HATCHER)

Calgary (1947-1975)
Calgary Transit System

One of the earlier adopters of trolley buses, the Stampede City system was one of the survivors that lasted into the Seventies. And except for Vancouver (still operating), only Edmonton, Toronto, Hamilton, and Montreal bested Calgary for total operating span. Not bad for a city that was cautious about embracing this new form of transportation.

Like many Canadian transit operations, Calgary dabbled with using motor buses for lightly-travelled routes as early as the 1930s, but remained a firmly-committed streetcar operation throughout the decade and the subsequent war years. With the return to peacetime conditions, Calgary, like many other cities, was faced with the choice of rehabilitating the tram system or converting to one or more of the alternatives available. These included additional gasoline or diesel motor buses, or moving to the electric trolley coach which was being promoted as the latest thing in municipal transit.

Such a difficult and important decision was not to be made without proper consultation, so several transit studies were undertaken. The first of these began in October 1944, when traffic experts from the Ford Motor Company were asked to make a survey. One wonders just how unbiased they could be.[462] In February 1945, W. H. Furlong, KC – who was also the Chairman and General Manager of the Sandwich, Windsor & Amherstburg Railway Company, operator of Windsor's transit – reported to the Calgary council on behalf of the Ford Motor Company. His report recommended the purchase of a fleet of ninety-nine, 27-passenger motor buses, presumably from Ford. He estimated the cost of trolley coach operation to be from 14.19 to 30.79 cents a mile. Mr. Furlong said he understood Edmonton's (trolley coach) costs were about 24 cents per mile. The Ford motor buses he claimed could be operated for 20 cents a mile. He did not offer to explain the economics of a difference in capacity between the 27 passengers which the Ford bus held, and those of a 44-passenger trolley bus.[463]

Fortunately, cooler and presumably less biased heads prevailed. Norman D. Wilson, of Toronto, an urban transportation expert who had recommended a similar conversion from streetcars to the City of Edmonton, was retained. In June 1945, he presented his report, which proposed a three-stage plan mixing gasoline buses and trolley coaches, with the latter as the mainstay. Ten years earlier, Mr. Wilson had recommended to Calgary that it wait to see what the transit supply industry had to offer before phasing out the streetcar. Now, he said, the trolley coach had established itself as the modern streetcar. It was standardized and had combined the flexibility of the automobile with the mechanical simplicity of the streetcar. It had minimum maintenance, high power and hill-climbing ability, was noiseless, odourless and held 44 seated passengers plus 30 standees. It was five cents a mile cheaper to operate than a gasoline bus and better at hill climbing than the diesel-hydraulic bus. Inexpensive electric power produced from hydro or gas-fired plants favoured the trolley coach. The disadvantage of overhead wires, he argued, was actually an advantage, as it stabilized routes, hence property values. The life of a trolley coach was at least fifteen years; that of the wire, twenty. In comparison, the Ford spokesman had put his bus's life at ten years, and even suggested that it was a "throw-away" vehicle, to be discarded as newer designs came along. Obviously, while this would be good for Ford, it would be the contrary for the Calgary taxpayer.

Mr. Wilson, as quoted in a newspaper article, said, "Calgary was a difficult city to provide with public transit because of its topography. Street railway traffic had increased 100 to 120 per cent over the pre-war years and, he estimated one-half of this increase would remain given a reasonable measure of prosperity and an attractive and convenient transportation system." He then detailed the proposed phase-in of a modern transportation system for Calgary. First would be the conversion to trolley coaches of the ELBOW PARK–MOUNT PLEASANT and TUXEDO PARK streetcar lines, followed by the CRESCENT HEIGHTS and RIVERSIDE lines.

The second stage would include conversion of the KILLARNEY, SOUTH CALGARY, EAST and WEST CALGARY, SUNALTA and SUNNYSIDE lines. The last two would be linked via First Street SW. The third stage would see the complete abandonment of streetcars. Trolley coaches would replace them on the BURNS AVENUE and MANCHESTER routes, with gasoline or diesel units on the OGDEN and BOWNESS lines. Ultimately a trolley coach route was suggested for Fourth Street W, Elgin Avenue, Premier Way, 10th Street, Council Way and 33rd Avenue to the RCMP Barracks.[464]

Superintendent Charles Comba of the Calgary Municipal Railway lost no time in submitting his own report to Council. In it, he too assumed that rehabilitation of the existing street railway system in any form was not practical. The Dominion Transit Controller, Mr. Gray, had indicated that no new equipment would be available before 1946, and even then delivery would likely be unpredictable. As a result, Mr. Comba recommended a start should be made to convert those routes that were on level ground,

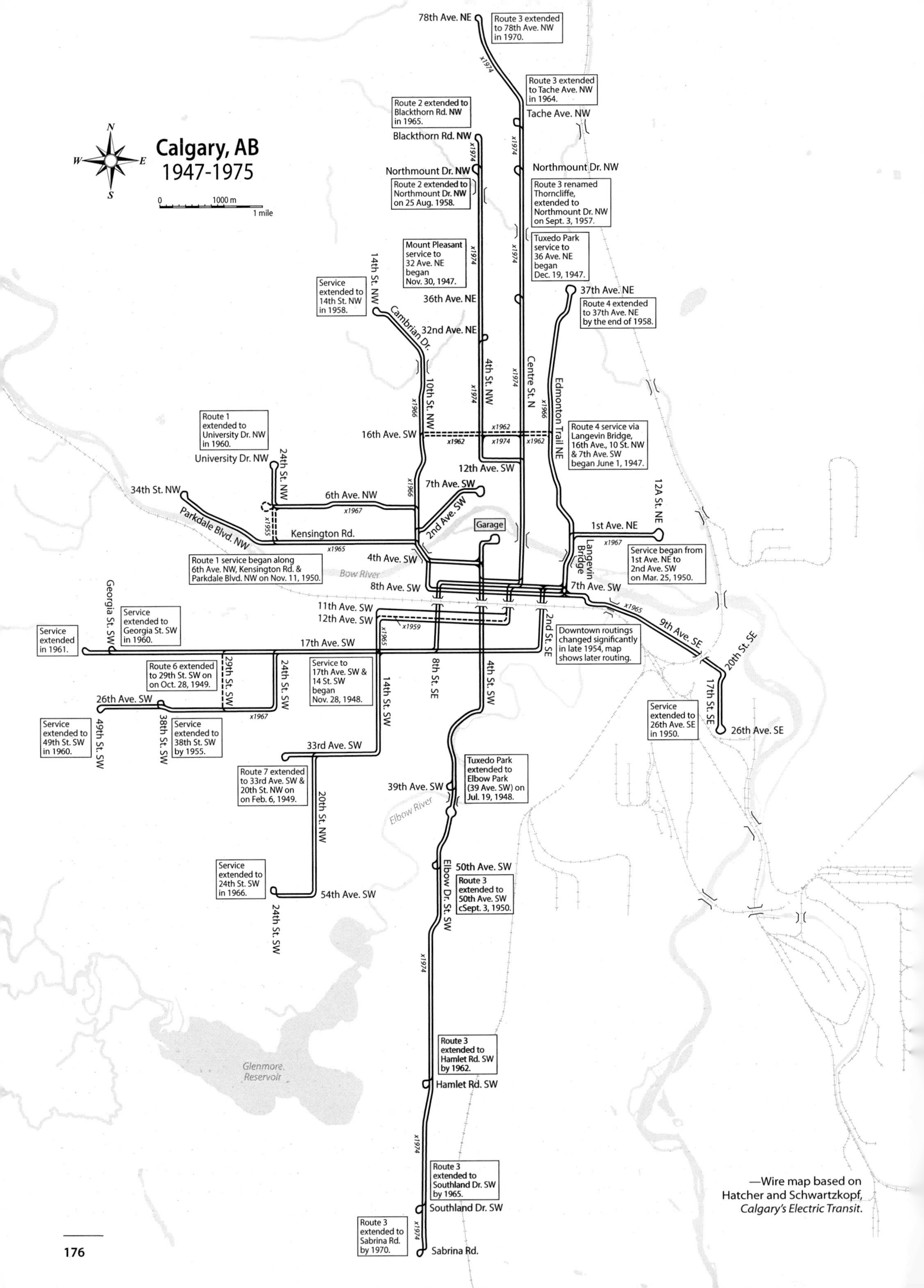

—Wire map based on Hatcher and Schwartzkopf, *Calgary's Electric Transit*.

Left: This ad highlighted both gasoline and electric coaches being ordered from Can Car's Fort William plant.
(OHIO BRASS COLLECTION, THE STRAHORN LIBRARY, ILLINOIS RAILWAY MUSEUM)

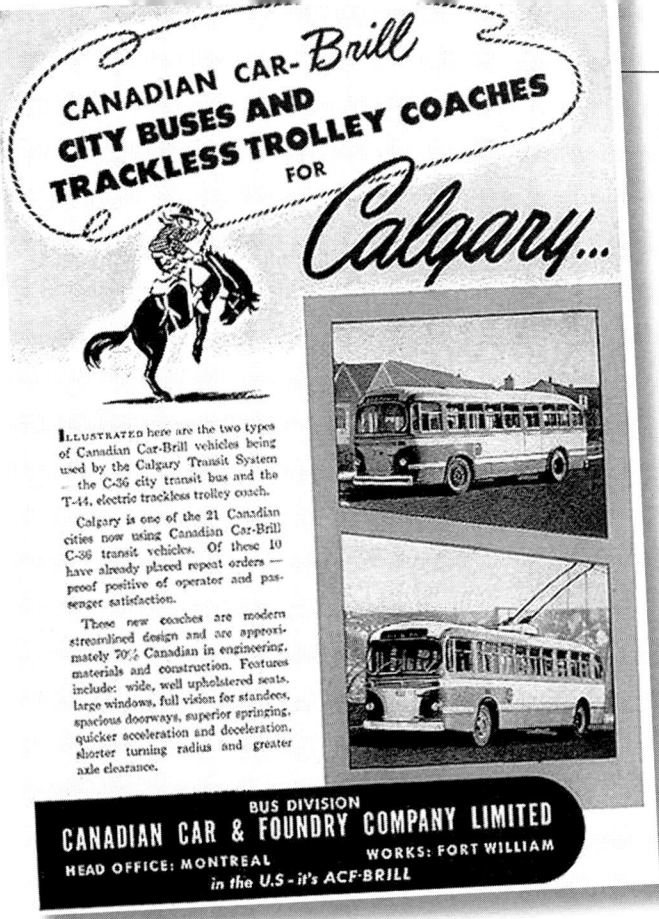

and where track intersections were in the worst shape, with conversion of the CRESCENT HEIGHTS, BELT LINE and MANCHESTER–RIVERSIDE routes to follow later. Proposed equipment for these routes would be thirty, modern, 44-passenger trolley coaches; these would use up all of the allotment Calgary was likely to get from the Transit Controller for the next year.

Conversion of the Capitol Hill routes to buses would follow as soon as the CRESCENT HEIGHTS line was changed over. The remaining routes would be converted in this order: SOUTH CALGARY, KILLARNEY, SUNNYSIDE and BURNS AVENUE, depending on availability of equipment. EAST and WEST CALGARY routes would be the last to be converted.

Total cost of the conversion plan was estimated at $811,508, of which $600,000 would be for the purchase of the trolley coaches at $20,000 each. Removal of ties and rail would cost $20,525, and overhead trolley construction would be $190,983, including installation north on First Street SW to Seventh Avenue and east to Centre Street. Lighter rail would be taken up, but the heavy steel embedded in concrete would be paved over. Rail special work at seven intersections would also be taken up for a total, including the light rail, of 110,250 feet.[465]

The members of the Elbow Park Residents Association were invited to a series of presentations from Council and other experts, in order to inform them prior to a vote on the form of transit they desired. Less than a hundred persons showed up. They were treated to talks on gasoline, diesel and trolley buses, and saw a film on trolley coach operation in the United States. City Commissioner V.A. Newhall represented the views of the Wilson report. Unbiased engineers, he said, have established the trolley coach as being more economical to operate than the motor bus. Alderman McCullough, who owned Maclin Motors, a Ford dealership, argued for the gasoline bus, stating more of these vehicles were in operation than trolley coaches "even though most of the transportation companies were electrical concerns."[466] He harkened to the fact that seventeen per cent of the city's prosperity was due to the oil industry, and then tried to compare the small capacity gasoline buses with the more expensive, but larger capacity, trolleys. The savings, he added with a political flourish, would build a civic auditorium, swimming pools and many other projects.

The new diesel-hydraulic bus was then presented by Mr. Mervyn Johnson as being clean with no fumes outside or inside the bus. (One doubts whether he had ever ridden one!) Safety features of the diesels were emphasized, without mentioning that these were also available on the trolley buses. Moreover, the costs of diesels were claimed to be less. The last speaker, Mr. Peele said it was peculiar that the reports presented by Mr. Wilson, the trolley coach manufacturers and Mr. Comba, were all similar in recommending a combination of trolleys, diesel and gasoline buses to best meet the city's needs. However, in defence of the trolleys, he stated that where they were used, passenger loads had increased due to the buses' popularity. In Edmonton, an 81 per cent increase had been recorded, the city had twenty such vehicles, and had ordered an additional ten. Edmonton hoped to have a complete trolley coach system by 1950.

Perhaps the comparison with the city to the north stung the assembly. At any rate twenty members voted for the trolley coaches while fourteen said they would abide by whatever City Council would decide.[467] Subsequently, Council authorized the purchase of thirty Can Car-Brill 44-passenger trolley coaches, ten Can Car-Brill 36-passenger gasoline buses and ten GMC diesels. The total cost of the trolley coaches was $519,000, with an additional $190,983 to be spent on overhead wires. The routes approved for conversion were: ROUTE 3 ELBOW PARK–TUXEDO … ROUTE 2 ELBOW PARK–MOUNT PLEASANT … ROUTE 5 BELT LINE and ROUTE 4 CRESCENT HEIGHTS.

Routes from the north were to travel through the city centre on 8th Avenue and those from the south on 7th Avenue SW.[468] On May 27th 1946, Council instructed the commissioners to order thirty additional trolleys, so as to have them manufactured in groups of ten, as funds become available. This would give Calgary sixty trolley coaches and ten gasoline buses by July. The ten diesels (presumably still on order) were expected when available. A few aldermen tried to delay the motion with the result they were accused by the others of being prejudiced in favour of the gasoline bus and, therefore, trying to stall the orders.[469]

Finally, on August 8th, a firm order for the additional thirty trolley coaches was placed. The *Calgary Herald* quoted Commissioner Newhall: "This direction of council seems to be in accord with all the major cities of Canada which are adopting trolley coaches."[470] On July 19th, Calgary Municipal Railway was re-branded as Calgary Transit System.

By mid-October, five of the Brill gasoline buses had arrived. Superintendent C.V.F. Weir, who had replaced Charles Comba on the latter's retirement in August was the first "passenger" on the motor buses. The sixty trolley coaches were expected by December, but there was no word on the delivery date of the ten GMC diesels.[471]

The *Calgary Herald* of October 17th quoted Commissioner Newhall saying he had received word from Canadian Car-Brill in Fort William that the first dozen trolley coaches would be shipped in early December. All the necessary overhead wire and fittings would be delivered from the Ohio Brass Company to the city by November. This would be sufficient to equip the BELT LINE and CRESCENT HEIGHTS routes. "However," the article went on, "Calgary citizens will not have to wait until December to ride and inspect the new type trolley as an exhibition pilot model will arrive here about Nov. 4 after being exhibited in Winnipeg.

"So that this exhibition unit can be put in operation one mile of overhead will be installed shortly on a belt route on 8th Ave. W. from 4th St. to 9th St. W., north on 9th St. W. to 4th Ave., east on 4th Ave. to 4th St. W. and then south to 4th St. W. to 8th Ave. W."[472] This route was selected because the overhead could be installed permanently for connection with future routes, including the CRESCENT HEIGHTS and BELT LINE. The demonstration coach would give free rides around that belt run.

Above: Coach 405 is turning off 7th Avenue SW south into 1st Street SW on the SOUTH CALGARY route. The iconic building on the left is the Hudson's Bay Company department store. The facade extends the full block along 1st Street SW between 7th and 8th Avenues SW and close to half the block along 7th and 8th Avenues SW. The tall brick structure behind the trolley coach is the Calgary Herald building. It is now gone.
(OHIO BRASS COLLECTION, THE STRAHORN LIBRARY, ILLINOIS RAILWAY MUSEUM. LOCATION INFORMATION – COLIN HATCHER)

The article continued to describe the furious activity preceding the start-up of Calgary's first trolley coach lines. CRESCENT HEIGHTS and the BELT LINE were now the first candidates for conversion, as the roadway was suitable. The car tracks were to be left for the time being, and paved over the following year. Every available lineman was to be rushed into service to speed the work. The new overhead was to be strung from the old poles, and new poles would replace them as work proceeded. The existing positive power wire from the streetcar overhead could still be used by streetcars, so there would be no major disruptions of service. Most of the major work was done at night to keep interruptions at a minimum.

Two of the Brill gasoline buses were placed in service on October 17th 1946, one each on the ROSEDALE and MOUNT ROYAL routes. Three others were being "broken in" to be used possibly on the SUNALTA run. This line, according to Superintendent Weir quoted in the *Calgary Herald*, would be converted eventually to trackless trolleys, however, like many plans for Calgary's trolleys, this never materialized.[473]

Finally the grand day arrived. The first Calgary trolley coach route went into operation Sunday afternoon, June 1st 1947. The ROUTE 4 CRESCENT HEIGHTS line had the honour, and was a belt line service running both ways from 7th Avenue SW, north along 4th Street SE, over the Langevin Bridge, up Fourth/Third Street NE, west on 16th Avenue, south on 10th Street NW, east on

Right: An Ohio Brass Ad from 1948 boasts that "64 per cent of Calgary's Mainline Service" is trolley coach. (OHIO BRASS COLLECTION, THE STRAHORN LIBRARY, ILLINOIS RAILWAY MUSEUM)

4th Avenue SW, south on 4th Street SW, and east on 7th Avenue SW again. The trolley coaches had to be parked on 7th Avenue between 3rd and 4th Street SE at night as the connection with the Victoria Park car barns was not yet installed. This route had been chosen as the first trolley coach route because all the streets were paved.

Public reaction to the service was positive, with both riders and civic officials remarking on the almost noiseless mode of electric transportation. Ridership increased noticeably. Conversion of ROUTE 2 MOUNT PLEASANT and ROUTE 3 TUXEDO PARK was not to be completed until August as delivery of the fittings was delayed. By July 1947, streetcars were taken off the north portions of these routes to allow overhead construction and road improvements to start on the North Hill. Motor buses were used in the meantime on Centre Street on these halves of the two routes.[474] These interim motor buses may have been new GM diesels assigned primarily to the MANCHESTER route, but also they were heavily involved in the streetcar-to-trolley bus interim services on several routes, along with the Fords and Can Car-Brill C36s.

However, the MOUNT PLEASANT route wasn't to be ready for trolley coach use until November 30th, and the TUXEDO PARK run didn't open until Friday, December 19th. A trial run was made on the previous day and the route declared fit to have the gasoline buses replaced by the quiet trolley buses. Coaches ran every fifteen minutes during the day and twice as often during peak hours.[475]

By the end of 1947, Calgary Transit System boasted that 42 per cent of its passengers – 2,250,000 per month – were now carried on rubber-tired vehicles. Nearly eighteen of the 82 miles of streetcar track had been torn up or covered over. There were 27 miles of motor bus routes and 24 miles of trolley coach lines. An ELBOW PARK route, which would link with the MOUNT PLEASANT and TUXEDO PARK routes on the North Hill, was next in line for trolley coach conversion, to be followed by ROUTE 5 BELT LINE, then ROUTE 7 SOUTH CALGARY and ROUTE 7 KILLARNEY which would link with the BELT LINE. Twenty-four of the thirty trolleys were in service, with ten more expected to be delivered in July of 1948. Another ten were to come later for the last two routes. The streetcars had not fared as well; eight were scrapped for parts to keep the remaining 74 alive for a few more years.[476]

By mid-June 1948, five of the second order of thirty trolley coaches had been delivered and the rest were to be in the city by the end of July.[477] On Sunday July 11th, the motor buses left the ELBOW PARK section of the line and the trolleys took over on this part of ROUTE 3, now linking ELBOW PARK with TUXEDO PARK in direct service. The motor buses were now deployed on the BELT LINE, whose conversion was to be more complicated as it involved stringing trolley coach overhead on sections still being serviced by streetcars.[478]

The streetcar's days were numbered though. Saturday, November 27th marked the last rail runs on the BELT LINE, SOUTH CALGARY and KILLARNEY lines. The next day, testing was completed by noon and the trolley coaches started operating in the afternoon, except for the southwest ends of the routes from the 17th Avenue and 14th Street SW intersection. Here, they were met by gasoline and diesel buses until the route paving would be completed.

That August, the *Calgary Herald* wrote in glowing terms about the city's new Eau Claire transit garage, even though it was in reality two former aircraft hangers, hauled into the city from the old RCAF training school at De Winton and placed back-to-back. The four trolley coach lanes could accommodate 32 units and there was room for forty more outside. The latest in repair and maintenance facilities had been installed: bus washers, pits, a 24,000-lb. hoist, as well as a battery room and carpentry shop. The 2nd Avenue and 2nd Street SW structure also housed a number of administrative functions for the growing Calgary Transit System.[479]

February 6th 1949 saw ROUTE 7 SOUTH CALGARY extended to operate from 17th Avenue and 14th Street SW, along 14th Street SN to 33rd-third Avenue SW, and then west to the South Calgary terminal at 20th Street SW. In September of that year, R. H. Wray became Transit Superintendent, succeeding C.V.F. Weir who retired in August.

Above: Northbound on 10th Street NW, coach 467 climbs a considerable hill showing that Calgary is not all flat.
(G.M. ANDERSEN PHOTO, KRAMBLES-PETERSON ARCHIVE)

The first of the new order of trolley coaches had arrived by October 20th, sporting some improvements over the previous ones. There were four additional vertical stanchions or handholds, and the earlier-style sliding window sashes had been eliminated in favour of conventional lifting sashes. The route signs were located behind double glazing, which avoided the problem of them steaming up in winter leaving the poor passengers wondering on what route the bus was travelling.

Below: Downtown Calgary in the summer sun. Number 417 picks up passengers on 8th Avenue near 4th Street. In the background is the Eaton's building.
(G.M. ANDERSEN PHOTO, KRAMBLES-PETERSON ARCHIVE)

However, these new vehicles couldn't yet be used on the full KILLARNEY route as bad weather had held up black-topping, resulting in service on the southwest leg being delayed. Finally, on the following Wednesday, October 28th, full service began on the run. The paving was still not complete due to wet weather, but the trolley coaches were put in service anyway while the paving awaited until better weather.[480]

December 7th was the day streetcar service ended on ROUTE 1 WEST CALGARY. West Hillhurst residents who had long used the trams as a meeting place and club room as they wended their way downtown, had now to contend with "somewhat garish, brightly-lit and speedy vehicles (that) would be far removed from the swing and sway, rattle and bang, and somewhat drafty club quarters of the past." These "garish" vehicles were, however, new Twin Coach gasoline buses, temporary replacements for the streetcars until the New Year, when the trolley would return, albeit with rubber tires and less "sway, rattle and bang."[481]

Wire was to be strung along the SUNNYSIDE and BRIDGELAND routes immediately with trolley coaches slated for operation early in 1950. BOWNESS would be the next to get buses, with OGDEN as the final route to change over. That was, however, optimistic planning; the OGDEN carline's interim conversion to motor buses seemed to take forever[482] and trolley coaches never did operate all the way to Bowness.

Trolley coaches were finally installed on ROUTE 1 WEST CALGARY, on November 11th 1950 – Remembrance Day. It had taken eleven months from the retirement date of the trams until their final replacement was in place. Trolley coaches serviced ROUTE 9 RIVERSIDE (BRIDGELAND)–SUNNYSIDE effective March 25th 1950.[483] By the end of 1950, the trolley coach fleet had expanded with the arrival of four more buses costing $24,363 each, freight included.[484]

The latest in modern urban transport was not without its share of incidents. On July 20th 1950, a CTS trolley bus driver, no doubt trying to keep up with a tight schedule, was making good time up the Tenth Street Hill when he noticed a flashing red light in his rear view mirror. A moment later, the ever-vigilant Calgary Police had pulled him over and charged him under the Alberta Vehicles and Highway Act of 1911 for exceeding the speed limit by going 42 miles per hour in the city. The *Calgary Herald* gleefully commented as it only being fair "that bus-drivers are just as subject to the law as anybody else." However the *Herald*'s glee was short lived. Six days later in an editorial, it revealed that the Act specifically excluded trolley coaches and streetcars. The paper commented, "if a Rosedale bus (which is gasoline or oil-powered) and a Crescent Heights trolley are going up Tenth Street N.W. together at 40 miles per hour, the police can prosecute the Rosedale driver for speeding but cannot touch the trolley bus driver. It is hard to see by what process of reasoning this sort of thing can be justified." The paper went on to point out that in case of an accident, the onus would be on the injured to prove negligence of the trolley driver, rather than the driver having to prove that it wasn't his fault, as is required by law. Since there was ever the one case quoted in the editorial, it would appear the newspaper's consternation was somewhat exaggerated.[485]

On December 18th 1953, four T-48A CCF-Brill trolleys, fleet numbers 481-484, were shipped. Their cost was $27,158 each, freight included, an increase in price from the 1950 order. These buses were equipped with Grant fareboxes, double-glazing on the standee windows to prevent frosting up, and a swing-down driver's sun visor. These four trolleys, which arrived in the first week of the New Year, brought the fleet to a total of 83 vehicles. This gave the system a greater margin of reserve buses.[486]

The week after the Calgary Stampede in July 1954, work started on an overpass at 8th Street and 9th Avenue SW. This overpass would carry 9th Avenue traffic over 8th Street and permit installation of a one-way street pattern. By October/November 1954, the one-way pattern was in full use, trolley routes adjusted, and the problems associated with Calgary's narrow streets, wide buses and heavy traffic were eased.

ROUTE 3 was extended 1¼ miles north on Centre Street from 36 Avenue NW to Northmount Drive NW and renamed THORNCLIFFE on Tuesday September 3rd 1957. The south terminal ELBOW DRIVE was at Elbow Drive and Sifton Road (50th Avenue SW).

In February 1957, CTS purchased twenty 1948 ACF-Brill trolley buses from the Baltimore Transit Company.[487] Now that Canadian Car was no longer building Brill trolley coaches, it was necessary to source used ones.

The *Calgary Herald* of March 10th 1958 announced that the trolley coach system would be extended an additional five miles during the year at a cost of $117,000. Direct trolley coach service was to be extended to Highwood, Edmonton Trail, Mountain View, Cambrian Heights, Collingwood, Rosemount, the eastern part of Capital Hill, and Renfrew. ROUTE 2 MOUNT PLEASANT was to be extended 1½ miles along 4th Street NW from the existing terminus at 32nd Avenue NW to Northmount Drive at a cost of $30,000. Service in Crescent Heights was to be revamped also. ROUTE 4 was to be extended from 16th Avenue NE northward along the Edmonton Trail to a new terminal at the foot of a hill near 37th Avenue NE. "A complementary western terminal will be extended north on 10th Street NW to a new terminal at Cambrian Place and 14th Street NW."[488] These improvements were expected to cost $67,000. The MOUNT PLEASANT extension went into service on Monday August 25th,[489] retaining the same route name. The new ROUTE 4 CAMBRIAN HEIGHTS–EDMONTON TRAIL extension was also in service by the end of 1958.

The March-April 1959 issue of Ohio Brass (OB) *"Traction News"* featured the Calgary trolley coach system. As a supplier of overhead switches and

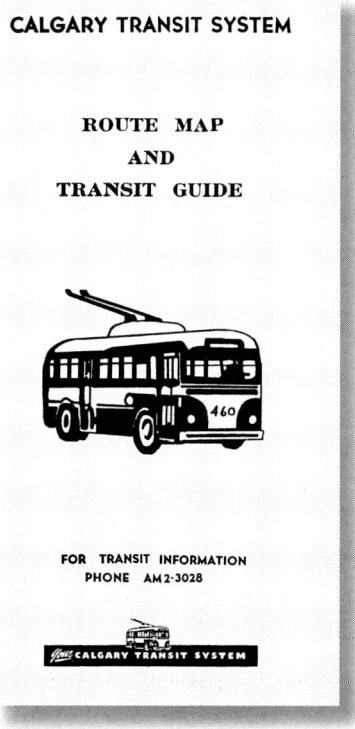

Above: CTS was proud enough of their trolley coach fleet to feature one on their Transit Map and Route Guide sometime in the early 1960s.

Above: In June of 1973 one could catch coaches in rapid succession navigating the overhead at 14th Street SW and 17th Avenue SW. Unit 421 leads, going to South Calgary, while 473 follows on the Belt Line. (TED WICKSON)

Below: Threading its way through the specialwork at 1st Avenue at 17th Street in 1973, coach 454 passes the urban clutter that defines a thriving city. The Calgary Tower, then called the Husky Tower, looms on the horizon. (MAC SEBREE PHOTO, KRAMBLES-PETERSON ARCHIVE)

fittings, OB had a bias in favour of the trolleys, but the article recorded faithfully their heyday in Calgary.

"Four miles of new overhead have been added to two lines of its 86.6 miles of round-trip trolley coach route, extending straight-through services into residential areas once covered by feeder motor buses. CTS has today a total of 105 trolley coaches and 67 motor buses for a total of 182.3 round trip miles." Ridership had been maintained since 1947, even with the increase in automobile traffic.

"In 1957 over 31-million passengers rode the CTS system – equal to the entire population of greater Calgary riding twice a week. Of this total 22,877,596 persons rode trolley coaches as compared to 8,329,355 on motor buses.

"Heaviest travelled of the eight lines is the Thorncliffe line, [i.e. #3] carrying over 3.7-million white collar workers, shoppers, and students from the southern station northward into densely populated residential areas."

The article went on to state, despite the congestion of narrow two-way streets, the trolley coaches maintained an average operating speed of 11.1 miles per hour. By that time, many of the coaches were eleven years old, having travelled about 400,000 miles. Nonetheless, many more years of service was expected from these vehicles. Trolley coach operating expenses were 39.86 cents per mile, of which 3.42 cents was power, 1.73 cents overhead maintenance, and 5.82 cents equipment maintenance. This represented a saving of 5.23 cents per mile over motor buses. The article also commented that the CTS kept its wire well maintained, thereby minimizing damage from dewiring and keeping expenses down.

A word about this is in order. CTS has been often accused of poor trolley wire maintenance. This in turn is shown as one of the reasons why the electric transit system was allowed to die. However, at least in the 1950s, maintenance seems to have been exemplary. Transit files record regular meetings of CTS staff responsible for overhead, where problems were aired and solutions put into effect. Trolley shoe wear was recorded and carefully monitored. Dewirings were investigated and wire tightened if that was the cause. Careful attention was paid to the trolley coach system during these boom days of postwar Calgary when the automobile had not yet made its major attack on public transit. For a few more years at least, the trolley coach would reign supreme in the Stampede City.[490]

But, despite the boom years of the 1950s and the optimistic plans for trolley coach line expansions, by 1960 the first shots had been fired in the diesel/trolley bus war. In a letter sent to C. E. Patton, Wilkes-Barre Transit Corporation in March of that year, Superintendent Wray stated that City Council had decided to extend the diesel fleet. Consequently, there would be no additions to the 105 trolley coaches then in use, for the time being.[491] However, Wray had written to British United Traction Ltd. earlier in that year, asking for a comparative quote on six British-built trolleys coaches.[492]

By 1958, the trolleys only covered 37.8 route miles one way, the reductions due to rerouting. During that year, they travelled a total of 3,069,738 miles. Only 6.04 passengers were carried per trolley coach mile, revenue was 72.80 cents/mile, while expenses were 57.82 cents. Despite route expansions in 1958, passenger riding in general was on the decline.[493]

Bureaucracy reared its head in February 1960. The Bay (Hudson's Bay Company) department store rented the CTS for an hour on a sale day to give the citizens "free rides" downtown. All was in readiness, including full-page ads in the paper and promotional covers for the fare boxes. The Alberta Department of Industry and Development then intervened, ruling that the free rides were the equivalent of 'green stamps', thus contravening one of the Acts. The newspapers were not very charitable towards the Department's attempt to "protect" the public from such promotions. Though CTS was even unhappier, it said nothing publicly.[494]

In January 1961, the beginning of several cost comparisons of operations between motor and trolley buses was published. It gave some hints as to the eventual fate of the trolley system. Total costs in cents per vehicle mile in the first nine months of 1960, as compared with 1958-59, were:[495]

	Motor bus	Trolley	Diff.
1960 Average	59.25	58.42	+0.83
1st nine months 1959 cost	61.55	57.36	+4.19
1958 cost	61.21	57.79	+3.42

The transit system was exempted from the previously imposed provincial fuel tax effective April 12th 1960, resulting in the immediate reduction of motor bus operating costs by two cents per mile. The trend, cited in the report, was toward lower operating costs for motor buses as compared to higher costs for trolley coaches. The newer motorbuses were 52-passenger models, compared with 44 or 48 for the trolley coaches; in fact only eight of the 105 trolleys carried 48 passengers. The motor buses averaged out at 1.12 cents per seat mile; the trolleys at 1.30 cents. The purchase cost of electricity had also increased from a flat 0.82 cents per kilowatt hour from the City's Electric Light Department to a peak load demand rate (from Calgary Power) at an estimated sixty per cent higher. The effect was estimated to raise trolley coach costs by two cents a mile.

Motor buses were cited as being more flexible – able to be short turned at peak hours, allowing them to do the work of two trolley coaches on heavily-travelled portions of routes. The motor buses did not need overhead plant, and were able to pass stopped buses on the same route. Finally, the motor buses were presented as more attractive, more modern, and, when equipped with automatic transmissions, able to start as smoothly as the trolley coach. Finally, no new trolley coaches were being produced in

Above: CTS coach 472 is outbound on Elbow Drive at 32nd Avenue. The (now) classic cars and cigarette advertising date this shot to June 1973.
(TED WICKSON)

North America, the last Canadian Car-Brill units having been delivered in 1954. Adding in the cost of the overhead for the trolley coaches put the vehicle cost of a trolley at $921.48 per seat, while the 52-passenger motor buses came in at $582.69. Whether the report's authors included the cost of all the motor buses – some of which were fully depreciated, worn out and held only 36 passengers – or how the costs of overhead were calculated (depreciation, maintenance and repair) is not clear, but the direction, and the system's former enthusiasm for the trolley coach, was now clearly on the wane. It must be said in fairness to the report's authors that they recommended a blended bus fleet, with extensions to the trolley lines limited to the present main lines, but only after carefully studying economics and applicability of conversion to motor bus. The report concluded by recommending more diesels be added to the fleet, but the basic transportation vehicle was still to be the trolley coach.[496]

At the end of 1961, there were 115 miles of trolley bus routes, compared with 145 miles of motor bus routes. There were 72 miles of trolley overhead, while 87.4 miles of street had motor bus service.

The trolley routes left at the end of 1961 were:[497]

1: EAST CALGARY–PARKDALE
2: MOUNT PLEASANT–SUNNYSIDE
3: THORNCLIFFE–ELBOW DRIVE
4: CAMBRIAN HEIGHTS–EDMONTON TRAIL
5: BELT LINE
6: KILLARNEY
7: SOUTH CALGARY
9: BRIDGELAND–WEST HILLHURST
CRESCENT HEIGHTS
No number assigned to "Crescent Heights" route

On October 16th 1964, Superintendent Wray wrote to D. B. Ball of Goodyear, advising ten trolley coaches were to be removed from service effective immediately. In response to a questionnaire, Mr. Wray stated while there was no formal plan to discontinue trolley coaches, all new buses purchased since 1954 had been diesels. Trolley coaches were no longer manufactured in North America, and he repeated the argument that the fixed nature of their routes was now being cited as a disadvantage, as compared with the assertion that it was an advantage when trolley coaches were first introduced. He felt that modern diesels could handle peak loads better than a trolley coach could. A diesel bus' capacity had now grown to 52 passengers, and they were felt to be able to operate faster schedules than trolley coaches. However, he again stated that there was no formal abandonment plan for the trolleys.[498]

In May of 1965, an American consultant, John Curtin of Philadelphia, was asked by CTS to evaluate the system and suggest its future direction. In his initial report, he recommended more through-routes and improved service west of Centre Street. He also suggested an immediate change in the mix of the bus complement – from 101 trolley coaches and 87 diesels, to 85 trolley coaches and 107 diesels. The report was considered by the CTS but, for the time being, more modest changes were made.

Many transit properties experienced passenger decline in these years and tried various means to attract the bus patron. The wait for a bus in Calgary's noted winter conditions was not a something very appealing, so a novel way of keeping ridership up was tried – 1500-watt electric heaters were installed at some bus stops on ROUTE 7. They were intended to make the wait for the trolley more bearable, however, the results must have been inconclusive, as they were eventually removed.[499]

Proposals for extensions were many throughout the 1950s and 1960s, and seemed to imply a continuing commitment to the trolley coach, despite some conversions to motor buses. But this was not to be. By October 1965, ROUTE 4 CAMBRIAN–EDMONTON TRAIL was slated to become victim to the diesel, as was ROUTE 1 EAST CALGARY–PARKDALE and ROUTE 2 SUNNYSIDE. Conversion of ROUTE 9 BRIDGELAND–WEST HILLHURST to diesel was set for March of 1967; thereafter no further conversions were planned. In fact, the CTS stated that the trolley coaches were good for another ten years. Despite the conversions, costs were estimated for an extension of ROUTE 9 to the University of Alberta, Calgary. ROUTE 4 was permanently converted to diesel sooner than planned, on Monday May 6th 1966, because the new diesel buses were delivered earlier than promised. Trolley wire was subsequently removed from unused portions of the route, and some intersections rebuilt to simpler configurations to accommodate the remaining lines.[500]

The trolley fleet stood at 99 units, despite the earlier plan to remove ten from the original 105. Of the 99, only 70 were required in regular service. Fourteen of the second-hand ACF-Brill trolleys were left; the remainder were of Canadian Car-Brill manufacture. Only eight were the larger T-48 models. By 1970, only three trolley coach routes still served the primary transit arteries of the city. These were routes 2, 3 and 7. Nonetheless, trolley coach expansions continued. An extension of ROUTE 3 THORNCLIFFE for a half mile, north along Simons Valley Road to 78th Avenue NW, was planned for completion by late 1970.[501]

In keeping with its modernization, the name of the system was changed from "The Calgary Transit System" to "Calgary Transit" on July 7th 1970, and a two-tone blue colour scheme officially adopted. Two of the trolley buses were repainted in the new colours, but concurrently, twelve of the ex-Baltimore trolley coaches were sold for scrap. Six more were stored as unavailable for revenue use, and two were re-painted in a candy cane striped pattern for use as portable passenger shelters. Despite these scrappings, the THORNCLIFFE extension opened into the Huntington Hills area on December 7th 1970. The new trolley coach service was favourably received by the area residents.

Responding to enquiries about the fate of the trolley coach network, Calgary Transit stated ROUTES 2, 3 and 7 would remain electrified, at least until the advent of rapid transit; after that time, they would be under review. The lack of spare parts, added to the high cost of those parts that *were* available, as well as the expense of maintaining such an operation were cited as reasons why many transit properties, including Calgary, were looking seriously at eliminating trolley coaches. By mid-1971, the working fleet was reduced to 65 vehicles, with twenty in reserve.[502]

January 26th 1972 dawned as a clear, crisp day. For trolley coach aficionados, this day had special significance, for the long awaited candidate for salvation of the trolley bus had arrived in Calgary. Built by Flyer Industries Ltd. in Winnipeg, and on loan from the Toronto Transit Commission, TTC No. 9213 was intended as the modern trolley coach with which transit companies would replace their aging Brills. At last, there was (again) a trolley coach manufactured in Canada, with all of the latest features, and readily available spare parts. The next day, the demonstrator coach was operated on the on ROUTE 3 ELBOW DRIVE–THORNCLIFFE. It was then used on several routes until February 29th, when it left for a demonstration in Hamilton, Ontario. A letter to *Trolley Coach News* magazine from Calgary Transit said, "the trolley coach functioned well during this demonstration. Calgary Transit is now preparing a report comparing the operating costs of modern trolley coaches with the new diesel buses. The operating costs of these new units are very similar. At this time the City of Calgary has made no final decision with respect to the policy to be followed for the replacement of our present trolley equipment which will likely occur within the next five-year period." [503]

By the end of the year, that report was in draft form, but had not been released. Finally, late in 1973, the report was presented to City Council. Considering the success of the demonstrator, the Council, in a startling move, voted to phase out trolley coaches over the next three years. The reasons given were that all the overhead, feeder wires and power supplies would have to be replaced at an estimated cost of $800,000. "Improved maintenance costs of the modern diesel bus lets it compete much more favourably with trolley coaches than the diesel buses of ten and twenty years ago." said a letter to *Trolley Coach News*. It continued, "At the end of 1973 the … cost-per-vehicle mile for diesel fuel was less than 50% of the powered cost per mile for trolley coaches." [504]

The final nail was driven into the trolley coach's coffin on the 26th of April, 1974. Construction work on the Centre Street bridge put all trolley coach operation north of the bridge in suspension. The old span poles on the bridge were removed and replaced with widely-spaced lamp standards, obviously not designed for trolley coach overhead. These changes placed ROUTE 2 MOUNT PLEASANT and ROUTE 3 THORNCLIFFE under diesel power at last. ROUTE 7 SOUTH CALGARY remained electric, as did the south parts of ROUTE 3 ELBOW DRIVE and ROUTE 2 KILLARNEY/17TH AVE. Twenty coaches were sold to Edmonton for parts, while ten went to Vancouver. Thirty-nine were still in use and the remaining sixteen were retained as spares.[505]

Trolley coach service ended abruptly almost without public announcement. While the remaining routes had been scheduled for abandonment in July after the Stampede, a threatened strike which would involve overhead line crews setting up pickets which bus operators would honour, forced Calgary Transit to move more swiftly. Seventeen Can Car diesel buses in storage were pressed into service, along with the 82 General Motors modern diesels that had arrived earlier than expected. This gave the system sufficient capacity to discontinue trolley coach service permanently.

In the early morning hours of March 8th 1975, electric passenger transit service came to an end in Calgary.

Coach 446 carried W. Kuyt, Director of Transportation, R. H. Wray, Director of Operations, and Messrs. L. Armour, D. Miller and S. Foffenroth to the barns, where, at 12:20 AM, revenue service ended.

Some form of official last run was felt to be in order, so coaches 422 and 465 were selected for the honour. Number 422 was repainted inside and out, and on May 8th 1975, the overhead was energized for the last time. At 6:34 AM, trolley coach 465 left the garage with Ted Kendricks, badge number 1, at the wheel. Five trips were made along ROUTE 3 ELBOW DRIVE. All passengers boarding the coach were given a souvenir folder and a free trip. After three trips, number 465 had to have its trolley shoes changed; one last kick at the system that had let it down. It arrived back at the garage at 1:20 PM. Then, at 1:50, coach 422 rolled out into the sun in its gleaming new paint, with "last run" banners on its sides. Ted Kendricks was again at the wheel, as the coach left for downtown carrying officials and invited guests. As a backup, coach 465 followed at a discreet distance, piloted by instructor Milt Anderson.

They proceeded to 6th Avenue and 2nd Street SW, where they met a charter diesel bus carrying officials and guests from City Hall. At 2:10 PM, both coaches departed for Downtown with 422 leading. At Windsor Place and Elbow Drive, 422 pulled over and 465 ran quickly to Sabrina Road loop, so the photographers could catch the arrival of No. 422 pulling into the loop for the last time. Both coaches then left the loop and returned to 6th Avenue and 2nd Street SW. Trolley coach 465 then left for the garage as the speeches began.

B. H. Cornish, Commissioner of Transportation and Planning, presided over the ceremony. Alderman Virnetta Anderson spoke on behalf of City Council, and then, with help from Operator Kendricks and Chief Supervisor of Personnel Services, H. Parsons, pulled down the poles. The officials then adjourned for refreshments, and the poles were raised for the final trip to the garage. On board were H. L. Simons, Supervisor of Maintenance (at the wheel); L. J. Penny, Night Maintenance Supervisor; Don McDermid, Passenger Services Representative; and the chronicler of the event, trolley coach fan Chris Radkey. At Fourth Street and Second Avenue SW, a stop was made for Mr. Penny and Mr. Simon to photograph each other at the wheel. Then Mr. Penny drove the bus down 2nd Avenue SW to the garage. At 4:17 PM, the poles were lowered forever. An era of fast, silent, electric transportation in Calgary had ended.[506]

Twenty-eight non-operational coaches were sold to Vancouver for $500 each; 25 additional coaches in working order, at $1000 each, also went to the west coast, shipped by CP Rail in September of that year. Spare parts, as well as usable overhead including a great deal of the specialwork, was sold to Edmonton. One coach, No. 432, was sold to a private buyer[507] and last run CTS coach 422 was preserved, eventually joining the collection in the Reynolds-Alberta Museum in Wetaskiwin.

Rumours of renewed trolley coach activity surfaced from time to time, but were just that – rumours. Eventually the wires came down and the trolley coach, along with its forerunner the streetcar, became only a memory.

Footnotes:

This account is extracted from *Calgary's Electric Transit*, Colin K. Hatcher and Tom Schwarzkopf, Railfare*DC Books Toronto, ON, 2009 Ch. 9 and 10, authored by Tom Schwarzkopf.

462. *Calgary Herald*, August 11, 1944.
463. *Calgary Herald*, February 16, 1945.
464. Calgary Public Library clipping file, June 6, 1945.
465. *Calgary Herald*, June 8, 1945.
466. *Calgary Herald*, June 27, 1945.
467. *Calgary Herald*, June 27, 1945.
468. *Ibid.* May 10, 1946.
469. *Ibid.* May 28, 1946.
470. *Ibid.* August 8, 1948.
471. *Ibid.* October 15, 1946.
472. *Ibid.* October 17, 1946.
473. *Ibid.*
474. Calgary Public Library, CTS clipping file, July 30, 1947.
475. *Calgary Herald*, Friday December 19, 1947 p. 16.
476. *Ibid.* December 31, 1947.
477. Calgary Public Library, CTS clipping file, June 19, 1948.
478. Calgary Public Library, CTS clipping file, July 12, 1948.
479. *Calgary Herald*, August 31, 1948.
480. *Ibid.* October 21 and 25, 1949.
481. *Ibid.* November 30, 1949.
482. *Ibid.* November 30, 1949.
483. Glenbow Archives, Calgary Transit records: File 537 Note H-1 by RHW (Wray), "Conversion to Trolley Coach and Extensions." Second page (not numbered) April 29, 1966.
484. Glenbow Archives Calgary Transit records: file 22 July 16, 1953.
485. *Calgary Herald*, July 20, 1949, p. 16 and July 26, 1949, p. 4.
486. *Calgary Herald*, January 2, 1954.
487 Glenbow Archives File 174.
488. *Calgary Herald*. March 10, 1958.
489. *Ibid.* August 18, 1958.
490 Glenbow Archives File 685.
491. *Ibid.* File 106 letter, March 3, 1960.
492. *Ibid.* File 106, January 6, 1960.
493. *Ibid.* File 2 and 7 *Canadian Transportation* annual trolley coach review, June 1959, p. 58.
494. *Ibid.* File 144.
495. Glenbow Archives Calgary Transit records "Calgary Transit System Comparison of Operation and Costs of Motor Buses and Trolley Coaches", January, 1961.
496. *Ibid.*
497. Glenbow File 279 system route data as of December 31, 1961, dated May 15, 1962.
498. *Ibid.* File 382, Questionnaire of Trolley Bus Operation on the Calgary Transit System, October 11, 1963.
499. *Ibid.* File 476 and File 382. August 15, 1964.
500. Numerous accounts in Glenbow files.
501. *Trolley Coach News*, Vol. 6, #13, May 1970.
502. *Ibid.* #12, January/April 1971.
503. *Ibid.* #15, February/June 1972.
504. *Ibid.* #24, Winter 1973.
505. *Trolley Coach News*, #28 Fall 1974; #30, #32, and #33, 1975, and UCRS *Newsletter*, March-April 1974, p. 56.
506. *Trolley Coach News*, #33 Summer 1975, including Radkey report and updates from McDermid.
507. *Ibid.* 34 Fall/Winter 1975.

Above: At the north end of Route 2, even though it's a nice day – even a moving day judging from the action in the background – this gentleman is probably glad the coach has arrived and he can be inside rather than waiting at the minimal shelter. Taken June 29th 1972, this trolley route was abandoned the next April when all routes north of the Bow River were severed due to bridge construction. (TED WICKSON)

Below: Angus McIntyre stopped over on a trip home to Vancouver from Winnipeg on "The Canadian" in March 1975 for 24 hours to take a quick look at Calgary's trolley coaches, and discovered it was the last day of operation. Here is his shot taken during the last few hours of that system. He met a few other fans riding around that night who knew that if the overhead crews went on strike the system would close. Note the fibreglass trolley poles. It was very cold (-18c) and the overhead crews went on strike the next day. CTS had a farewell day several months later.

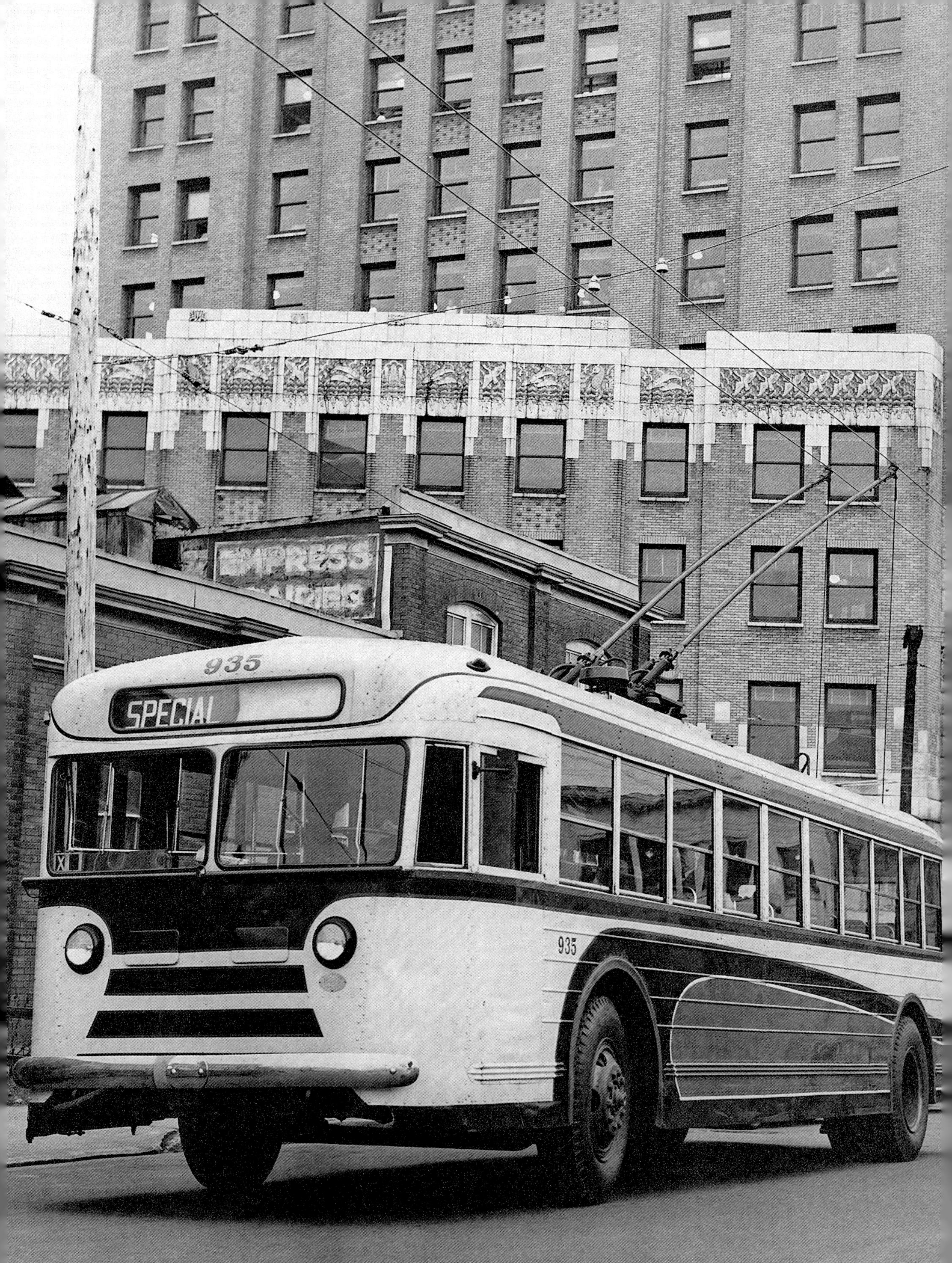
935
SPECIAL
EMPRESS
935

Vancouver (1948-present)
British Columbia Electric Railway Company/ British Columbia Hydro and Power Authority/ Urban Transit Authority of British Columbia – Metro Transit Operating Company/ BC Transit/TransLink–Coast Mountain Bus Company

With the last operating trolley coach system in Canada, Vancouver has embraced this form of transport and led the way with new innovations.

As was the case with many of Canada's transit systems, Vancouver was severely affected by the Second World War, with curtailment of streetcar production and rationing of gasoline and rubber tires. Canadian Car & Foundry (CCF) switched from making the Presidents' Conference Committee (PCC) streetcar to war production, so Vancouver saw only 36 PCCs added to their fleet. With wartime industries running 24 hours a day, the port of Vancouver bursting with shipping, and the rationing that affected personal vehicles, transit ridership doubled, tripled, and tripled again. The result, predictably, was that the streetcar system was worn out by the war's end and needed either rebuilding or replacing.

As early as 1912, the British Columbia Electric Railway Company (B.C.E.R. or simply 'B.C. Electric'), operator of public transit in Vancouver (and Victoria), considered using motor buses and trolley coaches to serve some of the sparsely populated areas of Vancouver. But those early trolley coaches had unreliable motors, solid tires – much like the early automobiles – and rough suspensions. Certainly, they were not suitable for the unpaved and gravel roads in those areas. However, by 1923, the situation had changed with the new Grandview area developing quickly on Vancouver's east side being a considerable distance from public transit.[508] [509] Rather than extend streetcar service, B.C. Electric tried their first motor buses, purchasing two from the White Motor Company. B.C. Electric continued to add more buses over the next twenty years, and by the late 1930s converted all of the streetcar lines in New Westminster to motor buses.

During World War II the company's President, W.G. Murrin, and transportation manager E.W. Arnott studied all the options. The Beeler Organization of New York was brought in to do a study, and from this a plan was developed: the company would re-track and re-wire the major routes, order 100 PCC streetcars, and test the new trackless trolley coach. Then W.R. Hubka, the Northwest Representative of The Twin Coach Company of Kent, OH, arrived at Mr. Arnott's door. B.C.E.R. operated some of the company's motor buses, and Twin Coach was eager to enter the Canadian market for trolley coaches. Since Twin had delivered 177 of its coaches to Seattle in the previous few years (converting all streetcar lines there to trolley coach), Hubka suggested it would be a simple matter to ship one for a trial in Vancouver and Victoria (where B.C.E.R. ran both transit systems).[510]

In November 1945, Arnott wrote to Vancouver's Alderman Thompson, Chairman, Harbours Utilities and Airport Committee requesting that, since Victoria City Council had approved the importation of a demonstration trolley coach under special licence from the Department of National Revenue, it made sense to conduct a similar trial in Vancouver. "Our company will assume all responsibility and costs for the erection of the necessary electrical overhead as well as respect the operation of the trolley coach itself and in addition will remove the said electrical overhead work immediately following the demonstration." In addition to promising the coach would operate in non-revenue service, he suggested a route "Starting point – Northwest corner of Burrard and Pender Streets. Thence west on Pender and Georgia Streets to Bidwell Street. Turn-around loop via Bidwell, Alberni and Cadero Streets. Thence east on Pender Street to Thurlow Street. Turn-around loop via Thurlow, Seton and Burrard Streets to starting point." Since the Victoria test was scheduled for the end of November, and the bus was on loan for only a month, B.C.E.R. postulated an early December trial.[511] The committee responded promptly, recommending such an arrangement.[512] This demonstration attracted the attention of Major J.S. Matthews, City Archivist, who requested from Mr. Arnott details on the coach and the trial operations, as well as photos which he would add to the clippings he was gathering for inclusion in the archives. The coach on loan from Seattle was a 1942 Twin

Opposite: In December 1945, the Seattle trial trolley coach was being demonstrated in Vancouver. The photographer was standing in the 400 block of Burrard Street, between Hastings and Pender streets, and the Marine Building can be seen in the background. (CITY OF VANCOUVER ARCHIVES, TRANS P112, PHOTOGRAPHER GEORGE YOUNG. LOCATION INFORMATION – ANGUS McINTYRE)

Detail: Downtown Vancouver

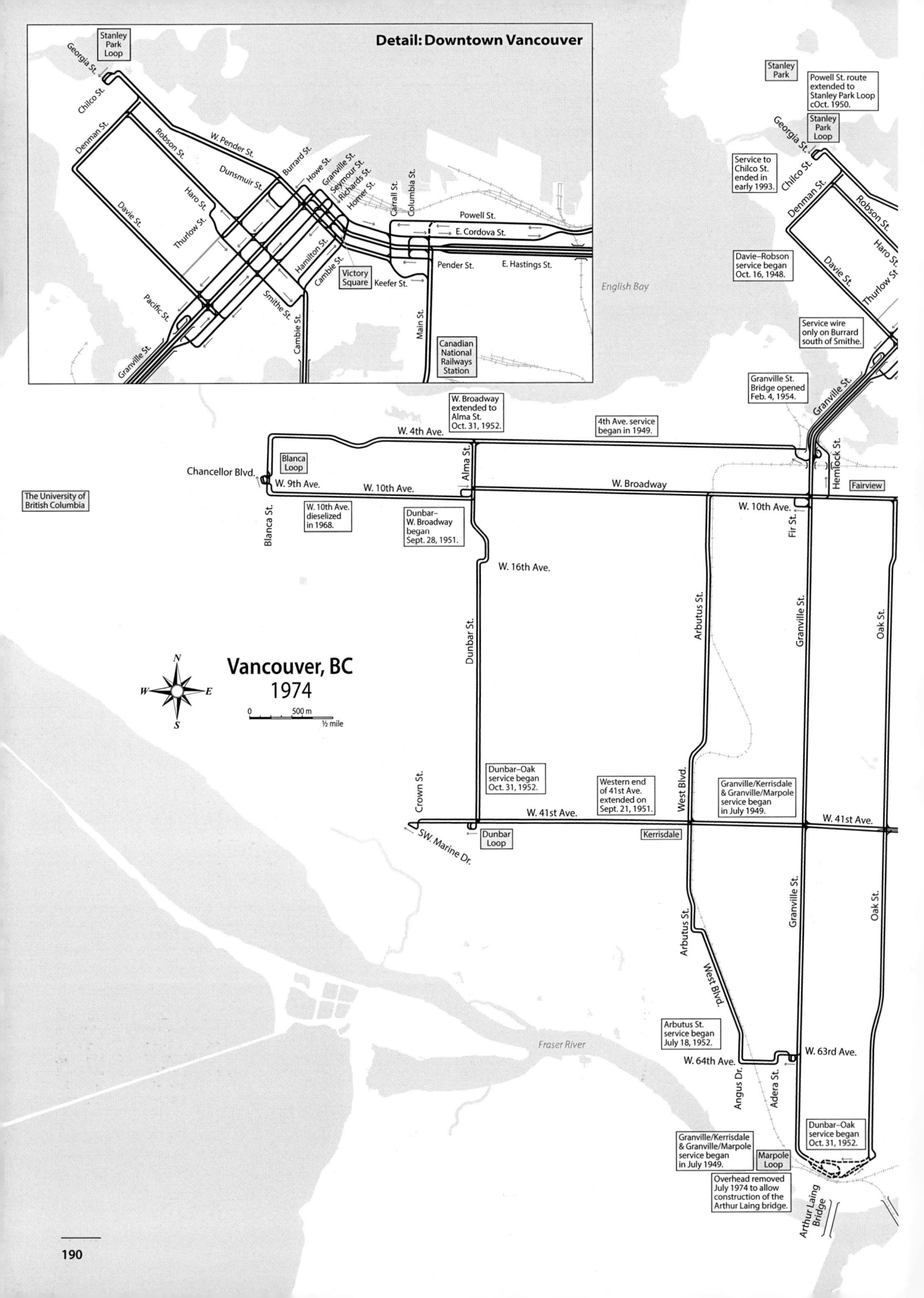

Vancouver, BC
1974

191

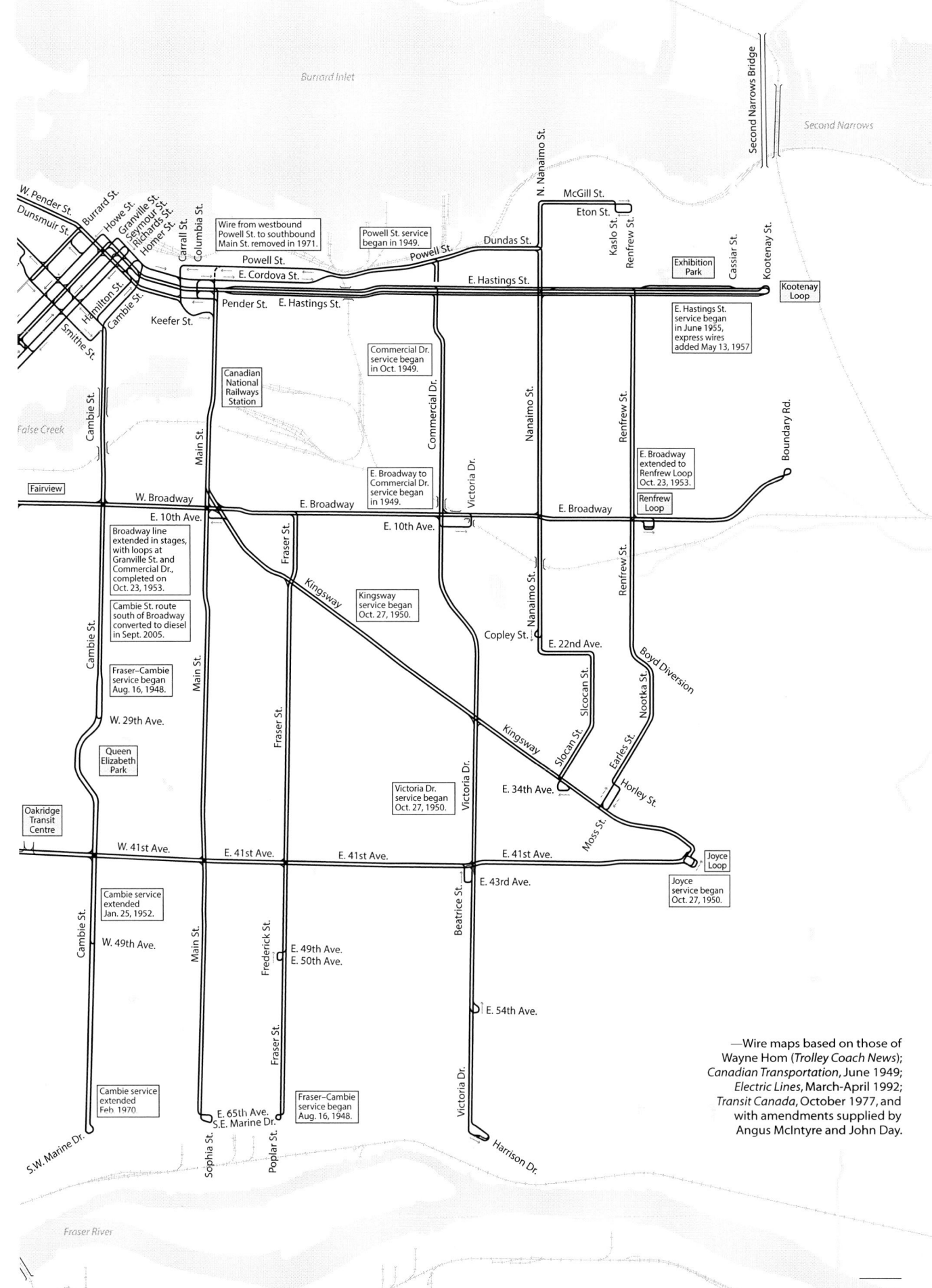

B.C. Electric Railway Company to operate
300 TROLLEY COACHES
in Vancouver

Left: By June 1949, four streetcar lines had been converted, four conversions were in progress, and B.C. Electric Railway was projecting fourteen lines and 300 coaches.
(OHIO BRASS COLLECTION, THE STRAHORN LIBRARY, ILLINOIS RAILWAY MUSEUM)

After an extensive survey of operations in several trolley coach cities, The B. C. Electric Railway Company, Ltd., decided to install these popular electrics in Vancouver. Four lines, the Fraser, Cambie, Robson and Davie, were changed over during 1948. They total 35.5 round trip miles and are operated with 76 trolley coaches. Four more lines, totaling 47.4 round trip miles, are being converted this year. Vancouver's program also calls for the conversion of six more major lines. When all changeovers are completed, Vancouver will be operating more than 300 trolley coaches over 14 lines, totaling 160 round trip miles.

Ohio Brass
TROLLEY COACH AND STREET [RAILWAY] MATERIAL AND CAR EQUIPMENT
CANADIAN OHIO BRASS CO. LTD. NIAGARA FALLS ONTARIO
MANSFIELD, OHIO

Coach, 41-passenger model. It began free service on December 5th 1945 and ran until the 14th.[513]

Passengers were treated to a brief spiel by announcer Teddy Lyons, a locally-famous observation car conductor. He had notes on his script to carefully maintain a tone of friendliness and hospitality, since as the host he was the face of the Company. In his commentary, reference was made to B.C.E.R.'s post-war plan, ready since V-E Day, and its eagerness to order thirty coaches at a cost of a million dollars as soon as the City approved the program. It also alluded to "air conditioning" which keeps a continuous flow of clean air in the bus. This was probably a reference to a forced air system, not air-conditioning as we know it today. Finally the announcer told the passengers that, if approved, trolley coaches would operate on Powell Street out to Hastings Park, on Macdonald Street, run across the Burrard Bridge to downtown and around the Davie-Robson loop. Trolley coaches would also be used on the Oak–Cambie routes. He ended by asking if any of them would like to see the vehicle's electric motor.[514]

On its return to Seattle, Twin Coach sent B.C.E.R. an invoice for the costs incurred and expressed their hope that "you are successful in obtaining permission from the Vancouver city authorities to operate trolley coaches in your city."[515] B.C.E.R. was convinced, especially since the costs of streetcar rail rehabilitation were mounting, and the union was complaining about conversion from two-man to one-man cars. The public's and politicians' acceptance of the trolley coach was also in their favour. However, B.C.E.R. had no rights to operate trolley coaches in Vancouver (or Victoria, for that matter), and those franchises were being renegotiated in 1946. City Council did adopt the report of a special committee on modernization of transit, and approved in principle the operation of three trolley coach routes. These were routes on which motor buses currently ran, but the company also saw a future for the trolley coach on streetcar routes that could not be economically justified for rail and rolling stock replacement. The coaches' reputation for being quiet, odourless and curb-loading were cited as plusses, and especially their hill-climbing ability, given the steep, sustained grades some routes had to contend with. Further, not having to make outside fuel purchases was a big factor for an electric company to consider in the trolley's favour.[516]

Worried that Vancouver might go south for their coaches, Canadian Car & Foundry dispatched a salesman from their Montreal head office who, after making a great pitch, invited Ivor W. Niel, B.C.E.R.'s General Manager of Transportation, to come to the Fort William plant and see the first coaches come off the line. Convinced, B.C.E.R. signed off on thirty model T-44 coaches. However, the company was now in the queue at the plant behind Edmonton, Kitchener, Cornwall, Montreal, Regina, Fort William, Port Arthur and Toronto. Two coaches were rushed through production and delivered to Vancouver in July 1947, in time to be displayed at the Pacific National Exhibition. The coaches were in a new paint scheme: all cream, with the letters BCE on a red background, topped by a symbolic west-coast totem pole. The red background, rounded shape, and the thunderbird totem sticking out of the top of the logo, soon gave it the nickname of "The Tomatobird". B.C.E.R. announced a $6-million expansion program including the installation of two trolley coach lines. Billed as one of the biggest programs in Canada and the biggest in the company's history, it added twelve more coaches to the thirty already ordered, then another forty.[517]

A trade press article in February of 1947 went on to detail delivery of thirty trolley coaches in the second quarter, 42 in the third quarter and 36 in the fourth quarter.[518] Obviously the writer of that article didn't do well in math class. The remaining coaches, expected in the summer, would replace the FRASER streetcar service from Marine Drive to downtown, and also would operate on Cambie from 29th Avenue to downtown, with eventual extensions to 41st Avenue. New company president A. E. "Dal" Garuer was quoted as saying "Trolley buses seem to be the most popular type of transportation vehicle. And from

Right: "They do things on a grand scale in Vancouver…" boasted this 1952 Ohio Brass ad, with 311 trolley coaches in just four years. (OHIO BRASS COLLECTION, THE STRAHORN LIBRARY, ILLINOIS RAILWAY MUSEUM)

what we can see, the most efficient. We will put many more of them in, but we want to learn about them first in certain areas by our own actual experience."[519] But things moved slowly, partly due to delays, strikes and shortages throughout 1946 that were cited in the Company's annual report as holding up both bus and copper wire deliveries. While the coaches were being delivered and stored, mechanics were sent to Seattle for training, substations converted, poles erected and wire strung.

A July 9th 1948 photo cutline stated "During the next two months, 400 British Columbia Electric Railway Co. operators will be taught how to pilot electric trolley buses…. The first step in the conversion of a number of routes from motor coaches and streetcars to trolley buses will take place in mid-August. It will be the first time that trolley bus service has been offered in Vancouver."[520]

On August 16th 1948, thirty Brill T-44 trolleys started Vancouver's service on the FRASER–CAMBIE line from Fraser Street and Marine Drive via Fraser, Kingsway, Main, Pender, Seymour, Robson and Cambie Street to 29th Avenue. Earlier, on August 13th, politicians, and trade and industry officials boarded the trolleys for an inaugural run following a ribbon-cutting ceremony and tour of the newly-opened Oakridge Transit Centre. As they set off to ride in the new coaches, B.C. Electric President A.E. "Dal" Grauer asked if he could pilot the coach. Taking over the driver's seat, Grauer, with a smile on his face, pulled out into traffic, dewired the coach and broke a pole.[521]

B.C.E.R. had also acquired a former army barracks at 41st Avenue and Cambie Street as a temporary bus depot for the new gasoline and trolley coaches. Dubbed "Little Mountain Garage", it was to serve until the new $1.75-million Oakridge Transit Centre was built a few blocks away.[522] This facility opened in August 1948, in time for the company's planned $16-million conversion from streetcar to rubber-tired vehicles. The new plant employed 110 mechanics on a 13½-acre site. There was a tarmac paved lot capable of holding 350 trolley coaches and motor buses, and inside could service nine trolley coaches at once over three inspection pits.[523]

On October 16th 1948, the second line (DAVIE–ROBSON) opened between Victory Square and English Bay on the Robson and Davie routes, replacing a temporary motor bus service.[524] The following year, in May, B.C. Electric took delivery of three T-48 Brill trolleys. The larger 48-passenger vehicles featured double-wide front doors and were to become the standard B.C. Electric model. In July of 1949, the GRANVILLE route, with branches to Marpole and Kerrisdale, was introduced using 34 coaches. This was followed by the BROADWAY EAST (to Commercial Drive), POWELL, and FOURTH AVENUE routes.[525] By the end of that year, 168 trolley coaches were operating in Vancouver. "The promise by Vancouver's city engineer that the new Granville Bridge would be ready before the end of 1952 had prompted the company to end service on the East Boulevard (Kerrisdale), Fourth Avenue and West Point Grey lines earlier than it had planned."[526] Eighty-eight more coaches were on order for the following year – all the bigger T-48 models.[527]

The next decade saw many more trolley coach conversions. On October 27th 1950, the JOYCE RD streetcar was converted to trolley coach, as were the two lines operating south of Kingsway on Victoria Drive, one of which ran to a wye at 44th Avenue, the other via single track to a still-extant loop at 54th. The trolley coach routes were operated as branches of the KINGSWAY–VICTORIA trolley coach line, while the POWELL route was extended to Stanley Park. At the year's end, an announced $5.3-million was to be expended and 55 more trolley coaches added,[528] giving B.C.E.R. more trolley coaches than any other transit utility in Canada. There were 15.4 miles of two-way wire added. There was also a new east end half million dollar garage to be constructed for motor and trolley coaches.[529] Many car and motor bus lines were converted to trolley coach as the service expanded. This included conversion of the DUNBAR–WEST BROADWAY car line and the 41ST AVENUE-CROSSTOWN bus on September 21st 1951.

Left: By March 1955, seven years after trolley coaches were introduced, Vancouver had built nineteen trolley coach lines.
(OHIO BRASS COLLECTION, THE STRAHORN LIBRARY, ILLINOIS RAILWAY MUSEUM)

Further routes came into operation in the 1950s, including CAMBIE (... it was extended to 50th Avenue, where previously there had been no service at all) on January 25th 1952; ARBUTUS (replacing the downtown–Marpole interurban) on July 18th 1952; and OAK (connected to the existing DUNBAR line) on October 31st 1952. In 1952-53, the BROADWAY line was initiated in stages so that by October 23rd 1953, it extended from Alma to Renfrew, with turnback loops at Granville and Commercial.[530]

Women became active participants in the trolley bus era in the fall of 1951 as 27 conductorettes were reassigned from streetcars. Still on the payroll after the male shortage of the war years, these ladies were being taught to rewind the 32-pound springs on the trolley retrievers as well as climb on the roof to replace trolley poles, or so the article in *Passenger Transport* would have us believe. Replacing a pole was likely a line truck maintenance job, male or female operator notwithstanding. Perhaps the writer meant re-wiring a pole when the rope had snapped.[531] Trolley coaches have two retrievers mounted on the rear of the bus. If a pole "dewired" (came off the trolley wire), the retriever would trip and a heavy spring inside the retriever would pull the pole down towards the roof of the bus, away from the overhead wires. Before rewiring the pole, the heavy retriever spring would have to be rewound and reset. In the event of a broken retriever rope, operators were trained to climb up fold-out steps onto the roof, walk down the pole and hook it under the pole hook. Returning to the ground at the rear of the coach, the rope ends could be tied together and the pole rewired. It was also possible to tie a short piece of rope to the other trolley rope, and rewire both poles using only one rope.

An Ohio Brass advertisement in June 1952 touted Vancouver as having, by year's end, 311 coaches and 130 miles of routes, with two more streetcar lines to be replaced.[532] In addition, a new converter station was built at Oakridge Transit Centre.[533] In October 1953, twenty-six (later reduced to just sixteen) more vehicles were ordered for service in the spring of the next year, new T-48A models.[534] That would leave only two streetcar lines, GRANDVIEW and HASTINGS EAST, remaining in 1953, but their fate was sealed in the next two years.

The August 1952 *Buzzer*, the take-away passenger newsletter, announced that turn signals were being installed on the left sides of all buses and trolley coaches. Although the buses did have turn signals on their rear and front ends, B.C. Electric put the new lights on to help motorists driving beside buses. However, signal lights would not be installed on the right side of buses, as most driving trouble came from left turns and moving left into traffic.[535]

On February 4th 1954, the Granville Street Bridge, a multimillion-dollar eight-lane structure opened, and the next day, trolley buses began service across it using four sets of overhead wires.[536] This was because two different routes used the bridge crossing. "One down – one to go," said *The Buzzer*, noting that with the conversion of the GRANDVIEW streetcar line to trolleys under the $1-million Transit Improvement Program, the HASTINGS line was now the last operating streetcar route in the Lower Mainland. While some mourned the loss of the streetcar, *The Buzzer* opined that: "Eight years of hard work and more than $25,000,000 have almost done away with the old rattlers. Canada's largest fleet of trolley coaches, 327 of 'em, now rolls over nearly triple the number of miles of route we had back in 1946."[537]

By 1955, nineteen lines had been converted using 327 trolley coaches, making Vancouver's fleet the seventh largest in North America and the largest in Canada. ROUTE #14, HASTINGS-EAST, the last remaining rail line, ended revenue service on April 22nd 1955, with trolley coaches replacing the trams that June. The streetcars made a final commemorative run on Sunday April 24th, carrying thousands of Vancouverites between Kootenay Loop and downtown Vancouver for free last rides as well as ceremonies at the Pacific Exhibition Grounds, involving the Vancouver Pioneers and specially-decorated cars.[538]

May 13th 1957 saw the inauguration of a new express trolley service introduced on Hastings Street between Kootenay Loop and Main Street, which required the installation of a second set of wires over the centre lanes in

Above: Sporting the B.C. Hydro logo, coach 2113 lays over at Blanca loop, the western terminus of the 4-FOURTH route, read to return as a 17-OAK, July 5th 1973. (TED WICKSON)

Below: You can count at least fifteen Brills queued up beside Empire Stadium/Pacific National Exhibition on Hastings Street when a nineteen-year-old Angus McIntyre took this photo. He recalls, "I took this photo of the 26 November 1966 Grey Cup game at Empire Stadium, and as you can see many people still rode transit to get to the game. 32,000 attended the game. Note TV camera on crane. These trolleys were filled to capacity, and a supervisor flagged down an inbound HASTINGS EXPRESS trolley and pulled it off the express wire to load more people. Saskatchewan won over Ottawa." The coaches are queued up on the layover wire, a fifth set on this part of East Hastings. In addition to this wire, there were two regular service and two express service sets of overhead (one of each in each direction).

TIRES AND WIRES

Right: A B.C. Hydro overhead truck, still in the B.C. Electric red paint scheme, works at Broadway and Oak in 1969 as a coach pulls away from its stop. Just behind the pole you can see another B.C. Hydro worker guiding the coach past the line truck.
(ANGUS McINTYRE)

Left: September of 1969 and coach 2319 looks a little tired on the exterior. The full load of passengers doesn't seem to mind just as long as they are safely and quietly delivered to their destinations along the KINGSWAY route.
(PETER COX, BILL LINLEY COLLECTION)

the street. This was the launch of one of the very few express trolley coach operations in North America.[539] Hastings Street between Rupert and Renfrew had a fifth set of overhead wires westbound along the curb lane for storing trolley coaches for Exhibition events. B.C. Electric took the opportunity to pose five coaches side-by-side near Hastings, east of Renfrew, during the Pacific National Exhibition in August.

As the mid-fifties rolled in, so did the recession. Money was tight so more people took to riding public transportation. With no more Canadian trolley coaches being produced, Vancouver looked south for good used units. With this in mind, B.C. Electric bought 24 used Pullmans from Birmingham, Alabama. Though they were a good price, the company would regret buying these coach-

es because they were steel framed, as opposed to the aluminum-framed Brills. Much effort and money was spent on rewinding the motors and remodelling them to suit local conditions, the first one entering service on March 8th 1975.[540] Somewhat heavier than the Brills, their stiff steering and frequent breakdowns made them unpopular with the operators. They were relegated to the relatively straight flat routes of 41st and Broadway, and since the anticipated surge in passenger traffic never materialized, they were scrapped within three years.[541]

In 1960, the B.C.E.R. was wound up into the British Columbia Electric Company Limited (BCE). In August 1961, the Province of British Columbia expropriated BCE, and – through a subsequent merger and after long court battles – created British Columbia Hydro and Pow-

Above: You young fellows just can't take it eh? Venerable T-48 Brill 2228, built in 1950, is ready to go back to work, while E800 Flyer 2647 (1976) has to take a rest at Oakridge Garage, September 12th 1981. (TED WICKSON)

Below: Doing the time warp? While it was December 5th 1982 in this view and E800 Flyer 2607 is now gone, it was the newest form of electric trolley in 1976. One supposes that the 1920s classic behind it was also the latest and greatest in its day. Unfortunately for 2607, after Expo86, its class was retired due to poor operation and single front doors, making it poor for heavy loading. Trolley route 15-CAMBIE is also history now. (TED WICKSON)

Above: Crossing False Creek on the Granville Street Bridge, Coast Mountain Bus Company (TransLink) 2854, a Flyer E902, looks spiffy in the blue, yellow and white paint scheme on July 10th 2006.
(TED WICKSON)

Right: Venerable Brill 2229, outbound on route 25-VICTORIA, stops to take on passengers on a sunny September day in 1981.
(TED WICKSON)

er Authority (B.C. Hydro) in 1962. Use of the thunderbird logo soon ceased, replaced by the stylized "H" logo, symbolizing forested mountains and abundant waters, that was being applied to all the company's assets. Subsequently, after much experimentation in the Kitsilano paint shop, 2227 emerged in a new off-white paint scheme, with narrow green and blue stripes reprising the colours of the logo, separated by the thin silver/grey of the belt rail.[542] While the paint scheme was being finalized, 2228 to 2232 were painted in the old cream paint, but every trolley painted afterwards, starting with 2233, emerged in the new off-white. (At the time, trolleys were repainted in strict ascending numerical sequence.)

The prosperity of the 1960s brought rising car ownership in Vancouver, and development of suburban areas outside the traditional trolley service area. These factors resulted in a precipitous drop in ridership, so that not only were the 24 Pullmans retired, but the first thirty of the 1947 Brills were also stored. Of these, ten were sold to Edmonton in 1962, while the others were cannibalized for parts and scrapped.[543]

Many properties in North America abandoned the trolley bus, and Vancouver started on that path in 1968 with the conversion of the Tenth/Hastings portions of the DUNBAR/TENTH/HASTINGS/RENFREW route. Conversion to diesel operation permitted through service to the University of British Columbia. Rising fuel prices and shortages put plans for any further conversions in abeyance. British Columbia had an abundance of hydroelectric generation, insulating electric transit from fuel price surges, and that made a compelling argument to at least try to maintain the status quo.

In 1969, B.C. Hydro said it would not prematurely abandon trolley coaches and looked to see how the Toronto experiment with a rebuilt Can Car/Flyer bus would work out. In the meantime, B.C. Hydro planned to extend the 15-CAMBIE line a mile, from 50th to 64th Avenue. Originally scheduled for implementation in October 1969, a strike at the steel pole plant delayed it until February 1970. It was the first trolley route extension in more than fifteen years. Some relatively minor overhead adjustments were made to accommodate one-way streets and construction of the new Pacific Centre. Meanwhile, the existing fleet was not forgotten – repainting, body work and repairs were done on a regular, programmed basis.[544] As other Canadian cities abandoned electric buses, Vancouver began to purchase usable trolley coaches for service and spare parts. Two ex-Winnipeg Brill trolley coaches soon graced Vancouver's streets. Public opinion was also on the side of the trolley buses, with two articles in the *Vancouver Sun* in the summer of 1970 advocating the retention of trolley coaches.[545] B.C. Hydro responded with an issue of its transit newsletter *The Buzzer*, stating that, as having the second largest fleet of trolley buses in North America, Vancouver had carefully maintained 296 vehicles in good condition.[546] Still, some trolleys had 600,000 miles on the odometer, motors were being rewound and some obtainable parts fabricated in B.C. Hydro's shops.

In January 1971, bus drivers went on strike, stranding 200,000 riders citywide. After 32 days of traffic jams and counter-offers, buses rolled again, including the reliable, aging trolleys.[547] Still, troubles were not over – in June, trolley linemen struck Hydro, causing delays and overhead failures. Otherwise, overhead improvements were quietly being made as the year progressed. The fleet stood at 282, with some other vehicles in storage.[548]

While the TTC rebuilding program was of some interest to B.C. Hydro management, there was little interest in embarking on a huge capital project in a corporation which by this time regarded its transit operations as a necessary nuisance.

The Greater Vancouver Regional District (GVRD) commissioned a transportation study which reported in the fall of 1971. Among many other things, the report highlighted the advantage of retaining and expanding electric bus service. It recommended several conversions, and contemplated that the GVRD eventually take over B.C. Hydro's transit operations. There was, however, nothing specific as to how the operation would be paid for.

In 1973, the newly-elected provincial government created the Bureau of Transit Services as an agency within the Ministry of Municipal Affairs. The Bureau took over the long-range and conceptual planning of transit, and took the first steps towards developing provincial-municipal cost sharing arrangements through service contracts. It embarked on a major province-wide expansion of services and uniform branding of services using common logos and naming conventions. In the traditional B.C. Hydro services areas of Greater Vancouver and Victoria, provincial plans were imposed on B.C. Hydro, which, as a provincial Crown Corporation, was forced to absorb the costs of service expansion. On August 31st 1973, the first new bus services under the provincial program were inaugurated in suburban areas. Although branded as "Greater Vancouver Transit System", these services were not funded or managed by the GVRD, but planning did take account of local and regional interests expressed by the various levels of government.

B.C. Hydro had, in 1973, placed an order for sixty diesel buses from Western Flyer. The intended use of these buses was to commence a wholesale trolley conversion program. Instead, the new government directed that these buses be used for suburban service expansion, that the trolley system be retained, and that steps be taken to commence a Toronto-style fleet renewal. Consequently, twenty used trolleys were purchased from Kitchener in May that year for use or spare parts.[549] These were to be followed by further coaches from Calgary. Another seventeen well-maintained T-48As were purchased from Saskatoon as it wound down its fleet, and repainted for Vancouver service.[550]

Above: Stereotypical Vancouver, snow capped mountains, a light drizzle and New Flyer 2215 on the OAK run, all demonstrating that trolley coaches are alive and well in at least one corner of Canada, January 2012. (TERRY DEJONG)

Part of busy Granville Street in the downtown core was converted to a pedestrian and buses-only thoroughfare, which entailed closure for a few months, with trolleys detouring via Howe, Seymour and Richards streets. Granville Mall opened in November 1974 and the trolleys returned to Granville.

Later in 1974, B.C. Hydro, in conjunction with Brown Boveri and the Metro transit system in Seattle, borrowed a Swiss-built Hess articulated trolley to test for several months. A small gasoline engine provided this vehicle with on-board power, allowing it to move when electrical power was interrupted. Even more revolutionary was the use of solid-state chopper controls which eliminated many mechanical parts and saved energy. There were plans to purchase this type of vehicle, but following a provincial election in 1975, they were shelved.[551] Prior to the change in government, B.C. Hydro had ordered fifty Flyer Industries model E800 trolley coaches in 1974 for delivery the following year.[552]

1975 started off with a group of youths taking over a trolley bus on an otherwise quiet Sunday, swerving through traffic, knocking down overhead lines, and finally smashing it into a tree. The youths took the bus when the operator was making a call to his supervisor to report unruly passengers – presumably the ones that hijacked the coach. No one was injured.[553]

In late 1975, tenders were called for twenty regular and forty articulated trolley coaches following public tests of three different coaches. However, the bids were rejected as too high and the rebidding process was stopped by the newly-elected provincial government.[554]

On December 31st 1975, the inaugural run of one of the two newly-commissioned Flyer E800 trolleys took place with company officials as passengers. A strike at the Flyer plant had delayed the order, but by the spring of 1976, the rest of the Flyer coaches arrived.

On August 4th 1976, Brill T-44 coach No. 2082, the last of the Canadian-built T-44 trolleys in service in Vancouver, made its final run after 28 years of service. The T-48 and T-48A Brills soldiered on.[555]

Vancouver also changed its unique route numbering system that year. In the past, through routing used different numbers, depending on the direction; for example, 20–GRANVILLE inbound and 25–VICTORIA outbound, both operating on Victoria Drive. This system made it easy to know what side of the street to stand on to get to a particular place. But this naming system was confusing for those unfamiliar with the city, and made it hard to draw transit maps, so the system was simplified by using the same number regardless of direction of travel, with only the destination name changing.[556]

The late 1975 change in government had precipitated a realignment of transit responsibilities. Some power had been returned to B.C. Hydro, although the erstwhile Bureau of Transit Services continued to exist as a secretariat of the Ministry of Lands, Parks and Housing. In 1977, B.C. Hydro eliminated the operating irritant of having fleets painted in multiple colour schemes and so the trolley buses received the orange-and-brown stripes formerly reserved for "FastBus" branding. The words "B.C. Hydro Transit" replaced "Greater Vancouver Transit System" on the side of the coaches. By this time, only the T-48s remained from the original fleet of trolleys.[557]

In 1978, B.C. Hydro conducted a major review of its trolley system, detailing the energy costs and future requirements for use. After months of uncertainty, the company announced that it would keep the quiet, pollution-free trolleys rather than abandon these electric vehicles as many other cities had done. Like Halifax, Vancouver was constrained by its geography. Wedged onto a peninsula, Vancouver was nearly fully-developed by the early 1950s, and the trolley coach system dating from that period had required little change. The city's grid street layout and early move to a comprehensive one-way street layout in the central core meant that the overhead remained largely unchanged and equally up to the task of the 1980s as it was in the 1950s. The low cost of hydro-electric power was also a positive factor, and a large fleet resulted in economies of scale. Finally, the hilly nature of Vancouver favoured the trolley coach's performance characteristics over that of diesel buses.[558]

In mid-August, B.C. Hydro wished their trolleys a happy 30th birthday of being in service. Described in *The Buzzer* as being the workhorse of the fleet, there were now 300 trolleys on twenty different routes. The accompanying picture showed T-48 Brill No. 2258 in pristine paint.[559]

At this time, B.C.Hydro built on the experience gained from the Swiss Hess demonstrator, and one Brown Boveri chopper and motor was installed in No. 2601, the first of the 1975 Flyer E800s. The installation was successful and well received, and it was clear that any future deliveries of trolley coaches would have solid-state controls along the lines of this unique experiment.

In July 1978, the Urban Transit Authority (UTA), another new Crown Corporation, was created, with a mandate to provide province-wide transit policy, planning and funding. This agency assumed the responsibility for public transit outside Victoria and Vancouver that had rested with the provincial government, and paved the way for the removal of the transit function from B.C. Hydro. The latter continued to operate transit in Victoria and Vancouver until April 1st 1980, when a new provincially-owned operating company, the Metro Transit Operating Company, was established to take over the staff and transit operations functions. For the first time, local governments in Vancouver and Victoria now contributed to the costs of transportation in their communities, and assumed a direct role in planning their services. The Board of Directors of UTA was composed of mayors appointed to the role by the Province.

One of the first tasks of the new authority was to take a lead position in finding a replacement for the aging Brill trolleys, some of which were now more than thirty years old. B.C. Hydro had made some tentative moves towards this, but lack of finance and an acceptable vehicle had stalled progress. As financier, the UTA viewed itself as the "customer" and thus entitled to lead the process, ensuring good value for its investment of taxpayer-provided funds. Other "stakeholders", in particular operations and maintenance staff of B.C. Hydro (later Metro Transit Operating Company) and the planning department of Greater Vancouver Regional District (which by this time had assumed an active advisory role on transit matters), provided relevant input on the project.

B.C. Hydro's experience with the Brown Boveri (BBC) chopper had been positive. The retrofitted coach performed well and its electrical system was easy to maintain. The experience with the Flyer coach in which the chopper had been installed was less positive, and B.C. Hydro staff's inclination was to negotiate a sole source procurement using, hopefully, a GM New Look bus body. Two major issues with this approach were that GM was not particularly interested in building trolley coaches, and sole source procurements were politically difficult if not impossible.

The UTA's involvement brought with it the political reality that public financing requires public input, and it became clear that the only way forward was a comprehensive review of the market and an open bidding process.

Simultaneously, Edmonton Transit System was looking to replace its Brill trolley fleet. Having had similar, less-than-satisfactory, experiences with Flyer E800s using rebuilt electrical equipment, ETS were anxious to obtain a modern coach, and, impressed by the performance of the BBC chopper in Vancouver, a joint procurement was discussed. With ETS seeking 100 coaches, and Vancouver between 150 and 220 units, some economies of scale were hoped for. After a few months of discussions it was clear that the ETS desire for a sole supplier was not compatible with the UTA's need to fully canvass the market, and the two agencies decided that a joint procurement was not feasible.

The bidding process began with approval from the UTA board resolving, on July 25th 1979, that "the existing trolley system be retained and … that a tender call be prepared and issued for 150 new standard trolley buses with the option for 70 additional vehicles and the retrofitting of 50 E800 Flyer trolley buses with new energy efficient electronic controls".[560]

In March 1980, a draft technical specification was circulated to all known suppliers of trolleybuses or trolleybus components world-wide. Suppliers were asked to comment on the feasibility and practicality of the specification, and many useful technical comments were obtained, enabling specifications to be modified to the advantage of the UTA.[561] The process yielded some interesting results, not all of which translated into bids: already-obsolete Soviet-built ZIU-682s, and poor quality Beijings that were informally offered at a bargain price.

Tenders were opened on August 21st 1980. Seven suppliers offered coaches, or electrical packages for installation into any coach, with a total of 22 choices. Prices per coach ranged from $181,650 for an Elroy Engineering (Australia) Townobile, to a high of $262,010 for a Flyer coach with Alsthom Freon-cooled electrical equipment.[562]

A complex price adjustment mechanism, adding freight charges, awarding bonuses for desirable features and penalties for undesirable ones such as excess weight, was applied.[563] The most striking penalty was one of $50,000 per coach assessed against the Flyer coach offered with traditional GE resistor controls.[564]

The bidding process had attracted some unexpected interest. Elroy Engineering offered a bus that was visionary, at least for its time, in that its use of hub mounted motors and roof mounted electrical equipment allowed for a 100% low-floor design, many years before even partial low-floor buses became the norm. Mack Trucks' new owners, Renault, offered the Renault ER-100 that was being delivered to several French cities (and which was later built under license in Poland by Jelcz). Such was the company's enthusiasm for its prospects that it arranged for a diesel demonstrator to visit Vancouver, allowing staff a hands-on inspection of Renault construction. Siemens Canada attempted to break into the Canadian market with an Austrian-built MAN bus.

Interesting for its absence was a Flyer coach with a Brown Boveri electrical package. Aware of the desire by B.C. Hydro maintenance staff for a GM coach with BBC equipment, Brown Boveri dealt with GM's reluctance to participate by making a bid with BBC as the prime bidder, with the bus body subcontracted to GM, (opposite of the usual process where the bus builder is the prime, with the electrical work subcontracted.) Now that BBC was a direct competitor, Flyer declined to bid on a coach that included BBC equipment.

After intensive evaluation, the Flyer E901A coach with Westinghouse equipment was selected. Westinghouse offered an electrical package that was convection cooled, eliminating low-voltage cooling fans which were anecdotally reported as being maintenance headaches. Ironically, cooling fans were later added to keep the Westinghouse electrical equipment cool, the passive cooling of the original design having proved inadequate. The UTA picked up an option for an additional fifty coaches, raising the order to 200, and also awarded Flyer/Westinghouse with a contract to retrofit the existing fifty E800 coaches with the identical electrical equipment. After an abortive attempt to retrofit one E800, it was deemed cheaper to simply build additional replacement coaches, so the contract was increased to 245 units. Five additional sets of electrical equipment were added as spares for the new trolley coach fleet.

The new E901A and E902 models featured double-stream front and rear doors, holding 38 seated and with a total capacity of eighty passengers. Equipped with solid-state electronic controls, the Flyer trolleys included energy-saving regenerative braking which saved twenty per cent in electrical power compared to the old Brill trolleys. The prototype of the new E901A trolleys arrived on April 2nd 1982, painted in the orange-and-white colours of the Urban Transit Authority ... but, the paint had scarely had a chance to dry when the Province in August changed the name of the UTA to BC Transit. Another new paint scheme, reflecting the then standard red, white and blue used by many provincial agencies, was chosen.[565] Metro Transit Operating Company continued to operate for two more years until it merged with BC Transit in 1985, completing the consolidation of transit services under one Crown Corporation. Also in August, production units of the E901A began service after a shakedown period involving extensive testing.

Not that life with the new coaches was smooth sailing: problems persisted with the chopper controls, and many other systems, despite the high expectations raised in *The Buzzer*'s article extoling the virtues of a smooth ride of the first coach so equipped in 1978 (i.e. 2601 fitted with Brown Boveri equipment).[566] In fact, it would not be until mid-1984 that BC Transit felt confident enough to retire the last of the Brills.[567] Meanwhile, in March 1983 the 34–HASTINGS EXPRESS was paired with the 10–TENTH–UBC, requiring use of diesel buses and, consequently, marking the temporary end of the only express trolley service in Canada. Several other trolley route pairings were adjusted at the same time, resulting in combinations that included FOURTH–NANAIMO, DUNBAR–POWELL, STANLEY PARK–OAK, and HASTINGS–ARBUTUS. RENFREW was left as an unpaired route terminating in the downtown area.[568]

Despite Vancouver's mild climate that obviated the need for winter-long use of road salt, an unusual icy spell in January 1984 made salting of roads essential. The combination of salt and moisture created an electrolyte solution that caused short circuits in the Flyer coaches, and put most of the fleet out of commission. At that time, only nine Brills were in service and about 100 Flyers. Flyer fixed the problem and returned the coaches to service.[569]

The end of Brill trolley service in Vancouver, as well as in Canada, was marked by a "Farewell to Brill" day on Sunday, January 15th 1984. More than 200 people enjoyed a luncheon and old movies at the Oakridge Transit

Above: Dual overhead, no problem passing, as 2134 wishes us a Happy Holiday in downtown Vancouver on a snowless day in December 2012. (TERRY DEJONG)

Centre, a three-hour tour of the system on six surviving Brills, post-cards and T-shirts and displays. A booklet was produced by historian and trolley coach operator Brian Kelly as a bonus and was included in the fare. Kelly recalls, "We used every single Brill that was still running ... Each and every coach was full ... When we planned the trip we thought two or three coaches, but once the press picked up on the whole theme of 'Farewell to Brill' people who loved these coaches literally came out of the woodwork. Oakridge was a zoo that day, believe me!" [570]

Some lingering problems with the new fleet meant the venerable Brills were retained in service for a short time after the official "last day".

Closure of the Connaught (Cambie Street) Bridge November 11th meant rerouting the CAMBIE and OAK lines, with the resultant conversion to diesel operation for a year. This also affected the STANLEY PARK and KINGSWAY trolley lines, which were through-routed in November. [571]

With the opening in late 1985 of SkyTrain (an elevated rapid transit rail service), a number of extensions to trolley coach service were initiated. First there was a two-mile addition to the KINGSWAY route, to the Metrotown SkyTrain station in Burnaby March 7th 1986. Other changes involved diverting the NANAIMO route (March 7th) and RENFREW route (May 30th) to SkyTrain stations, both changes resulting in a reduction in their lengths.

In 1988, on Labour Day (September 5th), trolley coaches began serving the University of British Columbia (also two miles in length).[572] The extension marked a conversion from diesel bus back to trolley service for the #10–TENTH as well as the HASTINGS EXPRESS which was through-routed with the TENTH. At the ceremony marking the opening of the UBC trolley extensions, those present were reminded that forty years ago, B.C. Electric President Dal Grauer and guests travelled on the inaugural trolley coach run. It was also a plus in that there was a surplus of trolley coaches in the peak periods, while there was a tight diesel fleet. Conversion to trolley coach freed up 27 diesel buses for allocation to other routes. As the boulevard linking the city to the University was tree-lined, care was taken

203

to minimize pruning, and bracket arm poles were used as well as underground feeder cables.[573]

The trolley fleet stood then at 244; trolleys were still the workhorse of the operation, running on 172 miles of wire and carrying more passengers than the system's 649 diesel buses.[574] On Vancouver's east side, the conversion of the HASTINGS EXPRESS back to trolley operation reintroduced regular trolley service on both the local and express wires on Hastings Street, the express running as part of the #10 route which included the newly-electrified portion to UBC.[575]

In the 1990s, most of the trolley coach fleet underwent repairs and improvements to improve reliability. In 1993, BC Transit decommissioned its last Hewittic mercury arc rectifier stations. These 600 v DC rectifiers were holdovers from the days of streetcars, and the last in public transit use in North America. Conversion to solid state achieved a nine per cent reduction in electricity consumption.

In early 1993, the STANLEY PARK route was converted to diesel bus operation. This was necessitated by the dangerous left-hand turn from Westbound Georgia Street into the Chilco Loop across three lanes of traffic coming off a blind curve. At first, service was provided by a short diesel bus route originating in downtown, avoiding the dangerous left turn through the use of Alberni Street; later it made use of a short detour within the park itself. In 1997, a new diesel route running along Hastings from Simon Fraser University in Burnaby was created, with its western terminus in the park. This eliminated the need for the diesel bus shuttle as well as ending, finally, trolley operation on the HASTINGS EXPRESS. In 2003, as part of a road improvement project in the park, the trolley route was reinstated, despite the need to string overhead wire where there is limited clearance at an underpass, and now enters deep into the park. Hence the conversion to diesel buses was only temporary and trolleys still serve Stanley Park.

August 16th 1998 marked the fiftieth anniversary of trolley coach service in Vancouver – now one of only seven cities in North America still operating trolley coaches and one of only two left in Canada. On April 1st 1999, responsibility for transit in the Greater Vancouver Regional District was transferred (yet again), this time from BC Transit to the Greater Vancouver Transportation Authority (GVTA), commonly known as TransLink. Trolley bus operation was entrusted to a wholly-owned subsidiary named Coast Mountain Bus Company (CMBC).[576]

In 2002, two temporary loops were built at UBC as there were plans to build a new underground loop to handle more buses. One temporary loop was for diesels and the other one was for trolleys. Some work started on the project, but had to be halted before it was finished due to a loss of TransLink funding. In addition, UBC wanted to go ahead with construction of the new Student Union Building to be located where the original UBC Loop was.

On October 29th 2003, TransLink awarded the contract for a total of 228 low-floor, accessible trolley coaches to New Flyer – 188 standard forty-foot buses and forty articulated sixty-foot buses – at a total cost of $273-million.[577] The first restyled low-floor bus placed in revenue service, No. 2101, came to Vancouver July 2nd 2005 as a pilot bus. The remaining 187 forty-foot units (model E40LFR) were delivered at a rate of four buses a week starting in August 2006. The articulated (model E60LFR) prototype arrived January 28th 2007,[578] and by June 2008, the Vancouver trolley fleet consisted of entirely low-floor accessible coaches. An additional 34 articulated units arrived in 2009.[579]

Labour Day, 2006 saw the closure of Oakridge Transit Centre (OTC), with a convoy of trolleys and other buses making a trip to the new multi-million dollar Vancouver Transit Centre in Marpole. The parade was led by one of the original 1947 Canadian Car-Brill trolleys in the B.C. Electric Railway Company livery, preserved Brill No. 2040, part of the fleet that was first to call OTC 'home' when it opened 58 years previously. Other vintage buses from the Transit Museum Society (TRAMS) collection were also part of the procession, along with one of the new generation New Flyer trolleys.[580]

In 2007, the provincial government renamed the Greater Vancouver Transportation Authority to the South Coast British Columbia Transportation Authority, headed by an unelected professional board. The TransLink name was kept.[581] Together with other TransLink-funded agencies – including SkyTrain, West Coast Express, West Vancouver Blue Bus, HandyDART and Albion Ferry – CMBC became part of a fully integrated transit system under the umbrella of the South Coast BC Transportation Authority.

On April 20th 2008, the last of the E901A and E902 trolleys, which were originally brought into service in 1982-83, were retired. Number 2805 did the honours on the 3–MAIN route, driven by veteran operator Angus McIntyre, who is also a member of TRAMS, the historical trolley coach preservation group. Despite having over 700,000 miles on them, many were still operable. They were retired because of accessibility issues for those with mobility impairments, having high floors, and poles in the middle of the doorways. Also, after 25 years, the trolleys had extensive wear and tear that would have cost TransLink too much to fix and maintain. Eighty of these buses were sold to the Mendoza trolley bus system in Argentina in September 2008.[582] A week after their official retirement, there was a farewell fan trip for the venerably Flyer coaches.[583] As a footnote, by 2017, the last Flyer trolleys in Mendoza had been retired.

More than a half-century of regional transit history took centre stage in Stanley Park on August 16th 2008, as TransLink and the Coast Mountain Bus Company marked the sixtieth anniversary of trolley bus service in Metro Vancouver. Six buses representing four generations of trolley buses were on display for a celebration that included transit executives, bus riders, trolley enthusiasts and nostalgia buffs.

Above: A forty-foot low floor New Flyer 2157 runs along Granville street advertising the Christmas market. Yes, it is November 2012, and this is (snowless) Vancouver.
(TERRY DEJONG)

Below: It looks like the first passenger is ready to elbow anyone who cuts into line as New Flyer E40LFR coach travelling south on Granville Street at West Georgia takes on passengers on April 6th 2014.
(KEVIN NICOL)

The sad story of the Seattle Twin Coach demonstrator

Brian Kelly of Vancouver tells of attempts to preserve the original Seattle Twin trolley coach demonstrated in Vancouver and Victoria.

The Seattle Twin Coach demonstrator sits at the Kitsilano Shops in Vancouver where most major work was done on B.C.E.R. streetcars and interurbans. (COLLECTION OF WALLY YOUNG)

After the 1962 Seattle World's Fair, that city began cutting back on trolleys. First to be scrapped were the PCF (Pacific Car and Foundry Company) Brills, then they started on the Twins. New Flxible diesels filled the streets.

We knew that a Seattle trolley had been the first to actually operate in Vancouver as a demo, and the only one to operate in Victoria. Peter Cox and I enlisted the help of the West Coast Railway Association (WCRA) to try and preserve the Vancouver demo coach before it was scrapped. I was only about 17 or 18 and Peter not much older, but we contacted the Vancouver archives and were given information on the Vancouver and Victoria runs, learning the trolley in question was No. 835. It turned out it was actually No. 935, but we didn't know.

We went to Seattle Transit and requested No. 835 be donated. Apparently No. 835 had been scrapped, so they offered us the next available bus, No. 842, which by then had been renumbered No. 617. We went down with a Buster's tow truck and brought her back, then obtained permission from B.C. Hydro to store it at Cambie Garage. This was before I worked for them, I was just a "bus enthusiast", but Hydro was very good to us.

Sometime later we learned of our error, but we now had No. 617 in Vancouver, so we kept it. Basically it was "my trolley" – the WCRA only loaned us their name to obtain the donation, but they really wanted no part of it.

Several years later, I was now a supervisor with Hydro, and plans were made to close the Cambie garage. I arranged to have No. 617 moved to Carrall Street for storage. I had made several attempts to get approval to get it operating for fan trips, but could not get to first base with that, and I couldn't push too hard less I jeopardize my position.

While all this was going on, there was an active public drive in Seattle to retain their remaining trolleys and order new ones. There was an organization known as COMET, the Committee To Maintain Electric Transit. They had enough political clout to force Seattle Transit to keep the trolleys and develop plans for new ones, but in the meantime there were not enough trolleys left to keep service levels going. So Seattle Transit obtained every trolley they could that had been donated to various museums, and that included wanting mine back. Their offer to me was, they'd repatriate it, rebuild it for service, use it, and when new coaches came they'd return it, all at their cost. How could I say no?

So a large Seattle Transit, (or "Metro Transit" as it was then known), tow truck came to Vancouver and hauled No. 617 back to Seattle, where it was rebuilt, renumbered No. 657, and saw service for the next few years. Then, when new trolleys arrived, true to their word, Metro brought the now No. 657 back to Vancouver for me. It was moved out to Hydro's new Burnaby garage and stored with other out-of-service vehicles.

Unfortunately, the story does not have a happy ending. BC Transit, as it was now named, decided to send several of its old buses to scrap. They brought the scrapper to Burnaby and showed them which buses were to go. This did *NOT* include the No. 657, but the tow truck drivers working for the scrapper made a mistake, and took No. 657 to the crusher along with several derelict diesels. By the time the mistake was discovered, the trolley had been crushed! There were lots of apologies, of course, but the damage was done. Sadly, the real Vancouver demo, No. 935, met a similar fate. On a positive note, a few Seattle Twins are preserved, and occasionally one will operate on a fan trip.

"Sustainable transit systems like the trolley bus make Vancouver – in fact, the whole region – one of the most livable in the world," said Deputy Mayor Heather Deal, who proclaimed that week "Trolley Week" on behalf of the City of Vancouver. "This is a key point of our history and heritage." The day kicked off with a parade of buses, provided by the Transit Museum Society, representing every type of electric bus but one used in Vancouver: No. 2040, one of the original 1947 Brill trolleys; No. 2416, a T-48A Brill built in 1954; No. 2649, a "triesel"(a Flyer E800 from 1976 that was converted to diesel operation and finally used for de-icing overhead wires); No. 2805, a recently retired Flyer E901A; and two New Flyer-Vossloh Kiepe trolleys: a forty-foot standard-length coach and a sixty-foot articulated trolley.[584] The missing member of the historic fleet would have been one of the ex-Birmingham Pullmans, none of which survive.

Vancouver had been the successful bidder to host the 2010 Winter Olympic Games, and the flurry of capital improvements made to show off the city had a direct impact on the trolley system. In September 2005, the 15–CAMBIE route was abandoned, to facilitate construction of the Canada Line rapid transit tunnels directly beneath Cambie Street. Although there was some thought that trolleys would be reinstated after the cut-and-cover work was finished, this was not to be, and surface transit on Cambie remained served by motor buses. The completed rapid transit line opened in August 2009, and trolley services on GRANVILLE, OAK and MAIN routes were adjusted to terminate at the new Marine Drive station. Newly-constructed overhead appeared on Marine Drive, Yukon and short stub of Cambie Street.

In December 2010, one of Vancouver's New Flyer E40LFR trolleys, No. 2242, went to Seattle to demonstrate new trolley technology of the King County Metro Transit agency. Two staff from the Coast Mountain Bus Company showcased the bus and fielded technical questions.[585] This coach had visited Edmonton a few years earlier for a year-long test of new trolley coach technology.[586]

After four years of detours, trolley buses returned to Granville Mall on Monday, September 6th 2010.[587] The trolleys had been moved in April 2006 for Canada Line rapid transit construction, and for redevelopment of the mall by the City of Vancouver. The reinstated routes 4, 6, 7, 10, 15, 16, 17 and 20 returned to using Granville Mall as part of their routes. However, Granville Mall is also an immensely successful entertainment zone, so at certain times, buses were re-routed to allow for the street to be totally closed. On Fridays, Saturdays, Sundays, holidays, and the day before a holiday, buses run along Granville each day until 9:00 PM, then are re-routed, travelling northbound on Seymour and southbound on Howe until the close of service on those days.[588] Shortly after the buses returned to Granville, signs were placed on the sidewalks to prevent pedestrians from getting run over by the buses that had been absent for so long.[589]

The Vancouver system has long been characterized by the pairing of routes ("through-routing") to facilitate travel through the downtown core. From time to time the pairings are adjusted to balance loadings based on shifting travel patterns; this can result in route number changes on some or all of the route. And so, on April 18th 2011, the #14 trolley, an iconic route that ran on Hastings from 1955 to 1997, returned. In its new form, it took over parts of the 10 and 17 routes running from Hastings to UBC. While "iconic" may seem like hyperbole, the #14 was ingrained in the minds of Vancouver's riding public so much that it even had a play named after it, in which performers sang and danced their way through various adventures aboard the #14 bus, earning the play several nominations and drama awards. The #14 had been a streetcar route that ran along Hastings Street and was converted to trolley bus service in June 1955. In 1997, when the #14 number was retired, the service was given different route number.

However, the #14 had been always linked to Hastings Street, an important east-west arterial. So, when changing travel patterns resulting from the introduction of the rapid transit Canada Line caused passenger loadings on the #17 – which went from Oak Street, through downtown, on Broadway to UBC and through Hastings – to become out of balance, and ridership demand on Hastings matched well with the demand on Broadway to UBC, the long-time pairing of Hastings/Tenth–UBC was restored, complete with its original number 14.[590]

On August 28th 2012, a new permanent trolley bus loop was installed on University Boulevard, replacing the temporary trolley route opposite.[591] The original loop was located west of the Aquatic Centre. Then a temporary trolley bus terminus (used from 2003-2004 until August 2012) was located in the little loop that is south of the War Memorial Gym.[592] The final configuration is basically a U-turn in the wide University Boulevard, with layover area and a passing track. A separate permanent motor bus loop was installed a short distance to the north.

Vancouver's trolley coach system is dynamic and vibrant, serving as a major contributor to the success of a busy transit system. Changes continue to be made: as late as December 19th 2016, the ROBSON and DAVIE routes were reconfigured to serve the newly-redeveloped area of Yaletown, involving several blocks of new overhead in an area which had previously seen neither trolley coach nor streetcar service. Challenges are looming: the disruption to be caused by the construction of the subsurface SkyTrain line under Broadway being one, which will require temporary reroutings and motor bus substitutions, and will lead to permanent route reconfigurations as travel patterns change. TransLink has committed to move to a 100 per cent zero-emission fleet by 2040 – whether the trolley coach will be a part of that remains to be seen. Regardless, no other Canadian city has felt the impact of the trolley coach like Vancouver, the iconic vehicle having been indelibly etched into the collective consciousness of several generations.

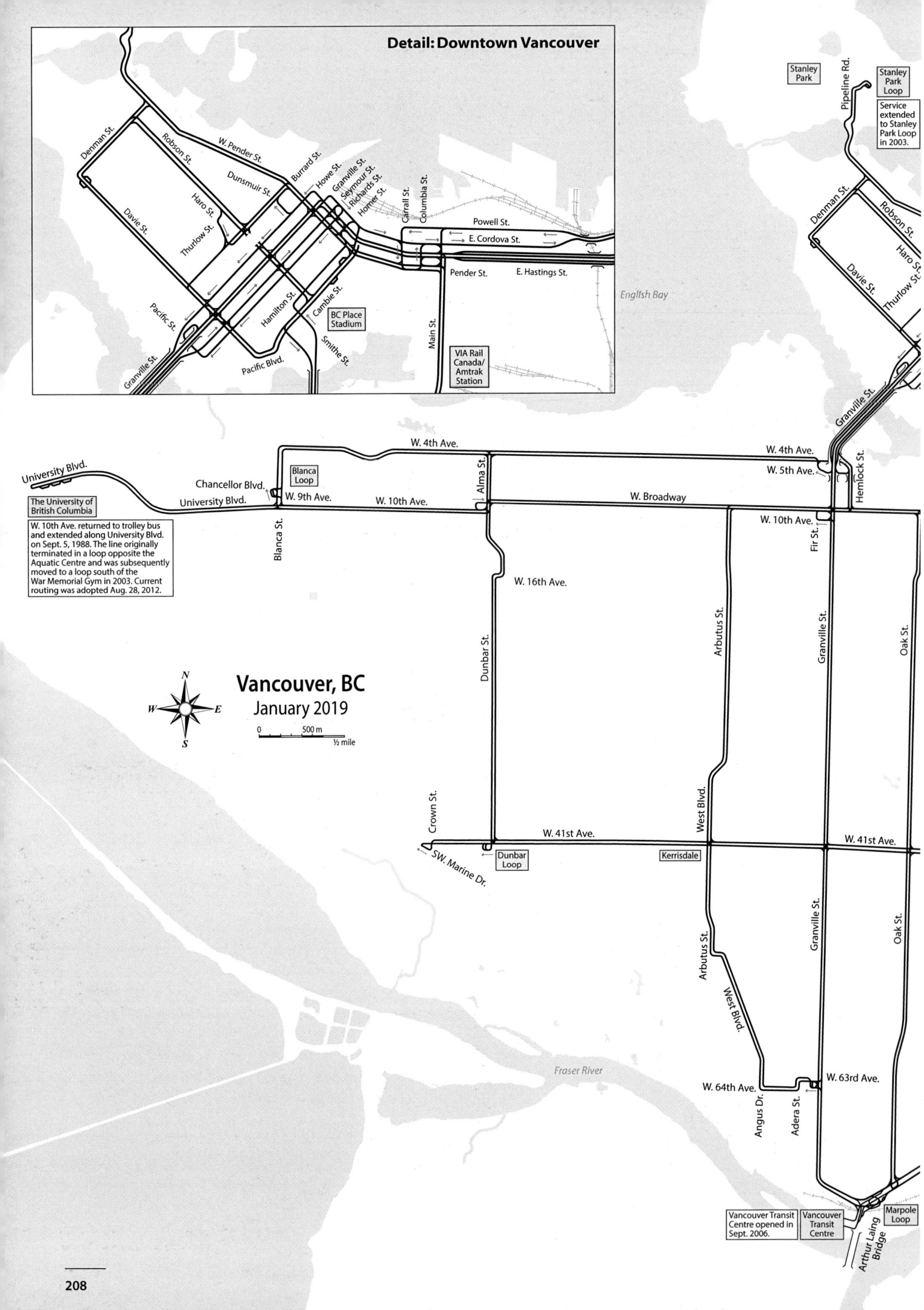
Detail: Downtown Vancouver
Denman St.
Robson St.
W. Pender St.
Dunsmuir St.
Haro St.
Davie St.
Thurlow St.
Burrard St.
Howe St.
Granville St.
Seymour St.
Richards St.
Homer St.
Carrall St.
Columbia St.
Powell St.
E. Cordova St.
Pender St.
E. Hastings St.
Hamilton St.
Cambie St.
Pacific St.
Granville St.
Pacific Blvd.
Smithe St.
BC Place Stadium
Main St.
VIA Rail Canada/ Amtrak Station
English Bay
Stanley Park
Pipeline Rd.
Stanley Park Loop
Service extended to Stanley Park Loop in 2003.
Denman St.
Robson St.
Haro St.
Davie St.
Thurlow St.
Granville St.
University Blvd.
Chancellor Blvd.
University Blvd.
The University of British Columbia
W. 10th Ave. returned to trolley bus and extended along University Blvd. on Sept. 5, 1988. The line originally terminated in a loop opposite the Aquatic Centre and was subsequently moved to a loop south of the War Memorial Gym in 2003. Current routing was adopted Aug. 28, 2012.
Blanca Loop
W. 9th Ave.
Blanca St.
W. 4th Ave.
W. 10th Ave.
Alma St.
W. Broadway
W. 4th Ave.
W. 5th Ave.
Hemlock St.
W. 10th Ave.
Fir St.
W. 16th Ave.
Dunbar St.
Arbutus St.
Granville St.
Oak St.
Vancouver, BC
January 2019
N
W
E
S
0
500 m
½ mile
Crown St.
W. 41st Ave.
SW. Marine Dr.
Dunbar Loop
Kerrisdale
West Blvd.
W. 41st Ave.
Arbutus St.
West Blvd.
Granville St.
Oak St.
Fraser River
W. 64th Ave.
W. 63rd Ave.
Angus Dr.
Adera St.
Vancouver Transit Centre opened in Sept. 2006.
Vancouver Transit Centre
Marpole Loop
Arthur Laing Bridge

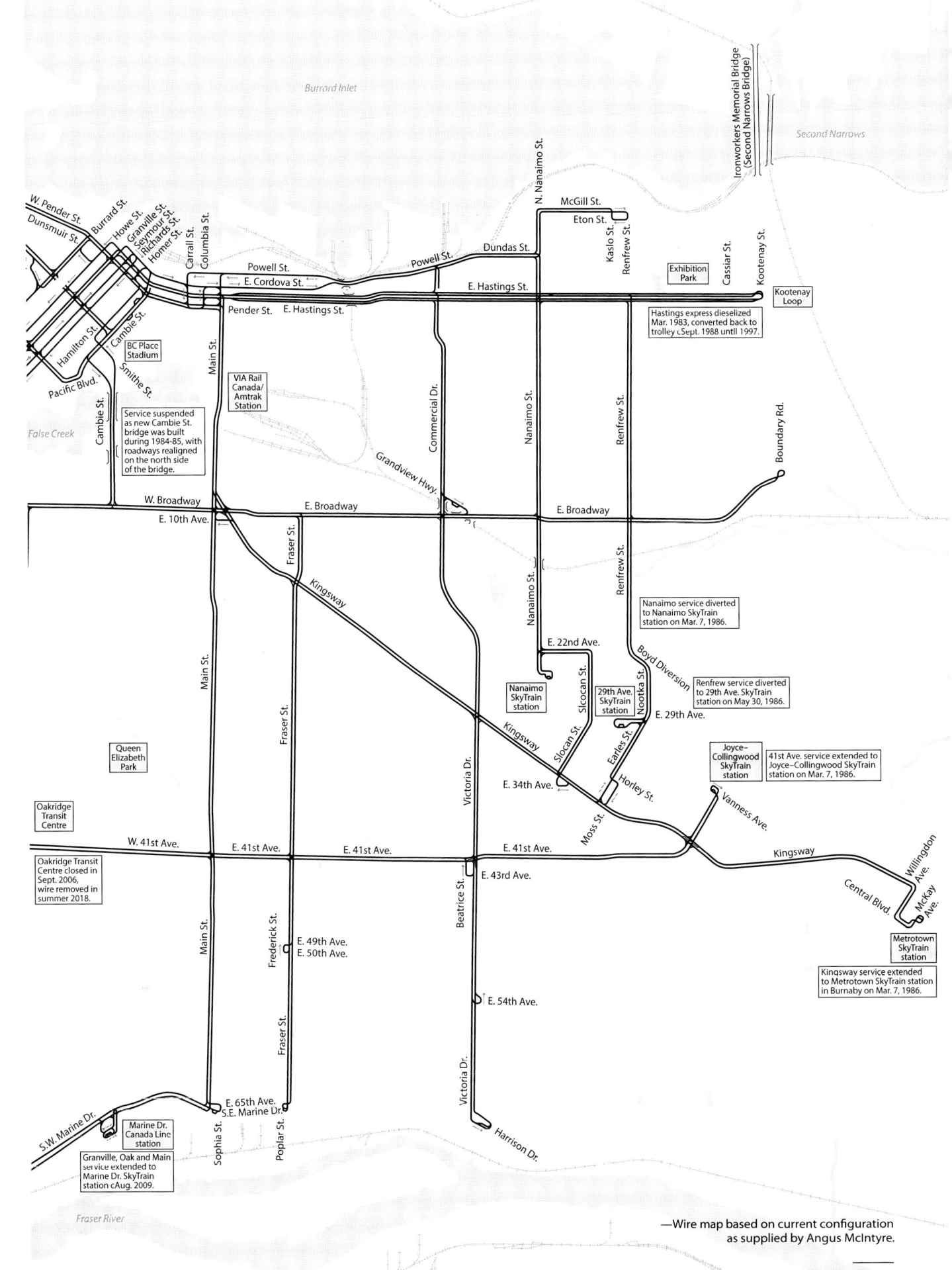

—Wire map based on current configuration as supplied by Angus McIntyre.

Footnotes:

508. *Transit History* – TransLink – Coast Mountain
http://www.coastmountainbus.com/transithistory visited August 2012; no longer active page.
509. *Transit History* – TransLink – Coast Mountain
http://www.coastmountainbus.com/transithistory visited August 2012; no longer active page.
510. Kelly, Brian, "Farewell to Brill", booklet 1983/4, self-published, pp. 1-3.
511. Vancouver City Archives, letter from E.W. Arnott to Alderman Thompson, November 3, 1945.
512. *Ibid.* Letter from R. Thompson, City Clerk to Arnott, November 13, 1945.
513. *Ibid.* Letter from E.W. Arnott to Mayor J.S. Matthews, December 13, 1945.
514. Collection of W. Young.
515. Collection of W. Young.
516. "The Place of the Trolley Coach in Urban Transportation," Canadian Transit Association symposium, June 12, 1946, pp. 25-7.
517. Kelly, Brill, p. 4-5.
518. *Bus Transportation*, February 1947, p. 47.
519. *Ibid.*
520. *Passenger Transport*, July 9, 1948.
521. Kelly, Brill, p. 6.
522. Kelly and Francis, *Transit in British Columbia*, p. 102.
523. *Canadian Transportation*, March 1950, pp. 141-2.
524. *Transit History* – TransLink, *op. cit.*
525. *Ibid.* and *Canadian Transportation* June 1949, p. 336.
526. Ewert, Henry, *The Story of the BC Electric Railway Company*, Whitecap Books 1986 p. 263.
527. *Passenger Transport*, September 23, 1949.
528. *Passenger Transport*, December 15, 1950.
529. *Canadian Transportation*, February 1951 p. 92.
530. *Passenger Transport*, September 28, 1951, p. 7, Transit History – TransLink *op. cit.*, and personal contemporary notes of V.L. Sharman, transit planning manager (and latterly Vice-President, B.C. Transit), provided by Mike Bergman.
531. *Passenger Transport*, November 23, 1951, p. 6.
532. Ohio Brass advertisement, June 1952.
533. *Passenger Transport*, December 28, 1951.
534. *Passenger Transport*, October 2, 1953.
535. *The Buzzer*, August 1, 1952.
536. *Passenger Transport*, October 2, 1953 and *Transit History* – TransLink *op. cit.*
537. *The Buzzer*, February 19, 1954.
538. *Canadian Transportation*, June 1955, p. 339?
539. *Transit History* – TransLink *op. cit.*
540. Kelly, p. 9
541. Kelly and Francis, *Transit in British Columbia* as quoted in *Trolleybuses in Vancouver* essay, Ian Fisher, Transport Action Group http://www.bc.transport2000.ca/learning/etb/trolleybus_essay.html Visited August 31, 2012.
542. Peter Cox, personal e-mail forwarded by W. Young.
543. *Transit History* – TransLink *op. cit.*
544. *Trolley Coach News*, Vol. 1 #6, December 1969 p. 55.
545. *Trolley Coach News*, #10 Vol. 2 #4, August 1970 p. 54.
546. *The Buzzer*, Vol. 55 No. 22, May 29, 1970 as copied in *Trolley Coach News*, #11 Vol. 2 #5, December 1970, p. 76.
547. *The Vancouver Sun*, Monday January 4th 1971 and Saturday February 6th 1971.
548. *Trolley Coach News*, #14 Vol. 3 #3 July-October 1971 p. 114-118 by John Day.
549. *The Province*, May 15, 1973, p. 11.
550. *Trolley Coach News*, #24 Winter 1973 p..89.
551. *Transit History* – TransLink *op. cit.*
552. *UCRS Newsletter*, January-February 1974, p. 24.
553. *Reading Eagle*, Monday, January 20, 1975.
554. *Trolley Coach News*, #34 Fall and Winter 1974 p. 94.
555. *Transit History* – TransLink *op. cit.*
556. *Transit Canada*, Vol. XII # 3 May-June 1976, p. 13 and *The Buzzer*, January 6, 1976.
557. *Transit History* – TransLink *op. cit.*
558. *Electric Lines* March-April 1992, p. 34.
559. *The Buzzer*, August 18, 1978, Vol. 63 No. 21.
560. Trolleybus Tender 80-4, Evaluation and Recommendation, Urban Transit Authority of British Columbia, November 1980 p. 1.
561. *Ibid.*
562. *Ibid.* p. 2.
563. *Ibid.* pp. 3-4.
564. *Ibid.* p. 7.
565. *Transit History* – TransLink *op. cit.*
566. *The Buzzer*, July 28, 1978, Vol. 63 No. 18.
567. Kelly and Francis, *ibid.*
568. *The Buzzer*, February 28th 1983, provided by Rob Chew.
569. *Kitchener-Waterloo Record*, Wednesday, January 11, 1984, p. A10.
570. Kelly, Brian, personal e-mail June 1, 2013.
571. *The Buzzer*. November 9, 1984, Vol. 69 No. 16.
572. *Electric Lines*, March-April 1992, pp. 34-36.
573. *Ibid.* p. 36.
574. *The Buzzer*, September 23, 1988.
575. *Transit History* – TransLink, *op. cit.*
576. *Transit History* – TransLink, *op. cit.*
577. New Flyer Media Release, October 31, 2003 http://www.newflyer.com/index/PR_Translink visited August 24, 2013.
578. Day, John M. captioned photo on Trolleybuses.net http://www.trolleybuses.net/van/htm/can_h_van_newflyer_2501_otc_20070128_johnday.htm.
579. TransLink Media, June 2, 2008 http://www.translink.ca/en/About-Us/Media/2008/June/Metro-Vancouver-buses-break-through-barrier-achieve-full-accessibility.aspx.
580. TransLink Media, August 18, 2006 http://www.translink.ca/en/About-Us/Media/2006/August/Would-the-last-bus-to-leave-OTC-please-turn-out-the-lights.aspx.
581. Taylor-Noonan, Michael, The Next Stop web page http://www.taylornoonan.com/nextstop/.
582. Buzzer blog, October 31, 2008 http://buzzer.translink.ca/2008/10/retired-trolleys-set-sail-for-argentina/.
583. Chew, Rob, e-mail correspondence with author August 24, 2013.
584. TransLink Media, August 16, 2008 http://www.translink.ca/en/About-Us/Media/2008/August/Trolley-service-begins-the-next-60-years.aspx.
585. Buzzer blog, December 13, 2010.
586. Cheung, Derek, e-mail correspondence with author, May 29, 2013.
587. Buzzer blog, August 11, 2010 http://buzzer.translink.ca/index.php/2010/08/trolley-service-returns-to-granville-mall-on-tue-sept-7/ and *The Buzzer* (paper) August 27, 2010, Vol. 34 #7.
588. Buzzer blog, September 7, 2010.
589. Chew, Rob, e-mail correspondence with W. Young, August 22, 2013.
590. Buzzer blog, April 7, 2011.
591. UBC Transportation Planning http://transportation.ubc.ca/2012/08/22/university-boulevard-set-to-re-open-to-busses-and-vehicles/ visited August 30, 2013.
592. Chew, Rob, e-mail correspondence with the author, August 30, 2013.
593. *The Ubessy*, September 5, 2012 http://ubyssey.ca/news/underground-ubc-bus-loop475/ visited August 30, 2013.

Above: Articulated New Flyer E60LFR 2548 glides along Main Street southbound at East 3rd Avenue, April 6th 2014. (KEVIN NICOL)

Below: The sun was setting as Vancouver's decommissioned E901A and E902 Flyers sail on the MV *Wisdom* under the Alex Fraser bridge on their way to a second life in Mendoza, Argentina, November 4th 2008. Mendoza bought eighty of TransLink's 1983 high-floor trolleys for use on their system. The coaches were landed at San Antonio, Chile and then transported across the Andes by road to Mendoza.
(TERRY MUIRHEAD/JIM MCPHERSON)

Above: The borrowed Seattle trolley coach is undergoing trials on Douglas Street passing in front of the Hudson's Bay Company store, nearing the intersection of Herald Street. The Hudson's Bay Building is still there today with the same facade, but the interior has been turned into condominiums and the ground floor is commercial.
(DUNCAN MACPHAIL IMAGE I-01213
COURTESY OF ROYAL BC MUSEUM AND ARCHIVES)

Below: A builder's photo of the interior of Seattle No. 943, identical to No. 935 which was borrowed by B.C. Electric for demonstration use in Victoria and Vancouver in late 1945.
(CITY OF VANCOUVER ARCHIVES, TRANS P110.4)

TWO BRIEF FLIRTATIONS WITH THE
TROLLEY COACH ON THE WEST COAST

Victoria (1945 demo)
British Columbia Electric Railway Company

Tried it, liked it, didn't buy it, might have been the slogan for Victoria, while across the strait, trolley coach activity became the most vigorous in Canada.

As early as 1923, B.C. Electric had operated buses (in Vancouver) to supplement the streetcar system. They were especially attractive in outlying areas where the expense of track and overhead could not be justified. B.C.E.R. also looked at replacing some streetcar lines with buses, but the motor buses of the day were not very powerful, nor did they have a large passenger capacity. An attractive alternative was the new trolley coach, able to utilize existing overhead spans, and with the capacity of a streetcar but none of the maintenance of track.

On August 14th 1945, the *Victoria Daily Colonist* reported that "Plans for the unification of Greater Victoria's transportation system on a basis which will broaden considerably services to all sections of the city and district, were announced yesterday by officials of the B.C. Electric Railway Company, following the decision of the Greater Victoria Transportation Committee to ask all interested companies to submit proposals and maps." It went on to say that Victoria's share in the company's $50 million investment in BC would put Victoria second to none in North America in transportation service. "Backbone of the system will be six trunk line trolley coach routes, ..." The cost was estimated at $1,630,750 for overhead and garage modifications in addition to the purchase of forty-two 44-passenger trolley coaches. This was said to follow on two years of research by the company with "leading transportation consultants." The trolley service would be complemented by twenty-four 36-passenger gasoline buses and ten 27-passenger gasoline buses for feeder service. The result would be sixteen main lines carrying up to twenty million passengers a year.

Proposed trolley coach routes were: Esquimalt–Fernwood; Gonzales–Hillside, Oak Bay–Downtown; and Mount View–Oak Bay.[594]

B.C. Electric Railway's proposal was not the only one, though. Vancouver Island Coach Lines (VICL), and Blue Line Transit – operated by the Veteran's Sightseeing and Transportation Company – said they would submit bids. Blue Line offered to use motor buses exclusively, with about 100 vehicles.[595] A vigorous campaign was waged in the local papers, with Blue Line refuting accusations that its low five-cent fares were because it paid low wages. Both companies also submitted applications for new (and competing) routes to City Council.[596] An open letter to the provincial government from Blue Line's union opined that the B.C. Electric service would not be as satisfactory or attractive as theirs, suggesting the matter go to the Public Utilities Commission. Added to the mix was the question of service to outlying areas such as Fairfield–Gonzales and Oak Bay Municipality. Blue Line played on the discontent of those residents who, they indicated, would not get service under the B.C. Electric proposal.[597] It then applied to the Commission for authority to operate bus lines in the Fairfield-Gonzales district.[598] B.C. Electric countered with the assurance that the GONZALES streetcar line would continue rather than be discontinued as their original bus plans had indicated.[599] Blue Line also approached City Council to acquire property downtown for a terminal which would shelter passengers waiting for MOUNT TOLMIE and FAIRFIELD–GONZALES buses.[600]

Despite the rhetoric, the B.C. Electric bid was accepted, prompting Blue Line to appeal the Commission's decision regarding the FAIRFIELD–GONZALES route to the Chief Justice in the Court of Appeal.[601] It appears that Vancouver Island Coach did not, in the end, bid. The Public Utilities Commission had refused the Blue Line application, ruling that it had a policy of refusing to allow one operator (Blue Line) into another's territory (B.C. Electric Railway) when the latter is prepared to offer similar service. It also allowed that the current situation should not be disturbed, in view of the temporary nature of the service, so the two companies' territories continued to remain exclusive. The Commission had also recognized that B.C. Electric had carried on with worn-out streetcars during the war when replacement buses were not available.[602]

It appeared that the idea of a unified Greater Victoria transportation service had become unravelled, as the municipality of Victoria gave its approval to the B.C. Electric plan, but the municipality of Oak Bay granted Blue Line operating rights.[603]

B.C. Electric forged ahead, promising a trolley coach trial in October, even though the Blue Line appeal was ongoing.[604]

Victoria was chosen as the first city in British Columbia to trial the trolley coach, and a Twin Coach bus was borrowed from Seattle in November 1945.[605] Twin was chosen as it had recently delivered eighteen coaches to Seattle, and the distance was not great, though there was the matter of importing the demonstrator coach. E.W. Arnott, Vice-President in charge of Transportation for B.C. Elec-

Victoria, BC 1945

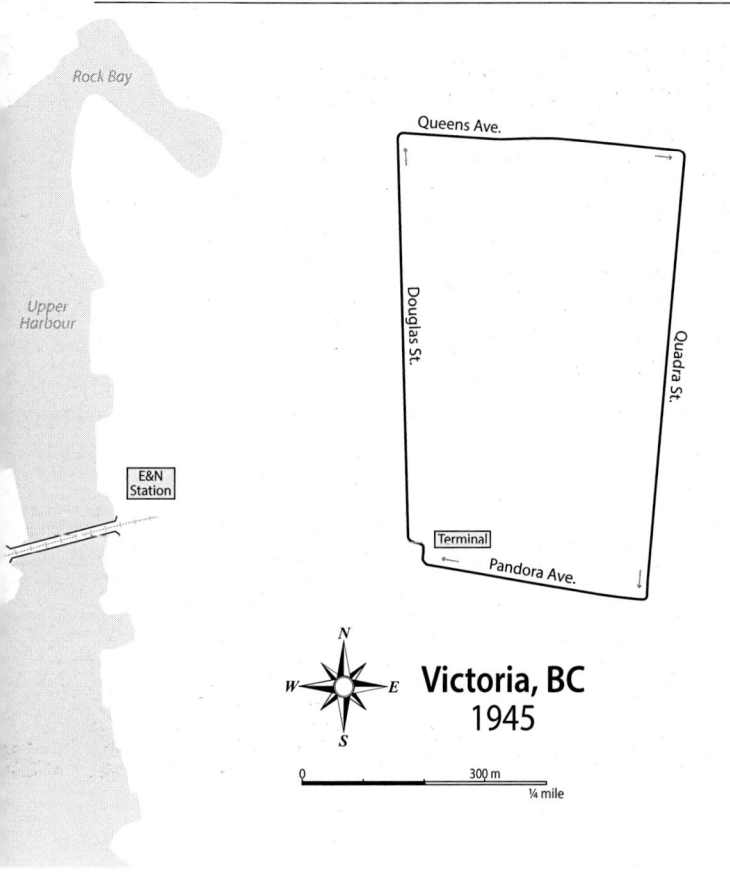

—Wire map compiled by author from route descriptions and note from Wally Young.

tric wrote on the matter to the Deputy Minister of Customs and Excise, asking for a duty exemption and mentioning that he had discussed the matter with Mr. George S. Gray, the Transit Controller for Canada. Gray had been the key to all transportation equipment requests during the war years and was still a powerful figure in urban transport matters in the immediate post-war period.

The coach was to be shipped by rail to Vancouver, and then by rail barge to Victoria. No fares were to be collected during the demonstration. The value of the coach quoted for customs purposes was $13,254 f.o.b. Seattle.[606]

The chosen route was a loop comprising Douglas Street, Queens Avenue, Quadra Street and Pandora Avenue, a total distance of 7,500 lineal feet. Douglas and Pandora had existing span wire; Queens needed spans added, as the poles were too short for mast arms, but Quadra used mast arms.[607] Despite optimism expressed earlier that a quick trial would be possible, it was pushed into November, with the trolley coach arriving November 15th 1945. The newspapers noted that the bus had already accumulated 250,000 miles in Seattle, but was practically new. A separate advertisement invited the public to "SEE IT – RIDE IT – TEST IT – SATISFY YOURSELF as to its ability to provide a transportation service in this district that will be second to none for safety, efficiency, convenience and comfort." The accompanying photograph was, however, of a San Francisco Brill coach![608] In addition to local offi-

B.C. ELECTRIC RAILWAY COMPANY
LIMITED
VICTORIA, B.C.

Dear Passenger:

The B. C. Electric is taking this opportunity of demonstrating to you just what an electric trolley coach system would mean for Victoria in the way of riding comfort and speedier public transportation service.

This coach has been secured on loan from Seattle for the express purpose of giving you a first-hand opportunity of seeing trolley coaches operate so that you may speak with expert knowledge on this latest type equipment in the public transportation field.

As you are doubtless aware, the installation of a trolley coach system in the Greater Victoria area has formed the basis of the B. C. Electric proposal submitted to the Greater Victoria Transportation Committee, this proposal now being under consideration by the committee with other competitive bids.

Your trip during this demonstration ride has been specially selected in order that you may be able to fully appreciate such trolley coach features as curb loading, smooth operation in the downtown section, acceleration on grades and smoother travelling over rougher roads.

In addition to these we would like to draw your attention to the quietness of the ride as compared with the gasoline bus, the quick pick up of the coach from a dead stop and freedom from gasoline fumes. There is also an important feature of comfort in the excellent interior lighting during night riding which is embodied in new type coaches.

Safety factors, of course, are always of primary importance, and this coach embodies the latest improvements in this regard. It is impossible for the operator to put the coach in motion as long as the side doors are open.

It is these things which we think make the trolley coach appeal. But we are naturally biased. We would like you to judge for yourself. We hope you enjoy the ride.

Yours truly,
W. C. MAINWARING,
Vice-President.

This card was distributed to Victoria trolley coach riders pointing out the benefits of this newest form of public transportation. Unfortunately, politics and policy doomed the trolley coach experiment.
(WALLY YOUNG COLLECTION)

cials, the Pacific Northwest representative of Twin Coach also arrived to observe the demonstration.[609] The first run was held at 11 AM Friday November 16th for "members of the City Council, the school board and civic department heads …." On Saturday, the public was allowed to experience the latest in modern transportation from 10 AM to 10 PM daily, over the next two weeks.[610]

Passengers trying out the new coach were given a handbill extolling the virtues of the trolley coach, and drawing attention to B.C. Electric's ongoing bid submission before the Greater Victoria Transportation Committee. Well over a thousand adults and hundreds of school children were carried on each day's trips. An article in the transit employees' newsletter boasted that the coach received very enthu-

Above: This B.C. Electric window display touted "B.C. Electric Presents the Trolley Coach; The Modern Electric Carrier; Silent; Modern" in support of the trolley coach trials.
(DUNCAN MACPHAIL IMAGE, COLLECTION OF ROB CHEW)

Below: The trial (Seattle) trolley coach is on Douglas Street passing in front of the Hudson's Bay Company store.
(DUNCAN MACPHAIL IMAGE I-01212 COURTESY OF ROYAL BC MUSEUM AND ARCHIVES)

siastic reception from all who rode it. "It's the smoothest, quietest and most comfortable vehicle in which I have ever had a ride," one patron is quoted as saying.[611] The November 19th *Daily Colonist* cited that 2700 passengers had ridden it on the first Saturday alone.[612]

The trial ran from November 19th to 30th 1945.[613] The coach then was moved to Vancouver for trials there, and officials of B.C. Electric Railway settled in to await the Transportation Committee's decision. The trolley coach made sense for Victoria as in other cities. The high costs were in the infrastructure – overhead construction, power supply, trained maintenance staff – all of which B.C.E.R. had from the streetcar operation. Trolley coaches were far more economical to operate and maintain than the gasoline buses of the day, and the company had the staff to do that too. So for B.C.E.R. it made good economic sense to go with trolley coaches.

However, B.C.E.R. did not enjoy a transit monopoly in Victoria as it did in Vancouver. Competition from VICL city lines and Blue Line was on the horizon; appeals had been registered to cabinet and it was felt that either the courts or government would determine who had the rights to which routes. The fear was that the decision would allow B.C.E.R. to keep the fixed routes, but the other two companies could have all the non-fixed plus any new extensions. Historically, the bus companies had started up in competition against the fixed-route tramway franchise, and for a while, it looked as though Blue Line could take over the city routes. With either streetcars or trolley coaches, the routes would be deemed "fixed," leaving B.C.E.R. at a competitive disadvantage. With the more flexible gasoline buses B.C.E.R. could compete and lobby on an equal footing, and so B.C.E.R. submitted a proposal for a motor bus system.[614]

By mid-January 1946, members of the Transportation Committee were taken for a demonstration of a different sort – on a Blue Line motor bus, similar to twelve others to be delivered to Victoria, but delayed by strikes in the US.[615] By March, the papers were quoting transportation officials in Seattle and Tacoma, stating that trolley coaches would not be suitable for Victoria, according to Alderman Diggon, chairman of the Greater Victoria Transportation Committee. "In order to be profitable, trolley lines should operate under fairly heavy traffic conditions for long distances" these officials stated. They also pointed out that motor buses would still be needed, and that double maintenance crews and equipment was an unnecessary expense. These thoughts formed the basis of a report Alderman Diggon prepared for the Committee. It also noted that Seattle had a population of 480,000 and Tacoma 120,000, while the 1941 census showed the City of Victoria with only 45,000 (75,000 for greater Victoria).[616] In all fairness, the report did compare the lifespan of a motor bus (seven years and 280,000 miles) to that of a trolley coach (ten years and 400,000 miles).[617] But, in the end, the Committee opted for B.C. Electric's all-gasoline bus proposal, and the trolley coach was never again to operate in British Colmbia's capital city.

Footnotes:

594. *Victoria Daily Colonist*, August 14, 1945 – Young collection.
595. *Victoria Daily Colonist*, August 21, 1945 – Young collection.
596. *Victoria Daily Colonist*, July 24, 1945.
597. *Victoria Daily Colonist*, July 25, 1945.
598. *Victoria Daily Colonist*, July 28, 1945.
599. *Victoria Daily Colonist*, August 11, 1945.
600. *Victoria Daily Colonist*, July 28, 1945.
601. *Victoria Daily Colonist*, September 21, 1945.
602. *Victoria Daily Colonist*, September 7?, 1945 – Young collection.
603. *Victoria Daily Colonist*, September 7, 1945 – Young collection.
604. *Victoria Daily Colonist*, September 20, 1945 – Young collection.
605. Transit Workers of British Columbia web site http://www.transitworkers.novatone.net/PUBLIC/a_brief_history_of_transit.htm visited April 2, 2008.
606. Letter Arnott to David Sims Deputy Minister, September 13, 1945 – Young collection.
607. Copy letter from the General Superintendent (E.N. Horsey) to T. Ingledow, Vice President & Chief Engineer, (B.C. Electric) Vancouver, BC, September 29, 1945 – Young collection. Also *Victoria Daily Colonist*, November 14, 1945.
608. Young collection.
609. *Victoria Daily Colonist*, November 16, 1945 – Young collection.
610. *Victoria Daily Colonist*, November 14, 1945 – Young collection.
611. Young collection, source assumed to be B.C. Electric Employees paper.
612. *Victoria Daily Colonist*, November 19, 1945 – Young collection.
613. Wyatt, Dave, All-time List of Canadian Transit Systems, Victoria http://home.cc.umanitoba.ca/~wyatt/alltime/victoria-bc.html.
614. Kelly, Brian, correspondence re: research into why trolley coaches not accepted, March 19, 2010.
615. *Victoria Daily Colonist*, January 16, 1946 – Young collection.
616. Young, Wally, e-mail correspondence regarding Henry Ewert's B.C.E.R. book and its quoted census figures taken from the Victoria newspapers, April 18, 2010.
617. *Victoria Daily Colonist*, n.d. possibly March 10, 1946 – Young collection

Nelson (1945-1949 planned)
Nelson Street Railway

The public wanted trolley coaches; the politicians didn't. Guess who won?

This West Kootenay city, population 5000 in 1900, scarcely seemed to be the size that could support public transit of any form, much less a tramway, but on Boxing Day, 1899 it became the smallest city in the British Empire to have a street railway. Plagued with politics, beset with breakdowns and derailments, the streetcar system teetered on the edge of abandonment for decades, saved only by an avid citizenry that fell in love with the streetcars and fought for their retention. Not that it was easy riding; just a few years later, in 1904, the British company operating the tramway wanted out, so the city took over in 1914. It didn't get any better under city ownership; accidents, breakdowns, weather and fire all conspired to make the Nelson Street Railway an on-again-off-again enterprise.

By 1938, the system was so deep in the red that Mayor Norman C. Stibbs wanted to do away with it and replace the trams with buses. However, the idea of bus service was not popular with Nelsonites, and some consideration was given to the trolley coach, which was gaining popularity in the US, as well as seeing success in Montreal. After receiving a report by the street railway committee that a gasoline bus service could be substituted, or the streetcar system rebuilt, Nelson Council decided no changes should be made and that the streetcar system should soldier on.

The debate raged into 1939, finally ending in a public vote on a bylaw to modernize the system by replacing the streetcars with buses. The voters decided on May 17th, rejecting the scrapping of the street railway. With war looming on the horizon, bus and automobile restrictions gave the tramway a new life, despite material shortages and overcrowding of streetcars with war production employees.

May 7th 1945, the end of the war is in sight, but not the war of what form transit would take in Nelson. Council, ever eager to scrap the tramway, looked into purchasing a gasoline bus. The debate spilled over into the Nelson *Daily News*, with letters for and against buses. Also, the trolley coach had made further debuts in Canadian cities: Winnipeg and Edmonton had joined Montreal, with several more cities actively investigating or considering the electric bus. American properties reported that the trackless trolley was very popular, and that the pre-war motorbus did not compare favourably.

By the end of 1946, a consulting engineer, A.C.R. Yuill of Vancouver, determined that the Nelson streetcar system had reached its end. Most rails needed replacing, half the overhead was worn out, and the tracks no longer went where the people wanted to go. Since the cars predated World War I, parts were unobtainable. In fact, many replacement parts had been fabricated by Nelson machine shops or by the transit corporation itself. In an overkill comparison, the report compared the existing system, the PCC streetcar, light and heavy gasoline buses, diesel buses, and the trolley coach. While for a city the size of Nelson, gasoline buses would seem to be the choice, the high cost of fuel and the "free" electricity from the city plant made the trolley coach an attractive option. Yuill recommended the city purchase three 44-passenger trolley buses, or a small fleet of motor coaches.

The *Daily News* jumped into the fray by opining that motor buses were smelly, noisy, high in maintenance and costly for fuel. The trolley coach would be the best of both worlds – quiet, clean, and excellent on Nelson's steep streets. The report's options were put to the public on December 12th 1946 and the results of the voting were: purchase trolleybuses (43%), purchase new streetcars (30%), repair existing streetcars (13%), leave decision to Council (10%), and lastly, purchase gasoline buses (4%). Council retorted that purchasing such a small quantity of trolley coaches was impossible, conveniently ignoring that Edmonton had recently placed an order for only two trolley coaches. However, despite the bus bias in Council, nothing was decided immediately. Studies were made of Edmonton and Calgary trolley coach operations in 1947, and Ohio Brass was asked to prepare a report. In May 1947, Claude R. Kingsbury, district manager for Canadian Ohio Brass visited Nelson, drove the proposed route and provided an estimate for overhead and fittings. The costs were a bit daunting: $63,000 for poles and overhead, $8000 for negative return cables (since the streetcar rails provided the electrical return for the trams, this was an added expense) and another $5000 for switches in the car barn area. This did not include the cost of the coaches. By spring 1948, there was still no progress on replacing or revitalizing the aging streetcars. In June, the transit superintendent asked Ohio Brass for another estimate. This one came in at $71,650 for overhead, labour, and housing for the six-mile line – but again not including the cost of the coaches. Council was not impressed with the idea of incurring debt for a trolley coach system, but a bylaw to borrow the funds to purchase the trolleys was finally drafted, and a public meeting was scheduled for November 19th 1948, with a vote to take place in December.

But, before the bylaw was to be voted on, Interior Stag-

TIRES AND WIRES

es Ltd. of Trail, BC approached Council with an offer to provide bus service on a franchised non-subsidized basis. Council jumped at the opportunity to get out of the transit business and avoid a debt, and, with their long-standing love of motor coaches evident, scrapped the trolley coach bylaw, and cancelled public meetings. Savings of $14,000 per year were too tempting, prompting the Mayor and Council to ignore the previous plebiscite, and the fact that the profit either for the city to operate trolley buses or a franchise to run motor coaches was nearly the same – a tough sell to the electorate. The public was less than happy about the lack of consultation, so a revised bylaw was proposed and the vote postponed, to give Council more time to sell the public on motor buses. A demonstration of the motor coach was held in February 1949, with the streetcar service correspondingly reduced to favour the motor buses. Mayor Thomas H. Waters contended that although the city had proposed a trolley bus system, would have to borrow for the purchase of the coaches and the overhead, while an Interior Stages' bus service would effectively cost the city nothing to run. Public debate raged over abandoning their treasured though worn-out streetcars, and whether the shiny Twin Coach buses or the unseen trolley coach should replace them.

Council, on the other hand, had already negotiated an agreement with Interior Stages before the public vote, which was held on April 12th 1949. Council blitzed Nelson with pro-bus arguments on radio and through the press, and on voting day the citizenry voted in favour of the franchisee 943 to 341.

Accordingly, on June 30th 1949, Nelson's three beloved streetcars passed into history, as a pair of Twin Coach motor buses took their place... and somewhere in all the rhetoric, bylaw votes and politics, the public's favorite – the trolley coach – got lost.[618]

Footnote:
618. Complied with information from Parker, *Streetcars in the Kootenays*, pp. 117-121, and Joyce, *Hanging Fire and Heavy Horses*, pp. 112-142.

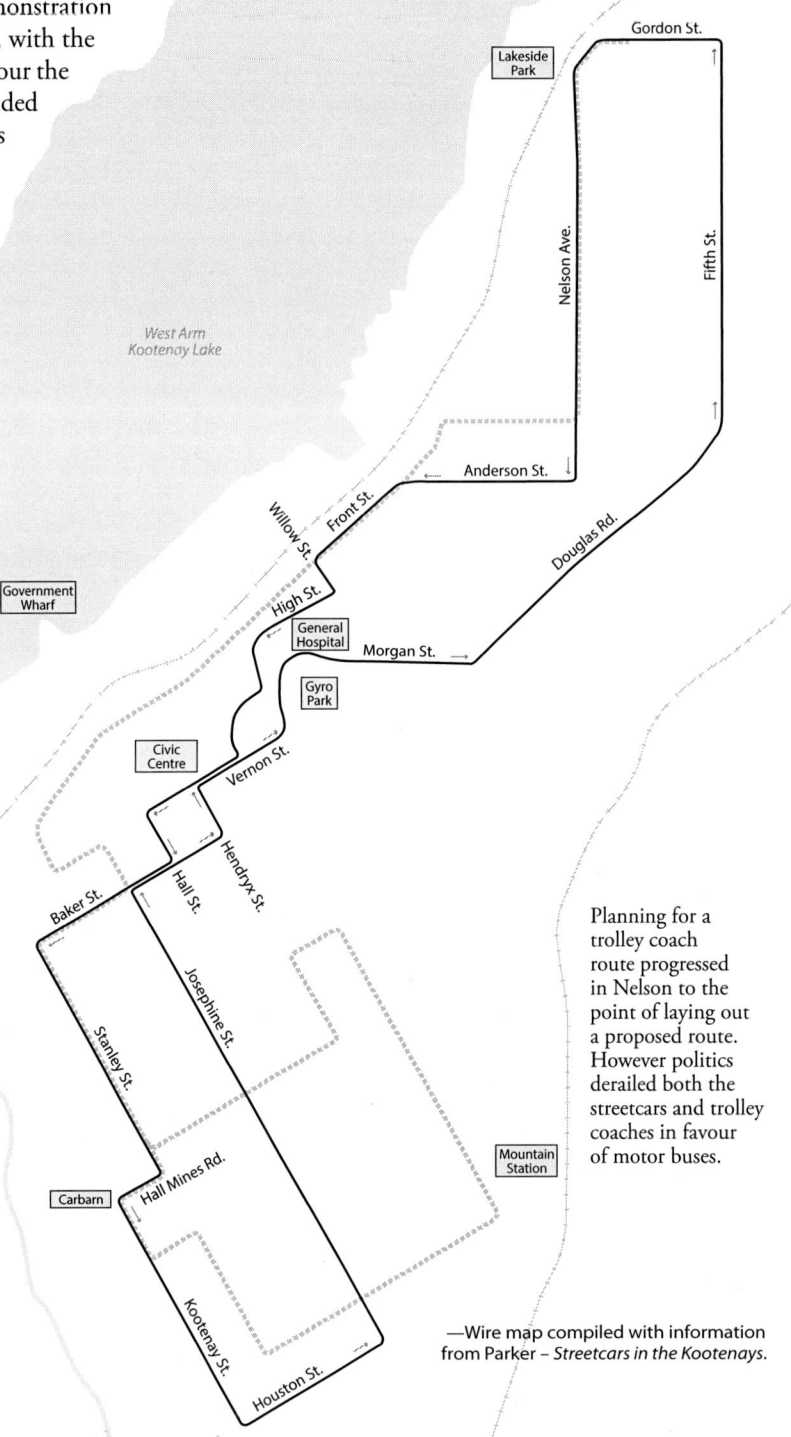

Planning for a trolley coach route progressed in Nelson to the point of laying out a proposed route. However politics derailed both the streetcars and trolley coaches in favour of motor buses.

—Wire map compiled with information from Parker – *Streetcars in the Kootenays*.

Nelson, BC Planned

Above: Nova Scotia Light and Power Brill 231 has just crossed the Angus L. Macdonald Bridge from the Dartmouth terminal and is headed to its downtown Halifax terminus on October 10th 1968. (TED WICKSON)

Below: Nova Scotia Light and Power T-44 Can Car-Brill trolley 238 lays over at the Halifax CNR station, the southern terminus for route 5. The Hotel Nova Scotian is in the background. (W.R. LINLEY/JBC VISUALS)

Above: It's 1966 in Montreal and coach 4108 rolls along the BEAUBIEN–12 AVE. route on Beaubien Street to the west of Iberville. The single wire overhead marks the end loop at 12th Ave. and the coach is headed back to Park on May 24th 1966. (PETER COX COLLECTION, CANADIAN TRANSIT HERITAGE FOUNDATION. LOCATION IDENTIFICATION – RALPH MARCOGLIESE/DAVE HENDERSON)

Below: Montreal Brill 4027 is on the AMHERST line in May 1966. The coach is coming off the loop from St-Andre turning left onto Craig. It will proceed north on Amherst and Christophe-Colombe to Villeray at the other end of the line.
(PETER COX COLLECTION, CANADIAN TRANSIT HERITAGE FOUNDATION. LOCATION IDENTIFICATION – DAVE HENDERSON)

Above: Few colour photos survived Ottawa's brief flirtation with the trolley coach so this one of OTC 2009 has to serve despite some shortcomings in quality. The coach is northbound on Bronson Avenue at McLeod heading downtown. The Eventide Monuments dealer is George Brown & Sons, still at 473 Bronson Avenue. Pattons Cleaners shirt depot is gone as is Phil's Restaurant. (SOURCE UNKNOWN)

Below: At the centre of the city, a Cornwall coach waits on the Second Street/Montreal Road run to continue east while BELT LINE coach 104 passes down Pitt toward Water Street, May 17th 1970. (TED WICKSON)

Above: CSR coach 104 pauses at the exit from Danis loop onto Cornwall's Montreal Road on a lovely morning in the spring of 1970. Perhaps the operator is taking a moment to drink in the peaceful St. Lawrence River setting before returning to the city bustle awaiting on the Second Street line. (TED WICKSON)

Below: Christmas Day 1966 with the sun shining, HSR coach 715 makes the turn onto Hamilton's Main Street West, as it begins its outbound trip on the KING route to the short turn east end Strathearne loop. (TED WICKSON)

Above: The new Flyer trolleys weren't the only ones sporting the Hamilton Tiger Cats colours. Can Car-Brill 748, one of a very few to receive the yellow and black livery, is westbound on King Street at Strathearne Avenue. It is early evening August 7th 1976 and this coach has likely operated in rush hour tripper service on the KING–STRATHEARNE route and is now running in to the Wentworth Street barns. Number 748 would be retired soon after the new E800 Flyer trolley coaches entered service in 1978-1979. (TED WICKSON)

Below: Hamilton Flyer 767 in Tiger Cat yellow is turning off King Street to enter the downtown McNab Transit Terminal (end/start point for BARTON and KING routes), June 1st 1974. The large building in background is the 26-storey Stelco Tower, completed in 1973 as part of adjacent Lloyd D. Jackson Square, Hamilton's major downtown indoor shopping mall, which opened 1970. (TED WICKSON)

Above: Kitchener coach 129 crosses the CNR tracks at King Street on March 25th 1973, a day before the end of trolley service.
(SCALZO COLLECTION, ILLINOIS RAILWAY MUSEUM)

Below: Kitchener trolley coach 121 loops around the back of the PUC Garage on its return trip to Waterloo, May 24th 1970. It was the only trolley to receive this modified repaint scheme, after being dressed in special livery as "Canada's Birthday Coach" in Centennial Year (1967).
(TED WICKSON)

Above: Toronto Can Car-Brill Coach 9106 passes sister T-44 Brill 9115 on the JUNCTION run, near Dundas Street and Humber Boulevard, April 11th 1971. (TED WICKSON)

Below: TTC Marmon-Herrington coach 9131 (ex-Cleveland 1351) leaves Blondin Loop on a threatening June 15th 1968. (TED WICKSON)

225

Above: Where else in Canada but Toronto could you see both forms of electric urban transit vying for space. TTC Flyer 9302 on the NORTOWN run lets PCC 4362 get out of the eastern terminus of the ST. CLAIR carline at Mount Pleasant and Eglinton Avenue on February 20th 1972. (TED WICKSON)

Below: Very little effort was made by the TTC to disguise where the leased General Motors/Brown Boveri (GM/BBC) units had come from. A few TTC stickers adding "9" to fleet numbers were sufficient, but the coach's Edmonton heritage still shone through. Unit 9197, recently delivered, is in the Doncliffe loop at the outer terminus of the NORTOWN EAST route on January 11th 1990. (TED WICKSON)

Above: Port Arthur coach 208 takes a time point at the end of the ARTHUR STREET line on a July 1966 afternoon.
(COLIN K. HATCHER)

Below: A clean Fort William PUC coach 46 showing the logo normally covered up by advertising signage sits at the garage on June 27th 1969.
(T.V. THOMPSON/TED WICKSON COLLECTION)

Above: Winnipeg Pullman 1582 travels down Salter Street in June of 1964. Bought used in 1956 from Providence, RI, the model 44CX was built in 1948 and lasted until the late 1960s.
(G.M. ANDERSEN PHOTO, KRAMBLES-PETERSON ARCHIVE)

Below: Winnipeg Brill 1800 at Main and McAdam on September 23rd 1969.
(SCALZO COLLECTION, ILLINOIS RAILWAY MUSEUM)

Above: Regina Brill 134 coasts along 3rd Avenue on a sunny day in July 1965. (COLIN K. HATCHER)

Below: Regina Transit coach 134 signed for PASQUA NORTH passes along 11 Avenue east of Lorne in June 1965. (COLIN K. HATCHER)

229

Above: Saskatoon Transit 152 on Route 2 PLEASANT HILL southbound on Lorne Avenue at Ruth Street captured on October 3rd 1963. The service station has been replaced by a 7-11 store, but a couple of the houses are still standing and look the same.
(PETER COX PHOTO,
 LOCATION IDENTIFICATION – MICHAEL P.J. KENNEDY)

Below: Saskatoon coach 164 in the new paint scheme on route 1 trundling through a quiet neighbourhood in September 1966.
(COLIN K. HATCHER)

Above: Edmonton Brill T-44 No. 132 cruises southbound into city centre along 101 Street at 103 Avenue on an April 1978 day. The 1947 coach sports the older ETS script on the front and an ET decal logo on the side. These coaches were kept in service and in shape in anticipation of the August Commonwealth Games traffic. (TOM SCHWARZKOPF)

Below: Edmonton E800 Flyer No. 217 whisks along 101 Street at 102 Avenue in July 1983. It only had three more years of useful life in Edmonton before being sold off to Mexico City. (COLIN K. HATCHER)

Above: Edmonton Transit System 128, a 1982 GM/BBC is wearing the final paint scheme applied to some of the trolley buses. This unique class of coach is eastbound on 102 Avenue NW, stopped at 124 Street NW, two miles west of downtown Edmonton. When the light turns green, 128 will turn right onto southbound 124 Street for a one-block jog down to Jasper Avenue, where the journey will continue through the city centre and the rest of the length of Jasper Avenue to a terminus at Stadium LRT station. The photo is especially poignant as it was taken on April 24th 2009, eight days before the end of all electric trolley bus service in Edmonton. (DAVID A. WYATT)

Below: Calgary coach 445 exits the loop at the north end of the #2 route, June 29th 1973. (TED WICKSON)

Above: Wearing the new paint scheme and a fair bit of prairie mud, Coach 460 exits the 24th Street and 54th Avenue loop on the SOUTH CALGARY run heading back into town.
(TED WICKSON)

Below: Vancouver's legendary, and now retired, trolley driver, Angus McIntyre hosted a few "trolley nuts" from Edmonton by taking refurbished coach 2040 out for a spin in June 2009. Part of the TRAMS (Transit Museum Society) historical collection, the Brill coach sports the famous "Tomato Bird" B.C. Electric logo.
(TERRY DEJONG)

Above: Laying over at Stanley Park Loop on a clear winter's night in February 1976, coach 2074 is resplendent in the Greater Vancouver Transportation System's grey and orange paint scheme.
(ANGUS McINTYRE/TED WICKSON COLLECTION)

Below: Southbound BC Transit No. 2929 passes a riot of spring colour while climbing the Arbutus Street hill at West 35th Avenue, May 12th 1997.
(TED WICKSON)

Colour postcards of Canadian trolley coaches

A transit curiosity is that in the late 1940s and early 1950s many postcard companies produced postcards featuring the new trolley coach form of transportation. Early ones had the original black and white photo hand-coloured before reproduction; later ones were made from colour slides or negatives which postcard collectors call "chromes." Standard cards were 3.5" x 5.5" on 12-point card stock with a matte finish before WWII. Photo cards often had a glossy finish (drum rolled during the drying process). Post-war cards (chromes) normally had a lacquer finish, but this process was outlawed in the 1980s due to the use of formaldehyde in the coating. Ultra-violet (U/V) finish then became the norm.

While the captions usually referred to only the city and occasionally the street, these featured the trolley coach prominently. On occasion, the colourist or photo editor would remove the unsightly overhead wires (how the coaches got their electricity was left a mystery) and other distractions such as telephone posts and wires, stray dogs and people. Sometimes there were two different versions of the same original photo, one with posts and dogs, and one without, and occasionally other more modern vehicles were added. Photo editing is not a recent phenomenon.

Following is a selection of these cards of Canadian properties from the Jeff Marinoff collection, with as much historical detail as could be ferreted out.

Barrington St., Halifax, Nova Scotia, Canada. -65

In this unique overhead shot there are at least four trolley coaches and judging from the Nova Scotia, Union Jack and American flags, it was probably the July holiday weekend in the early 1950s.

235

NSL&P 246 takes on passengers on Barrington Street in Halifax, probably in the late 1940s. The flags displayed suggest somewhere around the Dominion Day festivities.

Barrington Street, Halifax, Nova Scotia, Canada. -81

Compare this to the previous card – the Paramount Theatre is the same but not too much else is, with three Halifax trolleys going about their business while the locals enjoy a warm summer Saturday in the 1950s.

Barrington Street, Halifax, N.S. —81.

A 1951 T-48A Hamilton coach takes in the sun on a Bill MacDonald postcard. Coach 747 may not have been as fast as its namesake airliner, but it looks spiffy in as-delivered paint from the Fort William plant.

Hamilton — CCF — Brill Trolley Coach

Photo: Bill MacDonald

This coach is passing in front of Cornwall's Palace movie theatre on the BELT LINE on Pitt Street between First and Second Street looking north. The automobiles suggest that this is the early 1950s. Note the absence of overhead wires – retouched out!

New Electric Bus on Pitt Street, Cornwall, Ontario—10

VICTORIA AVENUE LOOKING WEST, FORT WILLIAM, ONT., CANADA

Fort William in the 1940s on Victoria Avenue. This rare linen postcard features a "made in Fort William" CCF-Brill. The bus in front of the trolley coach looks like a wartime Twin Coach with standee windows. The terminology "linen" was used to describe the paper texture used on post cards in that era but it's not actually linen.

Metropolitan Stores – a "Five and Dime" on the left, and a 1959, tail-finned Mercury Park Lane at right, as a Can Car-Brill trundles down Cumberland Street, which the postcard says on the back is "The Main Street of Port Arthur, Ontario". (MERCURY IDENTIFICATION, PAUL THEIREN).

Winnipeg – Portage Avenue probably shortly after 1953 when the Winnipeg Electric transit system was sold to the city and became the Greater Winnipeg Transit Commission. Brill 1700 in front has the new GWTC logo and paint while the vehicle behind may be the one and only MCI coach No. 1532 with the older paint scheme and the new GWTC logo over the old WEC one. The July 1st weekend seemed to be a popular time for trolley coach postcards. The brown brick building decked out in flags is the T. Eaton Company's store which was demolished a couple of years after Eaton's closed, and today the site is occupied by the "MTS Centre", Winnipeg's NHL arena. The Holt Renfrew building on the south side of Portage a block back at Carlton Street is still standing; today its main floor is occupied by a blue jeans store.
(LOCATION AND COACH IDENTIFICATION – DAVE WYATT AND MARK WALTON)

The trolley coach in the foreground has just passed SIMPSONS department store which was on Regina's 11th Avenue at Hamilton Street. On January 8th 1953, Simpsons was bought out by Sears, Roebuck and Company, Chicago. For a few years the former Simpsons stores were identified as Simpson-Sears and later just Sears. The store name shown in this postcard just shows the one name – Simpsons. Since the last BROAD NORTH trolley coach service was in 1954, this card can be dated to the early 1950s.
(DATING INFORMATION – WALLY YOUNG)

One of Edmonton's British-built Leyland trolley coaches is going north on 101 Street at 100 Avenue. The 1910 Post Office dominates the corner, while the iconic Macdonald Hotel (built 1915) is in the background on the crest of Bellamy Hill on the North Saskatchewan River.

One ETS Brill waits for the light while another pulls out on Jasper Avenue looking east. Another Edmonton landmark, Hudson's Bay Company department store looms in the front of the frame.

On Calgary's 7th Avenue in the late 1940s a lone coach plies its route in this rare 'tinted' black & white photo card. They were mass-produced that way, not individually hand tinted, and the process was very short-lived. The printer's art department had to be skilled to ensure the colour separations registered correctly where tinting was needed.

SEVENTH AVENUE, CALGARY, ALBERTA.

One block over on Calgary's 8th Avenue, coach 463 heads to Sunnyside on a Dominion Day and US Independence Day weekend.

Probably from a Kodachrome original, this card features at least five movie theatres. Just visible behind the "Tomatobird" logo-bearing trolley coach, a B.C.E.R. streetcar is heading north down Granville St. The last streetcars in Vancouver ran on April 24th 1955, so this card predates that historical event. (WALLY YOUNG, LOCATION AND DATE INFORMATION)

The landmark Hudson's Bay Company store looms over Vancouver trolleys at Georgia and Granville streets. The green over blue striped livery dates this as between 1961 and 1974 when the B.C. Hydro logo was replaced with the GVTS orange and yellow stripes.

This overhead view captures two B.C.E. Brills in the "Tomatobird" livery passing by the lawn of the Vancouver Courthouse on Howe Street just south of W. Georgia Street. The building on the left corner is the Vancouver Hotel. The parking lot was temporary, situated between Howe Street and Granville streets, and became the Pacific Centre which included Canada's iconic Eaton's department store. Judging from the cars it is probably the mid-1950s. The lead coach is a T-48, probably on route 5 or 8, followed by a T-44 on Route 4. (LOCATION AND DETAILS – RICHARD C. DEARMOND, DALE LAIRD AND WALLY YOUNG)

APPENDIX A:
Complete Equipment Roster for Each City

Note: CCF Brill serial numbers were of the form: CCB-TXX-YY-ZZZZ where XX is the model (44 or 48), YY was the year built and ZZZZ the serial number. Only the latter is shown in the tables below.

Similarly, Flyer Industries serial numbers took the form: E10240 0ZZZ and the leading 0 is not shown below.

HALIFAX

Fleet #s	Manufacturer	Model	Serial #s	Qty.	Year Built	Seats	Comments
201-260	CCF-Brill/GE	T-44	5395-5454	60	1948	44	
261-265	CCF-Brill/GE	T-44	5498-5502	5	1948	44	
266-271	CCF-Brill/GE	T-44	5787-5792	6	11-1949	44	
272-275	CCF-Brill/GE	T-44A	6734-6737	4	12-1950	44	
276-277	CCF-Brill/GE	T-44A	6763-6764	2	8-1952	44	
278-281	CCF-Brill/GE	T-44A	6765-6768	4	12-1954	44	
282-287	Pullman-Standard/GE	44CX	Vary – see Note 2	6	1947	44	Bought used in 1955

NOTES:
1. Sold to Toronto for cannibalization of parts: 204, 205, 209, 217, 227, 246, 251, 263, 264 and 272.
2. Pullman Coaches were ex-Providence, RI as follows:

Halifax #s	Providence #	Serial #
282	7411	5865
283	7212	5868
284	7407	5863
285	7408	5864
286	7409	5965
287	7410	5866

All had fiberglass dashes added to make them look like CCF-Brills. Retired Spring 1963, scrapped in 1965.

3. No. 273 preserved by Seashore Trolley Museum in May 1971

Sources: NATTA *Trolley Bus Bulletin 105* and amendments. Minor corrections from *Halifax – City of Trolley Coaches*.

MONTREAL

Fleet #s	Manufacturer	Model	Serial #s	Qty.	Year Built	Seats	Comments
4000-4006	A.E.C./MCW/E.E.C.	Electric		7	1937	38	Wt. 20,300 lbs.
4010-4049	CCF-Brill/GE	T-44	5355-5394	40	1947	44	Wt. 18,640 lbs.
4050-4089	CCF-Brill/GE	T-44	5824-5863	40	1950	44	13 del. June-July
4090-4114	CCF-Brill/GE	T-44A	6738-6762	25	1952	44	

NOTES:
1. CCF-Brills sold to Mexico City are as follows:

Mexico #s	Montreal #s
3300-3338	4010-4041 & 4043-4049
3339-3374	4050-4053, 4055-4066 and 4068-4087
3375-3399	4090-4114

2. No. 4042 preserved by CRHA (Exporail) until 1985, when it went to the Canada Science and Technology Museum in Ottawa, ON. No. 4067 was held by the MUTC until the early 1980s, then scrapped.

3. Nos. 4045 and 4088 scrapped after an accident, No. 4089 used as a diesel-electric experiment by a private party and scrapped in 1969.
4. No records exist as to the disposition of the English-built buses. They are assumed to have all been scrapped.

Sources: NATTA *Trolley Bus Bulletin 105* with amendments, and CRHA *Canadian Rail* #302. Also letter from D. Latour to W. Young, 2008-10-12.

Note 2 – from Exporail.

OTTAWA

Fleet #s	Manufacturer	Model	Serial #s	Qty.	Year Built	Seats	Comments
2001-2010	CCF-Brill/GE	T-48A	8220-8229	10	1951	48	Serial number preceded by CCB-T-48A-51-#

NOTES:

1. Units 2001-2005 sold to Kitchener in 1959* to become 133-141 (odd numbers only) in the following order:

Serial #	Ottawa #	Kitchener #
8224	2001	137
8220	2002	135
8221	2003	133
8222	2004	139
8223	2005	141

   *All Ottawa/Kitchener units were subsequently sold in 1973 to Vancouver as a parts source for its Flyer rebuild program.

2. Units 2006-2010 (serial #s 8225-8229) sold to Toronto in 1959 to become Nos. 9140-9144 in order.

Sources: NATTA *Trolley Bus Bulletin 105* and amendments.
Notes 1 & 2 from OTC files (TS) and confirmed in 2008 by Peter Newgard, OTC/OC Transpo Equipment Manager until 1988.

CORNWALL

Fleet #s	Manufacturer	Model	Serial #s	Qty.	Year Built	Seats	Comments
100-114	CCF-Brill/GE	T-44	5550-5564	15	1948	44	
115	CCF-Brill/GE	T-44	5000	1	1946	44	Demonstrator bought used in 1951

NOTES:

1. No. 115 was the original CCF-Brill demo unit that toured Canada, and the first post WWII trolley coach built in Canada.
2. Units 100-104, 106-108, 110-113 sold to Toronto in 1970 for use of parts. Remaining units Nos. 105, 109, and 114 were scrapped prior to May 1970 and one motor control unit sold to Toronto. No. 115 was sold to an employee (presumably minus motors and controls) for use at a rural camp.

Sources: NATTA *Trolley Bus Bulletin 105* and amendments.
Sale of No. 115 from J.D. Knowles

TORONTO

Fleet #s	Manufacturer	Model	Serial #s	Qty.	Year Built	Seats	Comments
20-23	Canadian Brill/WH			4	1922	29	Packard frames
9000-9024	CCF-Brill/GE	T-44	5045-5069	25	1947	44	
9025-9049	CCF-Brill/GE	T-44	5095-5119	25	1947	44	
9050-9074	CCF-Brill/GE	T-44	5285-5309	25	1947	44	
9075-9084	CCF-Brill/GE	T-44	5532-5541	10	1948	44	
9085-9124	CCF-Brill/GE	T-48A	8280-8319	40	1953	48	
9125-9139	Marmon-Harrington/GE	TC48	10365, 69, 371-380	15	1948	48	Bought used 1953 – see Note 1
9140-9144	CCF-Brill/GE	T-48A	8225-8229	5	1951	48	Bought used 1959 – see Note 2
9145-9152	Marmon-Harrington/GE	TC44	vary	8	1947-48	44	Bought used 1963 – see Note 3
9020-II later 9020	TTC–Western Flyer Coach/GE	E700/E700A	prototype	1	1968, revised model 1970	40	See Note 4
9201	TTC–Western Flyer Coach/GE	E700A	7181X	1	1970	40	See Note 4
9202-9222	TTC–Western Flyer Coach/GE	E700A	7181-7201	22	1970	40	Rebuilds, using motors etc. on new frame and body
9223-9230	TTC–Western Flyer Coach/GE	E700A	7203-7230	8	1970	40	Ditto
9231-9273	TTC–Flyer Industries/GE	E700A	See Note 5	42	1971	40	Ditto & see Note 6
9274-9276	TTC–Flyer Industries/GE	E700A	039-041	3	1971	40	See Note 6
9277-9299	TTC–Flyer Industries/GE	E700A	126-148	23	1972	40	See Note 7
9300-9332	TTC–Flyer Industries/GE	E700A	042-045, 051-060, 088-106	4 10 19	1971	40	See Note 8

APPENDIX A: COMPLETE EQUIPMENT ROSTER FOR EACH CITY

TORONTO (continued)

Fleet #s	Manufacturer	Model	Serial #s	Qty.	Year Built	Seats	Comments
9333-9351	TTC–Flyer Industries/GE	E700A	107-125	19	1972	40	See Note 7
9149-9199 See Note 9	GM/BBC	HR150G-T6H5307N-T9	vary	40	1980	40	Leased from Edmonton 1989-1993

NOTES:

1. ex-Cincinnati, OH coaches Nos. 1345-1359 in order; serial numbers in order.
2. ex-Ottawa, ON coaches Nos. 2006-2010 (serial #s 8225-8229) became Toronto Nos. 9140-9144 in the same order.
3. ex-Cleveland, OH coaches:

Toronto #	Cleveland #	Serial #
9145	1201	10291
9146	1205	10295
9147	1207	10297
9148	1209	10299
9149	1211	10301
9150	1212	10302
9151	1218	10308
9152	1224	10314

4. Second coach with this number. In 1967 the Commission had the original No. 9020 (then in dead storage) and No. 9144 (ditto) sent to different companies for a rebuilding experiment. No. 9144 was scrapped and No. 9020-II arrived back in 1968. After a year of trials the company decided to rebuild its whole 152-unit modern fleet (Nos. 9000-9152, less the scrapped No. 9144). No. 9020-II was further modified and renumbered 9200. There is no way, however, to correlate the new fleet with old numbers as rebuilt parts were pooled for use in new units.

    The TTC also bought a total of 23 units from Halifax and Cornwall in order to standardize components on the rebuilt fleet as some items on the 23 Marmon-Herringtons were not suitable. These units are: Halifax – Nos. 204, 205, 209, 217, 227, 246, 251, 263, 264 & 272 acquired in 1970. Cornwall – Nos. 100, 101, 102, 103, 104, 106, 107, 108, 110, 111, 112, 113, and a motor/control set from one of the remaining Cornwall fleet of 105, 109 or 114.

5. In 1971 due to Federal regulations, Western Flyer changed serial numbers to 7 digits; the first two showing the year of manufacture and month and the last three the individual unit number. For example 0171001 would be January 1971, unit 001. The following are the new serial numbers:

Toronto #/Serial #	Toronto #/Serial #	Toronto #/Serial #
9231 0171001	9246 0371010	9261 0471041
9232 0271002	9247 0371023	9262 0471048
9233 0271003	9248 0371024	9263 0471049
9234 0271004	9249 0371021	9264 0471013
9235 0271005	9250 0371031	9265 0471050
9236 0271015	9251 0471022	9266 0471014
9237 0371016	9252 0471025	9267 0471030
9238 0371017	9253 0471011	9268 0471034
9239 0371018	9254 0471012	9269 0371033
9240 0271006	9255 0471029	9270 0671035
9241 0371019	9256 0471026	9271 0671036
9242 0371007	9257 0471032	9272 0671037
9243 0371020	9258 0471046	9273 0671038
9244 0371008	9259 0471027	
9245 0371009	9260 0471028	

6. The numbering gap in the next series of E700As is artificial and when the full series was completed in 1972 it was erased.
7. Bodies for these units were turned out in 1971 but not readied by the TTC for service until 1972. Last unit finished on August 14, 1972.
8. Serials and fleet numbers are not in order for this series.
9. GMs leased from Edmonton Transit; returned to ET. Edmonton units Nos. 192 and 197 arrived in 1989, then Nos. 163, 164, 165, 166, 167, 168, 169, 170, 171, 172, 174, 176, 177, 178, 180, 181, 182, 183, 184, 185, 186, 187, 188, 189, 190, 191, 196 and 199 came in 1990. In 1991, Nos. 149, 150, 151, 152, 153, 154, 155, 156, 157 and 159 were also borrowed. All ET units had a 9 added to the start of their fleet number.

Sources: NATTA *Trolley Bus Bulletin 105* and amendments.
Note 2 OC Transpo files (TS)
Note 2 – confirmed in 2008 by Peter Newgard, OTC/OC Transpo Equipment Manager until 1988
Note 9 – *http://en.wikipedia.org/wiki/Toronto_buses_and_trolley_buses*

TIRES AND WIRES

HAMILTON

Fleet #s	Manufacturer	Model	Serial #s	Qty.	Year Built	Seats	Comments
701-718	CCF-Brill/GE	T-48	5804-5821	18	1950	48	14 delivered Aug.-Sept.
721-750	CCF-Brill/GE	T-48A	8246-8275	30	1951	48	See Note 4

NOTES:
1. No. 741 retired after accident with car September 22, 1969.
2. In 1972 Hamilton rebuilt their fleet but no direct correspondence exists between old and new fleet numbers:

Fleet #s	Manufacturer	Model	Serial #s	Qty.	Year Built	Seats	Comments
751-766	Flyer/GE	E700A	10722200-235	16	1972-73	44	Rebuilt 1982/3 with components from Brills
767-790	Flyer/GE	E700A	236-259	24	1974	44	Ditto, see Note 5
7801-7816	Flyer/GE	E800B		16	1978		See Note 6

3. In 1973 the 20 units left after Thunder Bay ceased operation were scrapped and the motor/control sets and other components sent to Hamilton to be used for rebuilding.
4. With the arrival of the first batch of Flyer coaches, ten older T-48A units were kept for rush hour use and repainted – fleet numbers: 727, 728, 730, 732, 735, 737, 745, 747, 748 and 750. HSR had originally decided to retire all of the T-48s after the arrival of the second batch of E700s, but decided to keep seven on the active roster (HSR Nos. 727, 728, 730, 732, 737, 745, and 750). These buses were repainted into the yellow and black 'Ticat' scheme, but were finally retired in 1979.
5. The last E700A coaches were retired and scrapped by 1989. No. 765 went to Halton County Radial Railway museum.
6. These lasted until the end of trolley service in 1992. The model "B" was only built for Hamilton; the main difference was the squared off rear end. Only three of these buses survived, numbers 7801 and 7802, which went to Halton County Radial Railway museum. No. 7809 went to Mexico City

Sources: NATTA *Trolley Bus Bulletin 105* and amendments
Last Flyer series from CPTDB Wiki site:
http://www.cptdb.ca/wiki/index.php?title=Hamilton_Street_Railway
Tom Luton's Hamilton Transit History pages:
http://hamiltontransithistory.alotspace.com/index.html
Tom Morrow's trolleybuses.net Mexico City page
http://www.trolleybuses.net/mex/mex.htm

KITCHENER

Fleet #s	Manufacturer	Model	Serial #s	Qty.	Year Built	Seats	Comments
101-119	CCF-Brill/GE	T-44	See Note 1	10	1946	44	
121-129	CCF-Brill/GE	T-44	5330-5334	5	1948	44	
131	CCF-Brill/GE	T-44	5793	1	1949	44	
133-141	CCF-Brill/GE	T-48A	vary	5	1951	48	Bought used in 1959 – Note 2

NOTES:
* All Kitchener units are odd numbered only.
1. Unit #/Serial # 101/5016, 103/5013, 105/5015, 107/5017, 109/5016, 111/5018, 113/5019, 115/5020, 117/5021, 119/5022
2. ex Ottawa as follows:

KPUC #	Ottawa #	Serial #
133	2003	8221
135	2002	8220
137	2001	8224
139	2004	8222
141	2005	8223

3. Number 119 destroyed by fire December 1970. All others sold to Vancouver in May 1973 and probably used for parts in the Flyer rebuilds. Number 103, Canada's first production trolley coach, was to be saved by B.C. Provincial Museum in Victoria, BC for preservation but was eventually scrapped.
4. Coaches 101 and 103 were decorated for Canada's Centennial with a white livery with red trim, the crests of the provinces – five on each side, the centennial logo on the front, and the advertising roof board which said "Welcome Aboard Canada's Birthday Coach".

Sources: NATTA *Trolley Bus Bulletin 105* and amendments
Note 2 from OTC files (TS) and confirmed in 2008 by Peter Newgard, OTC/OC Transpo Equipment Manager until 1988

WINDSOR

Fleet #s	Manufacturer	Model	Serial #s	Qty.	Year Built	Seats	Comments
1-4	St. Louis Car	T-T	Job 1267	4	1922	29	See Note 1

NOTES:
1. Sebree/Ward in *Transit's Stepchild, the Trolley Coach* state that the first of the order was the demonstrator Detroit coach, built in 1921.

Sources: NATTA *Trolley Bus Bulletin 105* and amendments.

APPENDIX A: COMPLETE EQUIPMENT ROSTER FOR EACH CITY

PORT ARTHUR–FORT WILLIAM/THUNDER BAY
PORT ARTHUR

Fleet #s	Manufacturer	Model	Serial #s	Qty.	Year Built	Seats	Comments
200-214	CCF-Brill/GE	T-44	5120-5127	8	1947	44	See Note 1
216-218	CCF-Brill/GE	T-44	5283,5284	2	1947	44	See Note 1

FORT WILLIAM

Fleet #s	Manufacturer	Model	Serial #s	Qty.	Year Built	Seats	Comments
40-47	CCF-Brill/GE	T-44	5168-5175	8	1947	48	
48-49	CCF-Brill/GE	T-48	5823,5822	2	1951	48	

NOTES:
1. Port Arthur units even numbered only.
2. The two cities amalgamated January 1, 1970 as Thunder Bay. Unit numbers were retained even through a new paint scheme that was applied to only PA 210 and 216. All units were operated by Thunder Bay Transit until end of service when they were scrapped, and motors, controllers etc. sent to Hamilton in 1973.

Sources: NATTA *Trolley Bus Bulletin 105* and amendments.

WINNIPEG

Fleet #s*	Manufacturer	Model	Serial #s	Qty.	Year Built	Seats	Comments
1500-1510	Mack Truck/GE	CR3S	1215-1220	6	1938	40	See Note 5
1512	Mack Truck/GE	CR3S	1234	1	1939	40	See Note 5
1514-1520	Mack Truck/WH	CR3S	1235-1238	4	1939	40	See Note 5
1522-1528	Mack Truck/GE	CR3S	1239-1242	4	1939	40	See Note 5
1530	Mack Truck/WH	CR3S	1249	1	1940	40	See Notes 1 and 5
1532	Motor Coach Industries/WH	TRLY	39	1	1942	40	See Note 2
1534-1538	Mack Truck/WH	CR3S	1271-1273	3	1943	40	See Note 5
1540-1542	Mack Truck/GE	CR3S	1274-1275	2	1943	40	See Note 5
1544-1558	Pullman-Standard/WH	44AS	5687-5694	8	1945	44	See Note 5
1560-1594	Pullman-Standard/WH	44CX	See Note 3	18	1948	44	Bought used 1956
1600-1648	CCF-Brill/GE	T-44	5070-5094	25	1947	44	
1650-1686	CCF-Brill/GE	T-44	5505-5523	19	1947	44	
1688-1726	CCF-Brill/GE	T-44	5335-5354	20	1948	44	
1728-1746	CCF-Brill/GE	T-48	5794-5803	10	1949	48	
1748-1806	CCF-Brill/GE	T-48A	8131-8160	30	1950	48	
1808-1826	ACF-Brill	T-46	063-072	10	1951	46	Bought used 1956. See Note 4

* all Winnipeg units are even numbered only.

NOTES:
1. Unit 1530, serial 1249, diverted from a Wilkes-Barre (US) order during WWII and used in W-B colors in Winnipeg from 1940-6 before being repainted.
2. Only trolley bus built by Motor Coach Industries as a wartime prototype. A contract for thirty coaches was signed by WEC, but the plant was turned to war production and no more were built.

3. ex-Providence, RI units:

Winnipeg #	Providence #	Serial#
1560	8503	7033
1562	8505	7035
1564	8507	7037
1566	8510	7040
1568	8511	7041
1570	8513	7043
1572	8514	7044
1574	8515	7045
1576	8516	7046
1578	8517	7047
1580	8518	7048
1582	8519	7049
1584	8520	7050
1586	8521	7051
1588	8522	7052
1590	8523	7053
1592	8524	7054
1594	8525	7055

WINNIPEG (continued)

4. ex-Flint, MI 867-876 bought November 1956. Units 1808, 10, 14-26 sold to A. Dallard Enterprises in November 1969 and most transferred to Mexico City as follows:

Winnipeg #	Flint #	Serial #	Mexico #
1808	867	063	3265
1810	868	064	3266
1812	869	065	scrapped
1814	870	066	3567
1816	871	067	3268
1818	872	068	3269
1820	873	069	3270
1822	874	070	3271
1824	875	071	parts
1826	876	072	parts

5. All the Mack units were scrapped in 1960 and the Pullmans in 1965 and 1969.

The remaining units at close of operations were dispersed as follows:
— 25 coaches: Nos. 1610, 14, 16, 18, 24, 28, 32, 34, 40, 42, 50, 52, 54, 56 and 1658 sold to Edmonton November 4, 1969 for parts.
— Nos. 1728, 30, 32, 34, 36 sold to Vancouver (B.C. Hydro) June 8, 1970. No. 1732 became BCH No. 2290 in 2/71; No. 1734 was scrapped in 1971; No. 1736 became BCH No. 2289 in December 1970 and No. 1728 & No. 1730 were scrapped in 1973 for parts.
— Units 1738 & 1740 were sold to Western Flyer on August 15, 1970 possibly for parts for MUNI Nos. 5001 and 5002.
— No. 1768 became the last unit to run in Winnipeg and was stored by Metro Transit for later display. It was then transferred to the Manitoba Transit Heritage Association.
All other coaches scrapped.

Sources: NATTA *Trolley Bus Bulletin 105* and amendments plus updated information from Baker *Winnipeg's Electric Transit*.

REGINA

Fleet #s	Manufacturer	Model	Serial #s	Qty.	Year Built	Seats	Comments
100-109	CCF-Brill/GE	T-44	5128-5137	10	1947	44	
110-119	CCF-Brill/GE	T-44	5201-5210	10	1947	44	
120-122	CCF-Brill/GE	T-44	5495-5497	3	1948-49	44	
123-146	CCF-Brill/GE	T-44	5651-5674	24	1949	44	
147-154	CCF-Brill/GE	T-48A	8123-8130	8	1950	48	

NOTES:
1. Numbers 100, 101, 103, 111, 115, 116, and 119-122 destroyed in a January 1949 car barn fire.
2. Coaches 125, 127-128, 133-137, 141 and 146 sold to Edmonton to become their second set of buses numbered 121-130:

Regina #	Serial #	Edmonton #
125	5653	125
127	5655	122
128	5656	124
133	5661	123
134	5662	121
135	5663	126
136	5664	127
137	5665	129
141	5669	128
146	5674	130

3. Unit 130 retained by city and subsequently scrapped; others scrapped in 1965-66 were Nos. 102, 112-114, 117, 118, 123, 124, 126, 129, 131, 132, 138, 139, 140, 142-145, 148-153.
4. Numbers 147 and 154 kept by RTS pending restoration. No. 154 subsequently transferred to Sandon collection.

Sources: NATTA *Trolley Bus Bulletin 105* and amendments.
Note 4 – Wally Young.

SASKATOON

Fleet #s	Manufacturer	Model	Serial #s	Qty.	Year Built	Seats	Comments
150-157	CCF-Brill/GE	T-44	5524-5531	8	1948	44	Delivered October 1948
158-159	CCF-Brill/GE	T-44	5680-5681	2	1949	44	Delivered November 1949
160-163	CCF-Brill/GE	T-48A	8119-8122	4	1950	44	Delivered September-October 1950
164-179	CCF-Brill/GE	T-48A	8230-8245	16	1951	44	Delivered October-November 1951

NOTES:
1. Nos. 150-159, 161, 163 retired in 1971. Seven cannibalized for parts October 1971.
2. Coaches 160, 162, 164-167, 170, 171 sold to Vancouver and shipped November 7 and 8, 1973.
3. Coaches 168, 169, 172-176, 178, 179 sold to Vancouver after abandonment and shipped May-June 1974.
4. Unit 177 donated to Western Development Museum in Moose Jaw for display 1973.

Sources: NATTA *Trolley Bus Bulletin 105* and amendments, and Wayman, *Saskatoon's Electric Transit*, p. 80.

EDMONTON

Fleet #s	Manufacturer	Model	Serial #s	Qty.	Year Built	Seats	Comments
101-103	A.E.C./E.E.C.	663T	087-089	3	1939	38	A.E.C. chassis/English Electric-Preston bodies/E.E.C. 115 HP motors/6 wheels, scrapped 1951
104-106	Leyland		302343-45	3	1939	38	Park Royal bodies/GE (U.K.) 135 HP motors/6 wheels, scrapped 1951
107-109	Leyland		305970-72	3	1942*	39	Same as numbers 104-6
110-112	Mack Truck Co.	CR	1276-78	3	1943*	40	Scrapped 1962. Serial numbers preceded by NOCR 1943
113-120	Pullman-Standard/GE	44T	5497-5504 (see Note 5)	8	1944	44	Retired 1963-66 and used for parts except #116 preserved in operating condition and renumbered 113
121-128	Pullman-Standard/GE	44T	5679-86	8	1945	44	Delivered 1946; retired 1963-66; used for parts
129-130	ACF/Brill	TC-44	164-165	2	1945	44	Scrapped 1965
131-152	CCF-Brill/GE	T-44	5023-44	22	1947*	44	131-135 serial numbers preceded by 46-, rest by 47. See Note 6
153-177	CCF-Brill/GE	T-44	5176-200	25	1947	44	See Note 4
178-179	CCF-Brill/GE	T-44	5503-04	2	1948	44	See Note 4
180-187	CCF-Brill/GE	T-44	5242-49	8	1948	44	See Note 4
188-192	CCF-Brill/GE	T-44	5675-79	5	1949	44	See Note 4
193-196	CCF-Brill/GE	T-48A	8276-79	4	1952	48	Double width front doors. See Note 4
197-202	CCF-Brill/GE	T-48A	8340-45	6	1954	42	Double width front doors. See Note 4
203-212	CCF-Brill/GE	T-44	5241-50	10	1947	44	Acquired 1962 from Vancouver Nos. 2001-2010 in order. See Notes 4 and 7
121-130 (2nd)	CCF-Brill/GE	T-44	See Note 1	10	1949	44	Acquired in 1966 from Regina. See Notes 1 and 4
213	Flyer Industries/GE	E800	E10240 395	1	1974	49	40' long/102" wide/rebuilt GE motors. See Note 8
214-237	Flyer Industries/GE	E800	396-419	24	1975*	49	All serial numbers preceded by E10240. See Note 8
238-249	Flyer Industries/GE	E800	420-431	12	1976*	49	All serial numbers as above. See Note 8
100-199 (2nd)	Brown Boveri/GM	HR150G	2B9546P D#BE001-BE100	100	1981/2	42	Last trolley coaches in Edmonton service. See Notes 9 and 10
6000 (CMBC 2242)	New Flyer Industries	E40LFR		1	2007		Leased from TransLink / Coast Mountain Bus Company for trial. Electronics by Vossloh Kiepe. Handicap accessible.

NOTES:

* Indicares the year delivered. Some units may have been partially or completely fabricated the year before.

1. Ex-Regina units:

Edmonton #	Regina #	Serial #
125	125	5653
122	127	5655
124	128	5656
123	133	5661
121	134	5662
126	135	5663 (serial plate reads CCF-T-44-47-5663)
127	136	5664
129	137	5665
128	141	5669
130	146	5674

2. Ex-Winnipeg 1947 T-44 units bought on November 4, 1969 for parts:

Winnipeg #/Serial #	Winnipeg #/Serial #	Winnipeg #/Serial #
1610 5075	1628 5084	1650 5505
1614 5077	1632 5086	1652 5506
1616 5078	1634 5087	1654 5507
1618 5079	1640 5090	1656 5508
1624 5082	1642 5091	1658 5509

3. Ex-Calgary T-44 and T-48 (†) units purchased July 1974 for parts:

Calgary #/Serial #	Calgary #/Serial #	Calgary #/Serial #
401 5139	416 5154	469 5691
403 5141	428 5166	477 8168†
404 5142	429 5167	479 8163†
405 5143	435 5216	480 8164†
412 5150	453 5234	481 8320†
413 5151	454 5235	482 8321†
415 5153	466 5688	

4. All CCF/Brills out of service as of November 17, 1978. The following remained: Nos. 121, 125, 127, 128, 129, 132, 135, 142, 144, 145, 148, 149, 153, 155, 161, 162, 163, 168, 170, 174, 176, 183, 185, 186, 189, 192, 195, 197-201, 203, 204, 208, 211, 212. T-44 Nos. 148, 191, and T-48A No. 202 preserved. Subsequently No. 191, the only unit in as-delivered coachwork, was vandalized, cannibalized for parts and scrapped. Balance sold to auto wrecker for scrap or storage sheds. Some 8-9 CC&F Brill T-44 trolleys were reported at A1 Auto Salvage, Stony Plain Rd. Edmonton at one time.

5. Serial number for No. 116 is 5500 (from serial plate, built June 2, 1944) and the balance of the series is extrapolated from this though not able to be confirmed. (Author's observation of No. 116 builder's plate)

6. Series probably built in late 1946 and continued into 1947 since serial numbers are in sequence.

EDMONTON (continued)

7. Garage records show no builder's plate for No. 209 but sequence is assumed to be continuous.
8. All Flyer Industries E800 Trolley Buses (Units 213-249) were sold to Mexico City in 1986. Five were still running in 2006, but all have been retired by now.
9. Nos. 149-157, 159, 162-172, 174, 176-178, 180-192, 196, 197 and 199 were leased to the Toronto Transit Commission. No. 155 also ran in Hamilton.
10. Disposition of BBC coaches: Units 109 and 110 were sold to the Greater Dayton Regional Transit Authority in 1994 as "gap-fillers" until the new SKODA ETBs arrived. They retained their same fleet numbers originally given by Edmonton. Dayton installed wheelchair lifts at the front door prior to their use. They were subsequently retired into Dayton's historical fleet.

    In October 2008, coach 143 was rear ended very badly, and in March 2009 No. 144 collided with a power pole and was scrapped. Coach 160 had an APU (Auxiliary Power Unit) which became inoperative because the charger failed.

    No. 100 (BBC prototype) and Nos. 119, 158-9, 194 stored in 2004; Nos. 115, 136 stored in 1998; Nos. 127, 132, 137, 157, 173, 175 stored in 2007; No. 170 stored in 2008; Nos. 165, 167, 178, 182, 185, 190 also stored on return from Toronto. Twenty-eight of these plus the then in-service units, with preservation exceptions, were sold to Plovdiv, Bulgaria. No. 100 preserved for Edmonton collection; No. 199 went to Reynolds-Alberta Museum in Wetaskawin; No. 189 went to Sandtoft, England; No. 182 donated to TRAMS in Vancouver; unit No. 125 donated for preservation to the Seashore Trolley Museum (Kennebunkport, ME) and No. 181 to the Illinois Railway Museum (Union, IL). In addition to No. 100, Nos. 113, 137 and 140 are stored in ET's Centennial Garage as of November 2018 (Hatcher).

    Nos. 103, 105-107, 118, 141, 142, 153, 171, 176, 187, 191 scrapped 2005; Nos. 117, 162, scrapped 2006; Nos. 116, 134, 154, 169, 196 scrapped 2007; Nos. 101, 108, 112, 114, 120, 123, 130, 146, 147, 149, 156, 163, 164, 166, 168, 177, 184, 186, 197 scrapped 2008; Nos. 104, 113, 122, 139, 151, 174, and 188 scrapped 2009. No. 158 decorated in an environmental paint scheme was kept after service, but subsequently scrapped. (Tucker).

    In service to the end: Nos. 102, 111, 121, 124, 126, 128, 129, 131, 133, 135, 138, 140, 145, 148, 150, 152 (see below), 155, 160, 161, 168, 172, 179-80, 183, 192-3, 195 and 198.

    There were a total of seven in-revenue-service BBC units for the last day: Nos. 111, 138, 148, 152, 155, 179, and 183. Also No. 195 was out, but as an overflow extra for Brill 202 on the final trip. The official last BBC in revenue service was No. 152 and it was also the last trolley to enter the garage.

Sources: Notes 1, 2 and 3 information from NATTA *Trolley Bus Bulletin 105* and amendments

Edmonton Transit: Don Mann, Supervisor, Ferrier Division; Jack Fleck, Superintendent Transit Services; Bob Rynerson, Marketing and Development (1983)

Notes 8 and 9 – Edmonton Transit Wikipedia page <http://en.wikipedia.org/wiki/Edmonton_Transit_System#Trolley_Buses>

Note 10 – James Mair, Edmonton, Terry Dejong, Edmonton Trolley Coalition, Wally Young and other correspondence with author, (Tom's Trolley Bus Web site http://www.daytontrolleys.net/history/rosters/2nd3rdhand.html#BBC)

Canadian Transit Discussion Board, Edmonton Transit All-Time Roster

http://www.cptdb.ca/wiki/index.php?title=Edmonton_Transit_System_All-Time_Roster
and CPTDB Edmonton Transit System 100-199
http://www.cptdb.ca/wiki/index.php?title=Edmonton_Transit_System_100-199

Confirmation of Edmonton, Reynolds, Sandtoft and TRAMS BBCs from Edmonton Transit, Ken Koropeski, Director of Service Development and Fleet Support, letter November 15, 2012. Confirmation of Seashore's BBC by e-mail from Tom Santarelli to author December 29, 2012; confirmation of IRM's BBC from Steve Scalzo.

Scrapping information on 191 and 158 verified by Brian Tucker, e-mail to author, June 24, 2013.

CALGARY

Fleet #s	Manufacturer	Model	Serial #s	Qty.	Year Built	Seats	Comments
400-429	CCF-Brill/GE	T-44	5138-167	30	1947	44	
430-459	CCF-Brill/GE	T-44	5211-240	30	1948	44	
460-470	CCF-Brill/GE	T-44	5682-692	11	1949	44	
471-476	CCF-Brill/GE	T-44	5693-698	6	1950	44	Del. July-August
477-480	CCF-Brill/GE	T-48A	8161-164	4	1950	48	
481-484	CCF-Brill/GE	T-48A	8320-323	4	1953	48	
485-504	ACF-Brill/GE	TC-44	vary	20	1948	44	See Note 1. Weight 20,760 lbs.

NOTES:

1. ex-Baltimore units purchased 1957:

Calgary #s	Baltimore #	Serial #
485	2172	581
486	2173	583
487	2171	585
488	2174	586
489	2177	587
490	2179	588
491	2178	589
492	2185	594
493	2187	601
494	2180	592
495	2182	598
496	2189	600
497	2175	590
498	2190	602
499	2176	593
500	2188	599
501	2184	595
502	2181	591
503	2186	596
504	2183	597

2. Removed from service October 1964: Nos. 485-489, and Nos. 495-499 inclusive.

3. In May 1973 stored as serviceable: Nos. 400-419, 491-493, 502 and 504†. Subsequently, Nos. 400-419 were disposed of as in notes 4, 5 and 10. Disposition of ACF coaches Nos. 491-3, 502 and 504 unknown, but assumed to have been scrapped.

4. Surplus coaches sold to Edmonton July 1974: Nos. 401, 403, 404, 405, 412, 413, 415, 416, 428, 429, 435, 453, 454, 466, 469, 477, 479, 480, 481, 482.

5. Surplus coaches sold to Vancouver July 1974: Nos. 402, 407, 408, 409, 410, 411, 414, 424, 438, 478.

6. Scrapped according to CTS records: Nos. 485-490 and Nos. 496-501 inclusive.

7. Used as portable passenger shelters: Nos. 494 and 503. (CTS)

8. As of February 1975 acquired by T.S. Holdings: Nos. 402, 407-411, 414, 424, 438, 478.

9. After close of system, last run coach No. 422 preserved by Reynolds-Alberta Museum in Wetaskawin, AB. (Walton)

    No. 432 sold to M. Vondrau, Preston, ON, in September 1974 and then donated to Halton County Radial Railway museum, Milton, ON. Subsequently it was sold to the Vintage Electric Streetcar Co. Windber, PA in July 1993. (Young/Sandusky)

    Nos. 446 and 459 preserved at Sandon, BC (via the Vancouver acquisitions).

10. All remaining coaches not previously sold or scrapped at close of system sold to Vancouver in August 1975, namely: 28 non-operational coaches @ $500 ea. – Nos. 400, 406, 417-421, 423, 425-427, 430, 431, 433, 434, 436, 437, 439-449. 25 operational coaches were sold @ $1000 ea. – Nos. 450-452, 455-465, 467, 468, 470-476, 483, 484.

Sources: Notes 1, 4 and 5 information from NATTA Databook II – *Trolley Bus Bulletin #109* with corrections by T.S.

Note 8 – *Transit Canada* January/February/75 p.32

Note 9 – Historic Sandon web site: Canadian Car & Foundry Brill Trolleys, July 10, 2006

http://www.sandonbc.com/brilltrolleys.html
visited February 2008

† information from NATTA – *Trolley Bus Bulletin #105*

Walton = Mark W. Walton, transit historian
Young = Wally Young, transit historian
Sandusky = Robert Sandusky, transit historian

TIRES AND WIRES

VANCOUVER

Fleet #s	Manufacturer	Model	Serial #s	Qty.	Year Built	Seats	Comments
2001-2042	CCF-Brill/GE	T-44	5241-5282	42	1947 new	44	See Note 1
2043-2082	CCF-Brill/GE	T-44	5455-5494	40	1948 new	44	
2083-2168	CCF-Brill/GE	T-48	5565-5650	86	1949 new	42	See Note 2
2169-2186	CCF-Brill/GE	T-48	5555-5582	18	1949 used	42	
2201-2225	CCF-Brill/GE	T-48	5699-5723	25	1950 new	42	
2226-2288	CCF-Brill/GE	T-48	5724-5786	63	1950 new	48	
2301-2355	CCF-Brill/GE	T-48A	8165-8219	55	1951 new	48	See Note 3
2401-2416	CCF-Brill/GE	T-48ASP	8324-8339	16	1954 new	42	See Notes 4 and 12
2501-2524	Pullman-Standard/GE	44AS	See Note 5	24	1945 bought used 1956	44	See Note 5
2289-2290	CCF-Brill/GE	T-48	5798, 5796	2	1949 bought used 1970	48	See Note 6
2355 (2nd)-2371	CCF-Brill/GE	T-48A	various – see Saskatoon roster	17	Built 1950/51, bought used 1973/74	48	See Note 8
2601-2650	Flyer/GE	E800	E10240 0527-0576	50	1976	40	See Note 10
2701-2774 2775-2799 2801-2899 2901-2902 2903-2946 2947* see notes	Flyer/Westinghouse	E901A E902	E10240 2316-2389 ..2390-2414 ..2415-2513 ..2514-2515 ..2974-3017 ..2772	74 25 99 2 44 1	1982-83	39	*2947 was originally numbered as 2700 as a prototype (no VIN) and returned to Flyer for rebuild then re-delivered, renumbered. Disposal of E901/2s see Note 11
2101	Flyer/GE	E40LF	2FYE5FJ15 5C027865	1	June 2005	29	Low floor prototype
2102-2289* see notes	New Flyer/ Vossloh Kiepe electrics & motor	E40LFR	2FYE5FJ15 6A029970- 2FYE5FJ16 6A030156	188	2006-7	31	2200 renumbered to 2289 See Note 13
2501-2540	New Flyer/ Vossloh Kiepe electrics & motor	E60LFR	2FYE5YJ14 6A030748- 2FYE5YJ14	40	2007	47	Articulated low floor 60' See Note 13
2541-2574			7A032467	34	2009		

NOTES:

1. Nos. 2001-2010 sold to Edmonton in 1961 to become Nos. 203-212 in that order. Nos. 2011-2030 scrapped in 1962.
2. Nos. 2083 thru 2100 were renumbered 2169-2186 in 1950. No. 2125 wrecked 1970 and stored.
3. No. 2328 was destroyed in an accident and scrapped in 1964, and No. 2355 of this series was renumbered to #2328.
4. Vancouver was the only city to receive T-48 & T-48A models with less than 48 seats and these 42-seat models were tagged SP or Special Production by CC&F. However, Nos. 2083-2225 were retrofitted to 42 seats from 48 in the mid-1950s, given the success of Nos. 2401-2416 which were built with 42 seats. Later, Nos. 2201-2225 were converted back into 48 seats although they retained the seat-mounted stanchions along the curb side forward-facing seats between the doors. (Day)
5. These were ex-Birmingham, Alabama units that were subsequently withdrawn December 1960 and scrapped spring 1961 *(see next column)*:

Vancouver #	Birmingham #	Serial#
2501	102	6052
2502	108	6058
2503	109	6059
2504	110	6060
2505	114	6064
2506	115	6065
2507	116	6066
2508	117	6067
2509	118	6068
2510	120	6070
2511	122	6072
2512	123	6073
2513	124	6074
2514	126	6076
2515	127	6077
2516	128	6078
2517	129	6079
2518	130	6080
2519	131	6081
2520	132	6082
2521	133	6083
2522	137	6087
2523	138	6088
2524	139	6089

6. These were ex-Winnipeg, MB units Nos. 1736 and 1732 respectively. Three other Winnipeg units, Nos. 1728, 1730 and 1734, were purchased and eventually dismantled for parts. Unit 1732 was refurbished in February 1971; No. 1736 in December 1970.

7. Twenty Kitchener units Nos. 100-141 (odd #'s), except for No. 119 that was damaged beyond use by a fire, were subsequently bought by BCH in May 1973 to be used for the rebuilding program. Unit 103, Canada's first CC&F production trolley coach, was to be saved to be preserved by the B.C. Provincial Museum in Victoria, but following a change in government and management, was eventually scrapped.

8. Saskatoon fleet Nos. 160, 162, 164-167, 170, 171 sold to Vancouver and shipped November 7 and 8, 1973. Nos. 168, 169, 172-176, 178, 179 sold to Vancouver after abandonment and shipped May-June 1974. See Saskatoon Roster for serial numbers. Vancouver fleet numbers correspondence to Saskatoon fleet #s unknown, however Wayman in *Saskatoon's Electric Transit* identifies B.C. Hydro No. 2360 as ex-STS No. 170. Also additional research into preserved coaches revealed that Vancouver No. 2355 was STS No. 160 and Vancouver No. 2357 was STS No. 164.

    However, The Next Stop database
    http://www.taylornoonan.com/nextstop/
    shows the following:

Vancouver #	Saskatoon #	Vancouver #	Saskatoon #
2355	162	2364	171
2356	160	2365	172
2357	164	2366	173
2358	165	2367	174
2359	166	2368	175
2360	167	2369	176
2361	168	2370	178
2362	169	2371	179
2363	170		

9. Of the Brill series Nos. 2001-2082, units 2031-2055 were stored in February 1971 following a long strike and service cut; some returned to service in May 1973 because of increased service levels; however wrecked units were stripped for parts for a rebuilding program in 1974. They were supposedly set aside for sale to Mexico City but that apparently fell through, and various scrap yards took on the fleet with the exceptions of: Nos. 2040, 2414 and 2416 acquired by TRAMS. Subsequently No. 2414 went to a collector in Edmonton. No. 2340 went to the Illinois Railway Museum, and several went to Sandon. Of these, BC Nos. 2355 and 2357 (ex-Saskatoon Transit Nos. 160 and 164 respectively), were acquired by Thunder Bay Transit and cosmetically restored and repainted to Port Arthur and Fort William liveries.

10. Flyer E800 units were withdrawn from service after end of Expo86 as a result of poor operation and obsolete electrical equipment. Most were converted to diesel buses using running units obtained from scrapped Flyer D700 diesel buses, which had undergone a mid-life rebuild with new engines and transmissions. Two retained trolley equipment for use as de-icing buses and one of these, No. 1109 (ex-2649) has been preserved by TRAMS.

11. The following trolleys were shipped to Mendoza, Argentina on November 4, 2008 on the motor vessel *Wisdom*:

    2703, 2704, 2705, 2712, 2713, 2714, 2716, 2727, 2741, 2743, 2744, 2746, 2751, 2755, 2761, 2763, 2765, 2767, 2769, 2772, 2774, 2777, 2780, 2782, 2785, 2787, 2792, 2793, 2796, 2798, 2799, 2803, 2806, 2808, 2811, 2819, 2820, 2822, 2825, 2826, 2832, 2833, 2834, 2836, 2838, 2840, 2841, 2843, 2845, 2846, 2847, 2852, 2853, 2855, 2858, 2867, 2868, 2869, 2870, 2871, 2878, 2884, 2889, 2892, 2893, 2897, 2904, 2905, 2907, 2910, 2912, 2915, 2916, 2919, 2924, 2926, 2941, 2943, 2946, 2947

    No. 2915 was not shipped and is assumed to have been damaged/scrapped. No. 2805 went to TRAMS.

12. ex-Vancouver Brill No. 2414 is at Sandon; No. 2402 was last reported at Three Valley Gap in poor condition (Day); No. 2411 is at the Oregon Electric RR Museum, Brooks, OR.

13. Serial numbers for Flyer E40 and E60 models are VIN numbers and are consecutive except for the 3 digits between the 2FYE5YJ and the A0XXXXX part of the number. These 3 digits seem to be in a recurring but random sequence. VIN numbers supplied by Derek (Ba See Lo) Cheung.

Sources: NATTA *Trolley Bus Bulletin 105* and amendments, and equipment rosters provided from bus records by Wally Young.

   Notes 4 and 10 – John Day correspondence with author.

   Note 9 – disposition from BARP Farewell to Brills web site
   http://www.barp.ca/bus/bctransit/farewell/index.html
   visited August 26, 2013

   Note 11 – Derek (Ba See Lo) Cheung and
   http://buzzer.translink.ca/index.php/2008/11/update-on-the-retired-trolleys-sailing-to-south-america/
   visited November 2008

APPENDIX B:
Preserved Equipment

Owner	Transit Company	Fleet #	Builder	Model	Built	Notes
Seashore Trolley Museum (Kennebunkport, ME)	Nova Scotia Light and Power Co. (Halifax)	273	CCF-Brill	T44A	1950	
	Edmonton Transit (ET)	125	BBC/GM	HR150G	1982	
Canada Science and Technology Museum (Ottawa, ON)	Montreal Urban Transit Commission (MUTC)	4042	CCF-Brill	T-44	1947	Originally sent to Canadian Railway Museum (now Exporail), Delson, QC.
Halton County Radial Railway (Milton, ON)	Hamilton Street Railway (HSR)	732	CCF-Brill	T-48	1948	
		765	Flyer	E700A	1972	
		7801 7802	Flyer	E800B	1978	Modified by GEC Alstom for dual power with diesel generator and chopper control for operating short distances without overhead
	Toronto Transit Commission	23	Packard/Brill	ED3	1922	Originally GE motors. Lacks motors, controllers and seats
Thunder Bay Transit/ Amalgamated Transit Union	Port Arthur Transit†	202	CCF-Brill	T-48A	1950	†Actually Vancouver Nos. 2355 and 2357, ex-Saskatoon Transit Nos. 160 and 164 respectively, cosmetically restored and repainted to Port Arthur and Fort William liveries.
	Fort William Transit†	45	CCF-Brill	T-48A	1951	
Western Development Museum (Moose Jaw, SK)	Saskatoon Transit System (STS)	177	CCF-Brill	T-48A	1951	Acquired 1973
Regina Transit System (Regina, SK)	Regina Transit System (RTS)	147	CCF-Brill	T-48A	1950	Under consideration to restore
Manitoba Transit Heritage Association (MTHA) (Winnipeg, MB)	Winnipeg Hydro	1768	CCF-Brill	T-48A	1950	Last unit to run in Winnipeg. Currently in Fort Rouge garage awaiting restoration.

Right: When you are a retired Brill, perhaps the closest to trolley coach heaven is sleeping in the sunshine in the hamlet of Sandon, BC with the Selkirk Mountains towering over you. This is some of the collection of trolley coaches maintained by Hal Wright. (JOHN M. DAY)

APPENDIX B: PRESERVED EQUIPMENT

Owner	Transit Company	Fleet #	Builder	Model	Built	Notes
Reynolds-Alberta Museum (Wetaskawin, AB)	Calgary Transit System (CTS)	422	CCF-Brill	T-44	1947	Last run coach
	Edmonton Transit System (ETS)	199	BBC/GM	HR150G	1982	
Edmonton Transit (Edmonton, AB)	Edmonton Transit System (ETS)	113	Pullman-Standard		1944	Original fleet No. 116, renumbered to simulate first in series.
		148	CCF-Brill	T-44	1947	
		202	CCF-Brill	T-48A	1954	Reportedly last T-48A built in Canada
		100	BBC-GM	HR150G	1982	
TRAMS (Transit Museum Society) (Vancouver, BC)	B.C. Electric (BCE) B.C. Hydro	2040	CCF-Brill	T-44	1947	
		2416		T-48ASP	1954	
	BC Transit	2649	Flyer	E800	1976	Delivered as a trolley coach, it was converted to diesel after the E800's last use for Expo86. This is one of two that retained the trolley collection equipment for use as an overhead de-icing bus.
	BC Transit	2805	Flyer	E902	1984	Non-operative
	Edmonton Transit (ETS)	132	BBC/GM	HR150G	1982	
Wrightway Charter – Sandon ETB collection (Sandon, BC)	Calgary Transit System (CTS)	446 459	CCF-Brill	T-44	1948	Sold to Vancouver in original blue & cream livery
	Winnipeg Hydro	1636	CCF-Brill	T-44	1947	
	B.C. Electric (BCE) (Vancouver)	2166 2201 2289* 2368** 2408 2301 2402***	CCF-Brill	T-48 T-48 T-48 T-48 T-48ASP T-48A T-48ASP	1949 1950 1949 1951 1954 1951 1954	*formerly Winnipeg No. 1736 **formerly Saskatoon No. 175 ***Removed from the collection for display at the 3 Valley Gap Resort Heritage Ghost Town in Revelstoke, BC.
	Regina Transit System (RTS)	154	CCF-Brill	T-48A	1950	
Illinois Railway Museum (Union, IL)	B.C. Electric (BCE) B.C. Hydro (Vancouver)	2340	CCF-Brill	T-48A	1951	
	TTC (Toronto)	9339	Flyer	E700A	1972	
	Edmonton Transit (ETS)	181	BBC/GM	HR150G	1982	
Oregon Electric Railway Museum (Brooks, OR)	B.C. Electric (BCE) B.C. Hydro (Vancouver)	2411	CCF-Brill	T-48ASP	1954	
Southeastern Railway Museum (Duluth, GA)	B.C. Electric (BCE) B.C. Hydro (Vancouver)	2207	CCF-Brill	T-48	1950	
Sandtoft, UK	Edmonton Transit (ETS)	189	BBC/GM	HR150G	1982	
Greater Dayton (OH) Regional Transit Authority	Edmonton Transit (ETS)	109 110	BBC/GM	HR150G	1982	Sold to Dayton in 1994. Both units are now in Dayton's historic fleet.

NOTE: The above is as accurate at the time of publication as the best of my sources. Preserved equipment does move through sales and transfers and occasionally is scrapped as beyond preservation – so the above information may have changed by the time you read this. Also, units occasionally surface and are acquired by interested properties. No attempt has been made to list units abandoned, in scrap yards, with private sources for resale or restoration, or modified for domestic/storage use. Some of that information has been captured accompanying the individual city rosters in the notes.

This table was compiled from the individual Company Rosters in Appendix A, which were drawn from the North American Trackless Trolley Association (NATTA) *Trolley Bus Bulletins 105* and *109* as well as other valuable trolley bus contacts. Some buses required considerable detective work to find their owner. To verify this information, my sources were: Edmonton Transit Public Relations as well as my personal observations; web site rosters for Halton County Radial Railway http://www.hcry.org/col_rubber.html, Seashore Trolley Museum http://www.trolleymuseum.org/collection/trackless.html, Manitoba Transit Heritage Association http://www.mts.net/~amregiec/Fleet%20Rosters.html, Illinois State Railway Museum http://www.irm.org/roster/trolley.html, Oregon Electric Railway Museum http://oerhs.org/oerm/roster/bct-etb-2411.htm, Southeastern Railway Museum http://www.srmduluth.org/exhibits/transit.shtml, and TRAMS http://www.trams.ca/buses.html. The E902s at TRAMS from Tom's Trolley Bus Web Site http://www.trolleybuses.net/van/van.htm. The MUCTC coach at Canada Science and Technology Museum was verified by ExpoRail – the former owner. Sandon's collection was verified by Hal Wright, owner of the Wrightway Charter – Sandon ETB collection http://www.sandonbc.com/brilltrolleys.html. Calgary's coach at the Reynolds-Alberta Museum was verified by Mark W. Walton, transit historian. The Western Development Museum and Thunder Bay coaches were verified by Wally Young, transit historian, who also verified, corrected and clarified many, many of the details in this chart. The Seashore collection was verified by Tom Santarelli, Seashore Museum in an e-mail December 29th 2012. Confirmation of IRM's BBC was by Steve Scalzo. Vancouver coaches corrected and verified by John Day.

TIRES AND WIRES

BOOMERS
Not as much preserved as these Canadian trolley coaches saw a second life running in service outside Canada.

Above: Ex-Edmonton BBC/GM coach No. 110 now retired into Dayton's historical fleet, poses June 6th 2018 on a fan trip. Unit 110 and sister No. 109 were used in daily revenue service by the Greater Dayton Regional Transit Authority from 1994 to 2004 until the ETI/Skoda coaches arrived. They retained their Edmonton fleet numbers. (ROB HUTCHINSON)

Tom Morrow comments:

In the early 1990s, the Miami Valley, OH RTA began to consider replacement of their Flyer fleet (Nos. 901-964), which had been delivered in late 1976-early 1977. While the number of trolleys needed on the street to serve the then operating lines was shrinking (and in fact there was some question as to whether trolleys would be continuing in Dayton), the remaining buses were aging at a fast pace.

A program to rebuild a few of the Flyers began in 1992. By 1994, approximately six had been rebuilt, and the Flyers in the worst shape had been put out to pasture. But, in 1994, after opening a few bids for the new trolleybus procurement, the RTA noted that the number of potential bidders was smaller than expected. The question was, if it takes longer for a new procurement, what alternatives are there for trolley operation besides rebuilding more Flyers?

While the Edmonton fleet was approximately twelve years old at the time, the buses had relatively low miles. Salt was not used much, so structurally the buses seemed to be in fairly good shape. The decision was made to explore what it would take to make an Edmonton BBC compatible with operations in Dayton, OH. The two major necessities were wheelchair lifts and air conditioning. Two candidate buses were picked, Nos. 109 and 110, and they were shipped to Dayton, arriving in the Spring of 1995.

Over the next few months, the RTA explored air conditioning (which would have needed more roof strengthening beyond that which was done for the pole bases – considered not economically viable), and managed to retrofit a wheelchair lift into the GM body. This was no small feat as there is not a real solid frame to easily attach a front door lift. But the job was very custom, and while they got it to work for two buses, it was not exactly clear how well they would have been able to deal with installing such lifts in about 35 buses.

During the run-ups to get the buses into service, the RTA discovered electrical issues with making these more modern buses co-exist with a Flyer fleet whose overvoltage relays had never been maintained, as the tried and true GE 1213 controls really weren't fussy about local overvoltage in a "non-receptive" regen situation, but the BBCs (and subsequently the ETI/Skodas) very much were.

While this experiment was going on, the new trolleybus procurement was moving along. The ETI/Skoda demonstrators were on their way, and the production run was starting, with local final assembly in Dayton. Considering the work to get more of the Edmonton BBCs into service, along with that needed for the ETI/Skoda fleet, it was decided to continue with just Nos. 109 and 110, and to get the production fleet into place as soon as possible. My understanding is that Nos. 109 and 110 went into revenue service in February 1996.

Above: Servicio de Transportes Eléctricos (STE) del D.F. No. 3359, an ex-Montreal 1950 T-44 CCF-Brill basks in the sun at a Mexico City Metro station, July 2nd 1980. (MICHAEL ROSCHLAU)

Left: Ex-Vancouver Flyer E901A No. 2769 running as Mendoza No. 24 in Mendoza, Argentina on January 23rd 2011. All the Mendoza Flyers were retired by 2017. (MICHAEL ROSCHLAU)

Bottom: Ex-Edmonton Flyer E800 No. 227, now as STE No. 3227, is marked "Azcapotzalco" in the windshield. Also written on the windshield is the fare of 300 pesos and the destination of Aeropuerto Metro station. Azcapotzalco, a municipality within Mexico City, served as a terminus of one of the trolley bus lines. Captured on May 16th 1991 near Mexico City International Airport. (JOHN PAPPAS)

APPENDIX C:
Trolley Coach Drawings

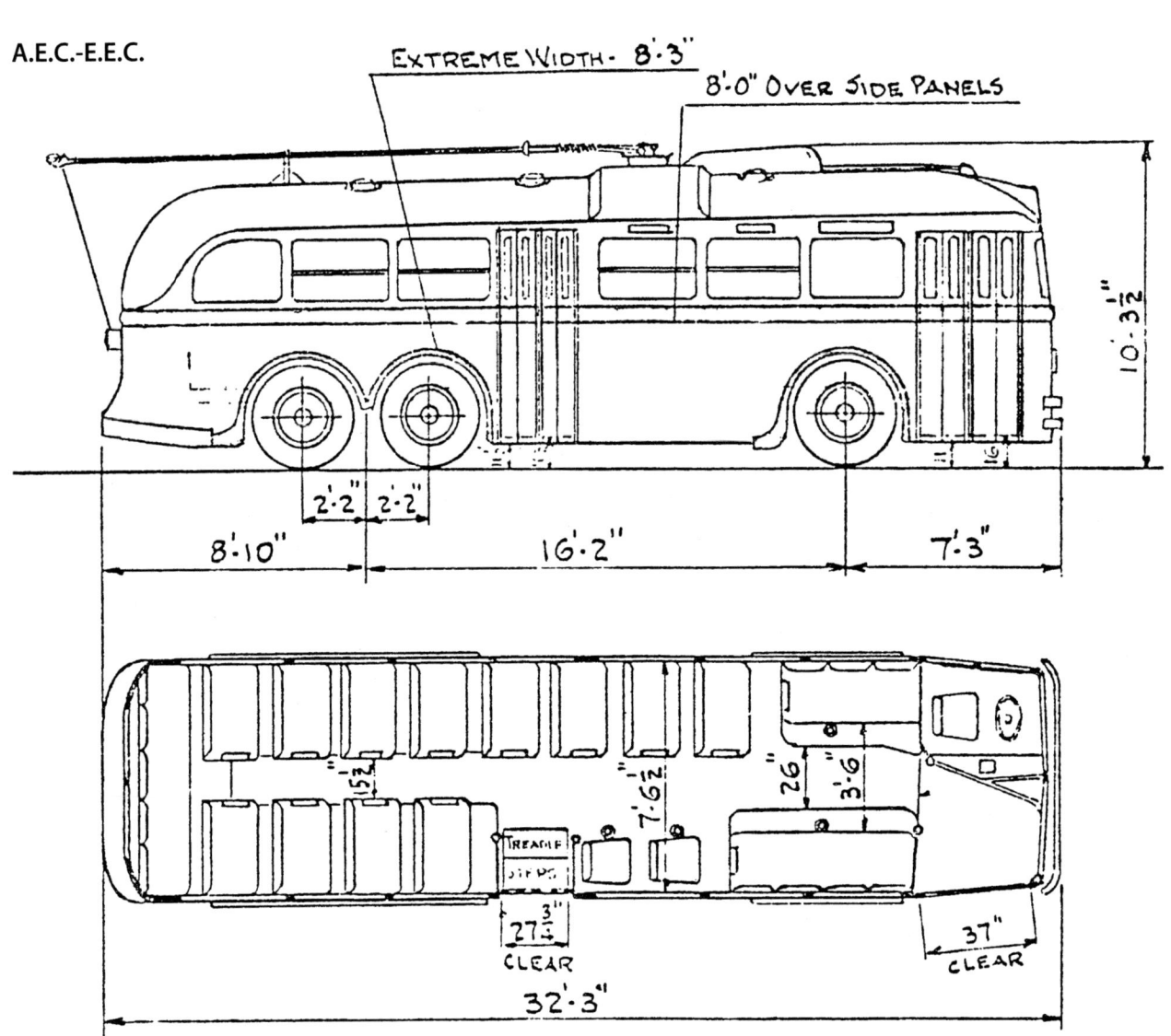

A.E.C.-E.E.C.

This A.E.C.-E.E.C. diagram, first published in *Canadian Rail*, March 1977, was likely drawn by Denis Latour.

APPENDIX C: TROLLEY COACH DRAWINGS

LEYLAND/PARK ROYAL

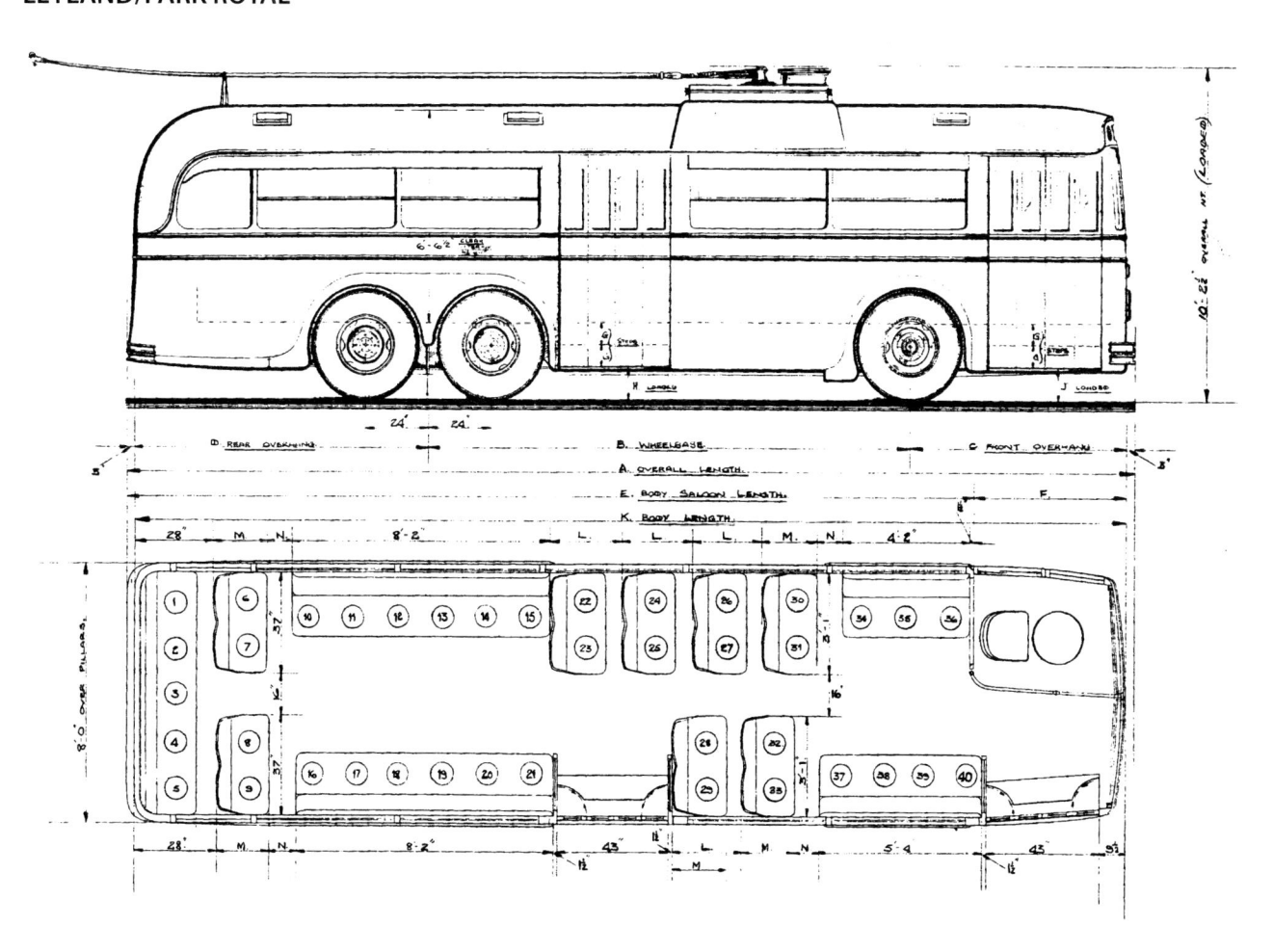

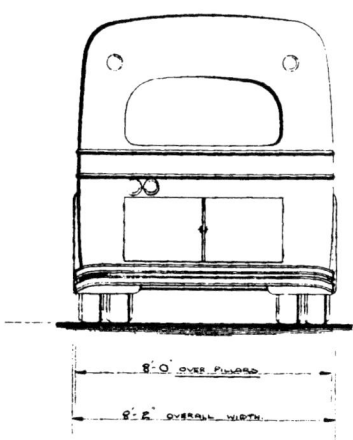

Leyland/Park Royal coach as proposed for Edmonton. Delivered units were similar.
(PROVINCIAL ARCHIVES OF ALBERTA, SCHWARZKOPF COLLECTION)

TIRES AND WIRES

MACK CR40

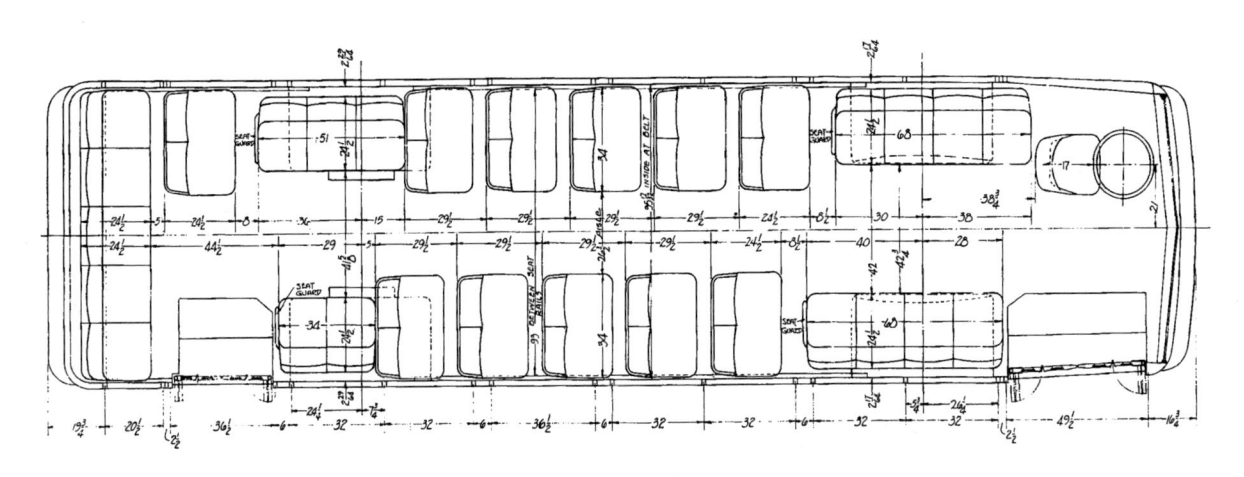

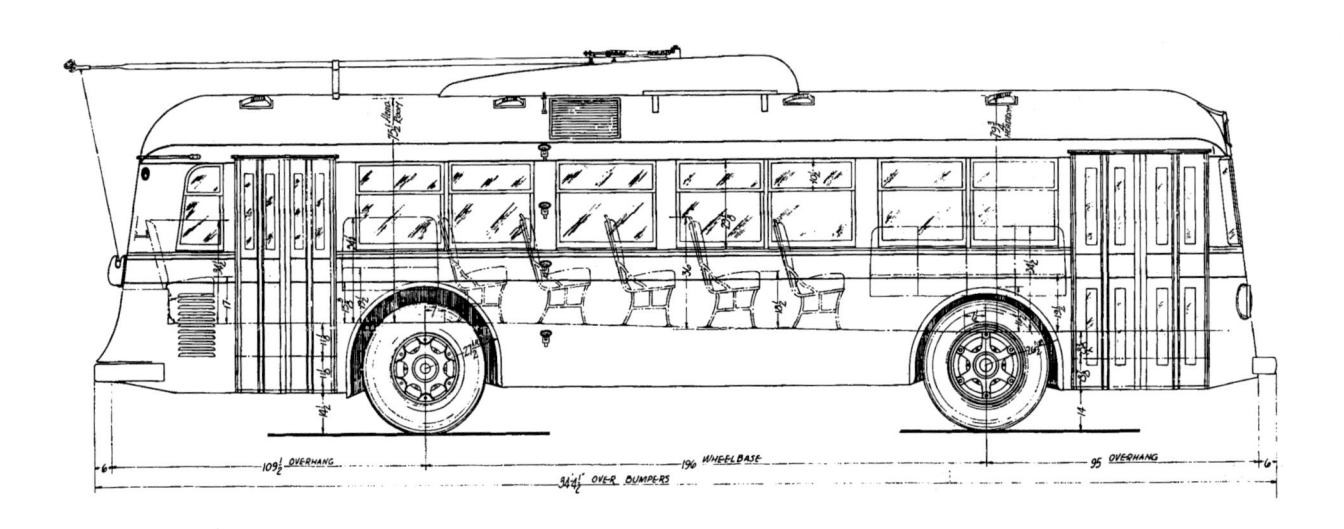

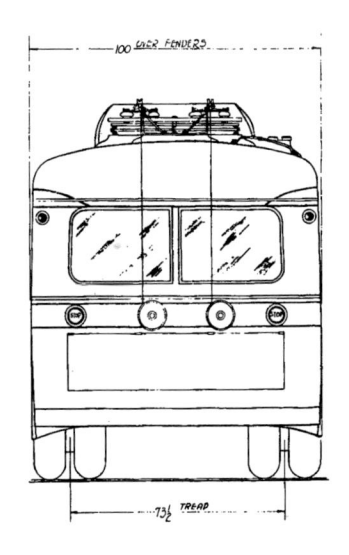

Mack CR40 as proposed for Edmonton, which is very similar to those delivered to Winnipeg.
(PROVINCIAL ARCHIVES OF ALBERTA, SCHWARZKOPF COLLECTION)

APPENDIX C: TROLLEY COACH DRAWINGS

PULLMAN

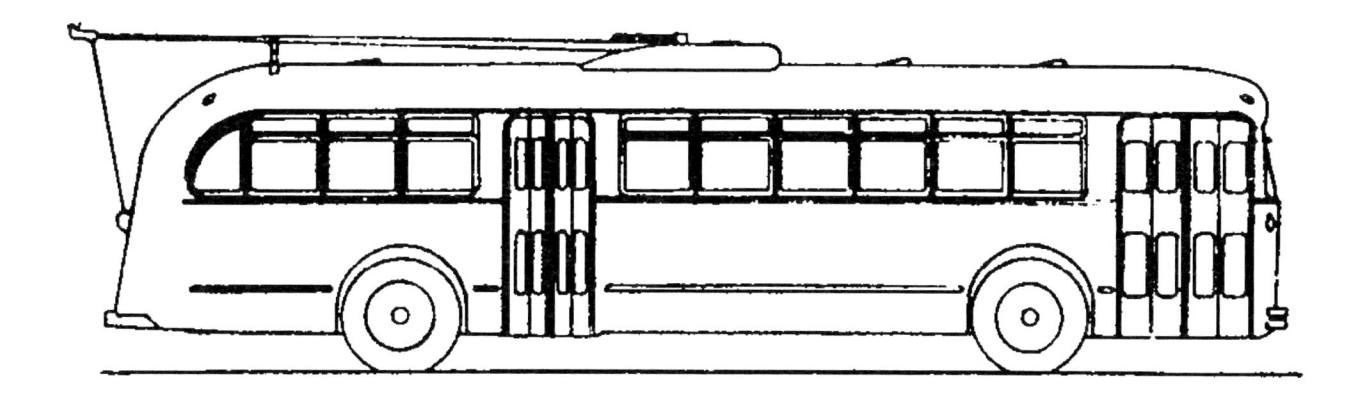

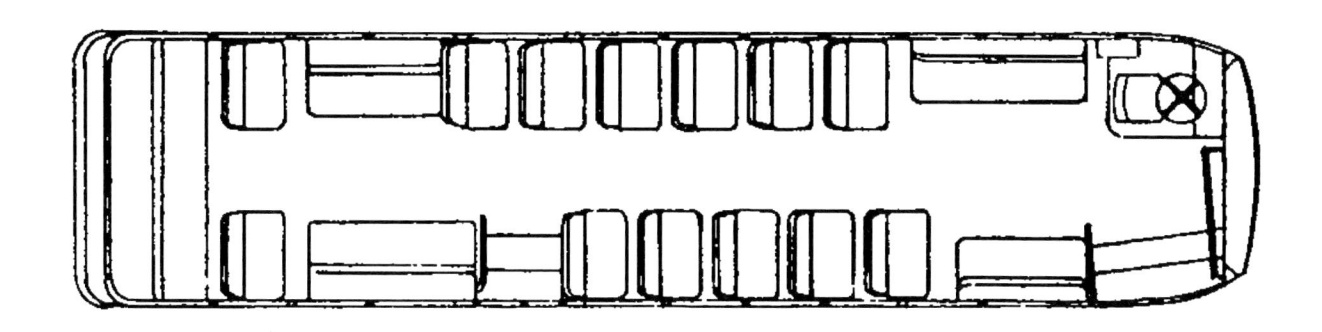

Pullman coach from Chicago Transit Authority, Staff Engineer's Office Trolley Buses drawing SEO-X 4103 as reproduced in *Trolley Coach News* #21 January-June 1973. This may not be exactly the same models as Canadian cities obtained.

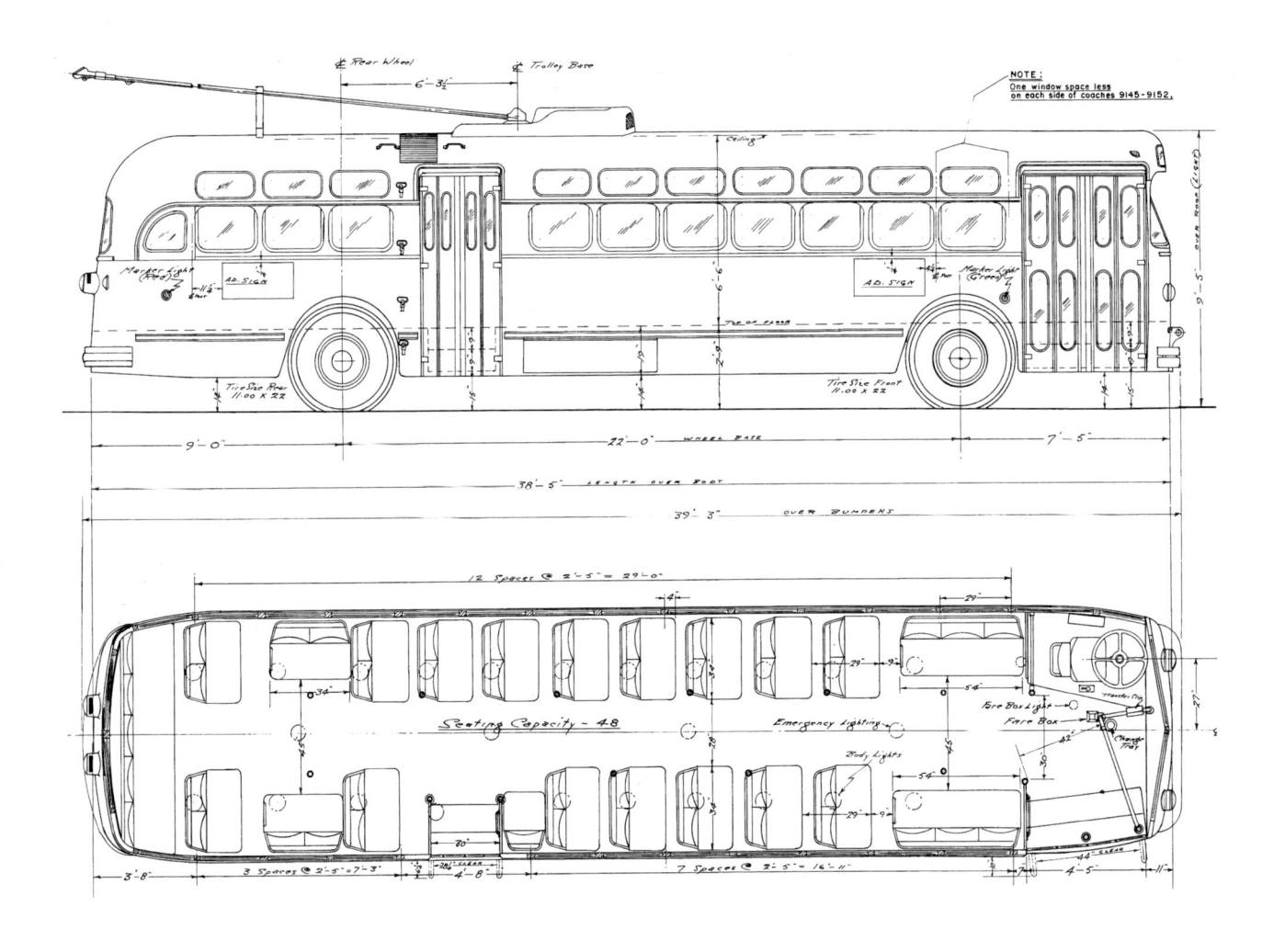

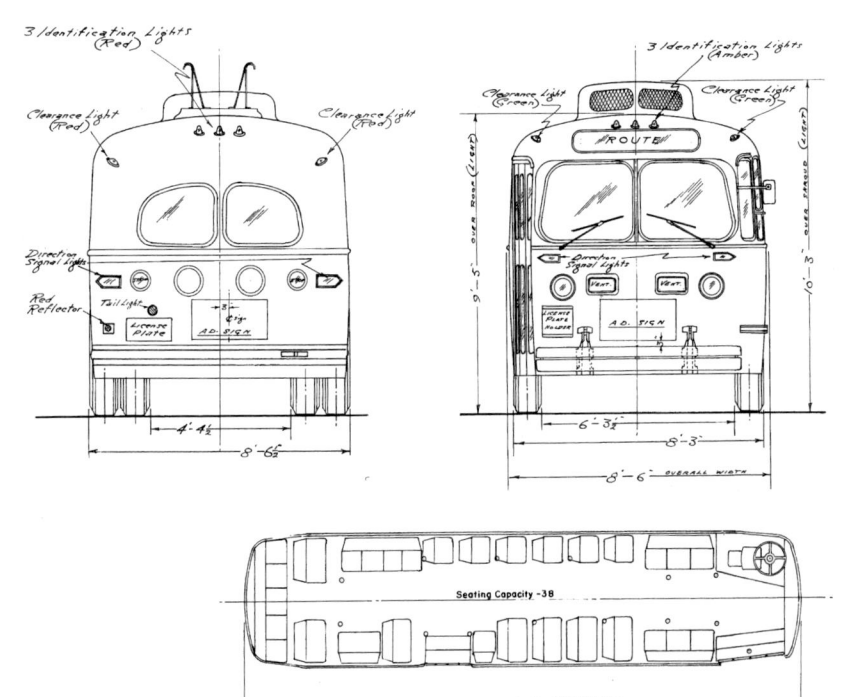

TIRES AND WIRES

MARMON-HERRINGTON TC48

Marmon-Herrington TC48 as bought used by TTC.
(COURTESY CHRIS PRENTICE)

Seating Layout for Trolley Coaches 9145-9152 only.

APPENDIX C: TROLLEY COACH DRAWINGS

ACF-BRILL T-44

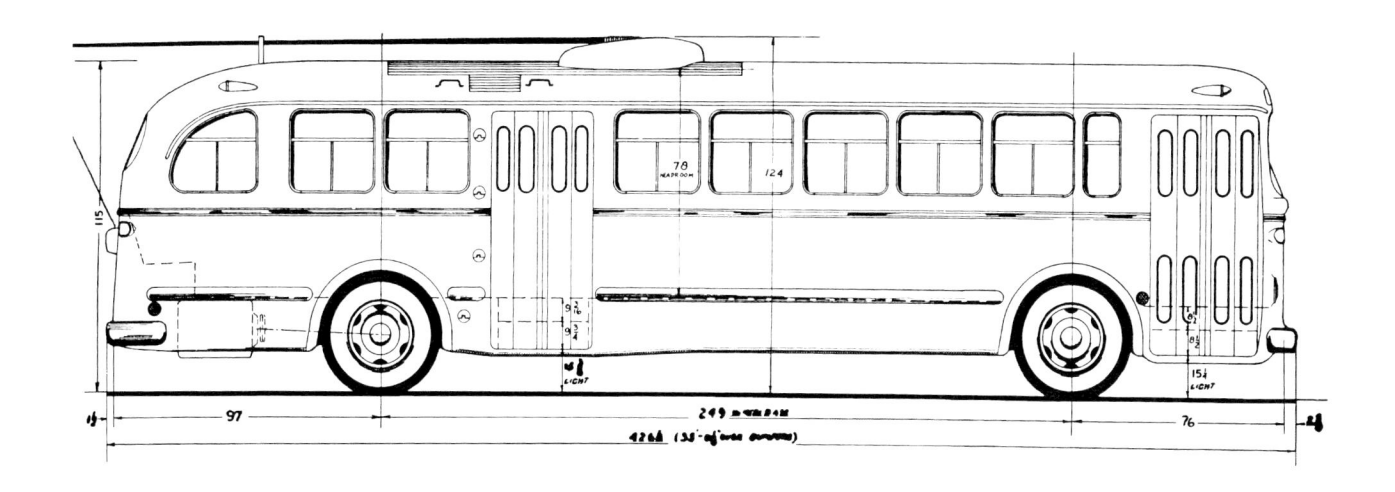

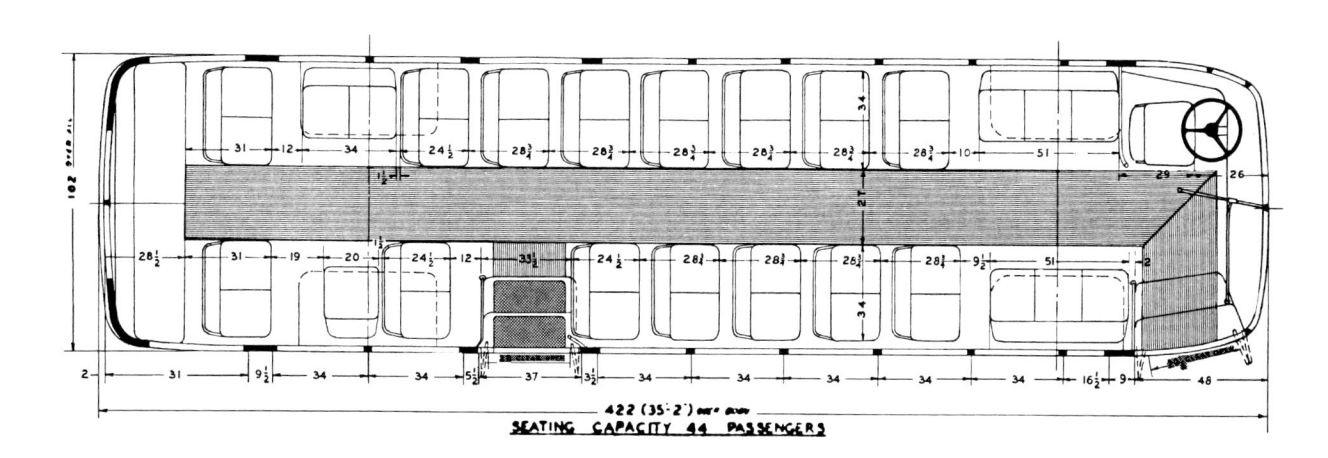

This diagram from Sebree, Ward's *Transit's Stepchild, The Trolley Coach* shows a T-44 series ACF-Brill. It is very similar to the model both Winnipeg bought new (T-46) and Edmonton and Calgary got used (TC-44). With the exception of some features on the front, it was identical to the CCF-Brills produced by Canadian Car.

261

TIRES AND WIRES

CAN CAR-BRILL T-44

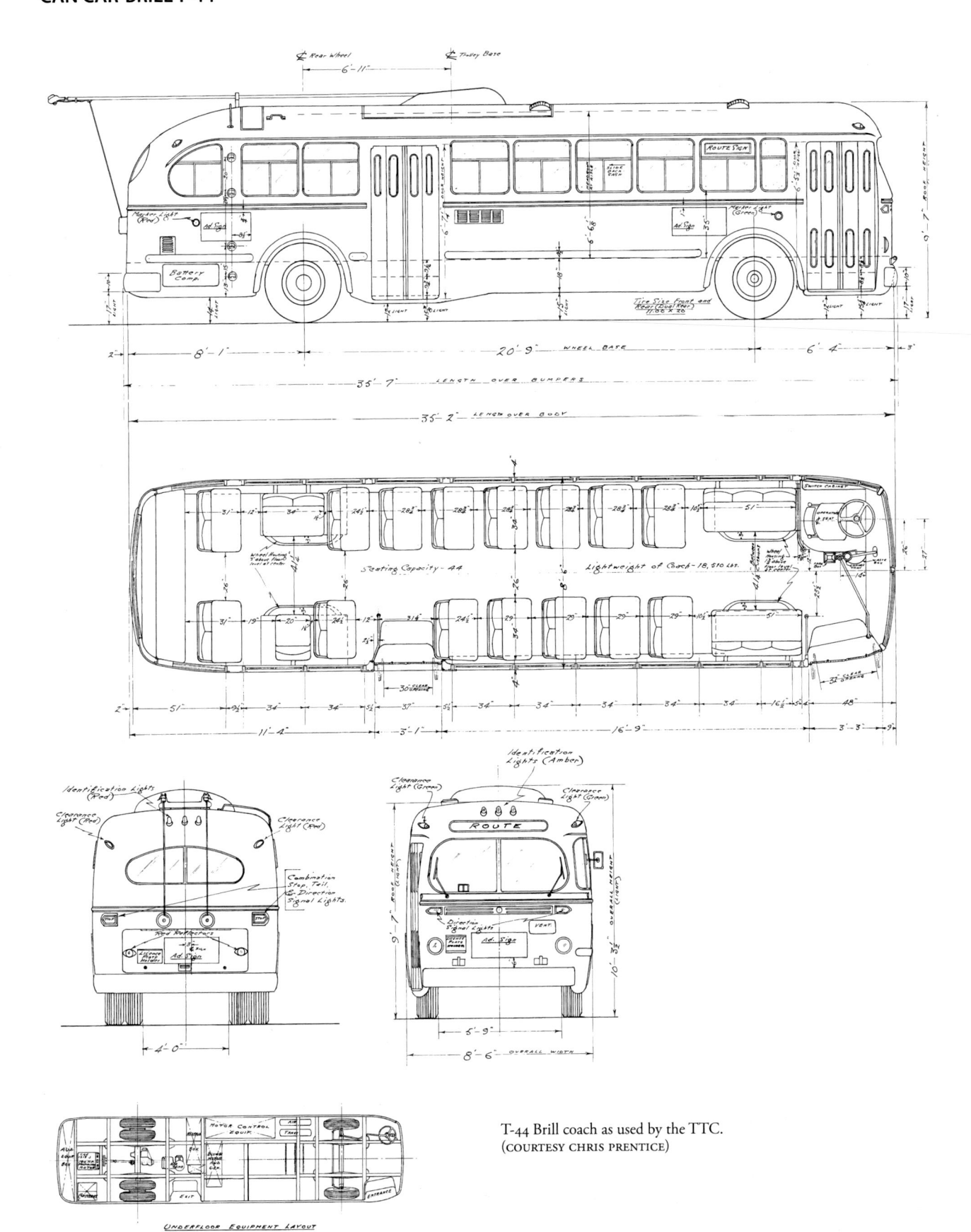

T-44 Brill coach as used by the TTC.
(COURTESY CHRIS PRENTICE)

APPENDIX C: TROLLEY COACH DRAWINGS

CAN CAR-BRILL T-48

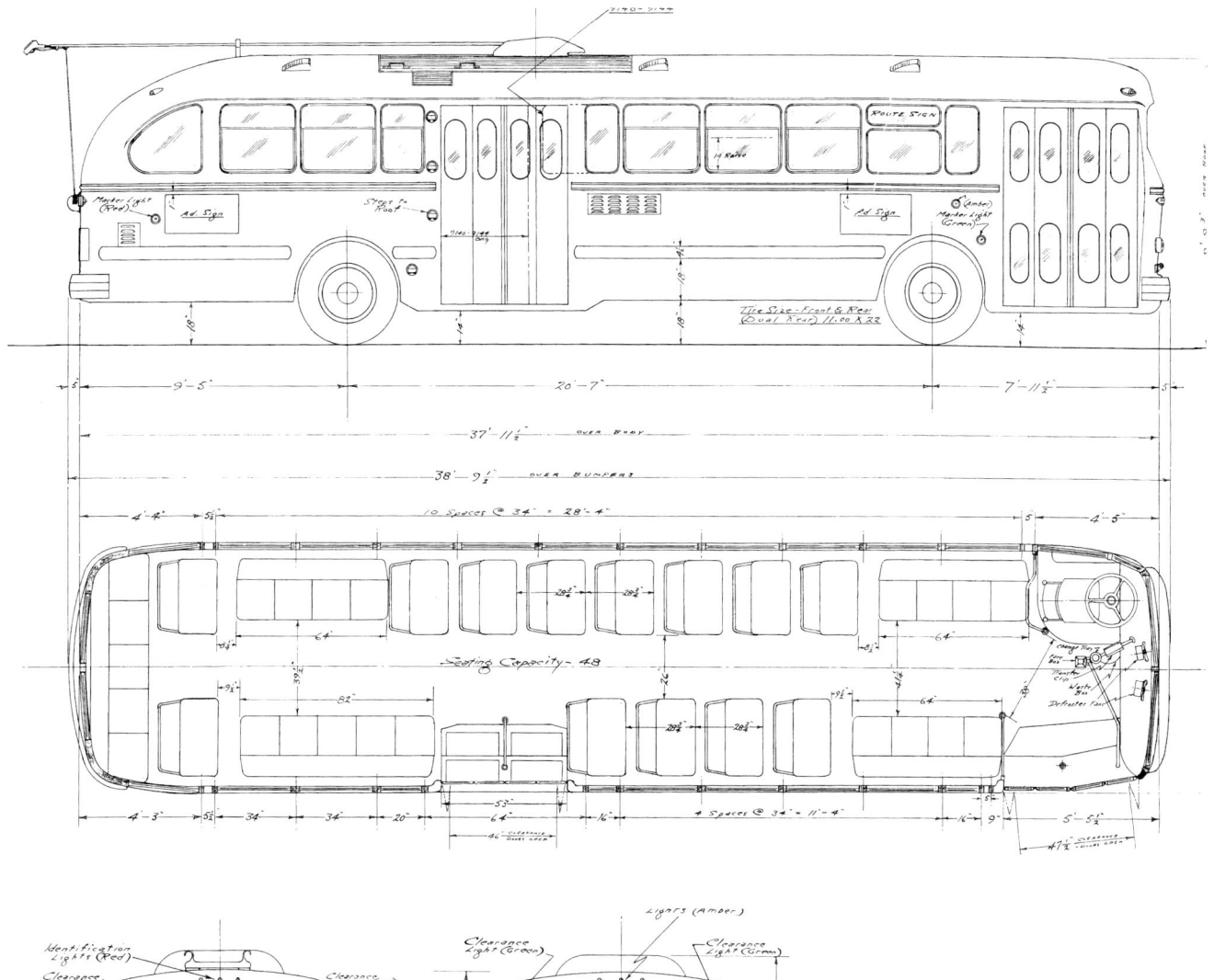

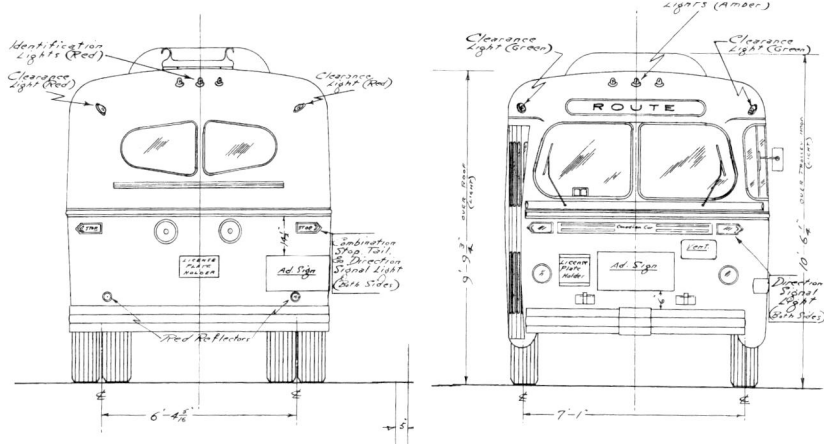

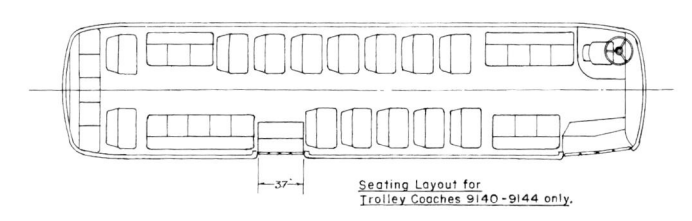

T-48 Brill coach as used by the TTC. The bottom inset refers to the used Cornwall coach bought by the TTC. (COURTESY CHRIS PRENTICE)

263

TIRES AND WIRES

BROWN, BOVERI & CIE/GMC HR150G

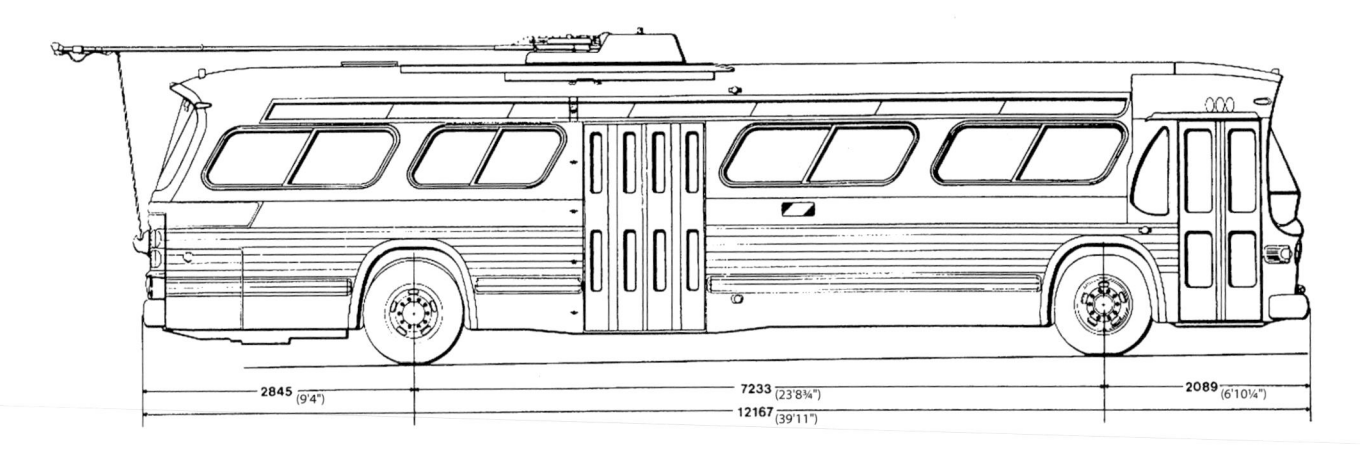

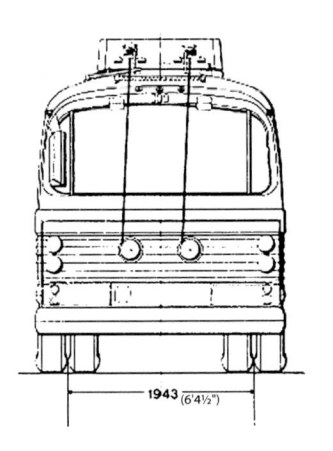

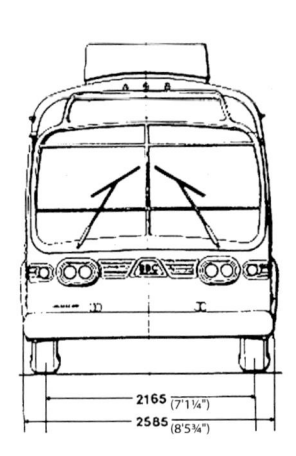

Brown Boveri/GMC HR150G trolley bus as built for Edmonton Transit. These were the only coaches ever built of this design. As a European enterprise, Brown Boveri normally utilized metric dimensions as shown in this official plan. For convenience of North American readers, approximate dimensions in feet/inches have been provided.
(*TROLLEY COACH NEWS* FALL 1981 BETWEEN PP.46-47, COURTESY EDMONTON RADIAL RAILWAY SOCIETY)

APPENDIX C: TROLLEY COACH DRAWINGS

FLYER E700A

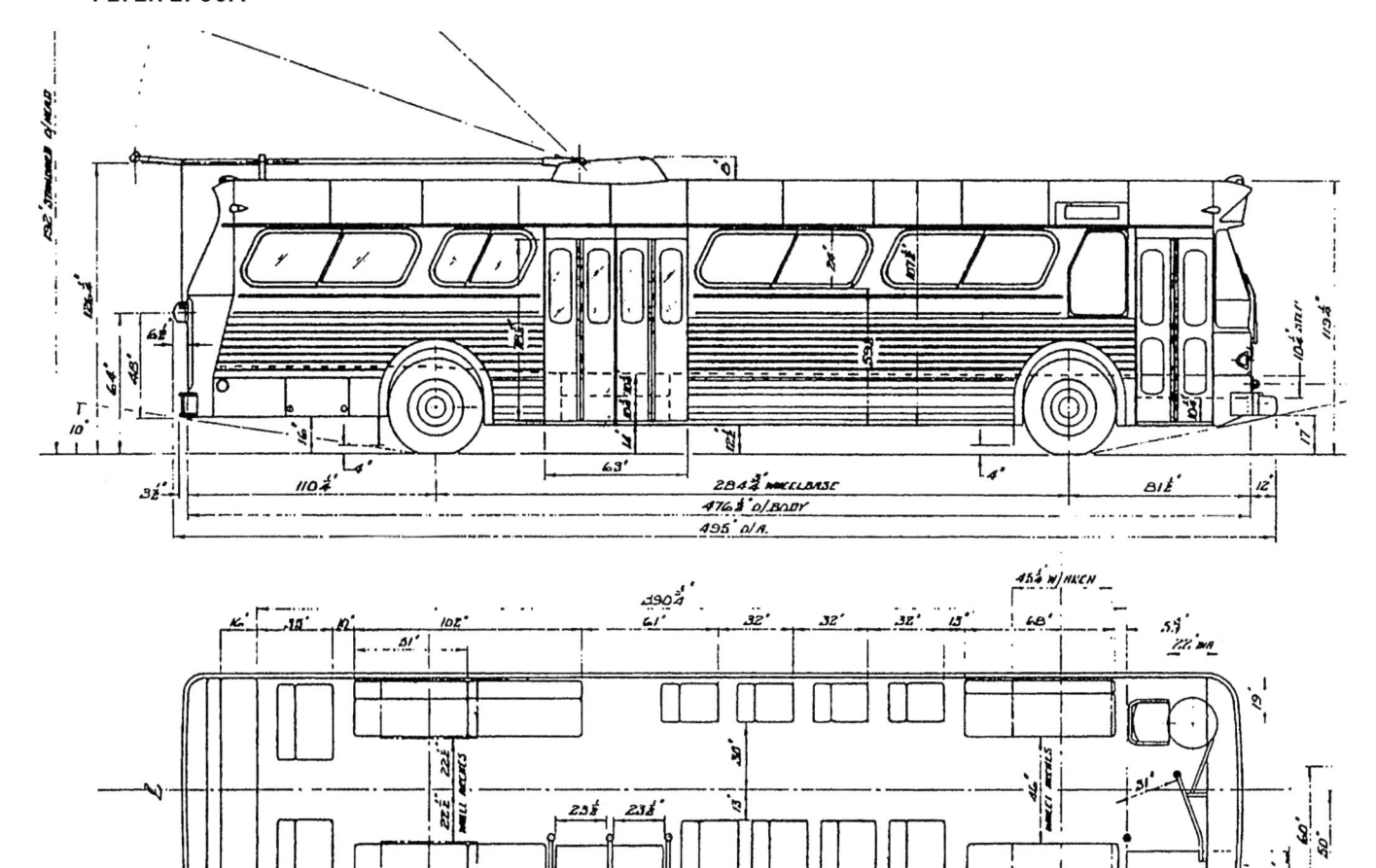

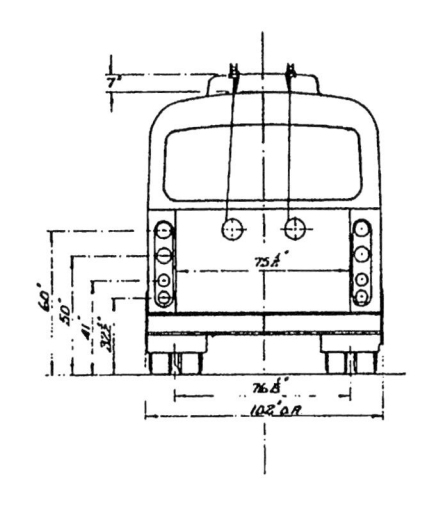

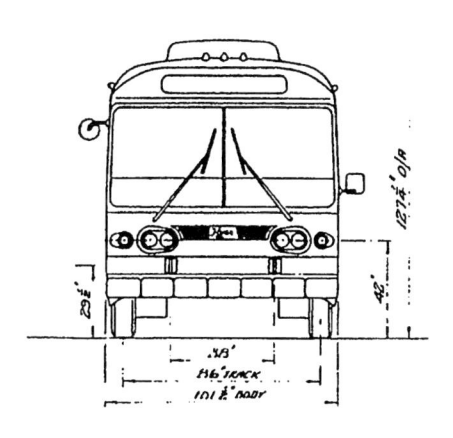

Elevation and plan views of the then-new Flyer E700A from the TTC pamphlet "Trolley Coach" April 1984.
(COLIN HATCHER COLLECTION)

265

TIRES AND WIRES

FLYER E902

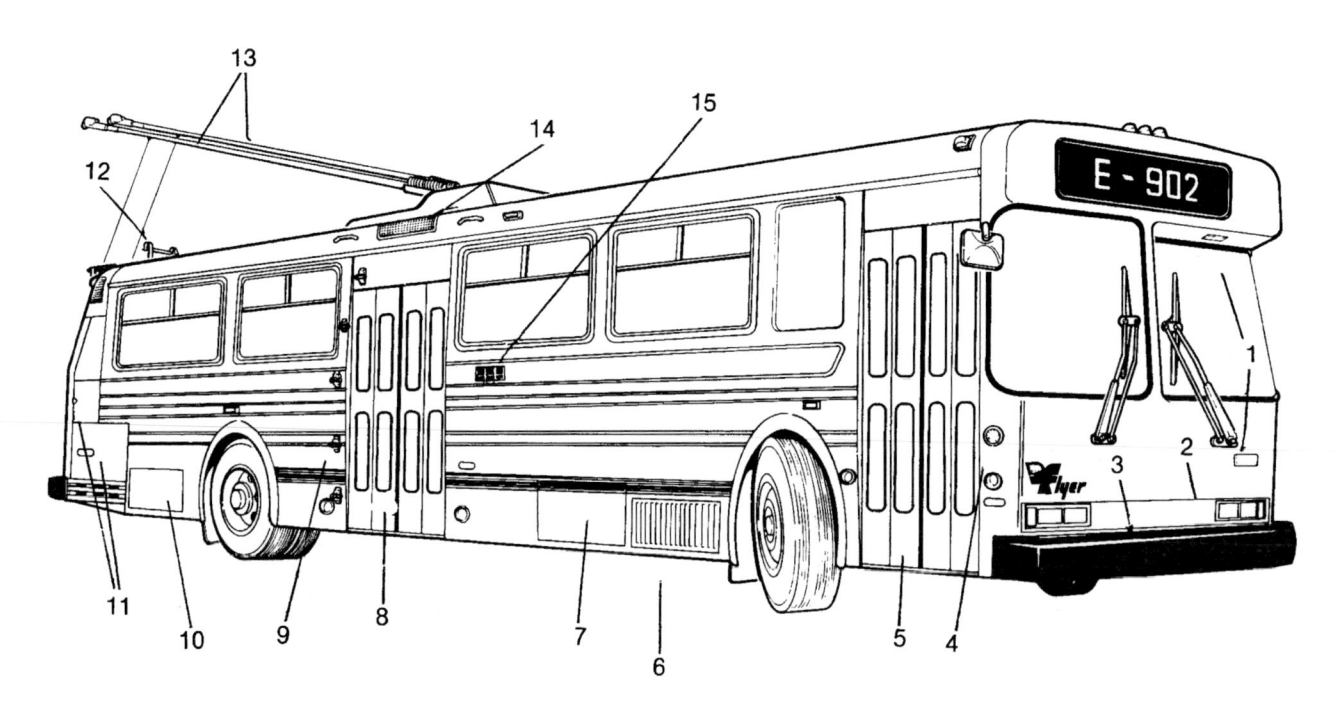

FRONT VIEW LEGEND
1. Fresh Air Intake
2. Front Access Door
3. Energy Absorbing Bumper
4. Kneeling Light Indicator
5. Entrance Door (Double)
6. Compressor Access Door
7. Auxiliary Battery Access Door
8. Exit Door (Double)
9. Steps, Roof Access, Folding
10. Battery Access Door, 12 Volt
11. Rear Access Door (Chopper)
12. Trolley Hooks
13. Trolley Poles
14. Rubber Insulator
15. Fresh Air Intake

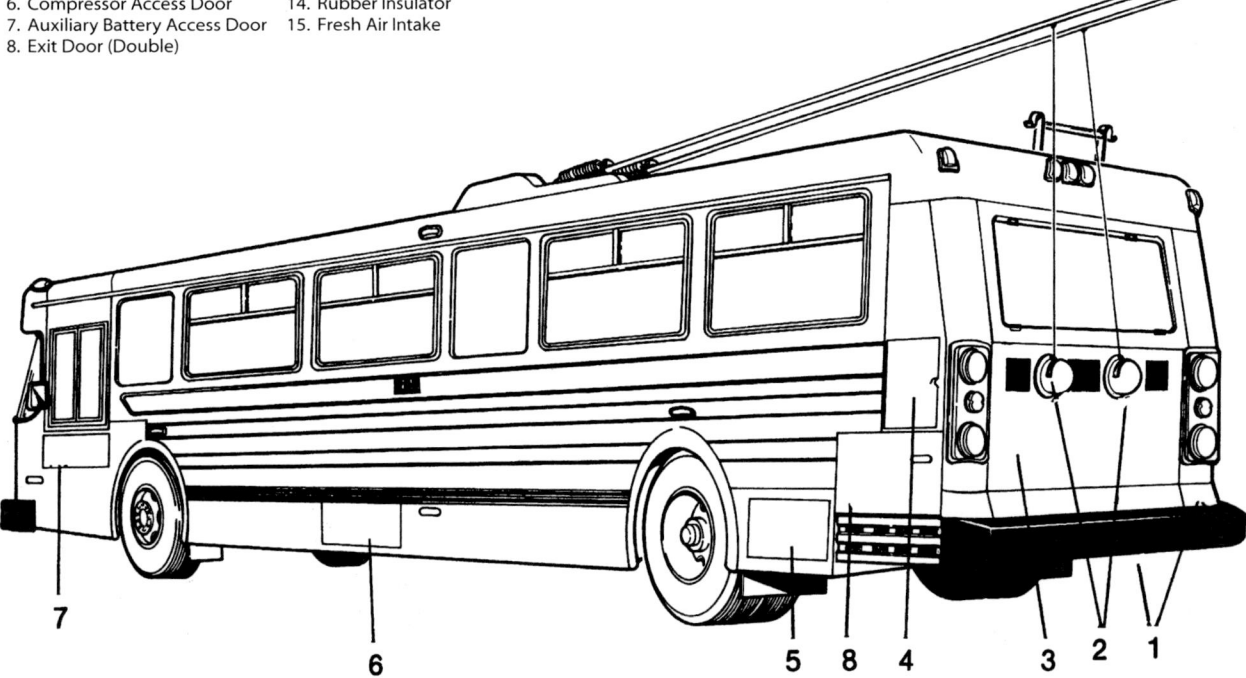

REAR VIEW LEGEND
1. Energy Bumper, Anti-Ride Shield
2. Retrievers
3. Chopper Access Door
4. Rear Access Door
5. Rear Control Box Access Door
6. Auxiliary Battery Access Door
7. Side Console Access Door
8. Contactor Access Door

Flyer E901/02 from New Flyer Operator's Manual.
(COURTESY ROB CHEW, USED WITH PERMISSION OF FLYER INDUSTRIES)

APPENDIX C: TROLLEY COACH DRAWINGS

FLYER E40LFR

LEGEND
1. Current Collector Poles
2. Roof Vent/Hatch
3. Heating & Ventilating Unit
4. Side Marker Light
5. Roof Mounted Equipment Enclosure
6. Exterior Speaker
7. Brake Resistor
8. Antenna (units 2102-2288)
9. Clearance Marker Lights
10. Front Route Sign
11. Headlight
12. Bike Rack
13. Defroster Access Door
14. Front Turn Indicator
15. Curb Lights
16. Kneeling/Ramp Warning Light
17. Side Turn Indicator
18. Side Destination Sign
19. Hubodometer
20. Battery Access Door
21. Battery Disconnect Switch Access Door
22. Air Intake Grille
23. Pole Hooks & Rope Guides
24. Contact Shoes

Flyer E40LFR from New Flyer Operator's Manual.
(NEW FLYER INDUSTRIES, USED WITH PERMISSION)

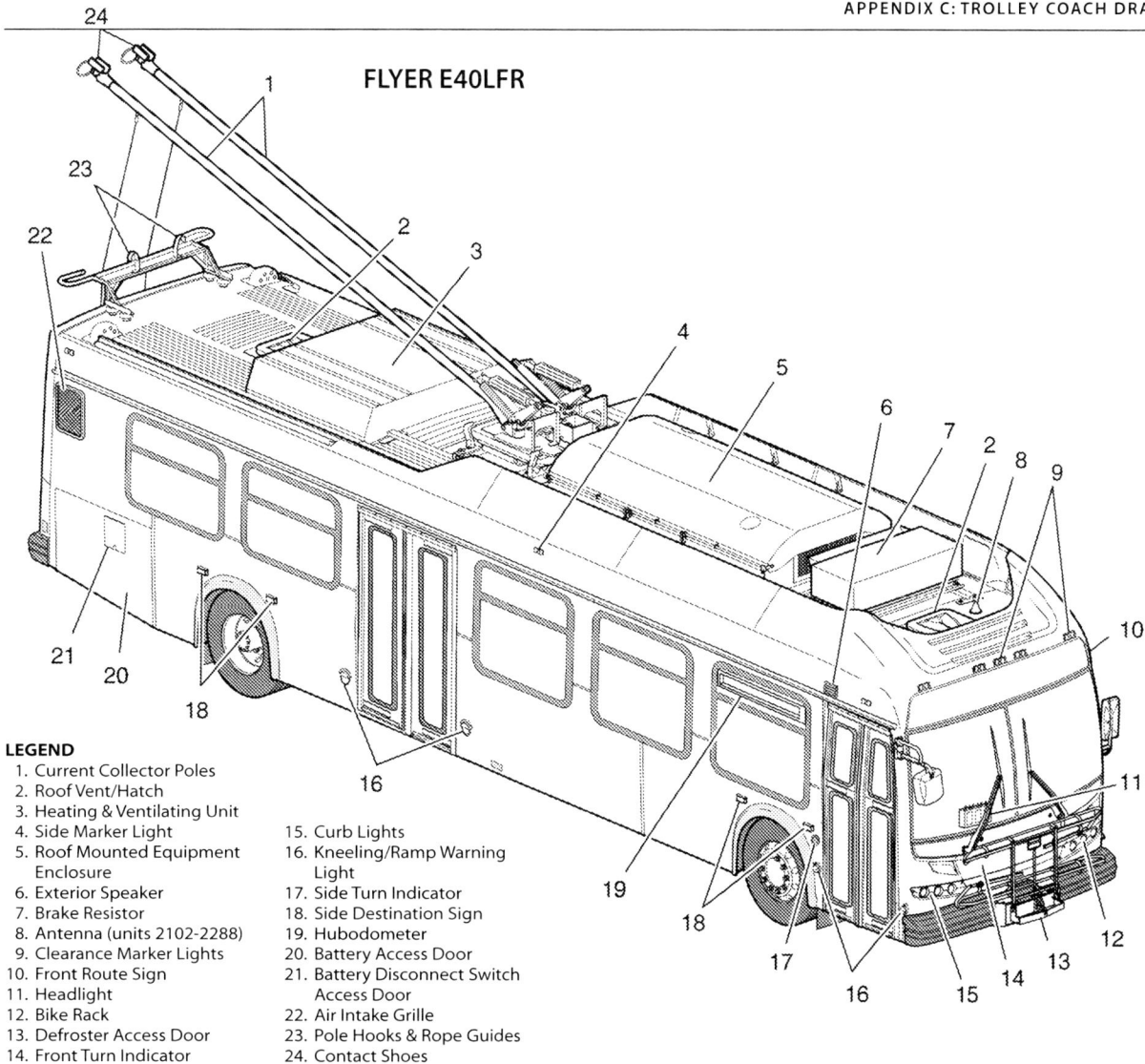

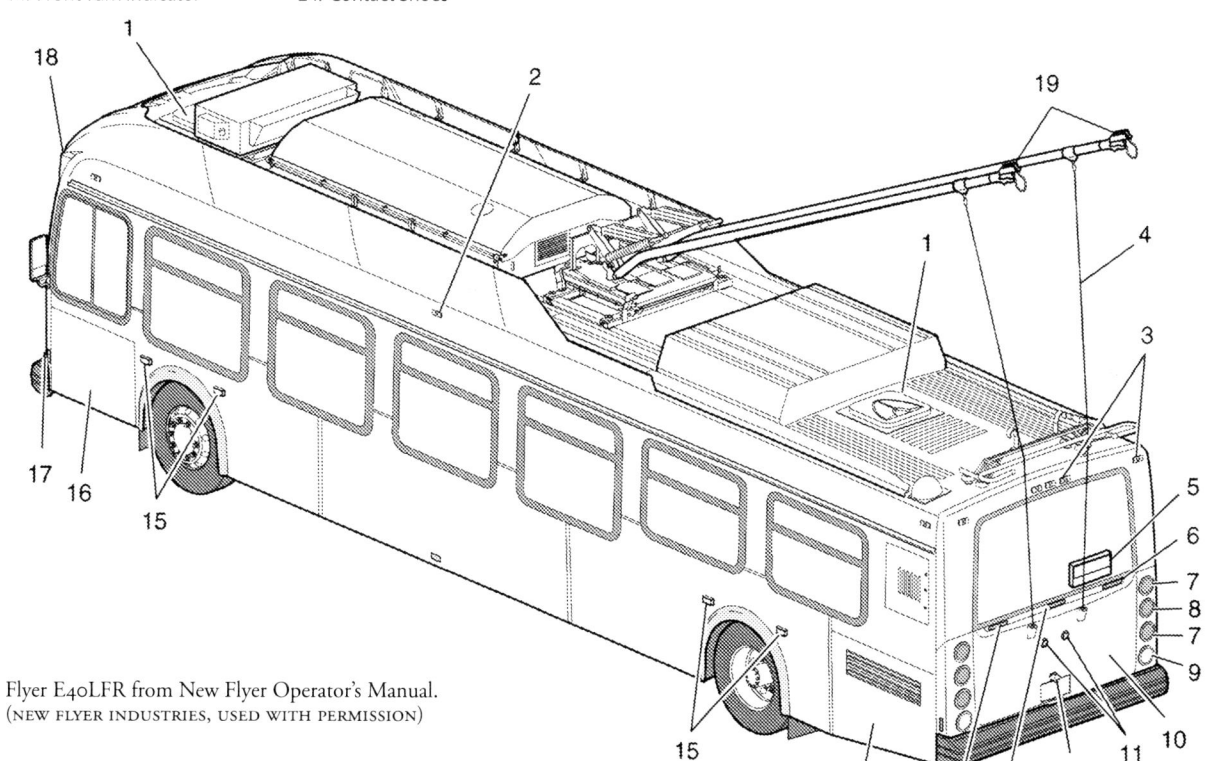

TIRES AND WIRES

FLYER E60LFR

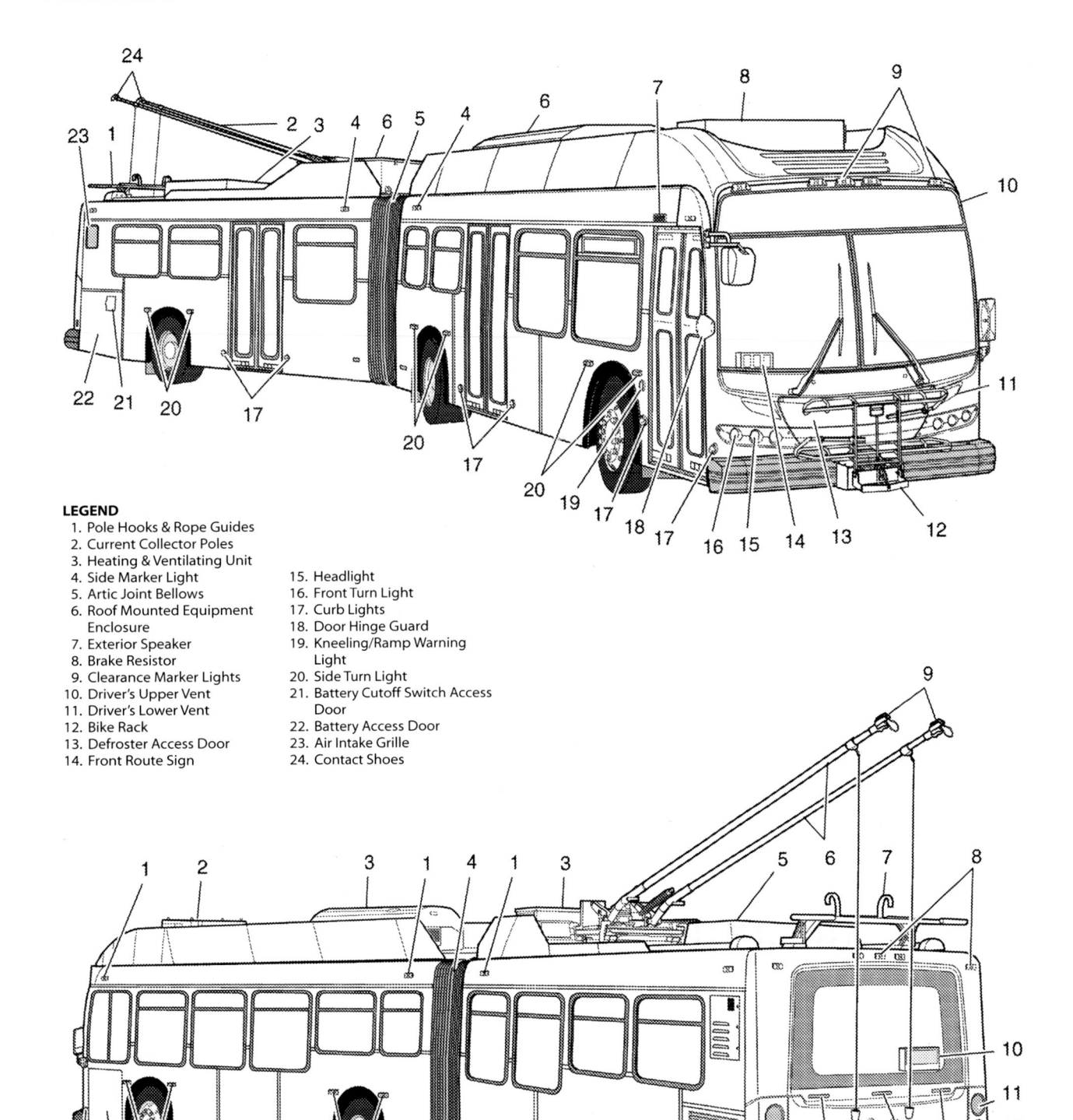

LEGEND
1. Pole Hooks & Rope Guides
2. Current Collector Poles
3. Heating & Ventilating Unit
4. Side Marker Light
5. Artic Joint Bellows
6. Roof Mounted Equipment Enclosure
7. Exterior Speaker
8. Brake Resistor
9. Clearance Marker Lights
10. Driver's Upper Vent
11. Driver's Lower Vent
12. Bike Rack
13. Defroster Access Door
14. Front Route Sign
15. Headlight
16. Front Turn Light
17. Curb Lights
18. Door Hinge Guard
19. Kneeling/Ramp Warning Light
20. Side Turn Light
21. Battery Cutoff Switch Access Door
22. Battery Access Door
23. Air Intake Grille
24. Contact Shoes

Flyer E60LFR from New Flyer Operator's Manual.
(NEW FLYER INDUSTRIES, USED WITH PERMISSION)

268

SELECTED BIBLIOGRAPHY

Baker, John E., *Winnipeg's Electric Transit – the story of Winnipeg's streetcars and trolley buses*, Railfare Enterprises Limited, Toronto, ON, 1982. ISBN 0-919130-31-3

Bain, D.M., *Calgary Transit: Then & Now*, Kishorn Publications, Calgary, Alberta, 1994. ISBN 0-919487-45-9

Brown, Robert R., *Halifax: Birney Stronghold*, CRHA, Montreal, revised by Richard Binns September 1964 and further revised and reprinted October1968

Carter Edwards, Karen, *100 Years of Service* (Cornwall Electric) (Beauregard Press), 1987. ISBN 0-9692908-0-2

Chemerys, Joseph, Rollsign Gallery web site
http://www.rollsigngallery.com/home.html

Clegg, Anthony and Omer Lavallée, *Cornwall Street Railway – The Insurance Company's Streetcars – an illustrated history of the transit operations of the Cornwall Street Railway Light & Power Company*, Railfare*DC Books, Pickering ON, 2007. ISBN 978-1-897190-26-5 (HC), 978-1-897190-25-8 (SC)

Davis, Donald F., *A Capital Crime? The Long Death of Ottawa's Electric Railway 1947–1999*. Paper presented to the "Construire une capitale – Ottawa – Making a Capital" Conference, University of Ottawa, November 20, 1999. Published as "Ottawa The Making of a Capital", University of Ottawa Press, Ottawa, 2000, as reviewed in Google Books at:
http://books.google.com/books?id=_Q9Bb4EiAyoC&pg=PA357&lpg=PA357&dq=Ottawa+transportation+commission&source=web&ots=3PAaG5sv3o&sig=Vv2JzVTP5IOmzNnRCUqCUwvLsb8#PPA359,M1

Drouillard, Bernard W., "Transit in Windsor," *Bus Industry* Vol. 9, #2, April/May/June 1982

Gryffe, Allan, Canadian Transit Information web site
http://www.angelfire.com/ca/TORONTO/index.html

Hatcher, Colin K., *Saskatchewan's Pioneer Streetcars – the story of Regina Municipal Railway*, Railfare Enterprises Limited, Montreal, QC, 1971. ISBN 0-919130-20-8

Hatcher, Colin K. and Tom Schwarzkopf, *Edmonton's Electric Transit – the story of Edmonton's Streetcars and Trolley Buses*, Railfare Enterprises Limited, Toronto, ON, 1983. ISBN 0-919130-33-X

Hatcher, Colin K. and Tom Schwarzkopf, *Calgary's Electric Transit – an illustrated history of electric public transportation in Canada's oil capital*, Railfare*DC Books, Pickering ON, 2009. ISBN 978-1-897190-55-5

Joyce, Arthur J. *Hanging Fire and Heavy Horses: A History of Public Transit in Nelson*, City of Nelson, Nelson BC, 2000 ISBN 0-9686364-0-3

Kelly, Brian and Daniel Francis, *Transit in British Columbia – The First Hundred Years*, Harbour Publishing, Madeira Park, BC, 1990. ISBN 1-55017-021-X

Leger, Paul A. and Loring M. Lawrence, *Halifax – City of Trolleycoaches*, Bus History Association, Windsor, ON, December 1994 (Vol. 15, No. 62 issue of Bus Industry). ISBN 0-9699267-0-7

McKeown, Bill, *Ottawa Streetcars*, Railfare*DC Books, Pickering ON, 2006. ISBN 0-919130-07-7

Mills, John, *Traction on the Grand*, Railfare, Montreal, QC, 1977. ISBN 0-919130-27-5. Re-issued and revised with additional material by Ted Wickson, as *Ontario's Grand River Valley Electric Railways*, Railfare*DC Books, Pickering ON, 2010. ISBN: 978-1-897190-52-4 (SC); 978-1-897190-53-1 (HC)

Morrow, Tom, Tom's North American Trolley Bus Pictures web site
www.trolleybuses.net

Parker, Douglas V., *Streetcars in the Kootenays*, Havelock House, Edmonton, 1992 ISBN 0-920805-02-7

Porter, Harry, *Trolleybus Bulletin No. 105* Trolleybus Databook I, North American Trackless Trolley Association (NATTA) Inc., Louisville, KY, 1973

Porter, Harry and Stanley F. X. Worris, *Trolleybus Bulletin No. 109* Trolleybus Databook II, North American Trackless Trolley Association (NATTA) Inc., Louisville, KY, 1979

Sebree, Mac and Paul Ward, *Transit's Stepchild, The Trolley Coach* (Interurbans Special 58), ASIN B0006C9ZOE. Interurbans, Los Angeles CA, 1973. LCCN 73-84356

Sebree, Mac and Paul Ward, *The Trolley Coach in North America* (Interurbans Special 59), ASIN B0006CEBZC. Interurbans, Ceritos CA, 1974. LCCN 74-20367

Wayman, Easten, *Saskatoon's Electric Transit – the story of Saskatoon's streetcars and trolley buses*, Railfare Enterprises Limited, Hawkesbury, ON, 1988. ISBN 0-919130-42-9

Wyatt, David A., All-time List of Canadian Transit Systems web site
http://home.cc.umanitoba.ca/~wyatt/alltime/index.html

INDEX

Photos and other graphic references are set in *semi-bold italic* type. To keep this Index to a manageable size, and for reader's ease of use, not every photograph or reference to the most popular coaches, i.e. Can Car–Brill and Flyer, has been included.

A

Acadian Lines ...28, 32
ACF-Brill ...12, 19, 20, 103, 121, 146, 148, 150, 156, *158*, 185,
advertising ...32, 118, 147
Alexander, E.R. ...58
Alstom S.A. ...6
AM General Corporation ...6, 15
Amalgamated Transit Union ...112
American Car & Foundry ...19, 20, 83, 148
Anderson, Garfield ...106
Archibald, George ...135, 137
Arnott, E.W. ...189, 213
Associated Equipment Co. (A.E.C.) ...15, 18, *38*, 39, *39*, 41, *43*, *140*, 143, *145*, 150, 153
Atkinson, Wally ...131

B

Baker, Henry ...131
B.C. Hydro ...86, 112, *194*, *196*, 199, 200, 201, 202, 206, *240*
B.C. Hydro Transit ...201
BC Transit ...202, 204, 206
Beeler Organization ...189
Binns, R.M. ...41
Birmingham, Alabama ...19, 196, 207
Bishop, S.L. (Syd) ...109, 110
Blue Line Transit (Victoria) ...213
Booz Allen Hamilton Inc. (consultants) ...166, 167, 168
Boutilier, R. (Bob) ...169
bridges
 Angus L. Macdonald (Halifax) ...*Front cover*, 28, 31, *32*, *33*, 219
 Belt Line Bridge (Toronto) ...76
 Cambie Street (Vancouver) ...203
 Granville Bridge (Vancouver) ...*193*, *198*
 High Level Bridge (Edmonton) ...146, 148, 149, 153, 154, 155, 161
 Low Level Bridge (Edmonton) ...141, 144, 145, 146, 149, 150, 155, 156
 Maryland Bridge (Winnipeg) ...118
 St. Vital Bridge (Winnipeg) ...120
 Walterdale Bridge (Edmonton) ...161
Brill, J.G. & Company ...19, 20
British Columbia Electric Railway Company (B.C.E.R.) ...*69*, 189, 192, 193, 196, *196*, 213, *215*, 216, *233*, *240*
 see also B.C. Hydro
Brown Boveri & Cie. (BBC) ...15, *18*, 76, 160, 162, 163, *168*, *170*, *173*, 200, *226*, *232*, *254*, Inside back cover
Bunnell, Arthur ...89
Bunnell, G.K. ...49
Bureau of Transit Services (British Columbia) ...199, 201

C

Calgary Municipal Railway ...175, 178
Calgary Transit System (CTS) ...*174*, 178, *178*, 179, *180*, 181, *182*, 183, 184, *184*, 185, 186, *187*, *232*, *233*, *239*
Canada Coach Lines, The ...89, 93, 95
Canada Wire and Cable Company Limited ...67, *67*, 106
Canadian Brill Company ...11, 18, 20, *20*, 22, *64*, 65, *66*
Canadian Car & Foundry Co. Ltd. (CCF, Can Car) ...9, *10*, 12, *13*, *14*, 22, 25, 35, *36*, *37*, 49, 51, 57, *66*, 71, 83, 103, 105, 106, 112, 118, *119*, 121, 127, 135, 143, 148, *149*, 150, 153, 155, 156, 181, 185, 189, 192, *272*
Canadian General Electric (CGE) ...*10*, 12, 36, *36*, 37, *37*, 74, 118, *118*, 144, *149*
Canadian National Railways (CNR) ...4, 59, 76, 137, 141, 146
Canadian Pacific Railway (CPR) ...4, 42, 45, 51, 103
Canadian Railway Museum (Montreal) see also Exporail ...45
Canadian Transit Association ...4, 41, 118, 142
carhouses
 see also garages, shops
 Cobourg Carhouse (Ottawa) ...54
 Eglinton Carhouse (Toronto) ...65, 74, 76
 Lansdowne Division (Toronto) ...*66*, 67, *70*, 71, 72, 74
 London Street Carhouse (Windsor) ...*100*
 Main Carhouse (Winnipeg) ...118, 124
 St. Denis Carhouse (Montreal) ...39, *44*
 Victoria Park Carhouse (Calgary) ...179
Carson, K. Gordon ...106
Chandler, R.B. ...105
Chaput, Hector ...52, 53
Checkel, Dr. David ...167, 168, 169
Church, Roy ...124
Cincinnati Transit Company ...19, *22*, 71, 110
Citizens for Better Transit (Alberta) ...166, 169
City Transit Company (Dayton, OH) ...79, *79*
City Transit Ltd. (Saint John, NB) ...35
Clark, Robert R. ...158
Cleveland, OH ...19, 67, 74
Coast Mountain Bus Company (CMBC) ...*Inside back cover, Back cover*, *173*, *198*, *200*, *203*, 204, *205*, 207, *211*, *234*, *252*
Comba, Charles ...175, 177, 178
conductorettes ...194
Confederation (Newfoundland) ...37
Cooke, Frank ...95
Cooke, Vernon ...63
Cornish, B.H. ...186

Cornwall Street Railway Light & Power Co., Limited (CSR)
...4, *5*, *6*, *12*, *56*, 57, 58, 59, *59*, *60*, 61, 62, *62*, *63*, *221*, *222*, *237*
Cox, Charles W. ...105, 106
Cox, Peter ...4, 206
Creighton, W.R. ...49, 51
Curtin, John (consultant) ...184

D

Dahl, C.H. ...115
Dayton, OH ...6, 7, 11, 79, 170, 254
De Leuw, Cather & Co. ...95
demonstrator trolley coaches
 see also trolley coach demonstrations
 Can Car-Brill ...12, *14*, 61, 63, *66*, 106
 ET 100 (BBC-GM prototype) ...15
 Motor Coach Industries ...22, *23*, 122
 St. Louis Car Company ...65, *98*, *100*
 Seattle Transit Twin Coach ...206
 Seattle Transit Twin Coach 835 ...206
 TTC 9020 (Western Flyer prototype) ...14, *16*, *17*
 TTC 9213 (Flyer production model) ...74, *94*, 95, 185
 (Vancouver, Victoria) ...*188*, 189, 192, 206, *206*, *212*, 213, *215*
Department of Defense Transportation (US) ...147
Department of Munitions and Supply (Canada) ...147
Department of Transport (Canada) ...150
Dominion Power and Transmission Company (Hamilton) ...89
Dominion Transit Controller see under Transit Controller (Canada)

E

Edmonton Power Authority ...162, 164, 165
Edmonton Radial Railway ...*140*, 141, *143*, 145, *145*, *151*, *238*
Edmonton Transit Historical Collection ...160
Edmonton Transit System ...*Inside back cover*, 15, *15*, *17*, 19, *140*, 141, *151*, *152*, 153, *157*, 158, *158*, 159, 160, *161*, 162, *162*, 163, *163*, 164, *165*, 166, *167*, *168*, 169, 170, *170*, *172*, *173*, *231*, *232*, *239*
Edmonton Trolley Coalition ...165, 166, 169
English Electric Company (E.E.C.) ...*42*, 143, 144, 146, 147
Exporail
 see also Canadian Railway Museum ...46

F

fare media (tickets, transfers)
 Cornwall (tickets) ...*59*
 Edmonton (transfers) ...*154*
 Montreal (transfers) ...*42*, *45*

"Farewell to Brill" (Vancouver) ...202, 203
Federal District Commission (FDC) ...51, 53, 54
Ferrier, Thomas ...141, 142, 144, 145, 157
fires
 Regina ...127, 153
 Saint John ...35
floods
 Winnipeg ...118
Flyer Industries Limited ...7, 14, 15, *15*, *16*, *17*, 123, 157, 158, 185, 200
Ford Motor Company ...175
Fort William City Council ...103, 108, 109, 110
Fort William Transit ...106, 110
Furlong, W.H. ...101, 175

G

garages, see also carhouses, shops
 Carruthers Garage (Winnipeg) ...121, 122, 124
 Cromdale Garage (Edmonton) ...141, 146, 154, 155
 Eau Claire Garage (Calgary) ...179
 Eglinton Garage (Toronto) ...76
 Lansdowne Garage (Toronto) ...79
 Oakridge Transit Centre (Vancouver) ...193, 194, *197*, 202, 203, 204
 PUC Garage (Kitchener) ...85, *87*
 Strathcona Garage (Edmonton) ...154
 Vancouver Transit Centre ...204
 Wentworth Garage (Hamilton) ...93
 Westwood Garage (Edmonton) ...155, 157, 158, 159, 162, 169
General Motors Company
 see also Brown Boveri ...15, 143, 160, 163, 185
Gibb, Robert J. ...141, 142, 143, 144, 146, 148, 149
Gill, David N. ...49, 51
Golden Arrow Coaches Limited (St. John's, Nfld) ...36, 37
Gorman, S.E. ...101
Granville Street Mall ...200, 207
Grauer, A.E. "Dal" ...193, 203
Gray, George S. ...147, 148, 175, 214
Greater Vancouver Regional District (GVRD) ...199, 201, 204
Greater Vancouver Transit System ...*82*, *198*, 199, 201, *234*
Greater Victoria Transportation Committee ...
Greater Winnipeg Transit Commission ...*119*, *120*, *123*, *125*, *228*, *238*
Gréber, Jacques ...49, 53

H

Halton County Radial Railway museum ...18, *20*, 65, 95
Hamilton Hydro-Electric Power Commission ...89

INDEX

Hamilton Street Railway Company (HSR)
...6, *88*, 89, *89*, 92, *92*, 93, *93*, *94*, 95, 96, *97*, *222*, *223*, *236*
Hamilton-Wentworth Regional Municipality ...95
Hamilton-Wentworth Transportation Services Committee ...96
Harrington, A.R. ...32
Hawker Siddeley Group ...14, 31
Horizon 2000 (Edmonton) ...164
Horovitz, Aaron ...58
Howe, Hon. Clarence D. ...12
Hu Harries and Associates ...160
Hudson's Bay Company (The Bay)
...*178*, 183, *212*, *215*, *239*, *240*

I

Illinois Railway Museum ...170
Interior Stages Ltd. (Nelson, BC)
...*217*, *218*
Irwin, W.F. ...67

K

Kates, Peat, Marwick & Company
...110
Kelly, Brian ...4, 203
Kiepe Electric ...5, 6, 207
Kuyt, W. ...186
Kyte, Ed ...163

L

Leyland Manufacturing Corp. Ltd.
...18, 74, 143, 144, 146, 153, 154, 165
light rail transit (LRT)
Edmonton ...159, 160
logos ...110, 159, 192, 199
Lyons, Teddy ...192

M

MacDonald, Donald L.
...155, 156, 157
MacDonald, John L. ...58
MacKeen, Col. J.C. ...27
Mack Trucks Inc. ...18, 21, *23*, *114*, 115, 117, 118, *119*, 121, *123*, 124, 143, 147, 148, 150, 156, 202
Manning, Fred C. ...35
maps
Calgary ...*176*
Cornwall ...*57*, *58*
Edmonton ...*142-143*
Fort William/Port Arthur/Thunder Bay ...*104*
Halifax ...*26*
Hamilton ...*90-91*
Kitchener ...*85*
Montreal ...*40*
Nelson ...*218*
Ottawa ...*51*
Regina ...*128*
Saskatoon ...*138*
Toronto ...*65*, 68
Vancouver ...*190-191*, *208-209*
Victoria ...*214*
Windsor ...*101*
Winnipeg ...*116*
Marcom Works (consultant) ...166
Marmon-Herrington Co. Inc.
...19, *22*, 71, *73*, 74, 110, 121, *225*
McAra, P.G. ...127, 131
McIntyre, Angus ...204
Mendoza, Argentina ...204
Metro-Cammell-Weymann (bus manufacturer) ...18, 39

Metro Transit Operating Company ...201, 202
Metro Winnipeg Transit ...121
Mexico City
...7, 11, 45, 124, 164, *255*
Miami Valley Regional Transit Authority (Dayton, OH)
...79, 254, *254*
Miller, E.V. ...160
Millican, Rick ...164
Montreal Tramways Commission ...39
Montreal Tramways Company (MTC)
...*19*, *38*, 39, 41, *41*, 42, *42*, *43*, *44*, 45, *45*, *46*, *47*, 142, 154
Montreal Transportation Commission (MTC)
...45, *46*, *220*
Montreal Urban Community Transit Commission (MUCTC) ...46, *46*
Morrow, Tom ...254
Motor Coach Industries (MCI)
...20, 22, *23*, 117, *122*, 124, 150
Municipal and Public Utility Board (Winnipeg) ...115
Murrin, W.G. ...189

N

National Capital Commission (NCC) ...51
natural disasters
see under floods, winter conditions
Nelms, George H. ...54
Nelson Street Railway ...217
New Brunswick Hydro Corporation ...35
New Brunswick Power Company ...35
New Flyer Industries Ltd.
...5, 6, 14, 15, 22, 204, 207
Newfoundland Light & Power Company Limited ...36, 37
Newhall, V.A. ...177, 178
New York Central Railroad ...58
NFI Group Inc. ...5, 22
Niel, Ivor W. ...192
North American Trackless Trolley Association (NATTA) ...4
Northern Electric ...106, 144
Nova Scotia Light and Power Company (NSL&P)
...*Front cover*, *12*, *24*, 25, 27, *27*, *28*, *28*, 29, *29*, 30, *30*, 31, *31*, 32, *32*, 33, *33*, *34*, *219*, *235*, *236*

O

Ohio Brass
...*8*, 28, *61*, 71, *71*, *83*, 85, 86, 106, *117*, 142, 144, 163, 178, *179*, 181, *192*, *193*, 194, *194*, 217
Ontario Hydro-Electric Railway, Essex Division ...*98*, 99, *99*, *100*
Ontario Municipal Board
...101, 106
operating costs
...95, 101, 110, 183, 185
Ottawa Electric Railway (OER) ...49, 53
Ottawa Transportation Commission (OTC)
...*48*, 49, *50*, 51, 52, *52*, 53, 54, *55*, *221*
Owen, Bill ...79

P

Pacific Car and Foundry Company (PCF) ...206
Port Arthur Civic Railway ...103

Postcards (trolley coaches)
...*235-240*
Presidents' Conference Committee streetcar (PCC)
...25, 57, 71, 118, 127, 141, 189, 217, *226*
Preston Car Company ...18, 20
Project Uni (Edmonton) ...161
Public Utilities Board
Halifax ...29, 31
Public Utilities Commission (PUC)
Fort William
...*102*, 105, 106, 108, 109, *111*, *113*, *227*, *237*
Kitchener
...*Inside front cover*, *82*, 83, *84*, 85, 86, *86*, 87, *224*
Port Arthur
...*103*, 105, *105*, 106, *107*, 108, *108*, 109, 110, *111*, *113*, *227*
Victoria ...213
Pullman-Standard Car Mfg. Corp.
...*19*, 117, *147*, *151*, *152*, 157, *162*, *163*, *228*

R

R.A. Malatest & Associates Ltd. (consultant) ...167
Regina City Council Post War Reconstruction Committee ...127
Regina Municipal Railway
...*126*, 127, *129*, *130*
Regina Transit System
...127, 129, *130*, *131*, *132*, *133*, *229*, *238*
Reynolds-Alberta Museum
...170, 186
Robin-Nodwell Ltd. (UK) ...74
Route maps ...*121*, *131*, *172*, *181*
Royal Commission on Canada's Economic Prospects ...54

S

St. Louis Car Company
...11, 18, 65, *98*, 99, *100*, 110, 143
Sandwich, Windsor & Amherstburg Railway
...65, 99, 100, 101, 175
Saskatoon Municipal Railway
...*134*, 135, *136*
Saskatoon Transit System (STS)
...*134*, 135, *136*, 137, *139*, *230*
Scharfe, Burt ...135
Schwarzkopf, Tom ...2
Seashore Trolley Museum ...33, 170
Seattle, Washington
...6, 11, 189, 192, 193, 200, 206, 207, 213, 214, 216
Seymour, Donald ...57
shops (streetcar, bus overhaul)
see also carhouses, garages
Hillcrest Shops (Toronto)
...14, *16*, *17*, 71, 74, 79, *79*
Kitsilano Shops (Vancouver)
...199
Youville Shops (Montreal)
...*38*
SkyTrain ...7, 203, 204, 207
SMT (Eastern) Ltd. ...35
Stibbs, Norman C. ...217
Stolte, Charles ...169
Streetcars for Toronto Committee ...76
Sun Life Assurance Company ...57, 61
Sutherland, Fred M. ...35

T

The Bay
see under Hudson's Bay Company
Thunder Bay Historical Transportation Committee ...112
Thunder Bay Transit ...110, 112
"Tomatobird" ...192, *233*
Toronto Transit Commission (TTC)
...*Inside front cover*, 5, *12*, 14, 15, *16*, *17*, 20, 27, 65, 67, 71, 72, *72*, *73*, 74, *75*, 76, *77*, *78*, 79, *80*, *81*, 95, 157, 164, 185, 199, *225*, *226*
Toronto Transportation Commission
...11, *20*, *22*, *64*, 65, *66*, 67, *67*, 70
Township of York ...71
Transit Controller (Canada)
...19, 83, 117, 147, 148, 149, 150, 175, 177, 214
Transit Museum Society (TRAMS) (Vancouver)
...170, 204, *233*
TransLink (Vancouver) ...204, 207
Transportation and Public Works Committee (Edmonton) ...166
Transportation and Streets Department (Edmonton) ...164
trolley coach demonstrations
see also demonstrator trolley coaches
...12, 14, *14*, *16*, *17*, 22, *23*, 61, 63, 65, *66*, *94*, *98*, *100*, 106, *122*, 188, *188*, 189, 190, 191, 192, 206, *206*, *212*, 213, *215*
Trolley Party (Edmonton) ...165

U

United Service Corporation (St. John's, Nfld.) ...37
Urban Transit Authority (UTA)
Vancouver ...201, 202
Urwick, Currie Limited (consultants) ...31, 54, 137

V

Vancouver Island Coach Lines (VICL) ...213, 216
Vigras, E.A. (Ed) ...108, 110
Vossloh Kiepe ...6, 207

W

Waters, Thomas H. ...218
Watt, R.N. ...39, 41, 42
Weir, C.V.F. ...178, 179
Western Flyer Coach Limited
...11, 14, 74, 79, 110, 121, 124, 157, 158, 199
Westinghouse Electric Corp.
...18, 22, 65, 99, 202
Whitton, Charlotte ...51, 53, 54
Wilson & Bunnell (consultants)
...141, 142, 146, 148
Wilson, Norman D. (consultant)
...7, 25, 49, 51, 53, 54, 142, 153, 175, 177
Winnipeg City Council ...121, 122
Winnipeg Electric Company (WEC)
...*21*, 22, *23*, *114*, 115, 117, *117*, 118, *191*, 120, *121*, *122*
Winnipeg Hydro ...122, 124
winter conditions
sleet storm (Kitchener) ...83
snow storm (Edmonton) ...146
snow storm (Winnipeg) ...118
Wishart, Eunice ...109, 110
Wray, R.H. ...179, 183, 184, 186

Y

Yuill, A.C.R. (consultant) ...217

271

Above: Taken with permission from scrapped Edmonton Brill coaches by the author, the round Brill maple leaf crest adorned the front of T-44 coaches. The T-48 models had a chrome script *Canadian Car* in its place. The long plate with the same crest in the middle was inside the coach mounted on the front near the door, and the brass serial number plate nearby. Can Car was proud to be a Canadian bus manufacturer and that extended even to the horn pushbuttons, two of which are shown here at top left and top right.